Sustaining Michigan

Sustaining Michigan: Metropolitan Policies and Strategies

EDITED BY

Richard W. Jelier and Gary Sands

Michigan State University Press • *East Lansing*

♾ The paper used in this publication meets the minimum requirements
of ANSI/NISO Z39.48-1992 (R 1997) (Permanence of Paper).

Publication of *Sustaining Michigan* was made possible
by the generous support of the Land Policy Institute.

Michigan State University Press
East Lansing, Michigan 48823-5245

Printed and bound in the United States of America.

15 14 13 12 11 10 09   1 2 3 4 5 6 7 8 9 10

LIBRARY OF CONGRESS CATALOGING-IN-PUBLICATION DATA

Sustaining Michigan : metropolitan policies and strategies / edited by Richard W. Jelier and Gary Sands.
    p. cm.
  Includes bibliographical references.
  ISBN 978-0-87013-850-8 (pbk. : alk. paper)
  1. Metropolitan areas—Economic aspects—Michigan. 2. Michigan—Economic policy. I. Jelier, Richard W. (Richard William) II.
Sands, Gary.
  HT334.U5S87 2009
  338.9774'07091732—dc22

                                                                                            2008029582

Cover design by Heather Truelove
Book design by Sharp Designs, Lansing, Mich.

Michigan State University Press is a member of the Green Press Initiative and is committed to developing
and encouraging ecologically responsible publishing practices. For more information about the Green Press
Initiative and the use of recycled paper in book publishing, please visit www.greenpressinitiative.org.

Visit Michigan State University Press on the World Wide Web at: www.msupress.msu.edu

Contents

Acknowledgments vii

Foreword by Soji Adelaja ix

Introduction.   Metropolitan Affairs and the Triple Bottom Line in
                Michigan *Richard W. Jelier and Gary Sands* 1

PART 1: ECONOMIC AND FISCAL PERSPECTIVES

Chapter 1.   The Economic and Fiscal Background of Metropolitan Policies
             in Michigan *Charles L. Ballard* 17

Chapter 2.   Michigan's Industrial Tax Abatements:
             Pyrrhic Victories? *Gary Sands and Laura A. Reese* .45

Chapter 3.   Abating Taxes, Abetting Sprawl: The Geographical Distribution of
             Tax Abatements in Michigan *Angela Lazarean and Katharine Trudeau* 63

Chapter 4.   Equity and Politics in Road-Spending Allocation in Michigan: Implications
             for Metropolitan Affairs *Soji Adelaja, Annalie Campos, and Yohannes G. Hailu* 85

Chapter 5.   Coming Together in Tough Economic Times: Workforce Development and
             Economic Development Move Closer in Michigan *Elsie Harper-Anderson* 111

PART 2: ENVIRONMENTAL CONCERNS

Chapter 6.   Flushing the Conflict: Wastewater Cooperation among Michigan's
Local Governments? *Eric S. Zeemering* 135

Chapter 7.   Best Practices in Protecting Green Infrastructure: Benchmarking
County Park Systems *Betty Gajewski* 159

Chapter 8.   The Impact of Policy Change in Local and State Environmental Policy:
Brownfield Redevelopment in Michigan *Richard Hula* 183

PART 3: SOCIAL/POLITICAL DYNAMICS

Chapter 9.   Explaining Horizontal and Vertical Cooperation
in Michigan *Jered B. Carr, Elisabeth R. Gerber, and Eric W. Lupher* 207

Chapter 10.   Regional Housing Policy: Can Crisis Spawn Collaboration? *Dale E. Thomson* 237

Chapter 11.   Michigan's Urban Policies in an Era of Land Use Reform and
Creative-Class Cities *June Manning Thomas* 261

Chapter 12.   The Brain Drain Wars: Characteristics of Recent Movers into and
out of Michigan *M. Curtis Hoffman and Jeremy Pyne* 281

PART 4: TOWARDS A TRIPLE BOTTOM LINE

Chapter 13.   Building a Triple Bottom Line Sustainability Model
in Michigan *Norman Christopher and Richard W. Jelier* 309

List of Contributors 331

Acknowledgments

This book is an outgrowth of the Michigan Higher Education Land Policy (MIHELP) Consortium. Rich and Gary would like to recognize the efforts of Soji Adelaja, the John A. Hannah Distinguished Professor in Land Policy, and others at the Land Policy Institute at Michigan State University to build and support an inter-university partnership around land use and metropolitan issues. Without Soji's leadership in advancing the MIHELP vision, this volume, directed towards pressing Michigan issues, would not exist. We hope this will be the first in a long series of projects aimed at promoting effective metropolitan strategies for Michigan.

Rich would also like to thank his former graduate assistant Daniel Petersen for his assistance on the volume and also support from the School of Public and Nonprofit Administration in the College of Community and Public Service at Grand Valley State University. Most important, we thank the authors of these chapters for their commitment to channeling scholarly research towards understanding and solving Michigan's endemic metropolitan problems.

Rich dedicates this volume to the three ladies in his life, Jaye, Jacqueline, and Natalie.

Foreword

Soji Adelaja

This book is one of the early products of the Michigan Higher Education Land Policy Consortium (MIHELP). The mission of MIHELP is to promote interuniversity partnerships in the development of science-based solutions to some of Michigan's pressing issues. Initial members of the partnership include Grand Valley State University, Michigan State University, and Wayne State University. This Route I-96 Corridor team is poised to focus the expertise of the partners on metropolitan policy strategies that can help better position Michigan's communities and regions to face the challenges of the New Economy.

In the New Economy, universities have been identified as a cornerstone of economic success in the twenty-first century. The need to expand the impact of the universities on the public cannot be limited to scientific innovation alone. Policy research, outreach, and education, especially in the areas of land use, must be at the center stage of the effect of higher education on the public. This is MIHELP's mission and vision.

This book explores a range of important land use issues. Not only are land use issues important, they are critical to the success of communities, regions, and states at this critical time when the U.S. economy must work to redefine itself. Academic institutions are vital to this repositioning. The research we do in Smart Growth, cluster-based economic development, Green Infrastructure, talent development and attraction, immigration, intergovernmental cooperation, farmland preservation, natural resource conservation, public finance reform, brownfield redevelopment, land banking, planning and zoning, urban revitalization, citizenry education, healthy communities, creative class, public spending patterns, metropolitan leadership development, water resource development, land use forecasting, decision support tools, land tenure, transit and public transportation, New Urbanism, mixed-use development, and farm viability must be stepped up to enhance the information available to society. This information can serve as the basis for a successful intervention strategy to restore the Michigan economy.

At the heart of any successful intervention strategy is science-based solutions; therefore, one of MIHELP's goals is to deepen the ability of partner institutions to conduct high-quality, nationally recognized scientific research on metropolitan issues. This is particularly needed in Michigan. Michigan's challenges are daunting. Many of Michigan's core communities place very poorly in national rankings of metropolitan areas. State leaders are looking for the best ideas for repositioning the state. A critical element to the success of our leaders in this effort is new smart tools that are unique to Michigan while relevant to other states. The MIHELP partnership shares a vision of an appropriate balance between scholarly excellence and maximum impact as a change agent. Even in the murky area of land policy, we must do this extremely well.

This book, as a MIHELP product, focuses on the promotion of scholarly excellence. It complements other products such as our recently published *State of Michigan Cities* and our ongoing work to complete case studies to support our Urban Core Mayors network. Universities are known not to collaborate well. In Michigan, MIHELP has debunked that paradigm. The contents of the book span contemporary issues in Michigan on which faculty from our partner institutions have been working. This book is only a first. MIHELP plans more academic volumes, more outreach products, and more education products.

We are grateful to the contributions of the W. K. Kellogg Foundation to our efforts as the angel investor in the MIHELP vision. Indeed it is fair to say that MIHELP, or this book, would have never happened without the foundation.

Metropolitan Affairs and the Triple Bottom Line in Michigan

Richard W. Jelier and Gary Sands

Some 80 percent of Michigan's residents live in the state's metropolitan areas. These areas are facing daunting challenges requiring regional approaches to improvements in municipal finance, rebuilding infrastructures, improving public services, ameliorating underlying racial attitudes, enhancing diversity, improving public education opportunities, and supporting local economies, a seemingly inexhaustible list of challenges. The health and future of these metropolitan areas are of urgent concern—explicitly and implicitly—to local and state government and policy makers. As a result of complex economic, environmental, and social interrelationships between the state's urban cores, inner-ring suburbs, outlying suburbs, and adjacent rural areas, Michigan represents a unique and complex research opportunity.

Specifically, Michigan is saddled with a $1.9 billion structural deficit that caused a brief government shutdown in 2007. Michigan has an infrastructure that is aging and costly to maintain. Michigan's economy is structurally dependent on manufacturing, which has been in absolute decline. Manufacturing employment decreased 29.06 percent between 1990 and 2006 (State of Michigan 2007). Build out projections anticipate small population growth accompanied by large increases in urbanized land. By 2040, the built areas of Michigan are expected to increase by 175 percent (Skole et al. 2002). Recent demographic changes and Latino immigration into many of the state's core cities present additional challenges.

This volume is the outgrowth of a new statewide consortium envisioned to address these and other problems by the director of the Land Policy Institute at Michigan State University and the John A Hannah Distinguished Professor in Land Policy, Soji Adelaja. The Michigan Higher Education Land Policy (MIHELP) Consortium was launched in 2005 with funding from the W. K. Kellogg Foundation. The foundation grant provided seed funding to support a sustainable partnership that would assemble multi-institutional, multidisciplinary teams of leading scholars and their academic institutions to deliver research results relevant to effective metropolitan policy making and local intergovernmental cooperation. The MIHELP Consortium addresses a fundamental research and outreach void in urban and metropolitan issues in the state of Michigan. It focuses on those issues that block or deny healthy growth in urban areas and their surrounding regions. It particularly addresses those issues associated with linkages between cities and their immediate and outlying neighbors.

The MIHELP Consortium provides Michigan universities with a vehicle that facilitates collaboration with other institutions on metropolitan issues that impact the state of Michigan. The overall objective is to mobilize university research and outreach resources to inform policy makers and decision makers in timely and relevant ways. As a statewide initiative, MIHELP takes full advantage of the key metropolitan regions that its component institutions represent—Lansing, Detroit, and Grand Rapids. MIHELP has the unique ability to marshal the resources of its component institutions—Michigan State University, Wayne State University, and Grand Valley State University—in concert with Public Sector Consultants, to execute an ambitious research and outreach agenda utilizing the talents and resources of over 200 academics. By fostering institutional collaboration among universities along with the private sector, MIHELP is defining an urban and metropolitan research agenda; disseminating research findings; promoting scholarship; facilitating seminars, symposiums, and research activities; and educating policy makers, stakeholders, and students to make Michigan's urban and metropolitan areas vibrant and successful communities.

One of the first major consortium accomplishments was the publication of the *State of Michigan Cities: An Index of Urban Prosperity* (2007), creating a comprehensive report on the well-being of Michigan's cities.[1] For virtually every indicator, this representative group of thirteen Michigan cities underperformed relative to the state as a whole. The condition of Michigan's cities is clearly unfavorable, whether they are benchmarked against other cities in the nation, the counties in which they lie, or the state in general.

The Index of Urban Prosperity, which served as the basis of the report, reflects a general deterioration in most measures for core cities in Michigan metropolitan communities. For instance, for the group of thirteen core cities, it is estimated that population declined 4.4 percent between 2000 and 2005, while the population of the state grew 1.8 percent. Poverty rates for that same period increased 4.8 percent to 26.2 percent for the thirteen core cities but rose only 2.7 percent for the state. Median household income decreased 2.2 percent for the thirteen core cities, but rose 3.1 percent for the state. Free and reduced lunch program eligibility increased from 49 to 58.1 percent eligible for the thirteen cities. Finally, unemployment in 2005 rose to 11.3 percent for the thirteen cities, nearly double the state average of 6.7 percent (Adelaja et al. 2007). The report indicates the critical need for scholarship directed at understanding metropolitan affairs in Michigan.

This book is part of the MIHELP Consortium's efforts to publish cutting-edge research by leading scholars addressing pressing problems facing Michigan metropolitan communities. It will be timely for use in the classroom by Michigan universities and for local and state practitioners and elected officials as well. This volume is in response to a call for papers that went out to nearly 400 academics in the state of Michigan and other scholars engaged in Michigan research. The chapters selected address a variety of high-priority areas related to metropolitan affairs in Michigan. They seek to share practices and lessons learned that have relevance for Michigan.[2]

Remarkable in the breadth of its collaboration, this volume includes seven scholars from Michigan State University, four from the University of Michigan, four from Wayne State University, and five from Grand Valley State University. Our hope is that this volume will enhance the MIHELP Consortium's efforts promoting engaged scholarship that addresses endemic issues and problems. The focus is on Michigan, but the lessons and implications of the research volume expand well beyond the state's borders. The chapters relate broadly to key programmatic themes suggested by the MIHELP Consortium partners that address the triple bottom line of sustainable development. Due to the nature of the interdisciplinary and collaborative research, the chapters often integrate multiple thematic areas of sustainable development.

The 1987 report of the Brundtland Commission defined sustainability as "meeting the needs of today without compromising the ability of future generations to meet their own needs." The European Union adopted sustainability patterns for future development nearly a decade ago. In Australia and New Zealand, sustainable development principles have been elevated to something akin to a national religion and pervade all public policy decisions. More recently, in the United States, cities such as Portland, Seattle, Chicago, and Denver serve as national models for enhancing sustainable futures.

The primary focus of sustainability centers on the triple bottom line (TBL) of environmental stewardship, economic prosperity, and social responsibility. Some refer to it as the 3 Es (economy, environment, equity), while others refer to it as the 3 Ps (profits, planet, people). By using a triple bottom line sustainability lens analysis, a balanced perspective can be obtained that helps us to look at systemic problems that our community is facing with a holistic systems-oriented analytical approach.

The Triple Bottom Line

Source: Adapted from Dyllick and Hockerts 2002.

3

This volume is organized around sustainability principles of the triple bottom line. These principles address many of the ten programmatic thrusts of Michigan governor Jennifer Granholm's Land Use Leadership Council in 2004.[3] The economic and fiscal framework of the triple bottom line is addressed through chapters on economic trends in Michigan, implications of tax abatement policies, current workforce development trends, and the connection between road grants to communities and sprawl. The environmental framework is explored through research on wastewater cooperation and management, protection of green infrastructure, and brownfield redevelopment in Michigan communities. The social/political/community framework is investigated through a study of regional cooperation in Michigan, an examination of urban and "creative class" policies, a study of the "Brain Drain Wars" regarding the characteristics of movers in and out of Michigan and an analysis of regional collaboration of housing policy in Michigan. Finally, a chapter evaluates efforts to holistically incorporate a sustainability TBL model in West Michigan that might serve as a benchmark for the rest of the state.

Our hope is that this volume will help to make connections between the academic audience and students, interested citizens, local government officials and administrators, and policy makers in Michigan. The sustainability framework that shapes this volume and the patterns of development in Michigan are in keeping with global trends toward adopting sustainability practices.

Economic and Fiscal Perspectives

In his chapter "The Economic and Fiscal Background of Metropolitan Policies in Michigan," Charles L. Ballard sets the stage for much of what will follow in the volume. Ballard asserts that Michigan is likely to face chronic structural deficits, resulting in deep cuts in public expenditures, making it difficult for the state to proactively address metropolitan issues. He attributes this crisis to trends in economic and population growth patterns over many decades. Indeed, Michigan has fallen to twenty-seventh in per capita income among the fifty states, and Ballard projects further decline.

Michigan's economy and population have grown considerably more slowly than the economy and population of the United States as a whole. Over the past century, on average, per capita income in Michigan has declined relative to the national average by about one-third of one percentage point per year. If this long-term trend were to continue for another two decades, Michigan would fall into the bottom ten states in terms of income level. Strikingly, Ballard asserts that if Michigan were to continue with the more precipitous pace of relative decline that we have seen since 1999, Michigan would be the poorest state in the United States in just twenty years.

Erosion of the manufacturing sector in particular has contributed to the decline of personal income in the state, which has significantly affected public revenues. Michigan has gone from slightly above the national average for taxes to slightly below the national average. If the percentage of personal income devoted to state and local taxes were still the same as it had been in the 1970s (before the steep decline of manufacturing in Michigan), then the state and local governments and public schools in Michigan would have about

$7 billion more per year than they have now. In addition, Ballard demonstrates how income inequality has also been exacerbated in Michigan. He concludes that it is likely the current budget woes for Michigan will continue as the state faces severe and chronic structural deficits.

The success of Michigan and its metropolitan areas is, at least in part, dependent on the ability to restructure state and local economies to adapt to changing economic imperatives at national and global scales. The long-term decline of manufacturing and the rise of the service and knowledge economies point the way to a vital economy in the twenty-first century. The chapter by Gary Sands and Laura A. Reese, "Michigan's Industrial Tax Abatements: Pyrrhic Victories?" examines the extent to which the state and local governments have facilitated this transition by their industrial property tax abatement policies. The authors focus on the use of PA 198 of 1974 during the 1990s and its effects on reshaping the Michigan economy. Sands and Reese vividly illustrate the shift both nationally and in Michigan toward a service economy. Michigan's employment profile more resembles the rest of the nation, with a declining manufacturing presence. Yet industrial development incentives crafted over three decades ago remain the chief economic development tool employed at the local level and do not enhance the economic prosperity component of the triple bottom line.

Sands and Reese conclude that, despite continuing to grant thousands of property tax abatements and foregoing millions of dollars in property tax revenue, Michigan has continued to experience a steady decline in manufacturing employment over the last decade. Moreover, the mix of industrial jobs in the state increasingly favors motor vehicle manufacturing and other heavy industries, most of which are anticipated to continue to further decline nationally. High-tech industries (such as pharmaceuticals, aerospace. and electronics manufacturing) were granted numerous abatements in return for promises of substantial job growth, but the end result is fewer jobs in these industries today than at the beginning of the decade.

If industrial property tax abatements are generally so ineffective, what are the public policy implications? While the net benefits of industrial tax abatements appear limited (and seem to accrue primarily to industries that provide a diminishing share of employment and have not generated the employment gains promised in the legislation), it is impossible to assess where Michigan and its metropolitan areas would be without them. Rather than simply eliminating these abatements, Sands and Reese argue that they should be used more judiciously. Limitations on the number of abatements that may be granted and on their repeated use for the same facility could lower costs, while some measure of performance guarantees could increase benefits.

Further, the collateral costs of clinging to past beliefs and practices need to be fully weighed as Michigan espouses movement toward attracting a knowledge-based class economy (see Thomas, chapter 11, and Hoffman and Pyne, chapter 12, this volume). The policy of continuing to use public resources to support stagnant or declining industries in Michigan has serious consequences for tax losses. Local government capacity to produce services, meet the needs of poorer residents, and generally enhance the public infrastructure to meet the challenges of attracting a "Creative Class" and making the state more regionally competitive are diminished. The $40 billion in industrial investment that received abatements during the 1990s cost municipalities more than $1 billion annually in foregone property tax revenue (Sands and Reese 2006).

The chapter by Angela Lazarean and Katharine Trudeau, "Abating Taxes, Abetting Sprawl: The Geographical Distribution of Tax Abatements in Michigan," considers another critical component of industrial property tax abatements: their geographic targeting. While the previous chapter raised questions about the overall effectiveness of the PA 198 program in promoting the repositioning of the state economy, the authors here consider the program's effects on the intrametropolitan distribution of manufacturing jobs. This is particularly important for Michigan, given that the state utilizes industrial tax abatements at much higher rates, 68 percent of cities granting at least one abatement, versus a national rate of 54 percent (Reese and Rosenfeld 2004). Other research on economic development policies has generally concluded that abatements and other incentives are, at best, effective at the margin, influencing location choices within a metropolitan area. Even when incentives are effective only in encouraging minor shifts in the location of jobs and investment, they may serve important policy objectives in encouraging firms to locate in disadvantaged communities.

An examination of PA 198 use at the county level finds little correlation between the granting of industrial property tax abatements and changes in the number of manufacturing jobs. Counties experiencing growth in manufacturing employment have provided numerous tax abatements; the same is true for counties where manufacturing is in decline. Within metropolitan areas, abatement activity, on a per capita basis, is greatest in communities on the developing urban fringe. Distressed central cities, like Detroit, have attracted fewer new jobs through abatements than more prosperous suburban municipalities. While the city of Grand Rapids, which generally enjoys a more healthy economy than Detroit and has made more extensive use of PA 198 abatements, has benefited from abatements, the suburban portions of its metropolitan area have enjoyed relatively greater gains.

Looking at the patterns of abatement activity in the Detroit and Grand Rapids metropolitan areas, it is easy to conclude that many of the firms have received tax benefits to do what they would likely have done anyway. The abatements granted by Canton or Holland Township probably had little actual effect on the location decisions of the firms that received them. Abatements by suburban townships not only represent an unnecessary public cost but also facilitate urban sprawl and the economic decline of central cities and older suburbs. The authors conclude that PA 198 tax abatements substantially contribute to metropolitan decentralization.

Despite the importance of metropolitan regions to the overall economic health of the state, there are few public policies in Michigan that explicitly address regional concerns. A wide range of policies, however, have significant indirect impacts on Michigan's metropolitan regions. The ways that the state of Michigan chooses to allocate its programs, services, and infrastructure investments impact the shape and health of the metropolitan areas, often with unintended consequences.

The chapter "Equity and Politics in Road-Spending Allocation in Michigan: Implications for Metropolitan Affairs," by Soji Adelaja, Annalie Campos, and Yohannes G. Hailu, examines the equity implications of the state's funding formula for the distribution of road maintenance and construction funds. Using data from Southeast Michigan, they model the distribution of these funds in the 1990s. Although the state formula relies on objective measures such as population and stock of existing roads, the authors' model finds that a number of equity-related factors are also significant, including class and race. They also conclude that the formula contributes to increasing dispersion of population and economic activity within metropolitan areas, to the disadvantage of central cities and older communities.

As the authors note, decisions concerning distribution of available funds for roads (or any other public resources) are subject to a highly political process. Because such decisions, whether direct allocations or the establishment of a formula for allocation, are not made in a vacuum, it is unlikely that the results will ever be entirely optimal. Nevertheless, it is important that the political decision-making process at least recognize and give some consideration to the equity consequences of decisions. The chapter illustrates one mechanism for doing this. Indeed, they conclude that the current formula rewards suburbanites, high-income households, and Republican communities. They assert that the inherent bias in road funding could exacerbate the spatial distribution of access to economic opportunities across communities, disadvantages lower income communities, and may interfere with urban revitalization programs statewide.

One area of public policy in Michigan that has been approached on a regional basis is that of workforce development. Implicitly, this recognizes the regional nature of labor markets and local economies. This broader perspective is manifest in regional workforce agencies (mandated by federal legislation dating back to the 1960s) and the state's system of community colleges, which provide a variety of vocational and technical training programs.

The chapter by Elsie Harper-Anderson, "Coming Together in Tough Economic Times: Workforce Development and Economic Development Move Closer in Michigan," examines the changing relationships between economic development organizations and workforce development in Michigan by studying twenty-five Workforce Investment Boards during the current economic downturn. The severity of the current recession, and the substantial economic dislocations that have accompanied it, appear to have encouraged workforce development professionals to adopt a more entrepreneurial and collaborative approach. They have begun to adopt many of the strategies of economic developers (emphasizing job development as well as job placement) and pursuing more collaborative approaches. The author finds that there are a range of collaborative models between the Workforce Investment Boards and economic development agencies and organizations that are relatively recent.

Harper-Anderson suggests the disconnect between workforce development and economic development has been a severe constraint in effective public policy in Michigan until recently. There seems little doubt that the observed increases in collaboration at the regional level have been fostered by the severity of the current hard times. While there is little indication of reverse learning (economic development professionals adopting strategies and tools of workforce development), the success of these regional collaborations does offer a model for future cooperative efforts in Michigan's metropolitan areas.

Indeed, Harper-Anderson concludes that there have been seven significant changes. The boundaries between workforce development and economic development have blurred. The key players in workforce development have changed dramatically, with much more

7

involvement by local business leaders. Networks have increased shared knowledge and social capital. Workforce development is now acting more like traditional economic development. Increased customization had led to new partnerships and collaborations in Michigan. State politics under the current governor has played a positive role in these developments. Finally, workforce development leaders have recognized the value of sector-based strategies to better respond to changes in a global economy. Understanding these trends is a critical first step in customizing further links between economic and workforce development.

Environmental Framework

An important aspect of metropolitan politics is how the public perceives issues, particularly whether regional politics is seen as collaborative or competitive. The media have an important role in shaping these perceptions. The chapter by Eric S. Zeemering, "Flushing the Conflict: Wastewater Cooperation among Michigan's Local Governments?" looks at four "frames" that shape the public discourse on wastewater issues in Michigan metropolitan areas—finance, political control, land use, and environmental concerns.

An extended case study of how regional cooperation in Grand Rapids gave way to a bitter fight over wastewater treatment facilities reflects the importance of these frames through the evolution of the policy debate over the five-year study period of wastewater issues. Initially, media coverage focused on the conflict between the city of Grand Rapids and the North Kent Sewer Authority (NKSA) over the cost of services. Over time, these issues were recast to reflect concerns over the management of the wastewater services and, to a lesser extent, the environmental aspects of the program. Once the NKSA decided to build its own system, the coverage began to have a more positive tone. Land use issues were only a minor aspect of the debates, however. The author observes similar patterns in other urban areas across Michigan.

Perhaps the most important contribution of this chapter is methodological. Decisions on how wastewater treatment services are to be provided, as well as many other complex metropolitan issues, can be viewed from a variety of perspectives. Moreover, the ways in which these issues are described in the media are likely to vary, depending on the particular frame that is being employed and the particular point in the evolution of the story. There is much that can be gained by a critical reading of media coverage and a careful assessment of the perspective that is being applied. Indeed, Hoffman and Pyne (chapter 12), suggest that media coverage of the "Brain Drain Wars" has greatly affected our perception of public policy around a knowledge-based economy in Michigan. Zeemering's chapter also reflects how the environmental and social components of the triple bottom line usually give way to being dominated by economic and fiscal concerns. The public finance frame appeared in 76 percent of the stories about interjurisdictional wastewater policy debate from 2001 to 2005. Ultimately, the "frames" of a public policy debate impact outcomes and proposed solutions to wastewater policies and other issues and help us to understand how environmental and social concerns are often relegated to secondary components of the triple bottom line.

There is growing recognition among Michigan residents regarding the importance of sustainability in planning for development. Initial efforts have tended to be place or community specific. Because sustainability is an issue that transcends political boundaries, regional- and metropolitan-level approaches are becoming more prominent.

In her chapter "Best Practices in Protecting Green Infrastructure: Benchmarking County Park Systems," Betty Gajewski argues that county governments can make a significant contribution to these efforts. In particular, county park systems can play an important role in protecting the green infrastructure aspects of sustainability. Based on a study of best practices of county park systems in Michigan and across the country, the author finds that, in addition to more traditional roles of providing recreational opportunities, county parks can be used for educational purposes, promoting the importance of sustainability, and to provide a green infrastructure network analogous to the gray infrastructure of roads and utilities.

Some of the earliest examples of regional cooperation have been in the areas of parks and open space. The Huron-Clinton Metropolitan Authority in Southeast Michigan is a prominent example of a regional approach. The existing county park organizations in Michigan provide a viable mechanism through which green infrastructure and sustainability policies can be encouraged. While individual counties can undertake such efforts on their own, there are also clear opportunities for promoting higher levels of regional cooperation. Gajewski describes Ottawa County as providing a leading example of how to effectively promote green infrastructure.

Finally, in his chapter "The Impact of Policy Change in Local and State Environmental Policy: Brownfield Redevelopment in Michigan," Richard Hula contends that states like Michigan have successfully challenged long-established federal dominance in environmental policy. One of the impediments to economic revitalization in Michigan, and other states in the Midwest and Northeast, is the abundance of contaminated sites that present not only hazards to health but also obstacles to redevelopment efforts. Federal initiatives, such as "Superfund," have impacted a limited number of sites, albeit ones that typically involve major contamination. Thousands of sites remain contaminated, however, with little in the way of public or private resources available for their remediation. The chapter explores efforts by the state of Michigan to craft a brownfield redevelopment initiative and assesses the affects of recent environmental policy reforms both through legislative action and executive order. Hula asserts that the magnitude of state efforts in brownfield initiatives is much greater than the federal initiatives. He finds that the Michigan brownfield initiative has, at a minimum, created a viable resale market for potentially contaminated sites.

As Hula points out, the state of Michigan has been a leader in dealing with contaminated sites as a result of its adoption of more flexible cleanup standards and limited owner liability, as well as the introduction of new funding mechanisms. Indeed, these efforts have been so successful that the state has broadened the definition of brownfield to include functionally obsolete but not necessarily contaminated sites. This set of policies has been successful in establishing a private market in contaminated (and obsolete) properties; it is not yet clear, however, that such policies are actually leading to increased levels of redevelopment.

Yet the empirical data cast doubt on many of the inflated claims advanced for brownfield initiative; with broad political support, however, the political success of the program is undeniable. This study provides conclusions that are admittedly tentative. Nevertheless, Michigan's suite of brownfield initiatives appears to have been successful in bringing substantial numbers of contaminated properties back onto the market. But making a site marketable is not the same as seeing it put to a productive new use or even eliminating environmental hazards. Renewing the interest of private investors in contaminated properties is an important, but only preliminary, step. There is a clear need for additional research to determine how public policy can be better used to achieve the important next steps in revitalizing older urban areas.

Social/Political Dynamics

Michigan municipalities face numerous impediments to intergovernmental cooperation on the provision of public services, including a strong tradition of home rule and competition for improving each community's tax base. Despite these obstacles, Jered B. Carr, Elisabeth R. Gerber, and Eric W. Lupher's chapter, "Explaining Horizontal and Vertical Cooperation in Michigan," finds that there are numerous instances of cooperation, both horizontal (between local units at the same level) and vertical (between the state or county and local units). Their research suggests that these two different types of cooperation are likely to result from differences in the nature of services and differences in the nature of the local government units.

Generally, public services that are capital intensive are more likely to be the subject of intergovernmental cooperation agreements, especially among similar local government units. Thus, libraries and water and sewer services are among the most commonly shared services. Services that required skilled personnel (legal, engineering, and planning, for example) are also likely to be subject to intergovernmental agreements. Cities and charter townships are less likely to participate in cooperative agreements than are general law townships and villages. This suggests that cooperation may be motivated more by the local ability to raise revenues than by the size of the local tax base.

From their findings, the Carr, Gerber, and Lupher draw conclusions with respect to how the state can encourage intergovernmental cooperation around service provision and how local units can more effectively identify candidates for cooperation. Based on the existing patterns of cooperation, local units may be able to discover service areas where cooperation is most likely and to identify potential partners. The state, even if it lacks financial resources to encourage cooperation, can provide information on the possibilities and benefits of cooperation and ensure that enabling legislation does not present impediments.

Dale E. Thomson's chapter, "Regional Housing Policy: Can Crisis Cause Collaboration?," identifies the problems of housing affordability in Michigan metropolitan areas and considers some particularly alarming trends in recent years in Southeast Michigan. Access to quality and affordable housing often forms the basis for economic opportunity. Housing is commonly the most important financial asset for households. It provides access to a bundle of private and public services that help to determine overall quality of life. While America is clearly a postshelter society (with most households enjoying very high standards of physical quality), substantial numbers of households still lack access to housing that is affordable. For many, excessive housing cost burdens leave them with insufficient resources for other necessities, such as health care.

Thomson asserts that housing affordability has become an increasing problem even in prosperous counties in Michigan. In 1989, only four of the nine counties of Southeast Michigan had more than 30 percent of households paying more than 30 percent of their income toward housing. By 2004, seven out of nine counties reached that threshold. In fact, since 1999, the cost burden grew by an average of 11 percent for each county. In 2004, an estimated 721,000 households within the region had affordability problems. This is 62 percent more than the 446,000 households with affordability problems in 1999. Even in relatively affluent areas like Oakland County, one of the richest counties in Michigan, the incidence of housing need is almost equal to that of counties where the average income is much lower. Even the most optimistic estimates of the cost of addressing these needs seems to be beyond the range of what can be achieved within existing budget constraints.

In addition, the national problems of foreclosure have deeply affected Michigan. By June 2007, Michigan had one of the highest foreclosure rates in the nation. Genesee, Macomb, Oakland, and Wayne counties had the four highest monthly total increases in foreclosure in the state (221, 404, 470, and 474 respectively) accounting for 60 percent of bank foreclosures statewide (Michigan Foreclosure Activity 2007). The number of elderly households in need of housing support has also skyrocketed. The picture is not entirely bleak, however. Thomson sees that the increasing prevalence of housing needs may provide sufficient political will to support the adoption of regional solutions. Because the population affected by affordability issues is changing in virtually every community, efforts to ameliorate these problems are less likely to be perceived as involving transfers of resources or providing benefits only to minority groups (inner-city residents of Detroit or Pontiac, for example). Similar to the arguments of Myron Orfield that natural coalitions exist among older municipalities, the widespread nature of housing need may lay the foundation for regional cooperative efforts. The author concludes that while changes are subtly beginning to shift the framing of the housing problem in Michigan in ways that can affect future solution sets, the current progress in creating regional solutions have not yet emerged.

The chapter by June Manning Thomas, "Michigan's Urban Policies in an Era of Land Use Reform and Creative-Class Cities," looks at two of the urban strategies that the state of Michigan has adopted in its efforts to reposition the state economy. One is to make an explicit link between land use policies, especially in metropolitan areas, and economic development. The efforts of the Michigan Land Use Leadership Council to connect urban revitalization with regional land use policies are cited as important examples of recognizing the need for greater state leadership in these areas. Although the implementation of specific recommendations of the council has been limited to date, the author considers the emphasis on land use to be important in framing policy discussions and initiatives. The second policy development also has an emphasis on place. Specifically, revitalization of Michigan's cities is seen as being critical to the state's ability to attract and retain the creative talent that is expected to drive the new economy. Operating primarily under the umbrella of the Cool Cities program, these policy initiatives attempt to use a variety of tools, many of them already in existence, to make cities more attractive to the "Creative Class." Thomas raises two fundamental concerns in Michigan's adaptation of Richard Florida's framework in patterning an urban economic development strategy. First, other analysts have found some

11

flawed analysis and erroneous conclusions in Florida's work. Second, no independent evidence yet exists that following his prescriptions will lead to central-city or metropolitan growth.

Thomas finds only limited examples of the success of these initiatives. Perhaps the most encouraging finding is that Michigan is attempting to utilize traditional planning tools to achieve objectives that serve the new economy. The effectiveness of inner-city redevelopment strategies is, however, limited by Michigan's lack of regional planning tools. Perhaps the greatest potential lies in strategies based on attracting larger numbers of immigrants to the state's cities.

Much has been made of the importance of educated young people to the future prosperity of Michigan. Richard Florida has argued that the new economy of the twenty-first century is especially dependent on the contributions of recent college graduates. Policy makers and researchers have suggested that Michigan is failing to attract and hold this population and is, in fact suffering a "brain drain." The chapter by M. Curtis Hoffman and Jeremy Pyne, "The Brain Drain Wars: Characteristics of Recent Movers into and out of Michigan," uses data from the American Community Survey to assess popular perceptions about the knowledge-based economy in Michigan, focusing on whether data supports common assumptions about the exodus of the Creative Class and suggests Michigan's future public policy must be firmly grounded in current realities if the state will make progress in transitioning to a more knowledge based economy.

The authors look at the migration in and out of Michigan between 2000 and 2005, focusing on the population cohorts identified by Florida as members of the Creative Class. They find that, although Michigan did experience a net loss of the Creative Class population broadly defined, the loss was actually less than that of the general population. The "Super Creative Class" and the gay and bohemian populations, however, did have even larger net losses to areas outside of Michigan.

From a policy perspective, even though the governor's Cool Cities initiative is cited as a mechanism for retaining and attracting Creative Class residents, the authors express concern about the effects of the current state fiscal crisis on the ability to adequately fund this program. While Cool Cities and other grant programs increase the capacity of local governments and other organizations to compete in the Brain Drain wars, these grants are dwarfed by the money lost in cuts to state revenue sharing to cities, which declined by $442 million in 2006 from the 2001 figure (Plante and Moran 2007: 2–3). Similarly, the Michigan Promise Scholarship program has been weakened by the state cuts in university funding and the perceived scarcity of jobs for college graduates in Michigan. They also argue that public policy developments in Michigan are likely to be perceived as being contrary to efforts to attract a diverse population to the state.

Towards a Triple Bottom Line

Finally, Norman Christopher and Richard W. Jelier's chapter, "Building a Triple Bottom Line Sustainability Model in Michigan," combines all three components of the triple bottom line by highlighting a first attempt in Michigan to create a regional model that could serve as a benchmark for the rest of the state. Christopher and Jelier focus on a few areas that are drawing national attention around the country, including certified and registered Leadership in Energy and Environmental Design (LEED) buildings and construction and sustainable manufacturing practices. More than 69 percent of LEED certified buildings in the state of Michigan have been built in West Michigan. Grand Rapids ranks first per capita nationally among all cities for the most LEED certified buildings.

Grand Rapids is also the first city in Michigan to create a sustainable development administrator, who directly serves the city manager and overseas the triple bottom line for the city. Further, the formation of a Community Sustainability Partnership (CSP), which has grown to include over 165 organizations in two years in Greater Grand Rapids, is significant. The CSP has endorsed and supported sustainability-guiding principles, and its members are applying sustainable development "best practices" into their respective organizations. The model has already been replicated in Muskegon, the Holland/Zeeland area, Spring Lake/Grand Haven and Kalamazoo, and may reach the east side of the state in the near future.

Fostering Sustainable Metropolitan Areas for Michigan's Future

Creating sustainable metropolitan communities in the twenty-first century will pose great challenges for Michigan, many of which are identified in this volume. These authors question existing policy related to the future course for Michigan. The findings, strategies, and policies presented here have applications outside of Michigan's metropolitan communities and should also be of interest to other states. Clearly, as the earlier MIHELP publication *The State of Michigan Cities: An Index of Urban Prosperity* so dramatically illustrated, Michigan's metropolitan communities are at risk (Adelaja et al. 2007). This volume goes a long way toward increasing understanding of the key economic, environmental, social, and political reasons why change is under way, the challenges to the current system, and the difficulty for Michigan in making substantive changes.

Collaboration by institutions of higher education through the MIHELP Consortium is a positive development. This volume links critical, cutting-edge scholarship to pressing issues facing Michigan's metropolitan communities. The well-being of our state may very well depend on the critical knowledge and understanding of the complex issues addressed in this volume to affect both the current and the next generation of decision makers.

Notes

1. This report can be accessed at http://www.mihelp.org.
2. An editorial committee reviewed each proposal and offered detailed comments on each draft. Chapters were selected based on methodological soundness encompassing quantitative, qualitative, or case-study research, and contribution to knowledge about metropolitan studies.
3. These include revitalizing Michigan cities; market solutions to land use problems; viable agriculture for the future; sustaining Michigan's water and natural resources and

13

related industries; enhanced planning and coordination in land use decision making; creating healthy communities; equipping state decision makers in land Use; empowering Michigan's citizens in land use; data collection, information, and analysis for improving land use policy; and national leadership profile.

REFERENCES

Adelaja, S., W. Rustem, G. Sands, R. Jelier, and J. Horner. 2007. *State of Michigan Cities: An Index of Urban Prosperity.* East Lansing: Michigan State University.

Dyllick, T., and K. Hockerts. 2002. Corporate Sustainability: Beyond the Business Case. *Business Strategy and the Environment* 11(2):130–141.

Plante and Moran, PLLC. 2007. Get Your Crystal Ball Out . . . What Will Michigan's Municipal Finance Model Look Like in the Years to Come? *Municipal Flash Advisor* (March):1–4.

RealtyTrac, Inc. 2007. Michigan Foreclosure Activity Increases 7 Percent in June. Press release, July 31. Http://www.realtytrac.com/ContentManagement/Library.aspx?ChannelID=13&ItemID=2845.

Reese, L. A., and R. A. Rosenfeld. 2004. Local Economic Development in the U.S. and Canada: Institutionalizing Policy Approaches. *American Review of Public Administration* 34:277–292.

Sands G., and L. A. Reese. 2006. The Equity Impacts of Municipal Tax Incentives: Leveling or Tilting the Playing Field? *Review of Policy Research* (January 23):71–94.

Skole, D., S. Batzli, S. Gage, B. Pijanowksi, W. Chomentowski, and W. Rustem. 2002. Forecast Michigan: Tracking Change for Land Use Planning and Policymaking. In *Urban Policy Choices for Michigan Leaders,* edited by D. W. Thornton and C. S. Weissert. East Lansing: Michigan State University Press.

State of Michigan, Department of Labor and Economic Growth. 2007. Current Labor Statistics (searchable database).

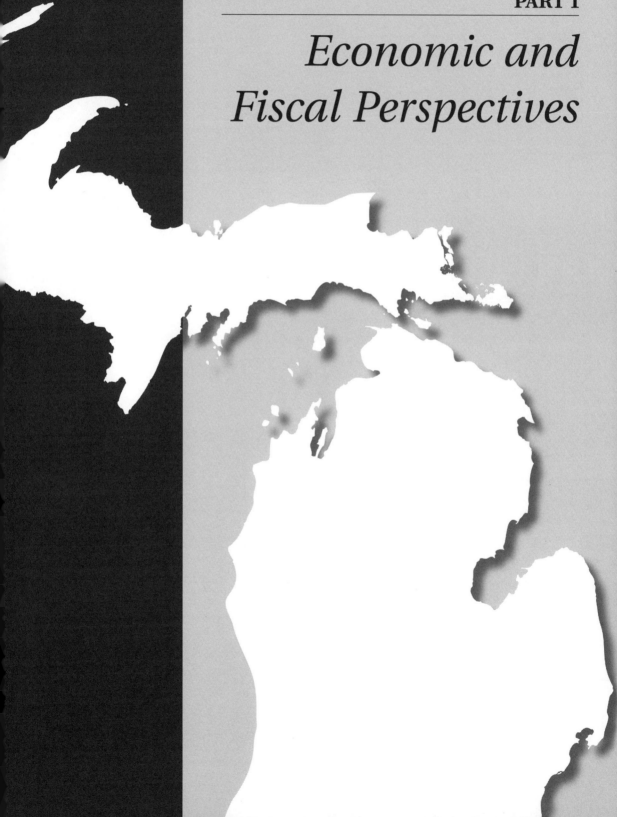

PART 1

Economic and Fiscal Perspectives

CHAPTER 1

The Economic and Fiscal Background of Metropolitan Policies in Michigan

Charles L. Ballard

Economic and Population Growth

In the first half of twentieth century, the Michigan economy became deeply involved in durable-goods manufacturing, with particular emphasis on the automobile industry. These industries were remarkably successful, especially in the three decades from 1940 to 1970. Workers flooded into Michigan from other states and other countries. During that thirty-year period, Michigan's population grew from 5.26 million to 8.88 million, an increase of about 69 percent.[1]

Since 1970, the economy and population of Michigan have grown much more slowly. If the rate of population growth between 1940 and 1970 had been maintained since 1970, Michigan's population would now be nearly 17 million. Instead, Michigan's actual population is about 10.1 million.[2] Thus, Michigan has nearly 7 million fewer people than it would have had if the rapid population growth from 1940 to 1970 had sustained itself. If that additional population growth had actually occurred, it is likely that it would have been heavily concentrated in the southern half of the Lower Peninsula, already the most densely populated part of the state.

That additional population would have put substantial pressure on the physical environment. More fields and forests would have been converted to residential, commercial, and industrial uses, and paved over for roads.[3] There would have been a few million more cars. Thus, when we consider economic development policies, it is useful to maintain perspective. Popular discussions of economic-development policy in Michigan tend to be strongly in favor of more rapid economic growth. The benefits of economic growth are undeniable. However, economic growth is also associated with a variety of costs. These costs

17

can be especially great if economic growth is not managed in a context that also places value on efficient land use and sensitivity to environmental issues. If the widely expressed wish for more rapid economic growth in Michigan is granted, then the people of the state will have to deal with an increased set of difficult land use and environmental issues. That will bring environmental stewardship to the fore.

The Level of Income

Figure 1.1 shows real (inflation-adjusted) per capita personal income in Michigan, and in the United States as a whole, from 1929, the earliest year for which these data are available, to 2007.[4] It is useful to see this long time series, to remind ourselves that Michigan has experienced phenomenal economic growth. The sluggish economy of the last several years should not obscure the long history of rapid growth. Figure 1.1 shows that, even after adjusting for inflation, personal per capita income was more than twice as high in 2007 as in 1965, and more than four times as high in 2007 as in 1940.

However, the *rate* of income growth, like the rate of population growth, slowed substantially after 1970. From 1940 to 1970, real per capita personal income grew at an annual rate of about 2.62 percent. From 1970 to 2007, real per capita income grew at an annual rate of about 1.72 percent. This may seem like a small difference in growth rates. However, when such a difference is compounded over a long period, it can have a very large effect. If real per capita personal income in Michigan had grown since 1970 at the same rate at which it

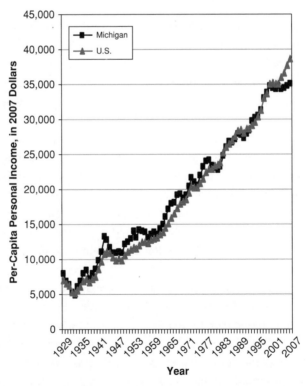

FIGURE 1.1
Inflation-Adjusted Per Capita Personal Income, In Michigan and in the United States, 1929–2007

grew from 1940 to 1970, it would have reached about $49,000 by 2007. Instead, per capita personal income in Michigan in 2007 was actually $35,086.[5]

This reduction in the rate of income growth has moved Michigan from above the national average level of income to below the national average. From the 1940s through the 1960s, per capita income in Michigan was typically a bit more than 10 percent higher than the national average. Michigan incomes stayed above the national average in the 1970s, although by a smaller margin. But the deep recession of the early 1980s was an especially severe blow to Michigan's manufacturing-based economy. As a result, in 1981 Michigan incomes fell below the national average for the first time since 1933. From 1981 to 2003, Michigan incomes were often very close to the national average, but usually a few percentage points below.

However, average real income levels in Michigan were essentially flat from 2000 to 2006. After a six-year period of negligible growth in real per capita income, the data indicate that Michigan finally saw a modest increase in 2007. Per capita personal income in Michigan rose to $35,086 in 2007. This is the highest level ever recorded, even after adjusting for inflation. (The previous all-time high had occurred in 2000.)

The upturn of real per capita income in Michigan in 2007 is an encouraging sign. However, this one year of modest growth came on the heels of a six-year period during which average incomes were stagnant. Moreover, while the income growth rate in Michigan between 2006 and 2007 was about 1.3 percent (higher than it had been in Michigan since 1999–2000), this was still only about half as large as the income growth rate for the United States as a whole. Thus, the ratio of Michigan incomes to the national average continued to fall. As a result, in 2007, Michigan's per capita income of $35,086 was only about 90.9 percent of the national average ($38,611). This is lower than the ratio of Michigan income to the national average has ever been.

According to the data from the Bureau of Economic Analysis of the U.S. Department of Commerce, Michigan ranked twenty-sixth among the fifty states in terms of per capita income (or twenty-seventh if we include the District of Columbia) in both 2006 and 2007. The rankings for 2007 are shown in table 1.1.

The preceding paragraphs certainly contain some bad news. However, they also contain some not-so-bad news, and even some good news. And yet popular accounts of the Michigan economy are often so negative that it may seem strange to hear that inflation-adjusted per capita income reached an all-time high in 2007. It may also seem strange to hear that Michigan is actually in the middle of the pack among the fifty states in terms of per capita personal income. In the midst of many negative stories about the Michigan economy, some may have assumed that Michigan was near the bottom of the fifty states in per capita personal income. It is true that Michigan's unemployment rate has been the highest in the country for a few years. However, the highest unemployment rate does not need to translate into the lowest level of income. Many Michigan workers are earning enough to keep Michigan's average per capita income level well above the average levels of West Virginia and Mississippi, for example.

The Distribution of Income

The data presented above are all for statewide averages. They do not say anything about the distribution of income among Michigan's people. In fact, many Michigan residents have

Table 1.1. Per Capita Personal Income for the Fifty States and the District of Columbia, 2007

Ranking	State	Income (dollars)
1	Connecticut	54,117
2	New Jersey	49,194
3	Massachusetts	49,082
4	New York	47,385
5	Maryland	46,021
6	Wyoming	43,226
7	California	41,571
8	New Hampshire	41,512
9	Virginia	41,347
10	Colorado	41,042
11	Minnesota	41,034
12	Delaware	40,608
13	Nevada	40,480
14	Washington	40,414
15	Alaska	40,352
16	Illinois	40,322
17	Rhode Island	39,463
18	Hawaii	39,239
19	Pennsylvania	38,788
	U.S. Average	**38,611**
20	Florida	38,444
21	Texas	37,187
22	Kansas	36,768
23	Vermont	36,670
24	Nebraska	36,471
25	Wisconsin	36,047
26	**Michigan**	**35,086**
27	Iowa	35,023
28	Ohio	34,874
29	North Dakota	34,846
30	Oregon	34,784
31	Louisiana	34,756
32	Missouri	34,389
33	Oklahoma	34,153
34	South Dakota	33,905
35	Maine	33,722
36	North Carolina	33,636
37	Indiana	33,616
38	Georgia	33,457
39	Tennessee	33,280
40	Arizona	33,029
41	Montana	32,458
42	Alabama	32,404
43	New Mexico	31,474
44	Idaho	31,197
45	Utah	31,189
46	Kentucky	31,111
47	South Carolina	31,013
48	Arkansas	30,060
49	West Virginia	29,537
50	Mississippi	28,845
	District of Columbia	61,092

done extremely well in recent decades. On the other hand, recent years have been difficult for a great number of Michigan's residents. One of the most important trends in Michigan (and indeed in the entire U.S. economy) in the last thirty years has been the rapid increase in the gap between those at the top of the income distribution and those in the middle and at the bottom. Nationally, income inequality has risen to levels not seen since the early part of the twentieth century.[6]

The rise in income inequality has been caused primarily by an increase in the inequality of labor-market earnings. (Most households get all or nearly all of their income from the labor market.) Rebecca Blank, who studied the increase in earnings inequality in Michigan (Blank 2003), documents the stark divergence between earnings for college graduates, which have risen rapidly, and earnings for those with less education, which have stagnated.

Along with Paul Menchik, my colleague in the Department of Economics at Michigan State University, I have analyzed the income trends for households in Michigan, and in the rest of the country, using detailed data from the Current Population Survey (CPS).[7] The CPS is an annual survey of households across the United States. In recent years, the CPS has typically had a sample of about 2,000 households in Michigan. Some of our results are shown in figure 1.2. In this figure, we compare the income level for households at the same place in the income distribution, in the 1970s and in recent years. (Specifically, we take averages for 1976–1978 and compare them with averages for 2003–2005. We use three-year averages, rather than data from a single year, in order to reduce fluctuations due to sampling variability.) We compare the real, inflation-adjusted income for the household at the 10th percentile of the income distribution[8] in 2003–2005 with the real, inflation-adjusted income for the household at the 10th percentile of the income distribution in 1976–1978.[9] We then follow the same procedure for the 20th percentile, 30th percentile, and so forth.

Figure 1.2 shows the percentage change in real, inflation-adjusted income for the 10th, 20th, and on up to the 90th percentile in Michigan, and also for the United States as a whole, between 1976–1978 and 2003–2005. Regardless of whether we are considering Michigan or the United States, we see a very strong trend toward greater inequality. The households at the lower part of the income distribution had much smaller gains than the households at the top of the income distribution. Figure 1.2 shows that the trend toward increased inequality in Michigan is fairly similar to the trend in the United States as a whole.

However, figure 1.2 also shows that Michigan residents did less well than the national average throughout the entire income distribution. In fact, the real income levels for the bottom half of Michigan households gained only about 2 percent over this period of nearly thirty years. (That is, 2 percent over the entire period, *not* 2 percent per year.) On the other hand, a Michigan household at the 90th percentile in 2003–2005 had about 33 percent more income than a Michigan household at the 90th percentile in 1976–1978, even after adjusting for inflation.

In the late 1970s, the top 5 percent of Michigan households had about 15 percent of the total income of the state, and the bottom 50 percent of households had more than 23 percent of the total income. Nowadays, however, the top 5 percent have about 22 percent of the total income, whereas the bottom 50 percent of households have only about 19 percent of the total income. This is a very substantial shift toward greater inequality. Thus, in terms of social equity, Michigan's performance has left a lot to be desired.

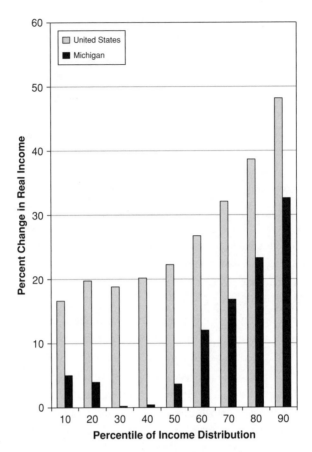

FIGURE 1.2

Percentage Change in Inflation-Adjusted Income, For Selected Percentiles of the Income Distributions of the United States and Michigan, 1976/78 to 2003/05

The rapid increase in inequality is one of the reasons why the adoption of a graduated income tax in Michigan would be desirable. Under a graduated income tax, the marginal tax rate is higher for those with larger amounts of income. Currently, Michigan is one of only seven states in which all taxable income is taxed at the same rate, whereas thirty-six states, the District of Columbia, and the federal government have a graduated income tax. Partly as a result of the state's flat-rate income tax, Michigan has one of the most regressive tax systems in the nation. Adoption of a graduated income tax would shift a portion of the tax burden to the most affluent residents of the state. These are precisely the people who, as shown by figure 1.2, have fared much better than their lower-income fellow citizens in the last three decades.

The gap between high-income and low-income residents of Michigan also has a geographical dimension. The most recent year for which income data are available on a county-by-county basis is 2005.[10] In that year, per capita personal income for the state as a whole was $32,804. Oakland County was by far the most affluent county in the state, with per capita income of $52,274, which is nearly 60 percent greater than the statewide average. In fact, per capita income in Oakland County was about 32 percent larger than in the second-most-affluent county in the state, Washtenaw County. Thus, the distribution of income by county is strongly positively skewed, so that only eight of Michigan's eighty-three counties are above the state average for income. At the other end of the scale, per capita income was below $20,000 in Oscoda County in the northern Lower Peninsula, and in Luce County in the Upper Peninsula. In 2005, per capita income in Luce County was $19,115, which is only about 58 percent as large as per capita income for the state as a whole, and only about 37 percent as large as for Oakland County. Table 1.2 shows the complete rankings for per capita personal income in 2005, for each of Michigan's eighty-three counties.

Table 1.2. Per Capita Personal Income for the Eighty-three Counties in Michigan, 2005

Ranking	County	Per Capita Income (dollars)	Per Capita Income as Percent of State Average
1	Oakland	52,274	159.4
2	Washtenaw	39,689	121.0
3	Midland	37,099	113.1
4	Leelanau	36,502	111.3
5	Livingston	36,140	110.2
6	Macomb	34,761	106.0
7	Emmet	33,896	103.3
8	Kent	33,627	102.5
	Michigan Average	**32,804**	**100.0**
9	Grand Traverse	32,089	97.8
10	Kalamazoo	32,089	97.8
11	Charlevoix	31,486	96.0
12	Monroe	30,873	94.1
13	Wayne	30,855	94.1
14	Ottawa	30,743	93.7
15	Clinton	30,685	93.5
16	Ingham	30,656	93.5
17	St. Clair	29,922	91.2
18	Barry	29,882	91.1
19	Dickinson	29,869	91.1
20	Eaton	29,257	89.2
21	Berrien	29,242	89.1
22	Lenawee	29,116	88.8
23	Huron	28,886	88.1
24	Lapeer	28,686	87.4
25	Mackinac	28,619	87.2
26	Cass	28,322	86.3
27	Calhoun	28,289	86.2
28	Allegan	28,259	86.1
29	Bay	27,984	85.3
30	Genesee	27,550	84.0
31	Antrim	27,333	83.3
32	Alpena	27,304	83.2
33	Jackson	27,299	83.2
34	Saginaw	27,256	83.1
35	Otsego	27,047	82.5
36	Delta	26,799	81.7
37	Benzie	26,676	81.3

(continued)

Table 1.2. Per Capita Personal Income for the Eighty-three Counties in Michigan, 2005 (*continued*)

Ranking	County	Per Capita Income (dollars)	Per Capita Income as Percent of State Average
38	Marquette	26,506	80.8
39	Mason	26,396	80.5
40	Sanilac	26,189	79.8
41	St. Joseph	26,078	79.5
42	Ontonagon	26,013	79.3
43	Keweenaw	25,740	78.5
44	Muskegon	25,692	78.3
45	Iron	25,458	77.6
46	Van Buren	25,290	77.1
47	Hillsdale	25,208	76.8
48	Menominee	25,094	76.5
49	Isabella	24,978	76.1
50	Shiawassee	24,916	76.0
51	Manistee	24,853	75.8
52	Cheboygan	24,765	75.5
53	Wexford	24,593	75.0
54	Schoolcraft	23,837	72.7
55	Gratiot	23,794	72.5
56	Gogebic	23,731	72.3
57	Newaygo	23,644	72.1
58	Presque Isle	23,547	71.8
59	Branch	23,502	71.6
60	Ionia	23,442	71.5
61	Oceana	23,404	71.3
62	Arenac	23,346	71.2
63	Roscommon	23,141	70.5
64	Osceola	23,093	70.4
65	Houghton	22,976	70.0
66	Tuscola	22,932	69.9
67	Iosco	22,792	69.5
68	Alcona	22,501	68.6
69	Clare	22,497	68.6
70	Gladwin	22,366	68.2
71	Alger	22,033	67.2
72	Montcalm	21,868	66.7
73	Ogemaw	21,768	66.4
74	Mecosta	21,658	66.0
75	Chippewa	21,632	65.9
76	Baraga	21,581	65.8
77	Missaukee	21,545	65.7
78	Crawford	21,204	64.6
79	Montmorency	21,153	64.5
80	Lake	21,041	64.1
81	Kalkaska	20,512	62.5
82	Oscoda	19,960	60.8
83	Luce	19,115	58.3

The heavily populated counties in metropolitan areas tend to have higher per capita incomes than the nonmetropolitan counties of Michigan. Macomb County ranks sixth in the state, Kent County is eighth, Wayne County is thirteenth, and Ingham County is six-teenth. Nearly all of the counties below the state median for per capita income are non-metropolitan. However, four nonmetropolitan counties are notable for their relatively high income levels. These are Leelanau (ranked fourth in the state), Emmet (seventh), Grand Traverse (ninth), and Charlevoix (eleventh). All are located in the northwestern part of the Lower Peninsula. These areas have achieved a relatively high degree of prosperity by attract-ing affluent tourists and retirees. If we look beyond these four exceptional counties, how-ever, the nonmetropolitan areas of Michigan tend to be much less affluent than the metropolitan areas.

The data presented above give us a very mixed picture. On the one hand, it is certainly true that Michigan remains a very prosperous place, both by historical standards and by comparison with most of the world today. Michigan is not Madagascar or Myanmar. On the other hand, for the last several decades Michigan's economy and population have grown considerably less rapidly than the economy and population of the United States as a whole. Since 1950, on average, per capita income in Michigan has declined relative to the national average by about one-third of one percentage point per year.[11] If this long-term trend were to continue for another two decades, Michigan would fall into the bottom ten states in terms of income level. If the more precipitous pace of relative decline that we have seen since 1999 continued, Michigan would be the poorest state in the United States in twenty years.

I do not predict that this will happen; I do not believe that Michigan will one day be the poorest state. As I have traveled around the state in the last few years, I have observed a real hunger for imaginative solutions, and a desire to work hard. I remain optimistic that the recent downward trends will be reversed. Thus, I am not trying to be alarmist or sensational. I am merely trying to show the situation clearly.

Reasons for the Economic Slowdown

Almost certainly, the vast majority of Michigan residents would prefer to reverse this trend of sluggish economic growth (even though doing so would put more pressure on the phys-ical environment). If we are to do so, it is imperative to understand how we got into this situation in the first place. These issues are discussed at considerable length in my book, *Michigan's Economic Future* (2006). In brief, the Michigan economy of today has been powerfully shaped by a series of events stretching back more than half a century. By the middle of the twentieth century, Michigan's economy was a manufacturing powerhouse. At that time, the manufacturing sector was the dominant force driving the economy. Con-sequently, Michigan's manufacturing-based economy was well positioned for rapid growth. For better or worse, however, manufacturing's share of the U.S. economy has been declining for several decades. According to the Bureau of Economic Analysis, manufacturing's share of U.S. gross product shrank from about 27.2 percent in 1963 to about 12.2 percent in 2006. The manufacturing share of Michigan's economy has been higher than that of the U.S. economy throughout this period, and it shows an even more dramatic decline. Manufacturing's share of gross product in Michigan fell from about 48.2 percent in 1963

25

to about 17.9 percent in 2006. Just as Michigan was relatively prosperous when manufacturing was at its peak, Michigan has been adversely affected by the relative decline of manufacturing.[12]

The lack of diversification of the Michigan economy is even more profound than the numbers in the previous paragraph might suggest. Michigan depends extremely heavily on only one sector within manufacturing. That sector, of course, is the automobile industry. But even that dependence does not fully tell the story of Michigan's undiversified economy. In fact, the automobile industry in the United States as a whole has not performed nearly as badly as the automobile industry in Michigan. U.S. installations owned by Japanese and other automakers (located in states such as Alabama, Kentucky, and South Carolina) are doing relatively well. Michigan's problem is that, with a few notable exceptions, the auto industry in Michigan is associated with the "Big Three" domestic automobile companies—General Motors, Ford, and Chrysler.

In the 1950s, these three companies had a cozy oligopoly, with very little competition. This was bad for consumers, but very good for the companies. The combination of high productivity and oligopoly pricing led to strong profitability. The United Automobile Workers union (UAW) succeeded in bargaining its way to control over an increased portion of the industry's revenues. This situation may have been sustainable if it had been possible to keep out competition, but competing companies began to penetrate the U.S. market strongly in the 1970s. This was good for American consumers, but the American auto companies found themselves in a very difficult situation. They were saddled with a bloated cost structure, at the same time that foreign-owned companies were producing cars that were very attractive to a wide segment of the American market. Between 1976 and 2004, the American companies lost half of their market share in the domestic market for passenger cars.[13]

The decline of manufacturing in general, and of the American-owned part of the auto industry in particular, is by far the dominant cause of the struggles facing Michigan's economy today. It is important to understand this, since alternative explanations are sometimes put forth in the public debate. Some have suggested that the difficulties are the result of Michigan's tax policies, but these suggestions are misleading. While tax policies undeniably have an effect on economic behavior, it is important not to overstate the case.[14] The location of economic activity is influenced by many things other than taxes, such as the availability of skilled workers, the availability of financing, proximity to customer base, proximity to resources, and the availability of transportation and communications infrastructure. My colleague Leslie Papke puts it succinctly in a research paper coauthored with Stephen Mark and Therese McGuire (Mark, McGuire, and Papke 1997):

> The economic effect of taxes tends both to be small and to be less important than other factors. Labor force availability and quality, for example, appear to be more important for explaining differences across locations in economic activity. How tax revenues are spent tends to be important enough that high relative taxes may not be a deterrent to economic growth if the revenues are used to finance services of value to business, such as education and transportation infrastructure. The studies do make clear that a policy of cutting taxes to induce economic growth is not likely to be efficient or cost-effective.

It is appropriate that Papke and her coauthors mention education, because human-capital investment plays such an important role in the modern economy. For many years, the portion of the Michigan population with a bachelor's degree has lagged behind the national average, typically by about three percentage points. As pointed out earlier, the earnings gap between those with a college education and those with less education has increased dramatically in the last few decades. Thus, the damage to the Michigan economy from having a low rate of college attainment is far greater now than it was a few decades ago.[15]

In a very real sense, Michigan's economy today is a victim of its past success. Half a century ago, during the heyday of manufacturing, large numbers of Michigan workers with less than a college education were able to earn middle-class or even upper-middle-class wages. Those opportunities are far less plentiful now. If the Michigan economy is to regain its former position, improved labor-force skills will be crucial. The skills of the labor force can be enhanced in a variety of ways, not all of which require public investment. However, public investment in education is certainly an important part of the picture. Thus, I turn now to an analysis of government budgets in Michigan.

Public Revenues and Expenditures in Michigan

Trends in Tax Revenues

Figure 1.3 shows some trends in the percentage of personal income devoted to state and local taxes.[16] The figure shows Michigan and the average for the United States as a whole, as well as New York (which has historically been among the states with the highest taxes) and Texas (which has historically been among the states with the lowest taxes).

Figure 1.3 shows a long-term trend, under which state and local taxes have accounted for a decreasing portion of personal income in the United States. Over the one-third of a century represented in figure 1.3, the U.S. average decreased from about 12.8 percent of personal income to about 11.3 percent. Throughout this entire period, the percentage of income devoted to state and local taxes in Michigan was quite close to the national average. In the 1970s and 1980s, this percentage was slightly higher in Michigan than in the United States as a whole. In recent years, Michigan has been slightly below the national average. In 2004–2005, Michigan ranked twenty-seventh among the fifty states in terms of tax revenue as a percentage of personal income, or twenty-eighth if the District of Columbia is included.

Thus, Michigan has gone from slightly above the national average for taxes to slightly below the national average, during a period in which the national average itself has been declining. Over the period shown in figure 1.3, state and local taxes in Michigan declined from about 13.2 percent of personal income to about 11 percent of personal income. In 2007, personal income in Michigan was about $353.4 billion (or a bit more than one-third of a trillion dollars).[17] Thus, if the percentage of personal income devoted to state and local taxes was still the same as it had been in the 1970s, the state and local governments and public schools in Michigan would have more than $7 billion per year more than they have now.

In presenting this information, I am not arguing for a sudden $7 billion tax increase. The point of these data is to show that the economy of Michigan has very substantial capacity. Our decisions to decrease the percentage of our income that goes to public purposes have

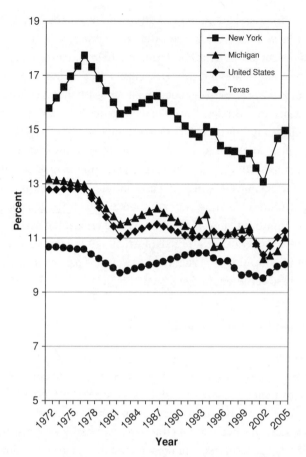

FIGURE 1.3
State and Local Taxes as a Percent of Personal Income, For Selected States, 1972–2005

been driven by the policy preferences of our elected leaders. They have not been driven by a lack of resources.

Explicit tax-rate cuts are one reason for the decline in tax revenues in the last decade or so. For example, the income-tax rate was reduced from 4.6 percent to 4.4 percent in 1994, and then it was reduced five more times from 1999 to 2004, eventually reaching 3.9 percent. (After a long legislative battle and a brief government shutdown in 2007, the rate was raised to 4.35. This helped to push toward a balanced budget for the 2008 fiscal year, and it will help to reduce, but not eliminate, the long-term structural budget deficit for the state of Michigan.)

However, changes in tax rates are not the only factor behind the long-term decline in tax revenues. Structural weaknesses in various components of the tax system are just as important. For instance, the sales tax in Michigan applies to relatively few services, but services have been growing more rapidly than the items that are subject to the sales tax. Thus, the sales tax applies to an ever-shrinking fraction of the economy.[18] In October 2007, during midnight sessions in an attempt to avert a government shutdown over a $1.9 billion structural deficit, the sales tax was extended to some services, but the extension was repealed before it ever went into effect. The sales tax on services was handled with an astonishing degree of political ineptitude. This is unfortunate, since it may mean that the idea of applying the tax to services will be off the table for a long time to come. Regardless of the political difficulties, the economic case for extending the sales tax to services remains extremely strong. As long as the sales tax is applied only to a declining portion of the economy, it will remain inefficient and inequitable, and it will contribute to the ongoing structural budget deficit.

The attempt to extend the sales tax to some services in 2007 was a part of a broader attempt to raise revenues to offset a large budget shortfall. Thus, the proposal was to increase the sales-tax rate from zero to 6 percent for some items, without giving a tax cut to any other items. The chances for political success might be higher in the context of a revenue-neutral tax reform. In that case, some services would see a tax increase from zero to, say, 4 percent, while many manufactured goods would see a tax cut.

Although the long-term trend is for state and local taxes to be a declining portion of personal income, figure 1.3 shows that the percentage actually *increased* slightly from 2002 to 2005, both for Michigan and for the nation as a whole. In Michigan, the most important factor contributing to these revenue increases was that property tax revenues increased substantially during this period, partly because of increases in property values and partly because of tax-rate increases. In addition, increases in the cigarette-tax rate led to sharp revenue increases. These revenue increases substantially offset the income-tax rate reductions. Even with these increases, however, the portion of personal income going to state and local taxes in Michigan in 2005 was still lower than it had been in any year from the 1970s until 2000, with the exception of 1995 and 1996.

The residential housing market in Michigan has suffered substantially in recent years, just as it has suffered in many other parts of the United States. Declining property values can be expected to lead to slower growth (or even to decreases) of property-tax revenues. Thus, when complete data for 2006 and 2007 become available, it is likely that we will see the end of the relative increases of 2002–2005.[19]

Earlier, it was noted that it is best to include both state and local revenues when making comparisons among the states. However, this does not mean that the distinction between state revenues and local revenues is unimportant. In particular, according to the census data, state tax revenues increased by only 7.6 percent from 2001–2002 to 2004–2005, while local tax revenues increased by 33.3 percent during the same period.[20] Thus, while local government tax revenues managed to stay ahead of inflation during this period, the tax revenues of the state government did not.[21]

State Government Expenditures

State government responded to the decline in tax revenue in a variety of ways. Asset sales figured very prominently in the state's response. According to a recent report by the Citizens Research Council of Michigan (2007a), the cash balances of the state's major funds deteriorated by $4.2 billion from the 2000 fiscal year to the 2006 fiscal year. As a result, these funds went from a positive net position to a negative one. The state is thus forced to make interest payments on borrowing to meet its cash needs, whereas the state used to be a net recipient of interest in the amount of approximately $200 million per year. The deterioration of the state's cash position is part of a broader trend toward relying on one-time resources to solve the state's budget woes. Other one-time fixes include securitization of tobacco-settlement revenues, changes in the timing of revenue collections, and accounting changes. As outlined in another Citizens Research Council report, the sum of all of these one-time resources is about $6.8 billion.[22] As soon as possible, the state of Michigan should find a way to match its recurring expenditures with its recurring revenues.

In addition to spending down its assets and engaging in one-time fixes, the state also engaged in substantial spending reductions. The spending programs over which the state government has control are concentrated in the School Aid Fund, which provides funding for K-12 education in Michigan, and the General Fund. Although elementary and secondary education is very important, the emphasis in this chapter is on other issues, and the paragraphs that follow will focus on the General Fund.[23]

The General Fund budget covers a wide array of departments within state government. Table 1.3 shows the General Fund/General Purpose (GF/GP) expenditures for the 2007 fiscal year.

In table 1.3, the three departments that are most associated with land use and the environment—Agriculture, Environmental Quality, and Natural Resources—have been highlighted. Together, these three departments make up only about 1 percent of the GF/GP budget. In fact, GF/GP expenditure in Michigan is strongly dominated by four departments. Community Health, Corrections, Higher Education, and Human Services account for about 85 percent of the $9.2 billion GF/GP budget for Fiscal Year 2007. No other departments involve remotely as much expenditure as these.[24]

Table 1.3 provides a snapshot, taken at a particular moment in time. Snapshots are useful, but motion pictures can sometimes be even better. Figure 1.4 shows the trends over time in the total amount of GF/GP expenditure on a per capita basis. The data are adjusted for inflation, so that they are in 2006 dollars.[25] Figure 1.4 covers the thirty-five-year period from 1972 to 2006.

In all but one of the years from 1973 to 2001, the inflation-adjusted level of per capita GF/GP expenditure fell between $1,170 and $1,400 (in 2006 dollars). However, the subsequent revenue squeeze led to very substantial reductions in GF/GP spending after 2001. If not for the aforementioned asset sales, it would have been necessary for the spending reductions to be even larger. Nevertheless, the spending reductions were very significant. From 2001 to 2006, inflation-adjusted per capita GF/GP spending fell from about $1,230 to a little less than $900. This is a decrease of nearly 30 percent, which is a very substantial decline over a period of only five years.

Figure 1.4 shows the time trends for total GF/GP spending. However, the aggregate trends mask some very substantial differences among the trends for different categories of expenditure. Figure 1.5 shows the very different spending trends for selected departments. (Figure 1.5, like figure 1.4, shows the data adjusted for inflation, and on a per capita basis.) One of the data series in figure 1.5 is for Corrections, and the other is for the combined spending in three departments—Agriculture, Environmental Quality, and Natural Resources.

Table 1.3. General Fund/General Purpose Expenditures for the State of Michigan for Fiscal Year 2007

Department	Expenditures (millions of dollars)	Expenditures as Percent of Total GF/GP
Agriculture	**28.8**	**0.31**
Attorney General	30.3	0.33
Capital Outlay	235.4	2.56
Civil Rights	11.4	0.12
Civil Service	5.8	0.06
Community Health	3078.1	33.51
Corrections	1866.4	20.32
Education	5.8	0.06
Environmental Quality	**30.5**	**0.36**
Executive Office	5.1	0.06
Higher Education	1612.5	17.55
History, Arts, and Libraries	38.3	0.42
Human Services	1220.3	13.28
Judiciary	157.6	1.72
Labor and Economic Growth	40.0	0.44
Legislative Auditor General	11.5	0.13
Legislature	114.0	1.24
Management and Budget	32.9	0.36
Michigan Strategic Fund	29.2	0.32
Military and Veterans Affairs	37.8	0.41
Natural Resources	**31.8**	**0.35**
School Aid	34.1	0.37
State	15.5	0.17
State Police	241.6	2.63
Treasury	266.5	2.90
Debt Service	4.8	0.05
Total	**9186.2**	**100.00**

NOTE: Detailed items do not add precisely to totals, because of rounding.

SOURCE: Executive Budget, Fiscal Year 2009 (http://www.michigan.gov/documents/budget/Budget_Book1_223972_7.pdf).

In figure 1.5, we see that Corrections spending was once of the same order of magnitude as spending on the three departments related to land use and the environment. However, between 1972 and 2001, while real per capita expenditure on Agriculture, Environmental Quality, and Natural Resources grew by about 50 percent, real per capita Corrections spending grew by nearly 800 percent.

After 2001, all but a few categories of GF/GP spending were reduced in nominal terms. The only two exceptions were Community Health and Corrections. When we add in an adjustment for inflation, the *real* level of expenditure was reduced in every department, including even Community Health and Corrections. As seen in figure 1.5, real per capita Corrections spending fell by about 11.5 percent between 2001 and 2006. However, relatively speaking, the reductions were far greater in the departments that are concerned with issues of land use and environmental quality. During the five years after 2001, real

31

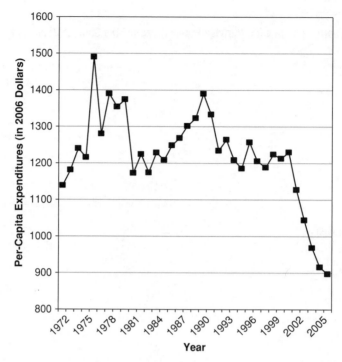

FIGURE 1.4

Inflation-Adjusted, Per-Capita, General-Fund General-Purpose Expenditures, State of Michigan, 1972–2005

per capita spending in the Department of Agriculture was cut by about 60 percent. Over the same period, spending in the Department of Environmental Quality was cut by about 73 percent, and spending in the Department of Natural Resources fell by about 64 percent.

The data discussed in the preceding paragraphs do not necessarily say that Michigan's Corrections spending is "too high," or that Michigan's spending in Agriculture, Environmental Quality, and Natural Resources is "too low." Calculating the "optimal" level of public expenditure is an exceedingly difficult task. Nevertheless, at a minimum, these data do show that while funding for Agriculture, Environmental Quality, and Natural Resources contributes to only a small fraction of the budget of the state of Michigan, these departments have been required to bear relative decreases that are extraordinarily large.

Revenue Sharing, Transportation, and Education

Local governments in Michigan face special challenges in funding their operations. The largest revenue source directly under the control of local governments is the property tax. However, there is a long history of resistance to high rates of property taxation in Michigan and elsewhere. This has led to legal restrictions on the ability of local units to raise their own revenues. Moreover, even if local governments were free to choose their own tax rates, they would do so in a world in which economic activity is highly mobile. In particular, mobility across local district boundaries is likely to be much larger than mobility across state lines. Thus, when a local government tries to raise tax revenue, its leaders have to be

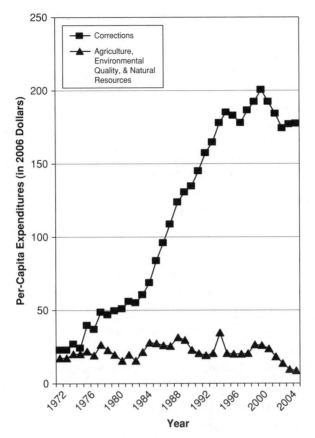

FIGURE 1.5
Inflation-Adjusted, Per-Capita Expenditures, for Selected Departments of the State of Michigan, 1972–2006

acutely aware of the disincentive effects. This is especially true of the poorer local jurisdictions, where even a relatively high tax rate does not provide a huge amount of tax revenue. Because of these special hurdles, the state government engages in revenue sharing in every state, including Michigan. The idea is that the state government can raise revenue more efficiently, but that local units may have a greater ability to respond to the needs of the citizenry.[26]

In recent years, however, the state of Michigan has chosen to reduce revenue sharing. Thus, while the state may give the impression of being fiscally responsible by balancing its own budget, the real effect may be merely to push the problems down to vulnerable local governments. This process is described in a report by the Task Force on Local Government Services and Fiscal Stability (TFLGSFS 2006). The authors of that report found that between 2002 and 2006, the constitutional portion of revenue-sharing payments actually increased in nominal terms, although not rapidly enough to keep up with inflation. Over the same period, however, the statutory portion of revenue sharing decreased by a staggering 58 percent.

As described in the report by TFLGSFS, the sharp reductions in statutory revenue sharing are particularly troubling on equity grounds. Statutory revenue-sharing funds are allocated on the basis of a formula that considers the tax capacity of the local unit. The formula is such that statutory revenue sharing has reduced disparities between poorer communities and more affluent communities. Thus, by reducing this type of revenue sharing, the state government has further exacerbated the growing gap between those at the top and those at the bottom.

One of the conclusions of TFLGSFS is worth quoting:

> There is an apparent difference in perception between state elected officials and local leaders. Many state legislators perceive revenue sharing as a line item among competing needs within the appropriations process. Local officials perceive the state's actions as a broken promise that has hamstrung local units of government and caused them to reduce police, fire, and other essential services that produce the quality of life necessary for communities of a vibrant state.

Thus, the overall level of revenue sharing is a serious policy concern. The allocation of revenue-sharing funds also presents potential problems. Gary Taylor and Carol Weissert (2002) discuss the ways in which revenue-sharing dollars are directed to high-growth jurisdictions, which tend to be on the fringes of metropolitan areas. The next three chapters of this volume are all concerned with various ways in which public policies in Michigan may encourage inefficient land use.[27]

Revenue sharing is an important feature of the relationship between different levels of government. Transportation is another. State and local authorities in Michigan make important decisions about the ways in which transportation funds are used.[28] Kenneth Boyer (2003) presents data showing that the quality of Michigan roads is relatively good for roads that see little traffic, but relatively poor for heavily traveled roads. For minor rural arterial roads, road quality is actually much better than the national average, and better than the average of other states in the Great Lakes region. Michigan's principal rural arterials are about average. However, when it comes to interstate highways, urban freeways, and other urban arterials, Michigan roads are far worse than the national average, and also far worse than the average of other Great Lakes states.

If Michigan's heavily traveled roads were worse than the national average, but comparable to the average of the other Great Lakes states, it would be possible to argue that the state's problems are caused by cold weather. However, since Michigan's major roads are worse than the major roads in neighboring states, the cold-weather explanation is inappropriate. The better explanation is that funds for road construction, maintenance, and repair are poorly allocated in Michigan. Many of the state's funding decisions are based on a law passed in 1951. Thus, the allocation of transportation funds has not kept up with changing needs.

Jurisdiction over roads in Michigan tends to be assigned to the level of government that originally built the road. Thus, as shown by Citizens Research Council of Michigan (2008), counties own 74 percent of the highway miles in Michigan, and the state of Michigan owns only 8 percent. However, 50 percent of the miles traveled are on state-owned roads, while only 32 percent of the miles traveled are on county-owned roads. Boyer (2003) shows that Michigan's pattern of road ownership is very unusual when compared with other states, in which state ownership of roads is much more prevalent. Part of the difference in quality between heavily traveled roads and lightly traveled roads has to do with the political pressures on county road commissions. Part of the difference is also due to the formula for allocating state revenues. In 1951, 44 percent of the state funds were allocated to the state, and the rest went to counties, cities, and villages. The formula was changed in 1984, and the amount going to the state was reduced to 39.1 percent. The formula has remained unchanged since 1984.

The Citizens Research Council of Michigan (2008) proposes a series of sensible reforms to the formula for allocating transportation funds. These involve changing the formula to reflect the extent of utilization, so that more dollars would go to the more heavily traveled roads. It has also been proposed to increase the tax on gasoline and diesel fuel, to provide additional funds for road repair. As of this writing, however, the prices of gasoline and diesel are at all-time highs, so that it may prove very difficult politically to increase the motor-fuels taxes. Another possibility would be to devote some general-fund dollars to road repair.

Spending on Agriculture, Environmental Quality, and Natural Resources, as well as revenue sharing and transportation, has been emphasized in this chapter because these expenditure categories are connected to land use and the environment. Before closing this section, however, I would also like to draw attention to the decline in one of the other most important categories in the GF/GP budget, namely, Higher Education. Between 2001 and 2006, real per capita spending on Higher Education in Michigan decreased by almost 30 percent. By 2006, the level of expenditure had fallen to about $184 per capita. This was the first time in the third of a century covered here that real higher-education spending per capita had fallen below $200 (in 2006 dollars). This policy of disinvestment in Higher Education is especially unwise at this time. As mentioned earlier, the importance of a college education has grown substantially in recent decades. Research universities also offer substantial benefits in terms of patents and licenses for new technologies. (For a thorough discussion of the economic effects of Michigan State University, the University of Michigan, and Wayne State University, see Anderson Economic Group 2007).[29] This also affects the "Creative Class" competitiveness outlined in future chapters in this volume by Thomas and by Hoffman and Pyne.

State Government Employment

In many parts of government, the largest expenditure is for employees. Thus, it is perhaps not surprising that the trends in state government employment in Michigan are reminiscent of the expenditure trends discussed earlier.

Figure 1.6 shows the total number of state government employees for fiscal years from 1966 to 2006. In 1981, the total number of state employees reached a peak of nearly 70,000, or about one state employee for every 132 residents. The fiscal crises of the early 1980s led to substantial decreases in state government employment, but the number of state employees rebounded in the late 1980s. By 2001, state government employment was a little above 62,000, or one state employee for every 161 residents. However, the fiscal difficulties of the

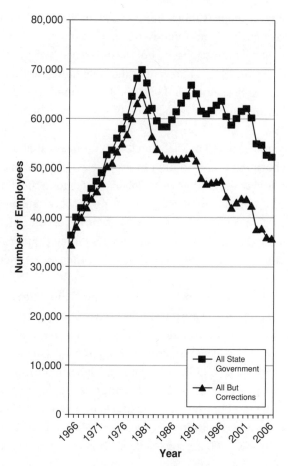

FIGURE 1.6
State Government Employment in Michigan, Fiscal Years, 1966–2006

twenty-first century led to a decrease of nearly 16 percent in the state workforce. As a result, by 2006 Michigan had slightly more than 52,000 state government employees, which is the lowest level since 1972. The 2006 state workforce comes to one state government employee for every 193 residents.

However, figure 1.6 also shows that, when we exclude the rapidly growing workforce in the Department of Corrections, state government employment fell even faster than would be suggested by the data described in the preceding paragraph. In the late 1960s, the Michigan Department of Corrections had fewer than 2,000 employees. In 2001, the Corrections workforce peaked at more than 18,000. By 2006, Corrections employment in the state government had fallen to about 16,500. Even after this drop, however, the state Corrections workforce was still more than 700 percent higher than it had been in 1970.

Thus, strikingly, the non-Corrections workforce in Michigan state government fell from a high of nearly 65,000 in 1980 to fewer than 36,000 in 2006, a decrease of about 45 percent. If we account for the population growth that occurred over the same period, the non-Corrections workforce decreased from about one worker for every 143 residents to about one

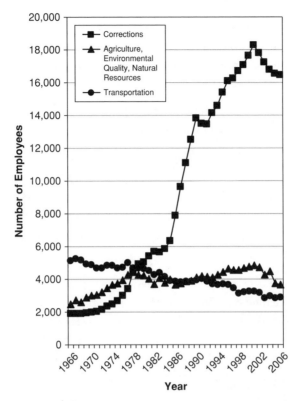

FIGURE 1.7
Classified Employees in Selected Departments of Michigan Government, Fiscal Years, 1966–2006

worker for every 282 residents. In other words, on a per capita basis, the non-Corrections state government workforce fell by almost exactly 50 percent over this period.

While figure 1.6 focuses on the overall level of state government employment, figure 1.7 looks at certain departments of particular interest. The growth of the Corrections labor force could be inferred indirectly from figure 1.6; it is shown directly in figure 1.7. Also shown in figure 1.7 are two other employment trends. One of these is for the combined employment in the Departments of Agriculture, Environmental Quality, and Natural Resources, and the other is for the Department of Transportation.

Figure 1.7 reveals that employment in the Department of Transportation has fallen fairly steadily over the last forty years. By 2006, the Transportation workforce was only about 56 percent as large as it had been forty years earlier. On the other hand, employment in both Agriculture and Natural Resources grew substantially in the 1970s, fell in the early 1980s, and then rose again in the late 1980s and 1990s. However, state government employment in these areas, as in other areas, has fallen quite noticeably since 2001. In the five years after 2001, employment fell by 18 percent in the Department of Agriculture, by 12 percent in the Department of Environmental Quality, and by 34 percent in the Department of Natural Resources. Thus, the employment reductions in the departments related to land use and the environment were substantial, although they were not relatively as severe as the spending reductions already noted in those departments.

Conclusion

In this chapter, a number of the salient factors that have affected the economic and fiscal background related to metropolitan policies in the Michigan economy in the last few decades have been highlighted. These include:

- The decline of manufacturing in general, and of the domestic automobile industry in particular, has had a powerful effect on Michigan's economy.

The economy of Michigan has been relatively undiversified, with very heavy emphasis on a single sector. As a result, Michigan turned in an excellent economic performance in the middle of the twentieth century. However, the very sectors that propelled Michigan so well at midcentury have contributed to the relative decline of the state's economy in the last forty years or so.

- Primarily as a result of the decline of key sectors, population and income have grown substantially less rapidly in Michigan than in the rest of the United States.

The successes of the mid-twentieth century helped contribute to the current situation, in which Michigan lags behind the national average in terms of college-education attainment. Thus, the Michigan workforce is not well positioned to take advantage of the ongoing changes in the global economy. If there is any silver lining to the cloud of slower economic growth, it is that the reduced rate of economic growth is associated with reduced pressure on the land and environment, relative to what would likely have occurred if the economy had grown more rapidly.

- Different groups in Michigan have fared very differently.

Income inequality has increased rapidly in Michigan, as in the rest of the United States. In particular, the inflation-adjusted earnings of those with at least a college education have soared, while the earnings of other groups have fallen. The most affluent citizens and regions in Michigan have prospered, despite the weakness in the overall Michigan economy. Oakland County remains one of the most affluent areas in the world. Average incomes are far higher in Oakland County than in any other Michigan county. With the exceptions of the tourist-oriented areas of the northwestern Lower Peninsula, the nonmetropolitan areas of Michigan lag far behind their counterparts in metropolitan areas.

- Governments in Michigan face chronic structural deficits.

Over the last thirty-five years, the proportion of income going to state and local taxes has fallen by more than two percentage points. This is partly the result of explicit cuts in tax rates, and partly the result of tax-base erosion. On the other side of the ledger, public expenditures on health care and corrections have grown rapidly. As a result, in the absence of explicit policy changes, governments face repeated fiscal crises.

- So far in the twenty-first century, Michigan has responded to budget crises mainly through shedding assets and cutting expenditure programs.

Adjusting for inflation, GF/GP expenditure fell by about 30 percent in a period of only five years. The expenditure reductions were accompanied by major reductions in the state government workforce. The departments of state government that are associated with land use and the environment have been the hardest hit. Revenue sharing to local governments has also been cut very substantially, so that a portion of the budget crisis facing the state government has merely been passed down to local governments.

Where do we go from here? If left unchecked, the trends of the last few decades in Michigan could eventually leave us with a state in which income is highly concentrated in a relatively small part of the population, and in which the economic prospects of the average citizen are very discouraging. Moreover, one of the responses to difficult economic times has been a drastic reduction in public expenditure in areas associated with land use and the environment. If this trend were to continue, the physical beauty and cleanliness of Michigan's land and water could be compromised. There is ample reason to be very concerned about the future of the Michigan economy and environment.

Nevertheless, beneficial changes can be made, but only if the people of Michigan change their attitudes and policies. The first priority is to recognize that we face long-term problems that are not easily solved by short-term gimmicks. Even if Michigan adopts the best possible combination of policies, it will still take years before we see a really substantial reversal of recent trends. The key to reversing the trends lies in improving the skills of the labor force. The evolving global economy has bestowed tremendous rewards upon the most highly educated and highly skilled workers. Thus, Michigan's recent policy of massive disinvestment in education is both puzzling and troubling.

A strong case can be made for tax reforms that will stabilize the revenue streams for state and local governments in Michigan, while at the same time making Michigan's tax system less regressive. However, this does not mean that policy reform should be concentrated exclusively on the revenue side. At the same time that we reform the tax system, it is also imperative that we bring greater control to spending on corrections and on health care (especially for public employees, schoolteachers, and retirees).

If reforms along these lines are made, it is very reasonable to believe that the rate of growth of income and population will increase (although it will take time). It might then be possible for the people of Michigan to turn more of their attention to land use issues, environmental issues, and better management of metropolitan affairs.

Notes

1. These data are taken from table 3.1 of Darga (2003).
2. Population estimates for 2000–2007 are available at http://www.census.gov/popest/ states/NST-EST2007–01.xls. The Census Bureau estimates that Michigan's population was 10,071,822 on July 1, 2007, which is 30,500 persons fewer than the estimated population in 2006.
3. Leholm, Vlasin, and Ferris (2003) provide an interesting look at the long-term development of land use in Michigan. Between 1920 and 2000, fully one-fourth of the land surface area in Michigan was removed from cultivation. Some of this formerly agricultural land was covered over with houses, roads, and factories. However, a very substantial portion reverted to forest.

4. The income data and the price index by which they are adjusted are both provided by the Bureau of Economic Analysis, which is one of the statistical agencies of the U.S. Department of Commerce. Data for per capita personal income can be found at http://www.bea.gov/regional/spi/default.cfm?satable=summary. The income data are deflated by the Personal Consumption Expenditures deflator, which can be found at http://www.bea.gov/national/nipaweb/SelectTable.asp?Selected=N.

5. These calculations are based on the previously cited income data and price-level data from the Commerce Department's Bureau of Economic Analysis.

6. See DeNavas-Walt, Proctor, and Smith (2007). Their report is available at http://www.census.gov/prod/2007pubs/p60-233.pdf.

7. Menchik and I received valuable advice from our colleague Steven Haider, and from Jay Stewart of the Bureau of Labor Statistics. We also received outstanding research assistance from Monthien Satimanon and Yao Hao-gen.

8. In 2005, a household at the 10th percentile of the Michigan income distribution had an annual income of about $12,000. A household at the 20th percentile had about $20,000; one at the 30th percentile had about $28,000; one at the 40th percentile had $36,000; one at the 50th percentile (the median) had about $46,000; one at the 60th percentile had about $57,000; one at the 70th percentile had about $71,000; one at the 80th percentile had about $91,000; and one at the 90th percentile had about $123,000.

9. The person at a given percentile in 2003–2005 is unlikely to be the same person as the one at the same percentile in 1976–1978. Some people who are in the sample for 2003–2005 had not been born yet in 1976–1978, and some people who are in the sample for 1976–1978 had passed away by 2003–2005. Nevertheless, these comparisons yield valuable information about the evolution of the income distribution.

10. County income data are available at http://www.bea.gov/regional/reis/default.cfm?catable=CA1–3&section=2.

11. In order to calculate this figure of one-third of 1 percent per year, I began by taking the ratio of per capita personal income in Michigan in each year to per capita personal income in the United States for the same year. Good-quality data are available for the fifty states and the District of Columbia since 1929. However, I used 1950 as the starting point, because the Great Depression and the Second World War were associated with some very large swings in the numbers. I then used the technique of ordinary least-squares regression to calculate the trend line that best fits the data for 1950–2007.

12. These data are taken from http://www.bea.gov/regional/gsp. The interpretation of the data is made more complicated by the fact that the sector classification system was changed in 1997. However, this change of definitions can only explain a small portion of the steep decline, either for the United States or for Michigan. The relative decline of manufacturing has been one of the most important trends in the American economy in the last half-century, regardless of which classification system is used.

13. The data for this calculation are from the Web site of Automotive News, at https://www.autonews.com, and from the American Automobile Manufacturers' Association Web site at http://www.economagic.com/aama.htm.

14. Most of my research career has been focused on understanding the economic effects of tax policies. For example, see Ballard, Shoven, and Whalley (1985); Ballard (1990, 2003); Ballard and Fullerton (1992); Ballard and Goddeeris (1999); Ballard and Kang (2003); and Ballard and Lee (2007).

15. In drawing attention to the rising importance of college degrees, I do not mean to imply that four-year colleges are the only really important parts of the educational system in Michigan. In my view, Michigan is underinvested in education, all the way from pre-school to Ph.D. Far too many of our children are unprepared when they enter kinder-garten. Far too many drop out before acquiring a high school diploma. (This problem is especially severe in Detroit and other older cities.) Far too many get a high school diploma, even though they have not really acquired a twelfth-grade education. Far too many who do get a high school diploma fail to go on to either a two-year or a four-year college. Far too many who do matriculate in college do not complete a degree. See chapter 2 of Ballard (2006) for more discussion of educational issues. See also Cullen and Loeb (2003).

16. It would be possible to show state taxes only, or local taxes only, but this would give a misleading impression. The finances of state government and local governments are closely intertwined in every state. However, there is substantial variation among the states in the degree to which local governments rely on state aid. Thus, to make mean-ingful comparisons among the states, it is important to include both state and local taxes.

17. This value for personal income, like several others mentioned earlier, is from the Web site of the Bureau of Economic Analysis. The data for 2007 are preliminary and subject to revision. However, the revisions are unlikely to be very large, so that the basic stories presented here are unlikely to be changed substantially.

18. Other structural problems in the Michigan tax system are discussed in Ballard (2003, 2006).

19. Proposal A, passed in 1994, put a cap on the amount by which the taxable value of a home could increase from one year to the next. Thus, for many homes in Michigan in the late 1990s and the first few years of the twenty-first century, the taxable value drifted farther and farther below the actual market value. Under Proposal A, a property is only reassessed to full market value when sold. This created an inequity, since neighbors in similar houses could pay very different amounts of tax, if one house had been sold recently and the other had not. Another consequence of the revenue drain caused by the cap is that in order to raise a given amount of tax revenue, the tax rate on the uncapped properties had to be higher than it would otherwise have been. When hous-ing values fell in many parts of the state in 2007 and 2008, many Michigan residents found their property taxes rising, even though their property values were falling. This is in full accord with the provisions of Proposal A. However, it does not appear to have been anticipated when the proposal was developed, since no one was predicting the large and widespread declines in residential property values that would occur thirteen years after Proposal A was passed. Of course, if the market value of a property decreases by a sufficiently large amount, the market value can fall beneath the cap. This has

happened to me: the assessed value of my home has fallen so far that my property taxes have actually declined.

20. The increase in local tax revenue is explained almost completely by increases in property tax revenues. Property taxes are by far the most important source of tax revenue for local governments in Michigan.

21. I adjust for inflation using the deflator for State and Local Government Consumption Expenditure and Gross Investment, tabulated by the Bureau of Economic Analysis of the U.S. Department of Commerce. These data are available at http://www.bea.gov/national/nipaweb/SelectTable.asp?Selected=N.

22. This report can be found at http://www.crcmich.org/PUBLICAT/2000s/2007/sbn200701.pdf. Also, see Citizens Research Council (2006), available at http://www.crcmich.org/PUBLICAT/2000s/2006/sbn200601.pdf.

23. For more discussion of educational issues, see chapter 2 of Ballard (2006), as well as Cullen and Loeb (2003). Because of the importance of education, it remains the subject of many proposals for reform. For example, (a) Governor Granholm has proposed that full-day kindergarten become mandatory in the state. Also, (b) there is ample evidence in the literature that prekindergarten programs can have very beneficial effects. (c) Proposal A increased the funds for operating expenses for many of the poorer school districts in the state, and this has resulted in some important improvements in student performance. See Papke (2005). However, substantial differences in per pupil funding remain, and members of the legislature from poorer districts have tried (unsuccessfully so far) to speed up the process of equalization. (d) Although Proposal A moved toward equalization of funding for public-school operating expenditures, the old inequities for capital expenditures remain in place. As a result, school facilities in many of the older and poorer school districts are substandard. Arsen et al. (2005) put forth proposals to ensure that every child goes to school in an acceptable physical environment. (e) While many countries around the world have a school year of 200 or more days per year, Michigan continues to have a school year of 180 days, just as in the nineteenth century. An expansion of the length of the school year could have an important effect on student achievement. The list could go on and on. The difficulty, of course, is that all of these proposals are likely to cost money.

24. There is widespread dissatisfaction with the performance of the Michigan legislature. This dissatisfaction often leads to calls for reductions in the legislative budget. In fact, I am a supporter of the Reform Michigan Government Now! proposal, which would have reduced pay and benefits for legislators. However, the data in table 1.3 should make clear that reduced spending on the legislature would only have a relatively small direct effect on the overall budget.

25. The expenditure data themselves are taken from various issues of the Executive Budget. As before, I have adjusted for inflation using the price deflator for State and Local Government Consumption Expenditures and Gross Investment, from the Bureau of Economic Analysis, at http://www.bea.gov/national/nipaweb/SelectTable.asp?Selected=N. The data for Michigan population are taken from the Bureau of the Census (http://www.census.gov/popest/states/NST-ann-est.html), and from various issues of the Statistical Abstract of the United States.

26. For more discussion of local government revenues and expenditures, and the relationships between state and local governments, see Ryan and Lupher (2003); Feldman, Courant, and Drake (2003); and Fisher and Guilfoyle (2003).

27. See also LeRoy, Lack, and Walter (2006).

28. The Department of Transportation is not included in the data on GF/GP expenditure in table 1.3. This is because the state of Michigan does not use any General Fund dollars for transportation purposes. Instead, state highway use taxes go to the Michigan Transportation Fund and are restricted to be used only for transportation; thus, these funds are not allocated according to the same budget process that applies to the departments shown in table 1.3. Federal funds are also used for transportation projects in Michigan.

29. This report is available at http://www.andersoneconomicgroup.com/modules.php?name=Content&pa=display_aeg&doc_ID=2162.

REFERENCES

Anderson Economic Group, LLC. 2007. Michigan's University Research Corridor: First Annual Economic Impact Report.

Arsen, D., T. Clay, T. Davis, T. Devaney, R. Fulcher-Dawson, and D. N. Plank. 2005. Adequacy, Equity, and Capital Spending in Michigan Schools: The Unfinished Business of Proposal A. http://www.crcmich.org/PUBLICAT/2000s/2005/schoolcapital.pdf.

Ballard, C. L. 1990. Marginal Welfare Cost Calculations: Differential Analysis vs. Balanced-Budget Analysis. *Journal of Public Economics* 41 (April):263–276.

———. 2003. Overview of Michigan's Revenue System. In *Michigan at the Millennium,* edited by C. L. Ballard, P. N. Courant, D. C. Drake, R. C. Fisher, and E. R. Gerber. East Lansing: Michigan State University Press.

———. 2006. *Michigan's Economic Future: Challenges and Opportunities.* East Lansing: Michigan State University Press.

Ballard, C. L., and Don Fullerton. 1992. Distortionary Taxes and the Provision of Public Goods. *Journal of Economic Perspectives* 6 (Summer):117–131.

Ballard, C. L., and J. H. Goddeeris. 1999. Financing Universal Health Care in the United States: A General Equilibrium Analysis of Efficiency and Distributional Effects. *National Tax Journal* 52 (March):31–52.

Ballard, C. L., and K. Kang. 2003. International Ramifications of U.S. Tax-Policy Changes. *Journal of Policy Modeling* 25 (November):825–835.

Ballard, C. L., and J. Lee. 2007. Internet Purchases, Cross-Border Shopping, and Sales Taxes. *National Tax Journal* 60 (December):711–725.

Ballard, C. L., J. B. Shoven, and J. Whalley. 1985. General Equilibrium Computations of the Marginal Welfare Costs of Taxation in the United States. *American Economic Review* 75 (March):128–138.

Blank, R. M. 2003. The Less-Skilled Labor Market in Michigan. In *Michigan at the Millennium,* edited by C. L. Ballard, P. N. Courant, D. C. Drake, R. C. Fisher, and E. R. Gerber. East Lansing: Michigan State University Press.

Boyer, K. D. 2003. Michigan's Transportation System and Transportation Policy. In *Michigan at the Millennium,* edited by C. L. Ballard, P. N. Courant, D. C. Drake, R. C. Fisher, and E. R. Gerber. East Lansing: Michigan State University Press.

Citizens Research Council of Michigan. 2006. Michigan's Budget Crisis and the Prospects for the Future. State Budget Notes 2006-01 (March).

———. 2007a. Michigan's Deteriorating Cash Position. CRC Notes 2007–02 (May).

———. 2007b. State Budget "Balance" for Fiscal Year 2007 Achieved with $1 Billion in Additional Non-Recurring Resources. State Budget Notes 2007-01 (June).

———. 2008. Improving the Efficiency of Michigan's Highway Revenue Sharing Formula. CRC Memorandum No. 1085 (February).

Cullen, J. B., and S. Loeb. 2003. K-12 Education in Michigan. In *Michigan at the Millennium,* edited by C. L. Ballard, P. N. Courant, D. C. Drake, R. C. Fisher, and E. R. Gerber. East Lansing: Michigan State University Press.

Darga, K. J. 2003. Population Trends in Michigan. In *Michigan at the Millennium,* edited by C. L. Ballard, P. N. Courant, D. C. Drake, R. C. Fisher, and E. R. Gerber. East Lansing: Michigan State University Press.

DeNavas-Walt, C., B. D. Proctor, and J. Smith. 2007. *Income, Poverty, and Health Insurance Coverage in the United States:* 2006. U.S. Census Bureau, Current Population Reports, P60–233. Washington, D.C.: Government Printing Office.

Feldman, N. E., P. N. Courant, and D. C. Drake. 2003. The Property Tax in Michigan. In *Michigan at the Millennium,* edited by C. L. Ballard, P. N. Courant, D. C. Drake, R. C. Fisher, and E. R. Gerber. East Lansing: Michigan State University Press.

Fisher, R. C., and J. P. Guilfoyle. 2003. Fiscal Relations among the Federal Government, State Government, and Local Governments in Michigan. In *Michigan at the Millennium,* edited by C. L. Ballard, P. N. Courant, D. C. Drake, R. C. Fisher, and E. R. Gerber. East Lansing: Michigan State University Press.

Leholm, A., R. Vlasin, and J. Ferris 2003. Michigan's Agricultural, Forestry, and Mining Industries. In *Michigan at the Millennium,* edited by C. L. Ballard, P. N. Courant, D. C. Drake, R. C. Fisher, and E. R. Gerber. East Lansing: Michigan State University Press.

LeRoy, G., A. Lack, and K. Walter. 2006. *The Geography of Incentives: Economic Development and Land Use in Michigan.* Washington, D.C.: Good Jobs First.

Mark, S. T., T. J. McGuire, and L. E. Papke. 1997. What Do We Know About the Effect of Taxes on Economic Development? Lessons from the Literature for the District of Columbia. *State Tax Notes* (August 25).

Papke, L. E. 2005. The Effects of Spending on Test Pass Rates: Evidence from Michigan. *Journal of Public Economics* 89 (June):821–839.

Ryan, E. M., and E. W. Lupher. 2003. An Overview of Local Government Expenditures in Michigan: Patterns and Trends. In *Michigan at the Millennium,* edited by C. L. Ballard, P. N. Courant, D. C. Drake, R. C. Fisher, and E. R. Gerber. East Lansing: Michigan State University Press.

Taylor, G. D., and C. S. Weissert. 2002. Are We Supporting Sprawl through Aid to High-Growth Communities? Revisiting the 1998 State Revenue Sharing Formula Changes. *Informing the Debate: Policy Briefs on Urban Issues.* Institute for Public Policy and Social Research, Michigan State University.

TFLGSFS (Task Force on Local Government Services and Fiscal Stability). 2006. Final Report to the Governor (May).

CHAPTER 2

Michigan's Industrial Tax Abatements: Pyrrhic Victories?

Gary Sands and Laura A. Reese

Pyrrhus, king of Epirus, invaded Italy in the year 281 B.C., defeating the Romans at Heraclea and Asculum. In these victories, however, his armies suffered heavy losses. Afterwards Pyrrhus is said to have stated "One more such victory and I am lost"—a Pyrrhic victory is thus any victory so costly as to be ruinous.

—*American Heritage Dictionary of Idioms*

In the latter years of the twentieth century, the United States experienced widespread deindustrialization (Alcaly 2003; Bluestone, Cowie, and Heathcott 2003; Sassen 2006). After reaching a peak in the late 1970s, the number of manufacturing jobs declined from more than 20 million to barely 14 million in 2005. Manufacturing's share of all jobs actually began declining two decades earlier, falling from 36 percent in 1945 to 13 percent in 2002, as manufacturing activity moved to overseas locations (Bluestone, Cowie, and Heathcott 2003).

This economic restructuring has had differential impacts across the country. The decline of the "Rust Belt" dates from the 1950s, as manufacturing jobs moved in large numbers to southern and western states for various reasons: relatively inexpensive land, fewer union restrictions, and more modern physical plants (Kasarda 1995). The decline in manufacturing employment in the Midwest seems likely to be permanent, with few prospects for reversal or significant improvement (Weil and Friedhoff 2006).

Overall, growth of services industry employment has been more than sufficient to offset declines in manufacturing jobs. Many areas dependent on traditional manufacturing industries, however, have seen their industrial base erode, without being able to replace lost jobs, either with services or high-tech manufacturing and knowledge-based employment opportunities (Florida 2005; Teaford 1994). As a result, these areas have experienced relative declines in both employment and incomes. Midwest manufacturing centers have been among the hardest hit (Hill 1987; Dandeneau 1996; Weil and Friedhoff 2006).

State and city economic development policies and incentives in response to these trends have been well documented (for recent examples, see Reese and Rosenfeld 2004; Peters and Fisher 2005). Academic observers and policy evaluators have focused on a relatively parsimonious set of recommended goals for economic development policies at the local level:

- Diversifying the economic base and focusing on areas of long-term competitive advantage (Voytek and Ledebur 1991; Hill and Brennan 2000)
- Shifting local employment sectors away from manufacturing and heavy industry to high-technology, knowledge-based, and creative industries (Florida 2005; Duderstadt 2005)
- Developing local capacity for entrepreneurship, business development, and human capital (Glazer and Grimes 2005)
- Improving the overall quality of life, culture, and urban amenities (Clark 2003; Florida 2005)

Yet the most common state and local economic development policies seem poorly suited to achieving these goals. Despite a call two decades ago by Eisinger (1988) for a shift to demand-side economic development policies, research over the 1990s and early 2000s clearly shows cities continuing (and increasingly) to focus on traditional industrial attraction incentives such as basic infrastructure and land development, promotion and marketing, and particularistic financial incentives (Clarke and Gaile 1992; Blakeley 1994; Peters and Fisher 2005; Reese and Sands 2006; Reese 2006).

Cities in the Midwest generally, and in Michigan in particular, have consistently relied on these policies. Further, Michigan cities are among the nation's most active in using industrial tax abatements (Reese and Rosenfeld 2004). The "high tax" image of Michigan is widely accepted and is frequently the basis for demands for tax abatements or reform (Citizens Research Council of Michigan 2006).

Given that Michigan's industrial tax abatement program is now more than three decades old, it is reasonable to ask how effective it has been in meeting the four primary economic development goals noted above, and at what cost? The goals of this analysis are to assess the impacts of industrial tax abatements on diversifying the economic base in the state of Michigan and shifting employment in the state to the New Economy. This chapter examines changes in the Michigan employment structure during the 1990s. The most recent decade has seen a severe decline occurring during a period dominated by a prospering national economy. First, a Shift-Share analysis of both total employment and the manufacturing sector in Michigan will be presented. Then the impacts of state economic development policies relative to manufacturing will be assessed. Finally, some public policy implications of these results are discussed.

Overall Employment Trends

The long-term restructuring of the U.S. economy, from agriculture to manufacturing to services, is widely recognized (Kasarda 1995; Sassen 2006). In 1992, primary industries

Table 2.1. Michigan and U.S. Employment, 1992 and 2002

	1992			2002		
	U.S.	Michigan	lq	U.S.	Michigan	lq
Forestry, Mining, Construction	6.2%	4.5%	0.72	6.2%	4.8%	0.77
Manufacturing	19.6%	26.3%	1.34	12.8%	17.8%	1.39
Retail, Wholesale	27.8%	22.3%	0.80	20.8%	28.0%	1.35
TCU	5.9%	4.5%	0.76	6.9%	5.3%	0.77
FIRE	7.5%	5.4%	0.72	7.5%	6.0%	0.80
Services	33.1%	36.5%	1.10	45.8%	48.2%	1.05
Total	92,750,000	3,320,000		112,401,000	3,890,000	

SOURCE: U.S. Bureau of the Census, *County Business Patterns,* 1992, 2002.

(including agriculture, forestry, fisheries, mining and construction) accounted for just over 6 percent of all U.S. jobs (table 2.1).[1] Manufacturing provided about 20 percent of jobs, down from 38.5 percent in 1945. Services industries provided one-third of U.S. wage and salary employment, with an additional 28 percent in wholesale and retail trade.

The 1992 employment profile for the state of Michigan also reflected a long-term decline in primary sector jobs. But the state was considerably different than the nation in other respects. Jobs in services were Michigan's largest single industrial category, accounting for 36 percent of total employment. Manufacturing industries, however, still provided more than one-quarter of Michigan's employment opportunities; the employment share in other industrial categories was often well below the national average.

Nationally, total wage and salary employment increased by 21 percent (19.7 million new jobs) between 1992 and 2002. The broad category of services added more than 20.8 million jobs, offsetting employment declines in manufacturing (3.8 million fewer jobs over the decade) and wholesale and retail trade (2.4 million fewer workers). Fully two-thirds of all U.S. jobs were in services or trade in 2002. The proportion of U.S. workers employed in manufacturing jobs declined from one in five to just one in eight.

For the state of Michigan, the rate of job growth, about 17 percent, was slightly below the national average between 1992 and 2002, resulting in an increase of some 570,000 jobs. During this period, the Michigan employment profile became more like the national one, with most location quotients shifting closer to unity. The largest absolute changes were in the services industries, which gained more than 650,000 workers, and in manufacturing, where 186,000 jobs were lost.

With a manufacturing location quotient of 1.39 in 2002, Michigan could still be described as a predominantly industrial state (table 2.1). Historically, manufacturing employment in Michigan has been highly cyclical, largely as a result of fluctuations in motor vehicle manufacturing activity (figure 2.1). A loss of more than 275,000 jobs between 1997 and 2002 represented the sharpest five-year decline since 1967. Previously, however, the state had been able to rebound, regaining most if not all of the manufacturing jobs.

47

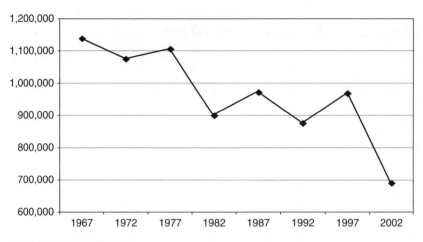

Source: County Business Patterns.

FIGURE 2.1
Michigan Manufacturing Employment 1967–2002

Manufacturing has also declined in importance in the state's two largest urban areas, Detroit and Grand Rapids. Strikingly, in 1992 one-quarter of the jobs in the tricounty (Wayne, Oakland, Macomb) Detroit area were in manufacturing (table 2.2). By 2002, the proportion had fallen to one-seventh. The Kent-Ottawa-Muskegon area was more reliant on manufacturing in 1992 (with 30 percent of all jobs); the Grand Rapids area experienced a slight increase in manufacturing jobs over the decade. Overall employment growth was greater, reducing manufacturing's share to 25 percent.

Figure 2.2 suggests that the current decline is perhaps not just cyclical but may represent a longer term, structural change. At best, the upturn in manufacturing employment that had occurred after each previous decline has not yet begun. Indeed, from 2002 through 2005 Michigan lost an additional 55,000 manufacturing jobs, almost 8 percent of the total. During the same period, other Michigan industries experienced job losses of some 37,000, about 1.2 percent.

Table 2.2. Manufacturing as a Percent of Total Employment, 1992 and 2002

	1992	2002
Michigan	26.3%	17.8%
Detroit Area	24.2%	14.4%
Wayne County	26.0%	15.1%
Oakland County	17.1%	9.5%
Macomb County	34.7%	24.5%
Grand Rapids Area	29.9%	25.3%
Kent County	27.2%	21.6%
Ottawa County	38.7%	36.9%
Muskegon County	29.8%	29.5%

SOURCE: U.S. Bureau of the Census, County Business Patterns, 1992, 2002.

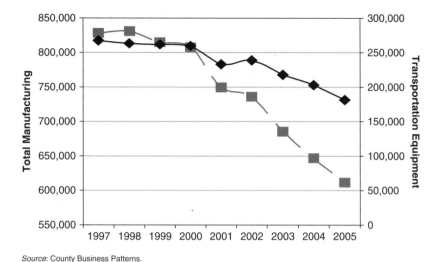

Source: County Business Patterns.

FIGURE 2.2
Michigan Manufacturing Employment 1997–2004

Table 2.3 presents U.S. and Michigan manufacturing job totals in five broad categories: transportation equipment, heavy industries, high-tech industries, consumer goods, and all others.[2] Michigan clearly differed from national averages in the types of manufacturing jobs. Well over half of Michigan manufacturing jobs in 1992 were in transportation equipment and heavy industries, compared to just 30 percent nationally. The location quotient for transportation equipment was quite high, exceeding 2.5; the figure for heavy industries was over 1.4. High-tech manufacturing jobs in Michigan represented barely 5 percent of the total, compared to almost 14 percent nationally.

Nationally, industrial employment declines in the 1990s were widespread, occurring in each of the broad manufacturing categories. Both transportation equipment and heavy industries recorded gains in their relative share of manufacturing employment. The greatest relative loss was in the manufacturing of consumer goods. High-tech manufacturing jobs declined by almost 38 percent. Despite the increasing importance of technology to the economy, high-tech firms employed only one of every eight U.S. workers in 2002.

Table 2.3. Michigan and U.S. Manufacturing Employment, 1992–2002

	1992			2002		
	U.S.	Michigan	lq	U.S.	Michigan	lq
Transportation Equipment	9.1%	23.1%	2.54	11.0%	32.4%	2.95
Heavy Industry	21.1%	30.0%	1.42	22.6%	29.1%	1.29
High Tech	13.9%	5.1%	0.37	12.7%	5.0%	0.39
Consumer Goods	15.1%	6.5%	0.43	13.9%	5.1%	0.37
Other	40.8%	35.2%	0.86	39.8%	28.4%	0.71
Total	18,162,480	876,724		14,393,609	736,259	

SOURCE: U.S. Bureau of the Census, *County Business Patterns,* 1992, 2002.

A similar pattern can be seen in Michigan, tempered by the state's traditional strength in heavy industries. Michigan's manufacturing base experienced a decline of just 18 percent, compared to the national decline of 21 percent. This slightly more positive performance is attributable entirely to an absolute increase in transportation equipment manufacturing jobs in Michigan. Transportation equipment jobs grew as a proportion of all manufacturing jobs from less than one-quarter to almost one-third. All other industrial categories experienced relative declines greater than the respective national average. Michigan manufacturing clearly became more reliant on the industries that had dominated in the previous century.

Shift-Share Analysis

Shift-Share is an analytical technique that assesses changes in local economic activity (in this instance, measured by wage and salary employment) relative to national trends (Hoover 1985). This methodology measures not just whether the local economy is growing or declining but also how the performance of local industries compares to national averages. By identifying the relative change in individual components of the local economy, a better understanding of strengths and weaknesses can be gained. The methodology provides three separate measures of economic change: National Share, an overall comparison of local to national trends; Industry Mix, a measure of how overall growth is affected by the initial mix of local industries (that is, how the local industry profile compares with the national mix of growing and declining industries); and Regional Share, a comparison of performance of local firms to national industry averages. The third statistic helps to identify the local industries leading and lagging in performance (Klosterman 1990).

The results of the Shift-Share analysis for all industries are provided in table 2.4. The first data column estimates the number of jobs in Michigan that would have existed in 2002 if the state had gained jobs at the same rate as the nation. The next column estimates the number of jobs gained or lost because of the mix of industries that existed in Michigan at the beginning of the period. The third column considers the impact of how well Michigan firms have done (relative to their national peers) with respect to employment. The last column is the sum of the previous three and represents actual employment in the state in 2002.

Table 2.4. Michigan Employment Shift Share, 1992–2002

	National Share	Industry Mix	Regional Share	Employment 2002
Forestry, Mining, Construction	182,498	(1,440)	5,008	186,066
Manufacturing	1,062,476	(367,680)	(4,174)	736,439
Wholesale, Retail	902,221	(226,682)	23,943	699,482
TCU	181,223	29,243	(4,662)	205,804
FIRE	219,813	1,658	10,481	231,952
Services	1,475,702	569,139	(168,921)	1,875,920
	4,023,933	4,238	(138,315)	3,889,846

Michigan and U.S. Total Employment

Overall, if employment in all Michigan industries had increased at the same rate as the national average, Michigan would have had over four million jobs in 2002, about 134,000 more jobs than it actually did (table 2.4). Estimates of 2002 employment reveal that if Michigan's manufacturing industries had added jobs at the same rate as the national growth trends for all jobs, the state would have had more than a million manufacturing jobs in 2002. In fact, the generally poor performance of Michigan manufacturing resulted in some 367,000 fewer jobs. Wholesale/retail trade also produced substantially fewer jobs (203,000) than would have been expected. Other industries had substantially more jobs than anticipated. Services employment, for example, provided an estimated surplus of almost 570,000 jobs.

The Regional Share estimates, which compare Michigan firms to national firms in the same industry, provide mixed results. Michigan's services industry experienced employment growth below the national average. As a result, Michigan had an estimated 169,000 fewer services industry jobs in 2002 than might be expected based on the national average growth of employment in services. The estimates of deviation based on Regional Share for other industries are much smaller in both absolute and relative terms.

The Shift-Share analysis provides insight into why overall employment growth in Michigan over the past decade has lagged behind the national average:

- Michigan had a high proportion of its total employment in manufacturing, a sector where employment declined; national declines in trade contrasted sharply with strong growth in wholesale and retail industry employment in Michigan.
- The state had a higher than average proportion of its jobs in the fast-growing services industry; Michigan firms in this category experienced much slower rates of growth than their national counterparts, however.
- As a result of these changes, the Michigan industrial employment profile became more similar to that of the country as a whole, although manufacturing continued to be one of the state's leading sectors.

Michigan and U.S. Manufacturing

A detailed comparison of Michigan's employment trends presents a different picture (table 2.5). In 2002, the state would have had about 695,000 manufacturing industry jobs based on the

Table 2.5. Michigan Manufacturing Shift-Share, 1992–2002

	National Share	Industry Mix	Regional Share	Employment 2002
Transportation Equipment	160,636	32,381	45,714	238,731
Heavy Industry	208,727	14,849	(9,958)	213,618
High Tech	35,628	(2,899)	4,221	36,950
Consumer Goods	45,458	(3,630)	(4,329)	37,499
Other	244,347	(6,008)	(28,878)	209,461
Total	694,796	34,693	6,770	736,259

SOURCE: U.S. Bureau of the Census, *County Business Patterns*, 1992, 2002.

national decline in manufacturing employment trends. However, because the rate of manufacturing job loss in Michigan was below the national average in the 1990s, Michigan actually had 41,000 more persons employed in this industry in 2002.

Within manufacturing, transportation equipment firms clearly made the largest contribution to employment growth. Michigan transportation equipment firms had a more positive growth rate than did all manufacturing firms or their national peer group. As a result, Michigan transportation equipment firms contributed a total of 78,000 additional jobs to the state economy.

In most other industry categories, Michigan manufacturing firms did not fare as well in national comparisons. Job growth in Michigan's heavy industries outperformed the national manufacturing average, although much of this gain was lost because of slower growth compared to all heavy industries nationally. High-tech industries in Michigan surpassed their national counterparts, despite an unfavorable industry mix (that is, they lost fewer jobs in high tech than occurred nationally). The remaining industry categories, consumer goods and other manufacturing, underperformed on Industry Mix and Regional Share measures.

While in the aggregate manufacturing declined both nationally and in Michigan, the Shift-Share analysis reveals:

- Nationally, employment in manufacturing declined in each of the five categories; the steepest decline occurred in high-tech manufacturing industries.
- Transportation equipment was the only Michigan manufacturing sector that experienced job growth during the decade.
- High-tech industries in Michigan, even though a much smaller proportion of the total than nationally, declined by almost 35 percent.
- Because of the strength of transportation equipment firms in Michigan, the state's manufacturing employment profile became less like that of the nation during the decade.

Michigan Manufacturing and Tax Abatements

Although employment in Michigan has been markedly cyclical in the past, the current trends appear more secular and likely to have substantial effects on the state's economy and long-term prosperity (Conboy 2001; Fulton and Grimes 2006). Given widespread recognition of the changing economic structure of Michigan (and the rest of the United States), it would be reasonable to expect that public investments in economic development incentives would reflect concerns about diversification of the employment base and attraction of New Economy job opportunities. There is broad consensus, however, that most traditional industrial development incentives have been at best marginally effective (Ahlbrandt and DeAngelis 1987; Schwarz and Volgy 1992; Fisher and Peters 1998; Peters and Fisher 2005; Reese and Sands 2006).

Michigan has a reputation for being a high tax state, especially with respect to property taxes.[3] The primary economic development incentive over the past three decades has been the granting of property tax abatements to encourage new investment in manufacturing plant and equipment (Sands and Zalmezak 2001; Sands and Reese 2006).[4] About one-third

Table 2.6. Abatement Investment, 1991–2001

	Number of Abatements	Real Property in Billions	Personal Property in Billions	Total Investment in Billions	Percent of Total Investment
Transportation Equipment	739	$2.817	$17.161	$19.978	49.1
Heavy Industry	3,453	$2.269	$6.297	$8.570	21.1
High Tech	418	$0.583	$1.342	$1.945	4.8
Consumer Goods	435	$0.390	$1.205	$1.561	3.8
Other Manufacturing	2,586	$2.419	$6.196	$8.615	21.2
Total	7,631	$8.478	$32.201	$40.66	

of all local governments in Michigan granted property tax relief to manufacturing firms through PA 198 Industrial Tax Abatements, with some 7,600 abatements granted between 1991 and 2001 (table 2.6). Michigan local governments used this type of incentive more often than localities in other states, and the proportion of localities granting abatements has increased over time (Reese and Rosenfeld 2004). The largest number of abatements (3,450) went to firms in the heavy industry category, while firms in the other manufacturing category received almost 2,600 abatements. Transportation equipment manufacturers received 739 abatements.

Abatements were granted to encourage over $40 billion in (projected) investment in new manufacturing plants and equipment. About half of this total represented investment by transportation equipment firms, where the average investment per abatement was just over $27 million. In the other industry categories, the average investment per abatement ranged from $2.5 million in heavy industries to almost $4.7 million for high-tech industries.

Firms receiving abatements promised that property tax relief would allow them to create more than 160,000 new jobs and ensure that an additional 490,000 manufacturing jobs would remain in the state (table 2.7). At least 30,000 new jobs were promised in each industry category, except consumer goods, where some 15,000 new jobs were promised. The 195,000 jobs retained by abatements granted to transportation equipment firms is double the number in any other industrial category.

Almost half of the abatements granted during this period were for investments in the state's two largest urban areas (table 2.8). Despite having a much smaller population, Grand

Table 2.7. Abated Jobs, 1991–2001

	New	Retained	Total	Percent
Transportation Equipment	44,143	194,901	239,044	36.5
Heavy Industry	30,173	71,524	101,697	15.5
High Tech	35,376	71,534	106,910	16.3
Consumer Goods	15,003	58,337	73,340	11.2
Other Manufacturing	38,931	94,197	133,128	20.4
Total	163,626	490,493	654,119	

Table 2.8. Abatement Activity in Detroit and Grand Rapids Urban Areas, 1992–2002 (millions of dollars)

	Detroit Area		Grand Rapids Area	
	Detroit	Tri-County	Grand Rapids	Tri-County
Certificates	153	1,244	274	1,992
Investment	$3,587.5	$18,971.7	$439.4	$5,346.7
Real Property	$174.2	$3.256.0	$121.0	$1,620.9
Personal Property	$3,413.4	$15,715.7	$310.4	$3,722.7
Jobs	22,471	168,647	15,662	163,202
New	2,713	47,816	3,311	35,736
Retained	19,758	120,831	12,351	127,466

Rapids-area municipalities issued more PA 198 certificates than did metro Detroit municipalities. Grand Rapids attracted much less investment than did Detroit but was promised a larger number of new jobs. PA 198 investments in the suburban portions of these urban areas attracted more new jobs in the Detroit area, but the numbers of jobs retained were about the same in both areas.

Industrial property tax abatements are clearly important to Michigan manufacturing firms. Overall, according to the abatement applications, almost 90 percent of the 1992 manufacturing job base would remain in the state as a result of abatement grants. Relative to total employment in 1992, abatement activity was greatest for high-tech and consumer goods manufacturing firms. In both of these industries, firms receiving abatements promised to retain more jobs than existed at the beginning of the period (table 2.9). Abatements granted to transportation equipment firms were projected to preserve almost the entire 1992 job base.

If all of the manufacturing jobs "retained" through PA 198 abatements had actually left the state (as certified in the abatement applications), there would have been fewer than

Table 2.9. Estimated Net Impact of Abatements on Employment

	Employment 1992	Retained	Retained as % of 1992	New	Total Abated	Actual 2002	Abated as % of 2002
Transportation Equipment	202,697	194,901	96.2	44,143	239,044	238,731	100.1
Heavy Industry	263,381	71,524	27.2	30,173	101,697	213,618	47.6
High Tech	44,957	71,534	159.1	35,376	106,910	36,950	289.3
Consumer Goods	57,361	58,337	101.7	15,003	73,340	37,499	195.6
Other Manufacturing	308,328	94,197	30.6	38,931	133,128	209,461	63.6
Total	876,724	490,493	55.9	163,626	654,119	736,259	88.8

SOURCE: U.S. Bureau of the Census. *County Business Patterns*, 1992, 2002.

60,000 manufacturing jobs left in Michigan by 2002. Without the new jobs promised by firms receiving PA 198 abatements, the total number of manufacturing jobs in the state would have declined to about 573,000 in 2002.

The above reasoning overstates the importance of abatements, however. An obvious concern is that the PA 198 jobs, both new and retained, are estimates and have generally not been verified. Even if all of the promises of new and retained jobs were fulfilled, declines in employment may still have occurred in firms that did not receive abatements. Because individual manufacturers (especially transportation equipment firms) received multiple abatements, jobs in these plants have, in effect, been "retained" multiple times. Some of the new jobs attracted by tax abatements might have been created anyway. Thus, while it appears that the gross jobs numbers attributable to PA 198 must be considered high estimates, it is just as difficult to estimate the low end of the range.

Has the use of PA 198 abatements been successful in expanding Michigan's manufacturing sector? The evidence suggests that this has not been the case. The new jobs promised in the PA 198 applications would have produced an increase of almost 19 percent in manufacturing employment. With the exception of transportation equipment manufacturing, however, employment has declined in manufacturing sectors. While the number of transportation equipment jobs rose by 18 percent, this is less that the 22 percent increase promised in abatement applications. The addition of new jobs as a result of tax abatements did not prevent staff reductions in other areas of these firms.

Data for Michigan's two largest urban areas reflect similar trends. Despite the promise of some 48,000 new jobs through PA 198 abatements, the tricounty Detroit area lost 130,000 manufacturing jobs over the decade. The modest (4 percent) increase in the number of Grand Rapid-area manufacturing jobs was equal to just 12 percent of the promised PA 198 jobs. For every new PA 198 job in the Grand Rapids area, seven existing jobs were lost.

What has been the impact of tax abatements on manufacturing job retention? Relative to total employment in 1992, high-tech and consumer goods manufacturing were the greatest beneficiaries of PA 198 abatements, with firms in these two categories receiving abatements that promised to preserve more jobs in these industries than actually existed in Michigan in 1992 (table 2.9). Abatements granted to transportation equipment firms promised to preserve almost the entire 1992 job base as well. Overall, the jobs covered by abatements equaled almost 90 percent of all manufacturing jobs.

With the exception of the transportation equipment industry, each of the other broad industry categories had fewer jobs in 2002 than in 1992. Consumer goods and the other manufacturing categories each experienced job losses of more than 30 percent. Heavy industries and high-tech manufacturers lost 19 and 18 percent of their workers, respectively. Michigan's job losses in these latter industry categories were steeper than the respective national rates.

Grand Rapids and Detroit fared little better in retaining their manufacturing jobs. Grand Rapids-area municipalities granted abatements to preserve more than 127,000 jobs during the 1990s; by 2002 there were only 123,000 manufacturing jobs left in the tricounty area. In southeast Michigan, even though abatements were used to retain 121,000 jobs, the area lost almost 130,000 manufacturing jobs, fully one-third of the 1992 total.

Has the use of tax abatements helped to diversify Michigan's manufacturing base and support elements of the New Economy? Abatements promised a substantial number of new jobs in industries with high growth potential (Florida 2005; Fulton and Grimes 2006). High-tech industries pledged 35,000 new jobs, about 21 percent of all new jobs attributed to abatements; the 71,000 retained high-tech jobs represent about 15 percent of all employment retained through tax abatements (table 2.9). High-tech firms, which received about 5 percent of all abatements, accounted for less than 5 percent of all investment. Based on the projected jobs, both new and retained, covered by tax abatements, Michigan should have had almost 107,000 high-tech jobs in 2002. The actual figure was less than 37,000. The proportion of Michigan manufacturing jobs in high-tech industries declined from 5.1 percent to 5.0 percent.

While all industrial categories benefited from tax abatements, the PA 198 program has had the greatest employment impact on transportation equipment manufacturing. Transportation equipment and heavy industries accounted for 70 percent of all PA 198 investment and 52 percent of all jobs covered by abatements. Thus, the primary focus of tax abatements has been on attracting and retaining jobs in Michigan's traditional manufacturing sectors.

In summary, then:

- Despite billions of dollars in foregone property tax revenues, manufacturing jobs have declined in Michigan in almost every category.
- Transportation equipment, where virtually every job benefited from abatements, was the only category where employment increased.
- In the high-tech category, some 70,000 promised jobs never materialized or left the state anyway; for consumer goods, the decline was almost 36,000.
- Michigan local governments have used tax abatements to preserve (at least temporarily and most certainly repeatedly) jobs in dying industries; efforts to attract new jobs in new industries have produced few lasting benefits.

Discussion

Duderstadt (2005: 1) argues that America's economic restructuring requires Michigan to adopt a new focus: "public and private sectors continue to cling tenaciously to past beliefs and practices, preoccupied with obsolete and largely irrelevant issues." This position is echoed by Glazer and Grimes (2004), who suggest that for Michigan to put itself in the best position for future sustainable economic prosperity, it must look to states like Massachusetts, Virginia, and Minnesota, all of which had above-average per capita income in 2001 and above-average growth in 1969–2001. These states have sustained their competitiveness through an emphasis on high-paying, knowledge-based industries (see Thomas chapter 11, and Hoffman and Pyne chapter 12, this volume, for a further discussion).

It does not appear, however, that the granting of tax abatements in Michigan has made much of a contribution to this effort. Clearly, the economic development strategies employed by local governments and state policies over the past decade have done little to diversify Michigan's manufacturing economy, which is now even more dependent on transportation equipment and other heavy industry than it was in the early 1990s. While some abatements were granted to attract new (and to retain existing) jobs in high-tech industries, total employment in this category declined by 36 percent in Michigan; nationally, high-tech manufacturing employment fell by just under 28 percent. The pattern is similar for consumer goods manufacturing jobs.

It would seem that the glass is, at best, half full. Michigan's manufacturing employment picture would certainly have been less favorable if no abatements had been granted. Industrial property tax abatements enabled the state to preserve a higher proportion of its manufacturing jobs than the national average. Michigan was able to gain employment in its transportation specialty, while losing jobs in all other categories. There are negative implications to these putatively favorable results, however. First, the increase (or retention) of transportation jobs might be declared a victory if heavy manufacturing generally, and transportation specifically, had good prospects for the future. The reality, however, is that significant financial incentives have been directed at industries suffering permanent structural decline.

Second, the policy of using public resources to support stagnant or declining industries has had significant collateral costs. The $40 billion in industrial investment that received abatements during the 1990s cost municipalities more than $2 billion annually in foregone property tax revenue. Although almost half of these tax expenditures benefited transportation equipment firms, all the other industry categories enjoyed reduced taxes while reducing their employment in Michigan. And this tax loss is very unevenly distributed across cities, typically to the detriment of those most economically stressed. For example, each abated job cost the city of Detroit about $925 annually in forgone property tax revenue, while the much healthier city of Grand Rapids lost less than $90 annually (Sands and Reese 2006).

There are a number of implications of these tax losses. Local government capacity to provide services, maintain public infrastructure, meet the needs of poorer residents, and generally enhance the quality of local life is diminished (that is, promoting the environmental and social equity components of the triple bottom line). In a state such as Michigan, which limits local property tax increases while cutting state revenue-sharing aid to municipalities, any loss of local tax revenue can have severe consequences, particularly if it occurs

Table 2.10. Net Impact of Abatements on Employment, Detroit and Grand Rapids Urban Areas, 1992–2002

	Detroit Tri-County	Grand Rapids Tri-County
Manufacturing Jobs 1992	386,536	118,765
PA 198 Retained Jobs	120,831	127,466
Retained/1992 Total	31.3%	107.3%
PA 198 New Jobs	47,816	35,736
Expected Jobs 2002 (1992 plus New PA 198)	434,352	154,501
Actual 2002 Jobs	256,950	123,183
Expected/Actual	59.2%	79.6%

SOURCE: U.S. Bureau of the Census, *County Business Patterns*, 1992, 2002.

in cities least able to afford it. The other effect of tax abatements is that necessarily the tax burden must shift from businesses receiving the abatement to other current residents and firms. Unless services are to be cut, someone must pay for the forgone tax revenue.

Of course, the granting of Industrial Property Tax Abatements is not the only factor in the current fiscal stress of Michigan's cities. The widespread use of residential property tax abatements by some cities (particularly Detroit) has affected local revenues. The implementation of Proposal A, limiting increases in taxable values and the ability to increase tax rates, has further reduced local revenue-generating capacity (Citizens Research Council of Michigan 2001). And the state's current fiscal stress has led to significant reductions in general revenue sharing and aid to cities.

Abatements could be more effective if they were not renewable and were allowed only for a limited time period, included requirements that recipients remain in the community well past the period of the abatement, and delete performance guarantees for jobs, investment, and the hiring of local workers. It might reasonably be argued that, eventually, revenue abated would accrue to the city in the future. However, none of this is the case in Michigan. These tax losses and incidence shifts represent a direct cost to the municipality.

Finally, there are significant opportunity costs to PA 198, such as missed chances for local governments to use other types of development strategies and policies that might better achieve a sustainable economic base that promotes diversity and new investment and jobs. While the value of industrial tax abatements as a tool for facilitating the restructuring of the Michigan economy seems questionable, it nevertheless represents the primary economic development tool available to local governments in the state. While other types of economic development policies are available and often widely used, tax abatements remain the most popular for a variety of reasons: businesses expect them because they are so frequently offered, they do not require actual cash outlays upfront and hence the political case is easier to make (half of something is better than nothing at all), granting of abatements does not require high levels of skill and numbers of development staff, and the retention or relocation of a large industrial facility as the result of an abatement is a very visible outcome occurring in the present. If the easiest and politically rational action that local economic developers can take is to offer property tax abatements, it should not be surprising that they do so with such frequency.

A broader look at Michigan's employment picture suggests that perhaps new local economic development initiatives, ones that focus on high-tech services and knowledge-based industries, might be more effective in repositioning the state's economy (Glazer and Grimes 2005). While Michigan has some incentive programs that might address this sector, these are not tools generally available to local governments (Conboy 2001; Michigan Economic Development Corporation 2004). The Michigan Economic Growth Authority (MEGA) grants and the more recent Cool Cities initiative operate primarily at the state, rather than the local, level. Strategies based on human capital and higher education have a long gestation period and often high upfront costs (Duderstadt 2005; Blank and Sallee 2006). What appears needed are state-level actions that limit abatements while encouraging (and likely subsidizing) other types of local development strategies.

Limits or restrictions on abatements have been suggested in other research (see Sands and Reese 2006, for example) but in summary could include:

- Targeting abatements to distressed communities
- Reducing the length of time for which abatements are granted
- Limiting the number of times a single firm can receive abatements from any local government or requiring a number of years between abatement requests
- Limiting the number of abatements individual municipalities can grant in a specific time period
- Limiting abatements to new investment or jobs
- Limiting abatements to particular targeted industries or sectors
- Requiring performance guarantees for recipients, including tenure after the abatement, investment and job creation levels, and hiring targets for residents of the community granting the abatement.

The issue of how to encourage other types of economic development strategies is complex. Research has identified a number of policies that might more effectively lead to new (as opposed to retained or relocated) business development that could be targeted toward high-tech or creative industries or be used to diversify the economic base generally: incubators, start-up loans, training, investment in education and amenities, export market development, and enhancements to art and culture, for example (Reese and Fasenfest 1999; Florida 2002). However, cities in Michigan tend not to use these policies, and the use of such policies has decreased over the past fifteen years. Development of business incubators has decreased by half during just the 2001 to 2005 time period (from 41 to 21 percent of cities using them); the use of foreign business attraction strategies and export market development also declined. Local investment in job-training programs has dropped even more significantly, from 57 to 16 percent of cities (Reese and Sands 2006). Tax abatement use, on the other hand, has remained steady.

State incentives encouraging the use of alternative economic development policies might logically lead to a shift in local policy. Such incentives are already included in the state's Cool Cities initiative, where state grants are available for local projects that enhance downtowns, culture and the arts, and other urban amenities. But the extremely limited funding for this program is not sufficient to affect local policies on even a moderate scale. State grants with matching requirements modeled on federal categorical grant programs might support local use of small business revolving loan funds, business incubators, job training, and so on. Given the financial conditions of the state, however, such an initiative is likely unrealistic.

The available policy options come back to changing the nature of state enabling legislation for PA 198. What happens to local economic development policies when a state limits or forbids the use of tax abatements? Research on U.S. states and Canadian provinces that prohibit local tax abatements has indicated that cities in those areas have increased the use of other, more entrepreneurial or innovative policies, more likely to increase new business development (Reese and Malmer 1994; Reese and Rosenfeld 2004; Reese and Sands 2006).

59

The most viable policy recommendations are thus for changes in state enabling legislation, with the expectation that this will precipitate shifts in local policy. If abatements are restricted, the local economic development policy vacuum could well be filled with different economic development initiatives more likely to lead to desired economic base diversification, ultimately shifting the state to the new economy. At the very least, forgone public resources may turn into investment in public amenities and local human capital, leaving individual cities, if not more competitive, at least more livable over the long term.

Notes

1. The year 1992 was selected as a starting point for this analysis because the data on tax abatements for the preceding years were incomplete; the subsequent decade, ending in 2002, incorporates periods of both economic growth and decline. Although the available data for 2003–2006 are limited, they indicate that abatements continue to be granted at about the same overall rate.
2. Transportation equipment includes all 336 North American Industrial Classification system codes except aerospace (3364); heavy industries include primary metals (331), fabricated metal products (332), and machinery (333); high tech includes pharmaceuticals (3254), computers and electronic products (334), aerospace products and parts (3364), and medical devices and equipment (3391); consumer goods include food (311), beverages and tobacco (312), apparel (315), leather products (317), and household furniture (3371). The balance of manufacturing NAIC codes constitutes the "all other" category.
3. According to the Citizens Research Council of Michigan (2006), Michigan is ranked twenty-first among the states in total taxes but fifteenth in property taxes.
4. PA 198 of 1974 allows local governments to reduce the property tax burden on new investment in manufacturing facilities (plant and equipment) by 50 percent for up to twelve years; in the case of a rehabilitated facility, new investment is completely exempt from taxes, while the taxes on the original property are frozen at their prerehabilitation level (Sands and Zalmezak 2001).

REFERENCES

Ahlbrandt, R. S., and J. P. DeAngelis. 1987. Local Options for Economic Development in a Maturing Industrial Region. *Economic Development Quarterly* 1:41–51.

Alcaly, R. 2003. *The New Economy.* New York: Farrar, Strauss and Giroux.

Blakeley, E. J. 1994. *Planning Local Economic Development Theory and Practice.* 2nd ed. Thousand Oaks, Calif.: Sage.

Blank, R. M., and J. M. Sallee. 2006. *Labor Markets and Human Capital Investment in Michigan: Challenges and Strategies.* Ann Arbor: University of Michigan, Gerald Ford School of Public Policy.

Bluestone, B., J. Cowie, and J. Heathcott. 2003. *Beyond the Ruins.* Ithaca, N.Y.: Cornell University Press.

Citizens Research Council of Michigan. 2001. *The Growing Difference between State Equalized Value and Taxable Value in Michigan.* CRC Memorandum 1058. Livonia, Mich.: Citizens Research Council of Michigan.

———. 2006. *Tax Revenue Comparison: Michigan and the U.S. Average.* CRC Memorandum 1080. Livonia, Mich.: Citizens Research Council of Michigan.

Clark, T. N., ed. 2003. *The City as an Entertainment Machine.* Greenwich, Conn.: JAI Press.

Clarke, S. E., and G. L. Gaile. 1992. The Next Wave: Postfederal Local Economic Development Strategies. *Economic Development Quarterly* 6:187–198.

Conboy, M. J. 2001. *The Evolution of Economic Development in Michigan.* Lansing: Michigan Economic Development Corporation.

County Business Patterns. 1992. www.census.gov.

———. 2002. www.census.gov.

Dandeneau, S. P. 1996. *A Town Abandoned: Flint, Michigan, Confronts Deindustrialization.* Albany: State University of New York Press.

Duderstadt, J. J. 2005. *A Roadmap to Michigan's Future:* Meeting the Challenge of a Global Knowledge-Driven Economy. Ann Arbor: Millennium Project, University of Michigan.

Eisinger, P. K. 1988. *The Rise of the Entrepreneurial State.* Madison: University of Wisconsin Press.

Fisher, P. S., and A. H. Peters. 1998. *Industrial Incentives: Competition among American States and Cities.* Kalamazoo, Mich.: W. E. Upjohn Institute for Employment Research.

Florida, R. 2002. *The Rise of the Creative Class.* New York: Basic Books.

———. 2005. *Cities and the Creative Class.* New York: Basic Books.

Fulton, G. A., and D. R. Grimes. 2006. *Michigan Industrial Structure and Competitive Advantage.* Ann Arbor: University of Michigan Institute for Industrial and Labor Relations.

Glazer, L., and D. R. Grimes. 2005. *A New Path to Prosperity? Manufacturing and Knowledge-Based Industries as Drivers of Economic Growth.* Ann Arbor: Michigan Future.

Hill, E. W., and J. F. Brennan. 2000. A Methodology for Identifying the Drivers of Industrial Clusters. *Economic Development Quarterly* 14:65–96.

Hill, R. C. 1987. *Deindustrialization and Racial Minorities in the Great Lakes Region USA.* East Lansing: Michigan State University Department of Sociology.

Hoover, E. M. 1985. *An Introduction to Regional Economics.* 3rd ed. New York: Knopf.

Kasarda, J. D. 1995. Industrial Restructuring and Changing Job Locations. In *State of the Union: America in the 1990s,* edited by R. Farley. New York: Russell Sage.

Klosterman, R. E. 1990. *Community Analysis and Planning Techniques.* Savage, Md.: Rowland and Littlefield.

Markusen, A. 1988. *Bowing Out, Bidding Down and Betting on the Basics.* Evanston, Ill.: Northwestern University Center for Urban Affairs and Policy Research.

MEDC (Michigan Economic Development Corporation). 2004. *Michigan's Cool Cities Initiative: A Reinvestment Strategy.* Lansing, Mich.: MEDC.

Peters, A., and P. Fisher. 2005. The Failure of Economic Development Incentives. *Journal of the American Planning Association* 70:27–37.

Reese, L. A. 1998. Sharing the Benefits of Economic Development: What Cities Utilize Type II Policies? *Urban Affairs Review* 33:686–711.

———. 2006. Do We Really Need Another Typology? Clusters of Local Economic Development Strategies. *Economic Development Quarterly* 20(4):368–376.

Reese, L. A., and D. Fasenfest. 1999. What Works Best? Values and the Evaluation of Local Economic Development Policy. In *Approaches to Economic Development,* edited by J. P. Blair and L. A. Reese. Thousand Oaks, Calif.: Sage.

Reese, L. A., and A. Malmer. 1994. The Effects of State Enabling Legislation on Local Economic Development Policies. *Urban Affairs Quarterly* (September):114–135.

Reese, L. A., and R. A. Rosenfeld. 2004. Local Economic Development in the U.S. and Canada: Institutionalizing Policy Approaches. *American Review of Public Administration* 34:277–292.

Reese, L. A., and G. Sands. 2006. Making the Least of Our Differences? Trends in Canadian and U.S. Local Economic Development, 1990–2005. Paper presented at the World Planning Congress.

Rosdil, D. 2006. Testing Cultural and Economic Explanations for Local Development Policies: The Competing Claims of Security, Distress, and Nontraditional Subcultures. Paper presented at the annual meeting of the Midwest Political Science Association, Chicago.

Sands, G., and L. A. Reese. 2006. The Equity Impacts of Municipal Tax Incentives: Leveling or Tilting the Playing Field? *Review of Policy Research* (January 23):71–94.

Sands G., L. A. Reese, and H. L. Khan. 2006. Implementing Tax Abatements in Michigan: A Study of Best Practices. *Economic Development Quarterly* 20:44–58.

Sands, G., and P. Zalmezak. 2001. Michigan Industrial Property Tax Abatements: A Summary of Activity under Public Act 198 of 1974, 1985–98. Paper presented at the Urban Research Seminar, Detroit.

Sassen, S. 2006. *Cities in a World Economy.* 3rd ed. Thousand Oaks, Calif.: Pine Forge Press.

Schwarz, J. E., and T. J. Volgy. 1992. The Impacts of Economic Development Strategies on Wages: Exploring the Effect on Public Policy at the Local Level. Paper presented at the annual meeting of the American Political Science Association, Chicago.

Teaford, J. C. 1994. *Cities of the Heartland.* Bloomington: Indiana University Press.

Voytek, K., and L. Ledebur. 1991. Is Industry Targeting a Viable Economic Development Strategy? In *Dilemmas of Urban Economic Development,* edited by R. D. Bingham and R. Mier. Thousand Oaks, Calif: Sage.

Weil, H., and A. Friedhoff. 2006. *Bearing the Brunt: Manufacturing Job Loss in the Great Lakes Region, 1995–2005.* Washington, D.C.: Brookings Institution Metro Economy Series.

CHAPTER 3

Abating Taxes, Abetting Sprawl: The Geographical Distribution of Tax Abatements in Michigan

Angela Lazarean and Katharine Trudeau

Central cities, particularly those in the Midwest, experienced great economic success in the early to mid-twentieth century due, in part, to booming industry and the resultant abundance of manufacturing jobs. More recently, economic circumstances have changed in central cities, and increasing numbers of manufacturing jobs are being outsourced to other countries every year. By the end of the last century, state and local governments across the United States were actively engaged in economic development efforts.

The policy cornerstone of many state and local economic development organizations in the United States has been an effort to attract private investment and replacement jobs that accompany this investment. Since the 1930s, states have actively competed to be selected as the location for a new plant or corporate headquarters, offering substantial incentives, including favorable financing, infrastructure improvements, training funds, and tax abatements (Eisinger 1988). In light of growing globalization, competition for jobs has grown more fierce, and bidding wars among states, even though there has been increasing criticism of the costs involved, nevertheless continue (Hovey 1986; Ledebur and Woodward 1990).

Despite the widespread deindustrialization of the U.S. economy, the challenges involved with diversifying and restructuring local economies are significant; thus manufacturing jobs continue to be a prime target of many economic development efforts. These jobs are also often viewed as largely serving export markets and are critical to economic growth (Miloslavsky and Shatz 2006). Manufacturing plants are seen as "big ticket" items, with substantial economic and political benefits; attracting an automotive assembly plant is a major coup.

Property tax abatements have for decades been utilized as the incentive of choice for state and local governments in efforts to hold on to manufacturing jobs. As of 2005, thirty-five states allowed local governments to offer property tax abatements, and, in general, some degree of property tax relief is one element of most major economic development incentive packages (Dalehite, Mikesell, and Zorn 2005; Reese and Rosenfeld 2004). This remains the case despite research suggesting that too often tax abatements are granted to firms with little consideration of costs and benefits, to the detriment of the community; costs appear to be significant while benefits are, at best, uncertain (Schwarz and Volgy 1992; Hood 1994; Wassmer 1994; Lynch, Fishgold, and Blackwood 1996; Wassmer and Anderson 2001; Peters and Fisher 2004).

Literature Review

From a municipal perspective, however, property tax abatements are perceived to have a number of advantages that account for their continuing popularity. They are typically granted for a limited period of time, thus offering the promise of revenue gains some time in the future. The cost of public services received by most industrial and commercial properties is less than the property taxes typically paid, so that any tax reduction may not have an adverse effect on the ability to provide necessary local services (Ladd 1998). Because tax abatements represent foregone revenues, as opposed to direct expenditures, they do not require appropriations. And the community generally receives some revenue from the facility, supporting the argument that some new revenue is better than none at all.

Tax incentives, such as the Michigan PA 198 Abatements examined here, have consistently evidenced mixed results in evaluations of their effectiveness. For example, surveys of recipients of tax abatements have generally reported that the incentives were effective in influencing the location decisions of firms and thus generating economic growth (Calzonetti and Walker 1991; Premus 1982; Rubin 1991). Other assessments, however, have concluded that incentives were basically ineffective in stimulating local economic growth (Schmenner 1982). Much of the conflict in the evaluation literature on tax abatements stems from: differing research methodologies, variation in the operationalization of "success" or effectiveness, differences in geographic scale of analysis, and the differing time periods evaluations have spanned.

Fisher and Peters (1998) and Goss and Phillips (2001) provide excellent meta-analyses of tax policy evaluations, categorizing methodologies into five types: surveys, case studies, general equilibrium models, hypothetical firm analyses, and econometric analyses. Overall, surveys, case studies, and econometric modeling have produced conflicting findings on the efficacy of tax abatements in stimulating development, however defined. Hypothetical firm analyses have suggested that tax incentives can increase company profitability, but do not allow for an assessment of the contribution to local economic growth (Goss and Phillips 2001).

Property taxes are typically only a small portion of business costs and are likely to affect financial decisions only at the margin. Location choices involve a host of factors, including ease of access to suppliers and customers, labor availability, and the quality of life offered in a particular location. Given that the proportion of property taxes to overall costs is typically negligible at best, the granting of property tax abatements ultimately encourages firms to do what they would have done in any case. Furthermore, tax abatements appear to have little long-term additive impact on overall business activity (Wassmer 1994), and any positive effects are short-lived, occurring only in the time period right after the tax incentive program begins. Even after four decades of research there is no consensus on whether tax incentives have any effect at all. Peters and Fisher (2004:32) conclude that "the best case is that incentives work about 10 percent of the time, and are simply a waste of money the other 90 percent."

Research has indicated that there *are* cases where, under the right circumstances, tax incentives can stimulate development. The necessary conditions for this success seem to be that the abatements are granted based on a careful assessment of costs and benefits and are accompanied by performance requirements that ensure local benefits in return (Bartik 1991; Calzonetti and Walker 1991; Goss and Phillips 2001; Gramlich 1997; Premus 1982; Rubin 1991).

Many studies, however, have documented that even when there are positive outcomes, tax abatements have not achieved the levels of growth desired, and they may have negative secondary impacts. For example, Hood (1994) concludes that because abatement packages offered to large corporations are so extensive, state and local burdens on the average small business owner or residential taxpayer increase because of the need for highways, access roads, water and sewer lines, and other infrastructure in anticipation of company relocation. Frequently, the relocated company fails to generate significant economic or employment gains, or it relocates again before local benefits can trickle down, thus distorting labor and consumer markets (Hood 1994).

If tax abatements and other business incentives do not significantly increase economic activity, they may be able to change the geographic distribution of this activity at the margin; that is, within a state or metropolitan region. By altering where firms choose to locate, the fortunes of specific local government units (and, possibly, their residents) may be improved. While society as a whole may not be better off, specific populations may enjoy some benefits (Bartik 1991). And as long as local officials *believe* that tax incentives must be a central component of local development strategies, their use is likely to continue with little regulation. Indeed, recent research on development incentives during the 1990s and into the early 2000s clearly indicates that the use of tax abatements remains popular in cities across the United States. For example, in the mid-1990s tax incentives were the seventh most commonly used economic development strategy; by 2001 they were the sixth most relied upon local technique (Reese, Rosenfeld, and Fasenfest 2002). Overall, 54 percent of cities in the United States were using tax abatements and other tax incentives at least to a moderate extent to attract and retain business investment (Reese, Rosenfeld, and Fasenfest 2002; Reese and Rosenfeld 2004).

For the past three decades, the state of Michigan has allowed its local governments to grant property tax abatements to firms investing in new or rehabilitated industrial facilities. Since its inception, Michigan's tax abatement program, PA 198, has been used more than 17,000 times. Most of Michigan's local governments are eligible to participate, and two-fifths have granted at least one industrial tax abatement (Sands and Zalmezak 2001). Michigan cities utilize industrial tax abatements at high rates, with 68 percent granting at least one abatement, according to data compiled by the Michigan Economic Development

Corporation. Abatement activity has been widespread, with one or more abatements granted in seventy-six of Michigan's eighty-three counties during the 1980s and 1990s.

An examination of the use of industrial property tax abatements in Michigan's two largest urban areas—Detroit and Grand Rapids—suggests that the abatement policies of local governments appear to have contributed to a pattern of metropolitan spatial and economic decentralization that is detrimental to central cities and older suburbs (Reese and Sands 2006). The majority of abatements were concentrated in the major metropolitan areas of the state. The tricounty areas around both Detroit and Grand Rapids accounted for 75 percent of the total number of abatements and 85 percent of the investment that resulted. These six counties also accounted for 84 percent of the promised new jobs (Sands and Reese 2006).

Despite this widespread use of industrial tax breaks for more than three decades, many Michigan cities currently face declining population and employment rates, and overall unfavorable conditions (Adelaja et al. 2007). Given the nature of the pathologies that exist in many Michigan cities, curbing sprawl becomes just one of many desired outcomes of policy to improve Michigan cities and metropolitan areas. This chapter addresses the role that property tax abatements play in patterns of metropolitan development.

Low-density, homogenous development at the urban fringe, characterized as urban sprawl, is considered by many as wasteful of resources, expensive, and inefficient to service (Rusk 1993). The adverse impacts of urban sprawl are many and include: redundant and declining infrastructure, environmental and resource degradation, duplication and inefficiencies in service provision, and inequities among municipal fortunes (Rusk 1993). Because the marginal cost of new development is below the average cost, the long-run sustainability of much of suburban development is questionable (Fulton 1997; Innes and Booher 1999).

As a direct consequence of urban sprawl, businesses and higher-income residents leave the central city, beginning a downward spiral in which municipal tax burdens grow as tax bases erode and the demand from low-income residents for services increases. High taxes and poor public services create barriers to attracting or retaining businesses and residents in central cities, thus perpetuating a vicious cycle of decline (Orfield 2002).

Michigan epitomizes the process of sprawling urban development. Despite limited growth in population, large areas of land have been converted to urban development in recent decades (Ballard et al. 2003). Michigan's larger metropolitan areas experienced an average growth of 8 percent in their urbanized area for every 1 percent increase in population. Metropolitan Bay City increased its developed area some twenty-seven times more rapidly than its population growth (Michigan Land Use Leadership Council 2003).

Some have defended the current trends as the natural consequence of market forces that reflect consumer preferences (Gordon and Richardson 1997). But this undesirable growth pattern is the result not only of individual choices by households and firms. Public policies related to transportation, housing finance, and development regulations have also been blamed for this situation (Jackson 1985; Kunstler 1993). Another potential policy cause of sprawl are the tax incentives used by local governments to encourage and retain economic development—PA 198 in the case of Michigan.

Property Tax Abatements in Michigan

From 1978 through 2001, 721 of Michigan's 1,773 local governments (40 percent of the total) granted one or more PA 198 tax abatements. Over this period, 137 municipalities granted only a single industrial property tax abatement, while an additional 72 provided only 2 abatements. At the other extreme, the city of Grand Rapids granted 522 abatements, an average of one new abatement every two weeks. The top five Michigan communities in terms of total abatements granted (Grand Rapids, Holland, Holland Township, Detroit, and Wyoming) gave 13.5 percent of all abatements. The thirty-five communities granting the most abatements provided over 6,000 abatements, almost 44 percent of the total.

Since 2001, abatement activity has declined, following the pattern observed in earlier periods of economic decline (Reese and Sands 2006). From 2002 through 2006, 429 of Michigan's 1,773 local government units (24 percent of the total) granted one or more tax abatement. There were no abatements granted in fourteen of Michigan's counties. Over this period, 142 municipalities granted only one industrial property tax abatement, while an additional 80 provided only 2 abatements. At the other extreme, Holland Township in Ottawa County granted 84, and the city of Cadillac in Wexford County granted 60. The top five Michigan communities in terms of abatements granted in this time frame were Holland Township, Cadillac, Zeeland, Walker, and Wyoming, accounting for 11 percent of all abatements. The thirty-five communities granting the most abatements provided 1,053, or 42 percent of the total. Counties and municipalities long established as manufacturing and business centers are the heaviest users of PA 198 as indicated by their frequency in different time periods in table 3.1.

Methodology

The data for this study come from several sources. First, data on tax abatements come from the files of the Michigan Economic Development Corporation and its predecessor agencies. These data cover all abatements awarded from 1985 to 2006 and include the number of abatements, projected real and personal property investment, and projected retained and created jobs. Second, census and property assessment information for the years 1980,

Table 3.1. PA 198 Abatements Granted, 1980–2005

	1980–85	1986–90	1991–95	1996–2000	2001–5	Total
Certificates issued	3,189	3,130	3,367	3,920	3,094	16,700
Total investment (millions)	$5,088.9	$8,636.0	$11,924.7	$23,333.2	$20,212.6	$69,195.4
Percent real property	26.8	21.4	19.2	22.1	na	21.8*
Total jobs	117,777	229,996	180,043	408,491	369,833	1,306,140
New jobs	19,843	37,427	56,654	81,989	90,171	286,084
Retained jobs	97,934	192,569	123,389	326,502	279,662	1,020,056

*1980–2000

SOURCE: Michigan Economic Development Corporation.

1990, and 2000 were added to the abatement data set. Third, the data set has been geo-coded to allow for the mapping of tax abatement use, the nature of firms awarded abate-ments, and various demographic and economic health characteristics of Michigan municipalities. These data were subsequently mapped to analyze the geographic location of tax abatements. Thematic maps, expressing abatement use at the statewide level by county, and at the countywide level by municipality in two tricounty areas, Grand Rapids and Detroit.

Previous research based on these data indicate that, in Michigan, abatement use does not appear to favor distressed areas, and, if per capita use is considered, generally healthy exurbs have offered more abatements per capita than central cities and inner-ring suburbs (Reese and Sands 2006). Investment patterns, particularly new development and new jobs, favor exurban areas. In short, the pattern where central cities and distressed areas make the greatest use of abatements to retain and generate new jobs and investment in order to "catch up" with their suburban and exurban counterparts does not appear to be present. Many communities, of all health profiles, are using abatements and new investment pat-terns that clearly favor exurban, greenfield areas (Reese and Sands 2006). Thus, it can be posited that abatement use among exurbs is supporting the movement of business, people, and infrastructure investment farther from existing central cities, thereby contributing to urban sprawl rather than urban redevelopment. Michigan's industrial tax abatements, because they are so widely available, do little to affect the patterns of private investment and job creation in the state. PA 198 Tax Abatements substantially contribute to metropolitan decentralization because of their extensive use by peripheral townships, exacerbating exist-ing intercity inequities in economic health.

Analysis of tax abatement use and outcomes utilizing visual (GIS) technologies will make the patterns clearer and more understandable for local officials, stakeholders, and state leg-islators and facilitate policy debate and revision. An examination of tax abatement data rep-resenting the history of abatements in Michigan concludes that abatement patterns can be best understood when past abatement behaviors and the nature of the local employment base are included in the analysis. With respect to the number of abatements granted, it appears that both these forces—along with the general economy and governmental struc-tural and process factors—are important in understanding abatement behavior. When the total value of abatements is considered, industrial mix appears most critical. Once munici-palities start giving tax abatements, they continue to do so. Municipalities having concen-trations of transportation-related industries and food/consumer products manufacturers are likely to be early users of abatements (Reese 2006).

While the majority of Michigan's eighty-three counties have experienced little change in manufacturing jobs over the past two decades, significant losses have occurred in Southeast Michigan and in counties along the Interstate 75 corridor from Detroit to Bay City and along Interstate 94 from Ann Arbor to Kalamazoo (figure 3.1). Some manufacturing job growth did occur, primarily in West Michigan (Grand Rapids and Holland) and in metropolitan fringe counties such as Lapeer, Livingston, and Allegan.

Extensive abatement activity occurred in counties that both gained and lost jobs (figure 3.2). The 1,309 abatements granted in Kent County accompanied a gain of 7,551 manufacturing

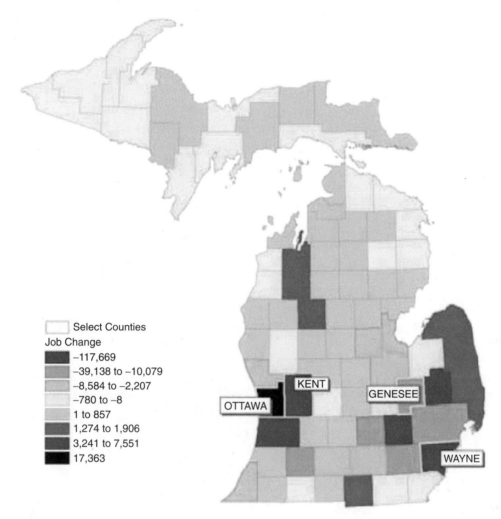

FIGURE 3.1
Manufacturing Job Change, 1982–2002

jobs. On the other hand, Wayne County lost more than 117,000 manufacturing jobs, despite granting 741 abatements.

Abatements have been used to attract more than $43.9 billion in investment from 1978 to 2001 and about $16.3 billion in the years 2002 to 2006. About 80 percent of the investment has been for machinery and equipment, rather than new building construction. Michigan's traditional manufacturing industries (motor vehicle, machinery, and fabricated metals manufacturing) have received the largest share of abatements granted and account for 80 percent of the total investment. High-tech industries, such as pharmaceuticals and electronics manufacturing, have received a disproportionately large share of abatements.

The tax abatements that have been granted are associated with a substantial number of retained jobs. While it becomes very difficult to verify that employment levels included on initial applications have actually been attained, PA 198 abatements are credited with directly affecting more than 489,000 jobs in the 1990s. This figure equals almost 60 percent of the

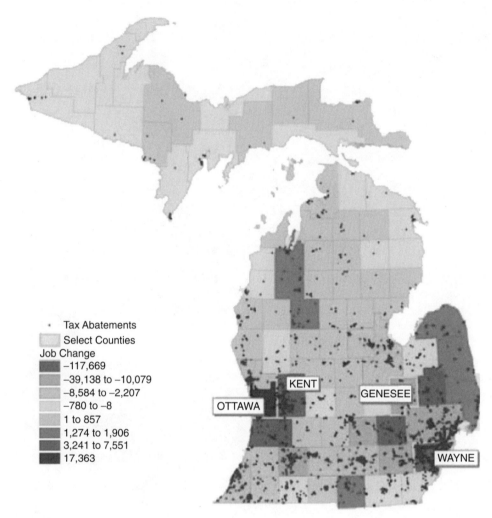

FIGURE 3.2
Manufacturing Job Change and Tax Abatements, 1982–2002

837,000 manufacturing jobs in Michigan in 1990. Only 20 percent of the PA 198 jobs were "new" employment opportunities, however. The number of retained jobs probably involves some double counting, since the same facility may have received multiple property tax abatements during this period. Regardless, allowing for new jobs that never materialized and the elimination of the double counting of retained jobs, the PA 198 program has had a substantial impact on Michigan manufacturing industries during the 1990s. For the time frame covering 2002–2006, 237,525 existing jobs were directly affected and retained, while 71,299 jobs were promised.

Metro Area Trends

The majority of the abatement activity has been concentrated in the largest metropolitan areas of the state. For this analysis, the Detroit urban area is defined as Wayne, Oakland, and

Macomb counties; the Grand Rapids urban area consists of Kent, Ottawa, and Muskegon
counties. Both of these definitions represent areas less extensive than the current U.S.
Bureau of the Census definitions of the respective Primary Metropolitan Statistical areas.
Using the more restrictive definition captures the largest concentrations of population,
economic, and abatement activity.

The six counties include a total of almost 200 local units of government, each of which
has the ability to grant industrial property tax abatements. The local governments include
cities, villages, and townships. Generally, cities and villages have more governmental powers
and responsibilities than townships. In the Detroit and Grand Rapids areas, incorporated cities
range in size from almost one million people in Detroit to fewer than 500 in Lake Angeles.
Villages generally range in population from about 1,000 to more than 10,000. Property tax
rates are typically highest in cities, with large older communities such as Detroit having the
highest property tax rates.

Most townships are large in area (thirty-six square miles), with low population density
and responsibility for few municipal services. Because they provide for only a limited range
of public services, townships generally have relatively low property tax rates. Some townships, especially in the Detroit area, have large populations (up to 90,000 persons) and function as cities in all but name.

PA 198 tax abatements promised new jobs in the majority of the municipalities in the
Detroit urban area (figure 3.3). While a substantial number of these jobs were promised for
the city of Detroit, three suburban municipalities—Auburn Hills, Sterling Heights, and

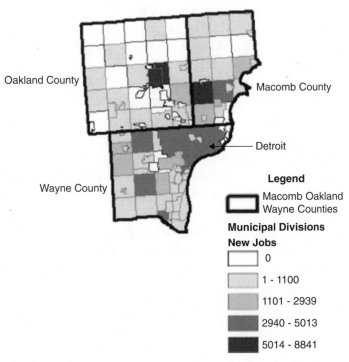

FIGURE 3.3
Detroit Tri-County Area New Jobs, 1978–2002

71

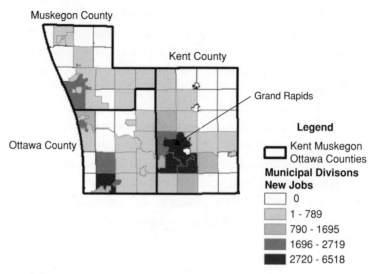

FIGURE 3.4
Grand Rapids Tri-County Area New Jobs, 1978–2002

Pontiac—attracted even larger numbers of new jobs. Livonia, Flat Rock, Romulus, and Chesterfield Township each attracted almost as many new jobs as did Detroit.

A similar pattern can be seen in the tricounty Grand Rapids area (figure 3.4). In addition to Grand Rapids, the communities that were most successful in attracting new PA 198 jobs were Wyoming, Kentwood, and Holland Township. Walker, Muskegon, Zeeland, Grand Haven, and Olive Township were not far behind in the total number of new jobs.

The distribution of jobs preserved by PA 198 abatements follows a similar pattern, with many of the same municipalities at the top of the list in both urban areas (figures 3.5, 3.6). In the Detroit area, several southern Wayne County municipalities (Woodhaven, Sumpter and Huron townships, and Gibraltar) used PA 198 only to attract new jobs, but did not use the program to retain existing jobs. Although the absolute number of retained jobs in Detroit was much larger than in these fringe communities, PA 198 clearly has contributed to the decentralization of manufacturing employment.

Most of the Grand Rapids-area suburban municipalities granted PA 198 abatements both to retain and attract jobs. Cedar Springs and Rockford used PA 198 only to retain existing jobs. The number of existing jobs retained in Tallmadge Township was substantially higher than the number of new jobs attracted by abatements. Blendon Township, along with half a dozen townships in Muskegon County, attracted new jobs with tax abatements, but did not use tax abatements to preserve existing jobs. While the core communities still provided the majority of manufacturing jobs, PA 198 clearly has contributed to increasing the number of jobs in peripheral municipalities.

Central Cities

It is a common perception in Michigan that Grand Rapids (along with other areas in West Michigan) has become a dynamic and prosperous urban center, while Detroit continues a period of decline that began half a century ago. And indeed, many statistical measures

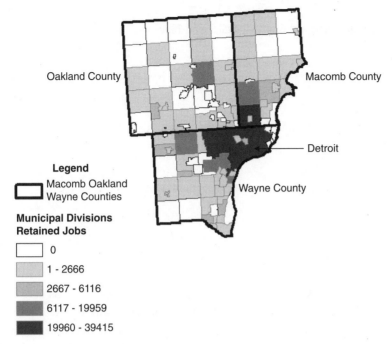

FIGURE 3.5
Detroit Tri-County Area Retained Jobs, 1978–2002

support this contention (table 3.2). In 1990, Detroiters had lower per capita incomes and higher unemployment and poverty rates than did residents in Grand Rapids. The per capita tax base in Detroit was only 43 percent of that in Grand Rapids.

Both cities were active in granting PA 198 abatements during the 1990s, with Grand Rapids providing more than twice as many of these tax breaks in total as did Detroit

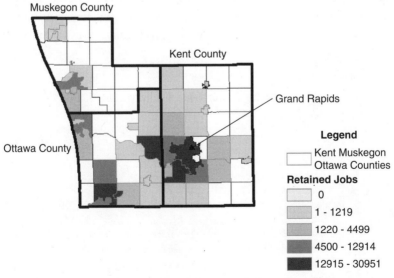

FIGURE 3.6
Grand Rapids Tri-County Area Retained Jobs, 1978–2002

Table 3.2. Demographic and Economic Indicators, 1990

| | Central Cities | | Older Suburbs | | Newer Suburbs | |
	Central Cities	City of Grand Rapids	Detroit	Grand Rapids	Detroit	Grand Rapids
Number	1	1	26	10	26	12
Population	1,027,974	189,126	986,844	198,029	390,553	72,131
Income per capita	$9,443	$12,070	$13,573	$13,773	$17,898	$15,782
Unemployment rate	19.7%	7.4%	10.4%	7.2%	5.8%	3.6%
Poverty rate	32.0%	15.0%	13.4%	13.4%	4.4%	4.7%
SEV per capita	$5,501	$12,709	$12,785	$1,586	$27,216	$22,541

SOURCES: U.S. Census of Population; Michigan Department of Labor and Economic Growth; Michigan Department of Treasury.

(table 3.3). The total investment receiving abatements in Detroit was more than $4.5 billion. Abatements involving real property (industrial buildings) represented less than 3 percent of this total. Grand Rapids granted $313 million in abatements, with over two-fifths going for new manufacturing plants. As a result, the actual investment in real property was about the same for the two cities. Detroit's abatements secured more than twenty-four times the amount of investment in personal property (machinery and equipment) than did Grand Rapids' abatements. With respect to employment opportunities, the patterns are similar. Overall, Detroit's abatements involved almost twice as many jobs as did those in Grand Rapids. In Grand Rapids, abatements promised a greater number of new jobs, but only half as many jobs were retained there as a result of abatements, compared to Detroit.

These differences are even sharper when the respective populations are considered. When related to population, Grand Rapids was twelve times more likely to grant a request for tax abatement than was Detroit. Investment per capita in Detroit was about $4,400, compared to about $1,650 in Grand Rapids. The number of employment opportunities in Grand Rapids relative to population was more than twice as high as it was in Detroit.

Table 3.3. Central City Abatement Activity, 1991–2001

	Detroit	Grand Rapids
Abatements	107	221
Number per 1,000	0.1	1.2
Total investment	$4.54 billion	$0.31 billion
% real property	2.9	41.2
Investment per 1,000	$4,412	$1,655
Total jobs	27,252	15,470
% new jobs	9.2	21.2
Jobs per 1,000	26.5	81.9

SOURCE: Michigan Economic Development Corporation 2006.

Older Suburbs

The state of Michigan has adopted a definition of "distressed communities" that is used as a basis for targeting benefits and eligibility for a number of assistance programs other than PA 198. The factors used in determining whether a municipality qualifies as distressed include population loss, high poverty, high unemployment, and slow property value growth. Currently there are some ninety-eight eligible distressed communities in the state (MSHDA 2006). This definition of "distress" has been adopted here to identify the older suburbs where economic revitalization is likely to be a priority.

The list of communities that have been designated as distressed generally conforms to expectations. It includes all of the state's larger central cities and many of its older suburbs. It also includes a number of municipalities that actually appear to be relatively prosperous and certainly would seldom be considered to be distressed in popular opinion. Among the "distressed" communities are Ann Arbor, Holland, Livonia, and Dearborn. These relatively prosperous communities meet the distress guidelines primarily on the basis of population loss and relatively slow growth in property values. (Holland is an exception; it qualifies as distressed based on its persistent high unemployment rate.)

The tricounty Detroit area includes twenty-six of the distressed communities, about 27 percent of the state total, including some of the lowest income municipalities in Michigan (see appendix 3.1). Some of these officially distressed communities include residents with relatively high incomes (Livonia, Trenton, Gibraltar) or have substantial property tax bases (Dearborn, Southfield). One characteristic that they do have in common with the more obviously distressed municipalities is that they are predominantly built up, with few opportunities for greenfield development. Despite their statistical qualification as distressed, these municipalities are, by most measures, better off than most of the other communities in this category. Several of these communities, notably Livonia, Trenton, Warren, and Dearborn, were active in granting abatements during the 1990s.

The Grand Rapids area includes seven suburban distressed communities, including the cities of Holland and Muskegon, the largest cities in Ottawa and Muskegon counties, respectively. These seven distressed communities were supplemented with three other municipalities that experienced population losses of more than 4 percent during the 1990s to constitute the list of older Grand Rapids suburbs. The lack of population growth during a period when other parts of the urban area, including more than half of the state's designated distressed communities, were growing suggests that economic development might be a priority in these communities as well.

Table 3.2 summarizes the characteristics of these distressed older suburbs in 1990. In both urban areas, older suburbs have an aggregate population roughly equal to that of their respective central city. Detroit's older suburbs fare much better than the city itself on most indicators. Per capita income was more than 40 percent higher in the suburbs, and suburban unemployment and poverty rates were less than half of Detroit's. The per capita tax base in the older suburbs is close to three times higher.

Even if the more prosperous (and dubiously distressed) municipalities are excluded, Detroit remains substantially worse off than its older suburbs. For example, if the per capita income of the six wealthiest distressed suburbs is excluded, the remaining municipalities

Table 3.4. Older Suburban Abatement Activity, 1991–2001

| | Detroit | | Grand Rapids |
	Active	Not Active	
Municipalities	20	6	10
Abatements	323	2	575
Number per 1,000	0.34	0.01	2.90
Total investment	$6.36 billion	$12.3 million	$1.66 billion
% real property	22.1	0.0	24.5
Investment per 1,000	$7,780	$86	$8,396
Total jobs	46,558	55	51,625
% new jobs	31.7	9.1	22.4
Jobs per 1,000	56.8	0.35	260.7

have a per capita income of $12,188, still 29 percent higher than the city's. Similarly, by excluding the richest older suburbs in terms of property tax base per capita, the average declines to $12,126, more than double the Detroit figure.

The older suburbs of Grand Rapids exhibit a similar pattern, although the differences are generally not as stark. There is only a 10 percent difference in per capita income and poverty rates. The unemployment rates are about equal, and the tax base per capita in the suburbs is about 23 percent higher.

Older suburbs in both metro areas were quite active in granting PA 198 abatements during the 1990s (table 3.4). On a per capita basis, the numbers of abatements in the older suburbs were more than two and a half times higher than in the respective central cities. Total investment in abatement projects was over $6.3 billion in the Detroit area and $1.66 billion in the Grand Rapids older suburbs. The average investment in real property was less than a quarter of the total investment in both the Detroit and Grand Rapids areas. On a per capita basis, tax-abated investment in the older suburbs was more than four times higher in the Grand Rapids area ($1.96 per capita in Detroit, $8.40 in Grand Rapids).

The older Detroit suburbs used abatements to retain almost 32,000 jobs and to attract a putative 15,000 new jobs; the comparable figures for the Grand Rapids older suburbs are 40,000 and 11,500. On a per capita basis, each abatement in the Grand Rapids area involved four times as many employment opportunities as in the Detroit area.

Not all of Detroit's distressed suburbs actually granted tax abatements during the 1990s. Five of the twenty-six municipalities granted no abatements during the decade, while another granted only a single abatement. The communities eschewing abatement activity generally are in the midrange of population and wealth among the older Detroit suburbs.

Newer Suburbs

Newer suburbs in both urban areas were defined to include those that experienced the most rapid population growth during the 1990s. With only limited exceptions, the municipalities falling into this rapid growth category are townships. Both their low initial populations and the generally large amount of vacant land in these communities are factors that contribute to their rapid growth.

Table 3.5. New Suburbs Abatement Activity, 1991–2001

| | Detroit | | Grand Rapids | |
	Active	Not Active	Active	Not Active
Municipalities	13	13	5	7
Abatements	252	6	506	0
Number per 1,000	1.05	0.03	13.68	0
Total investment	$1.47 billion	$185 million	$1.23 billion	0
% real property	35.0	27.6	22.8	0
Investment per 1,000	$6,282	$31	$3,324	0
Total jobs	1465	416	50974	0
% new jobs	35.1	32.2	14.4	0
Jobs per 1,000	61	3	101	0

In both urban areas, only about half of these new suburbs were active in granting abatements during the 1990s (see appendix 3.1). Among these communities, the ones that were active in granting abatements had, on average, lower incomes and tax base per capita than those that offered one or fewer abatements. In Grand Rapids, the differences were substantial; per capita income was 32 percent higher in the suburbs not granting abatements and the per capital tax base 39 percent higher.

Thirteen Detroit-area new suburbs granted a total of 252 abatements (table 3.5). Each of these abatements attracted an average total investment of almost $6 million. Thirty-five percent of the total investment was in real property, a much higher proportion than in either Detroit or its older suburbs. Total investment amounted to about $0.63 per capita. Each abatement involved an average of sixty jobs; 35 percent promised new jobs.

Among the newer Grand Rapids suburbs, only five were active in granting abatements during the 1990s. These municipalities granted an average of more than 100 abatements each. This represents an average of 13.7 abatements per thousand population, by far the highest rate for any group of municipalities. The average investment was about $2.4 million, less than one-quarter of which represented real property. These abatements were extremely productive in terms of employment opportunities, involving just over 100 jobs on average. The number of new jobs promised was less than 15 percent of total jobs.

Outcomes

The objective of granting property tax abatements is presumably to attract private investment and jobs in order to improve the economic well-being of the community granting the abatements. The indicators of improving economic health include higher incomes, lower poverty and unemployment rates, and higher housing values and property tax base. While property tax abatement activity is clearly not the only factor influencing these measures, it nevertheless is one that is within the control of the local government.

Among the Detroit-area municipalities, there was a general trend toward economic improvement between 1990 and 2000 (table 3.6). Per capita incomes increased by about half

Table 3.6. Detroit Area Outcome Measures, 1990–2000

Change in:	City of Detroit	Older Suburbs		Newer Suburbs	
		Active	Not Active	Active	Not Active
Population	−7.5%	−3.1%	−7.1%	46.3%	41.6%
Income	57.4%	48.1%	53.8%	61.7%	62.8%
Unemployment rate	−5.9%	−2.9%	−3.4%	−2.1%	−2.4%
Poverty rate	−6.0%	−1.2%	−0.8%	−0.3%	0.3%
Housing values	148.4%	109.8%	87.0%	101.2%	101.3%
SEV	94.0%	67.7%	71.5%	198.5%	178.0%

or better for each group of municipalities. Unemployment declined across the board, as did the poverty rate. The largest proportional increase in housing values occurred in Detroit, although from the lowest base. For suburban municipalities, median home values often doubled during the 1990s. Aggregate property values (SEV) almost doubled in the city of Detroit, again from a relatively low starting point. In the new suburbs, home values almost tripled in some instances.

Comparisons between groups of suburban municipalities that did and did not grant abatements during this period show generally mixed results. Even though there was considerable similarity in the initial values of the indicators for the older suburbs, it does not seem that granting property tax abatements led inevitably to greater economic improvement during the period. The older suburbs that were not active in granting abatements achieved greater increases in income and tax base and a larger reduction in unemployment rate. The older suburbs active in granting abatements enjoyed more favorable results in terms of population loss, reduction of poverty, and increased home values.

Among the new suburb communities, there were only minor differences between those municipalities granting abatements and those that did not. Income, unemployment, and housing values all changed at about the same rate over the decade for the two groups. The communities granting abatements saw their average poverty rate decline slightly, while the others saw a slight increase in the poverty rate; the result was a widening of the gap between the two categories. The trends in tax base per capita produced the opposite result—the higher growth rate in the suburbs that granted abatements narrowed the gap that existed in 1990.

In the Grand Rapids area, the changes in economic indicators are relatively more modest, especially considering that the initial values were, in most cases, lower (table 3.7). The city of Grand Rapids showed improvement in all of the indicators (except poverty rate, which did not change). But despite being much more active in granting abatements than Detroit, Grand Rapids residents experienced smaller relative improvement in most indicators.

The older Grand Rapids suburbs, all of which granted at least one tax abatement, generally experienced much more positive results than did the city of Grand Rapids. The rate of change in population, unemployment, poverty, median housing value, and tax base was much more favorable in the older suburbs than in the central city. Only in terms of income growth are Grand Rapids and its older suburbs comparable.

Table 3.7. Grand Rapids Area Outcome Measures, 1990–2000

Change in:	Grand Rapids	Older Suburbs	Newer Suburbs Active	Not Active
Population	4.6%	38.2%	58.0%	51.0%
Income	38.9%	38.2%	39.7%	50.7%
Unemployment rate	−1.0%	−1.5%	1.1%	0.7%
Poverty rate	0.0%	−3.7%	2.3%	−0.8%
Housing values	56.8%	71.9%	101.2%	101.3%
SEV	69.3%	108.1%	177.7%	146.2%

The results for the two categories of new suburbs were mixed, but generally favored those that did not grant abatements. Income and housing values rose at faster rates in municipalities that did not grant abatements. The gap in per capita income widened, while the difference in unemployment rates narrowed. There was also a narrowing of the gap in the tax base. The new suburbs that granted abatements experienced a substantial increase in poverty rate, with the result that the poverty rate in these communities came to surpass that of the communities that did not grant abatements.

Implications for Future Policy in Michigan

From a policy perspective, what should local governments consider before they decide to use tax abatements? The earlier review of the literature points to several issues. Abatements appear to be successful in certain circumstances—in cities with high fiscal stress or where the marginal costs of doing business are critically high, in limited or focused geographic areas, for firms that would not have located in a stressed city under normal market conditions, or for firms that serve an employment or skill niche compatible with the local population. This suggests, then, that processes need to be in place to assess whether those conditions are met. At a very minimum, a best practice would entail a policy spelling out guidelines or requirements to determine whether an individual firm should receive abated taxes. In other words, it is assumed that under best practice conditions, some firms would not be granted tax abatement.

Another integral part of a codified system for granting abatements might include "strings" or "claw backs" (Ledebur and Woodward 1990), which would impose sanctions if the conditions of the abatement—whether it be jobs, number of local hires, or length of operation in the community—are not met. Such claw backs might include returning some or all of the value of the abatement to the community or paying some other kind of "reparation." This implies that communities must actually evaluate the outcomes of the abatement. Did the firm hire the requisite number of local workers? Did it create the promised number of jobs? Were the jobs of the quality or nature anticipated? The answers to some of these questions should be quite obvious; that is, did the firm stay in town for the time agreed to? But other indicators, such as job creation or local population composition in hiring or contracting, would be more opaque and would require systematic evaluation on the part of the locality. Furthermore, changes in state enabling legislation targeting abatements to distressed areas and adding requirements for evaluation may produce more effective use of abatements at the local level.

The use of property tax abatements to attract and retain jobs and investments is likely to remain a staple of local government economic development policy in Michigan and other states for years to come. In many communities, abatements will continue to be offered with little regard for their effectiveness or efficiency in the use of public resources. But selectively reducing the burden of local property taxes seems to provide the greatest benefits to prosperous firms and prosperous communities, raising serious questions of equity. Requiring that local communities grant abatements only on demonstration of necessity (so-called but for requirements) or that abatements be tied to minimum levels of investment or employment could encourage communities to be more selective in their abatement activity and thus alleviate some equity concerns.

Whether industrial tax abatements are good public policy seems to depend a good deal on the perspective from which they are viewed. From the perspective of the state government, Michigan's PA 198 has been extremely successful in attracting new investments (especially for new machinery and equipment) and securing promises to keep jobs in the state. A disproportionate number of those jobs, however, are in traditional manufacturing and auto-related industries as opposed to "new economy" high-tech jobs (Reese 2006). From the point of view of local governments, investments resulting from tax abatements have generally been associated with positive economic indicators, although not necessarily more positive than if no abatements had been granted.

In cases of distressed cities like Detroit, the granting of abatements has not directly yielded positive economic outcomes; in fact, abatement use has coincided with the continued dispersal of employment and economic activity farther from the city center. While the revitalization of the state's older cities is not explicitly one of the objectives of PA 198, it is one of the overarching concerns of state policy, which appears not to be well served by PA 198.

APPENDIX 3.1
Abatement Activity in Detroit and Grand Rapids Suburbs, 1991–2001

Municipality	Certificates	Investment	Jobs	New	Retained	Population 2000
Detroit city*	107	$4,536,499,463	27,252	2,510	24,742	951,270
New Suburbs						
Addison township	0	$0	0	0	0	6,439
Bruce township	0	$0	0	0	0	8,158
Canton township	42	$323,394,632	3,358	1,517	1,841	76,366
Chesterfield township	87	$201,110,687	3,202	1,707	1,495	37,405
Commerce township	0	$0	0	0	0	34,764
Groveland township	0	$0	0	0	0	6,150
Huron charter township	1	$27,107,053	135	135	0	13,737
Independence township	0	$0	0	0	0	32,581
Lenox township	0	$0	0	0	0	8,433
Macomb township	28	$90,539,219	1,714	614	1,100	50,478

Abatement Activity in Detroit and Grand Rapids Suburbs, 1991–2001 (*continued*)

Municipality	Certificates	Investment	Jobs	New	Retained	Population 2000
Milford township	8	$306,239,533	1,109	290	819	15,271
New Baltimore city	8	$13,882,706	204	143	61	7,405
New Haven village	1	$0	0	0	0	3,071
Northville city	1	$1,832,000	26	26	0	6,459
Novi city	1	$12,000,000	230	120	110	47,386
Oakland charter township	0	$0	0	0	0	13,071
Orion township	1	$145,000,000	100	0	100	33,463
Oxford charter township	2	$2,195,000	85	30	55	16,025
Richmond township	1	$56,881	1	1	0	3,416
Rochester city	4	$18,942,128	185	75	110	10,467
Rose township	5	$6,639,330	530	18	512	6,210
Shelby charter township	10	$112,139,650	715	334	381	65,159
South Lyon city	34	$69,107,214	2,578	937	1,641	10,036
Springfield township	7	$5,135,330	105	68	37	13,338
Washington township	3	$2,017,623	105	65	40	19,080
Wixom city	8	$312,849,430	653	355	298	13,263
Older Suburbs						
Center Line city	5	$21,770,411	568	253	315	8,531
Dearborn city	33	$2,102,310,524	6,772	1,716	5,056	97,775
Eastpointe city	0	$0	0	0	0	34,077
Ecorse city	3	$242,266,275	87	75	12	11,229
Ferndale city	4	$3,708,704	40	30	10	22,105
Gibraltar city	1	$12,295,000	55	50	5	4,264
Hamtramck city	4	$124,044,152	514	70	444	22,976
Harper Woods city	0	$0	0	0	0	14,254
Hazel Park city	0	$0	0	0	0	18,963
Highland Park city	4	$21,001,684	360	290	70	16,746
Inkster city	0	$0	0	0	0	30,115
Lincoln Park city	1	$0	0	0	0	40,008
Livonia city	55	$333,157,867	5,069	1,789	3,280	100,545
Melvindale city	3	$2,774,678	80	40	40	10,735
Mount Clemens city	10	$49,235,031	709	659	50	17,312
Oak Park city	19	$46,093,013	863	193	670	29,793
Pontiac city	17	$860,548,233	14,525	4,205	10,320	66,337
Redford township	7	$29,873,852	583	329	254	51,622
River Rouge city	4	$168,920,275	96	14	82	9,917
Royal Oak charter township	11	$30,520,392	789	328	461	5,446
Southfield city	11	$58,036,555	1,405	521	884	78,296
Taylor city	18	$72,495,687	1,323	252	1,071	65,868
Trenton city	50	$125,027,257	1,669	1,039	630	19,584
Warren city	48	$1,542,245,125	9,440	2,232	7,208	138,247
Wayne city	10	$534,062,467	1,464	656	808	19,051
Wyandotte city	7	$11,216,271	267	124	143	28,006
Grand Rapids city	221	$312,765,953	15,470	3,286	12,184	197,800
New Suburbs						
Allendale township	0	$0	0	0	0	13,042
Alpine township	29	$50,214,282	2,593	843	1,750	13,976

(*continued*)

APPENDIX 3.1
Abatement Activity in Detroit and Grand Rapids Suburbs, 1991–2001 (*continued*)

Municipality	Certificates	Investment	Jobs	New	Retained	Population 2000
Bowne township	0	$0	0	0	0	2,743
Caledonia township	0	$0	0	0	0	8,964
Cannon township	0	$0	0	0	0	12,075
Courtland township	0	$0	0	0	0	5,817
East Grand Rapids city	0	$0	0	0	0	10,764
Holland township	289	$275,064,316	17,972	1,751	16,221	28,911
Olive township	22	$137,324,257	11,584	1,467	10,117	4,691
Port Sheldon township	0	$0	0	0	0	4,503
Robinson township	0	$0	0	0	0	5,588
Vergennes township	9	$80,702,475	651	209	442	3,611
Zeeland charter township	157	$686,617,624	18,174	3,050	15,124	7,613
Older Suburbs						
Grand Haven city	90	$122,181,073	8,230	1,424	6,806	11,168
Grand Rapids charter township	1	$461,041	6	6	0	14,056
Holland city	197	$656,577,706	19,982	3,669	16,313	35,048
Muskegon city	64	$233,240,659	7,475	1,081	6,394	40,105
Muskegon Heights city	11	$8,807,787	2,000	96	1,904	12,049
Norton Shores city	85	$152,340,278	2,816	1,451	1,365	22,527
South Haven city	34	$69,107,214	2,578	937	1,641	5,021
Spring Lake village	70	$216,195,219	7,327	2,034	5,293	2,514
Whitehall city	8	$77,571,009	802	651	151	2,884
Wyoming city	15	$126,637,234	409	233	176	69,368

*distressed communities in bold type

SOURCES: MEDC; U.S. Census of Population.

REFERENCES

Adelaja, S., et al. 2007. *State of Michigan Cities: An Index of Urban Prosperity.* Lansing: Michigan Higher Education Land Policy Consortium.

Ballard, C. L., P. N. Courant, D. C. Drake, R. C. Fisher, and E. R. Gerber, eds. 2003. *Michigan at the Millennium.* East Lansing: Michigan State University Press.

Bartik, T. J. 1991. *Who Benefits from State and Local Economic Development Policies?* Kalamazoo, Mich.: W. E. Upjohn Institute.

Calzonetti, F. J., and R. T. Walker. 1991. Factors Affecting Industrial Location. Decisions: A Survey Approach." In *Industry Location and Public Policy,* edited by H. W. Herzog Jr. and A. M. Schlottman. Knoxville: University of Tennessee Press.

Dalehite, E. G., J. L. Mikesell, and C. K. Zorn. 2005. Variation in Property Tax Abatement Programs among States. *Economic Development Quarterly* 19:157–173.

Eisinger, P. K. 1988. *The Rise of the Entrepreneurial State.* Madison: University of Wisconsin Press.

Fisher, P. S., and A. H. Peters. 1998. *Industrial Incentives: Competition among American States and Cities.* Kalamazoo, Mich.: W. E. Upjohn Institute for Employment Research.

Fulton, W. 1997. *The Reluctant Metropolis: The Politics of Urban Growth in Los Angeles.* Point Arena, Calif.: Solano.

Gordon, P., and H. Richardson. 1997. Are Compact Cities a Desirable Planning Goal? *Journal of the American Planning Association* 63:95–126.

Goss, E. P., and J. M. Phillips. 2001. Do Business Tax Incentives Contribute to a Divergence in Economic Growth? *Economic Development Quarterly* 13:217–228.

Gottdeiner, M. 1977. *Planned Sprawl.* Beverly Hills, Calif.: Sage.

Gramlich, E. M. 1997. Subnational Fiscal Policy. In *Perspectives on Local Public Finance and Fiscal Policy,* edited by J. M. Quigley, 3–27. Greenwich, Conn.: JAI Press.

Hood, J. 1994. Ante-Freeze: Stop the State Bidding Wars for Big Business. *Policy Review* 68:62–67.

Hovey, H. 1986. Interstate Tax Competition and Economic Development. In *Reforming State Tax Systems,* edited by S. Gold, 89–100. Washington, D.C.: National Conference of State Legislatures.

Innes, J. E., and D. E. Booher. 1999. Metropolitan Development as a Complex System: A New Approach to Sustainability. *Economic Development Quarterly* 13:141–156.

Jackson, K. T. 1985. *Crabgrass Frontier.* New York: Oxford University Press.

Kunstler, J. H. 1993. *The Geography of Nowhere.* New York: Simon and Schuster.

Ladd, H. 1998. *Local Government Tax and Land Use Policies.* Northampton, Mass.: Edward Elgar.

Ledebur, L. C., and D. P. Woodward. 1990. Adding a Stick to the Carrot: Location Incentives with Claw Backs, Recisions, and Recalibrations. *Economic Development Quarterly* 4:221–237.

Lynch, R. G., G. Fishgold, and D. L. Blackwood. 1996. The Effectiveness of Firm-Specific State Tax Incentives in New York. *Economic Development Quarterly* 10:57–68.

MSHDA (Michigan State Housing Development Authority). 2008. Eligible Distressed Communities. www.Michigan.gov/MSHDA/0,1607,7-141—181277—,00.html.

Michigan Department of Labor and Economic Growth. 2008. *Labor Market Information System.* Lansing: Michigan Department of Labor and Economic Growth.

Michigan Department of Treasury. 2000. *State Equalized Values.* Lansing: Michigan Department of Treasury.

Michigan Economic Development Corporation. 2006. *Industrial Facilities Tax Abatements Granted.* MichiganAdvantage.org/PA198.Michigan Land Use Leadership Council. 2003. Final Report. Lansing, Michigan: Michigan Land Use Leadership Council.

Miloslavsky, E., and H. J. Shatz. 2006. Service Exports and the States: Measuring the Potential. *Economic Development Quarterly* 20:3–21.

Orfield, M. 2002. *American Metropolitics.* Washington, D.C.: Brookings Institution Press.

Peters, A., and P. Fisher. 2004. The Failures of Economic Development Incentives. *Journal of the American Planning Association* 70 (Winter):27–37.

Premus, E. 1982. The Location of High Technology Firms and Regional Economic Development. Subcommittee on Monetary and Fiscal Policy of the Joint Economic Committee, Congress of the United States, Washington, D.C.

Reese, L. A. 2006. Not Just Another Determinants Piece: Alternative Hypotheses to Explain Local Tax Abatement Policy. *Review of Policy Research* (March 23):491–504.

Reese, L. A., and R. A. Rosenfeld. 2004. Local Economic Development in the U.S. and Canada: Institutionalizing Policy Approaches. *American Review of Public Administration* 34:277–292.·

Reese, L. A., R. A. Rosenfeld, and D. Fasenfest. 2002. The State of Local Economic Development Policy. In *The 2002 Municipal Yearbook,* 10–17. Washington, D.C.: ICMA.

Reese, L. A., and G. Sands. 2006. The Equity Impacts of Municipal Tax Incentives: Leveling or Tilting the Playing Field? *Review of Policy Research* (January 23):71–94.

Reese, L. A., G. Sands, and H. L. Khan. 2005. Implementing Tax Abatements in Michigan: A Study of Best Practices. *Economic Development Quarterly* 20:44–58.

Rubin, M. 1991. Urban Enterprise Zones in New Jersey: Have They Made a Difference? In *Enterprise Zones: New Directions in Economic Development,* edited by R. Green, 105–121. Newbury Park, Calif.: Sage.

Rusk, D. 1993. *Cities without Suburbs.* Washington, D.C.: Woodrow Wilson Center Press.

Sands, G., and L. A. Reese. 2006. Sustainability Strategies in North American Cities. In *Sustainable Development and Planning II,* Vol. 1, edited by A. G. Kungolos, C. A. Brebbia, and E. Beriatos, 133–142. Boston: WIT Press.

Sands, G., and P. Zalmezak. 2001. Michigan Industrial Property Tax Abatements: A Summary of Activity under Public Act 198 of 1974, 1985–98. Paper presented at the Urban Research Seminar, Detroit.

Schmenner, R. W. 1982. *Making Business Location Decisions.* Englewood Cliffs, N.J.: Prentice Hall.

Schwarz, J. E., and T. J. Volgy. 1992. The Impacts of Economic Development Strategies on Wages: Exploring the Effect on Public Policy at the Local Level. Paper presented at the annual meeting of the American Political Science Association, Chicago.

United States Bureau of the Census. 2008. Decennila Census of Population and Housing, Detailed Tables. www.Census.gov.

Wassmer, R. W. 1994. Can Local Incentives Alter a Metropolitan City's Economic Development? *Urban Studies* 31:1251–1278.

Wassmer, R. W., and J. E. Anderson. 2001. Bidding for Business: New Evidence on the Effect of Locally Offered Economic Development Incentives in a Metropolitan Area. *Economic Development Quarterly* 15:132–151.

CHAPTER 4

Equity and Politics in Road-Spending Allocation in Michigan: Implications for Metropolitan Affairs

Soji Adelaja, Annalie Campos, and Yohannes G. Hailu

The allocation of state funds to local communities is a contentious issue in most U.S. states, as is the case in many parts of the world (Cadot et al. 2006; GAO 2004; Kemmerling and Stephan 2002; Schneider, McClelland, and Guy 2005). Due to the limited availability of discretionary funds in state budgets, and the growing inability of communities to raise sufficient local revenues for needed programs (including services and infrastructure), local officials have vested interests in attracting and leveraging state funds. Communities therefore invest their political resources to attract state resources. Local communities are aware that, unlike expenditures on private goods, which are determined largely by market forces, the resources needed to provide public roads are significantly determined by a political process (Stiglitz 2000). The allocation of state funds for road maintenance and development is particularly contentious because roads represent a catalytic investment that can define future community growth and prosperity (Dilworth 2003).

A community's perspective about growth is likely to affect its stance about lobbying for state road allocations and how it would invest state funds coming in. On one hand, progrowth communities, which are dominated by advocates of growth and development (for example, land-based elites, housing developers, bankers, and mortgage lenders), believe that development is a universal good (Molotch 1976). To them, growth would create opportunities for jobs, improve the tax base, and consequently benefit society. On the other hand, antigrowth communities dominated by antigrowth advocates (for example, some homeowners, environmentalists, conservation enthusiasts) see the so-called job opportunities and benefits of development as accruing only to a select few, and believe that both quality of life and the environment are likely to be compromised by unfettered growth (Molotch and Logan 1984). Progrowth advocates should prefer road investments that would entice individuals and households to relocate to the community. Therefore, progrowth-dominated communities will spend state-allocated funds on road infrastructure that attracts growth. Antigrowth advocates, however, would prefer road investments that would deter relocation to the community. Antigrowth-dominated communities will, therefore, utilize allocated state funds to support antigrowth actions and similar objectives (Baldassare and Protash 1982; Molotch 1976; Schneider and Teske 1993).[1]

The linkage between community perspective and the deployment of received funds suggests that state- and local-level decision makers may not view road-spending allocations to local communities in the same vein as direct or indirect federal or state highway spending, both of which have been consistently shown to fuel sprawl (Carlino and Mills 1987). In other words, whether state-allocated funds fuel sprawl depends on the nature of the community involved and how it spends such funds. Similarly, lobbying efforts should also be endogenous to community perspective.

In cases where state allocation to communities is hotly debated, ranking systems, allocation formulas, or other formal mechanisms are often enacted. Presumably, this is to help balance competing interests, shield decision makers from constant pressure, and create the semblance of transparency. Such formulas are often based on simple parameters that appear on the surface not to be sensitive to factors such as race, class, and other socioeconomic and demographic factors. For example, in Michigan, Public Act 51 of 1951, popularly known as the Michigan Transportation Fund Act (MTFA), provides a formula for distributing road development, maintenance, and improvement funds based solely on population and existing road stock. While this simple formula established the "rules of the game," its initial setup and subsequent revisions often involved the types of political processes and posturing that characterized decisions about funds allocated without a formula (for example, earmarked funds). This raises questions about the distributional difference between formula- and nonformula-based allocations.

Is it possible that, in reality, seemingly simple formula-based allocations also incorporate socioeconomic and demographic, race, income, and locational considerations? If so, they represent masked political responses to socioeconomic and political pressures brought to bear by actors involved in the decision-making process. State decision makers (governor, senators, district representatives, lobbyists, and so forth) obviously have some interest in allocating state road funds in ways that maximize the returns to their constituents, whose interests may vary by community. To the extent to which a given formula is not sensitive to the changing needs of constituents, such formulas may not maximize the interests of state officials.

Michigan is an excellent case study of state-allocated funds to communities for the purpose of road development, improvement, and maintenance. The simple formula in Michigan distributes funds based on population and existing road stock. Despite the apparent fixity of the formula, one can envision built-in distributional impacts with respect to race, class, politics, and location. On one hand, a fixed formula rewards growing communities, which tend to be nonurban and have low population density. On the other hand, it rewards communities with existing road infrastructure, which are often urban communities with high population density. Therefore, over time, the net effect of a given formula has the tendency to gradually increase the proportion of the total allocated funds toward some nonurban areas that are growing and economically competitive or "destination areas," and away from central cities or urban areas and some nonurban areas that are not as economically competitive and attractive for the relocation of businesses and people as other areas. It is also possible that the allocation formula provides leverage and protection for central cities or more urbanized areas with established road infrastructure without totally ignoring the growth in other areas. Hence, by design, the formula is not likely to favor some communities, specifically central cities that tend to experience population loss over time and suburban areas that are affected by spillover effects whereby the growth of adjacent or neighboring areas affects their neighboring areas in a positive or negative way. The fact that urban communities generally tend to have more liberal, and perhaps less wealthy, constituents (Timpone 1988) clearly raises questions about the distributional equity and political implications of a given formula.

It is not surprising that since the adoption of MTFA, the underlying formula has changed a few times, in each case with minor modifications. The demand for revision suggests that despite its simplicity, the formula is not free from social, economic, demographic, and political pressures beyond what it currently captures (population and existing roads). An existing formula may therefore reflect a temporary agreement on allocation, subject to future changes as the balance of political power shifts.

Community criticisms that trigger formula change dynamics have tended to focus on the argument that the formula is not doing what it is mandated to do, which is to respond effectively to the fast-changing needs of the transportation consumers in today's society (Welke et al. 2000; LeRoy et al. 2006). Urban residents in particular invoke urban, suburban, and rural, as well as racial and economic distributional equity. Community location is likely correlated with race, income, class, and other socioeconomic and demographic factors (Schneider, McClelland, and Guy 2005). Therefore, despite the apparent fixity of a given formula, it appears to be endogenous and subject to changes in the goals and interests of competing interests groups.

In examining the distributional implications of formula-based schemes, it is important to recognize two effects. The first relates to the endogeneity of a given existing formula and the impacts on allocation through pressures to change the existing formula itself. The second relates to the pure distributional effects of a given formula during the time that it stays in place. The latter is particularly important because it can shed some light on whether a given fixed formula strictly distributes funds based on the variables explicitly incorporated into it, or if it implicitly incorporates other nonstated factors, particularly the socioeconomic, political, class, and location considerations. The focus of this essay is on the second effect. It evaluates the distributional impacts of a given formula, holding constant revisions to the formula.

An examination of the distributional outcomes of the existing formula for sensitivity to factors other than population count and road stock would reveal the equity implications of the formula. Such understanding is useful in predicting future political posturing and criticisms. Finally, given the current debate about the role of public spending in facilitating sprawl, such understanding could be useful in informing future debates on the role of distributional schemes on sprawl (Diamond and Noonan 1996; Jaret, Reid, and Adelman 2003; Katz et al. 2003; Lobao and Saenz 2002; MLULC 2003; Sauerzopf 1999a; Squires 2002).

To explain the allocation of state road funds to local communities, this essay investigates the possible relationship of road funds allocation, not only as it relates to population and existing road stock factors but also other equity-related factors (class, race, political, rural/urban, or locational variables). Recognizing the complexity of the underlying political process, a theoretical model is developed to help identify the factors that would normally affect funding allocation so that an empirical model can be constructed that would allow testing for the equity implications of the formula-based allocation. Such analyses have potential policy implications as well. Road-spending allocation could be tied to sprawl in communities, and hence the current fund allocation and its implication to sprawl could be one area of policy interest. Road-spending allocation is also tied to metropolitan and rural community growth. Accessible locations could have potential comparative advantages in attracting growth, and hence the nature of road-spending allocation could influence where growth happens and how growth affects poverty across locations and communities. Road-spending allocation could also have implications to urban revitalization, as one component of such revitalization is infrastructure investment and improvement. Road-spending allocation, as stated earlier, could also have potential fund allocation equity implications. These policy issues can be directly or indirectly discussed on the bases of analysis developed in this essay.

Literature Review

To develop a conceptual framework for analyzing the allocation of state funds to local communities for road development, improvement, and maintenance, it is important to review the general literature on such related issues as the motivation for state investment in infrastructure, the motivation of communities interested in seeking state investments, the interactions between state and local politics, and the distributional framework. The existing literature generally suggests that the underlying pattern of distribution of public spending is complex and necessitates an understanding of the competing goals and dynamic interactions between various actors at different levels. According to the General Accounting Office (GAO 2004), public spending on infrastructure such as roads is tied to growth, economic development, and equity goals.

The essay first examines the state rationales and motivations for state investments in infrastructure. The literature confirms that stakeholders have varied values, tastes, and preferences, and that the allocation process is laden with politics and political posturing (OTA 1995). From the state's perspective, the determinants of the magnitude of state funds to be distributed and the pattern of distribution should therefore include social, economic, and political factors at the state levels. The literature also identified debt limits, tax rate ceilings, spending caps, and the ability to levy increased sales and/or an income tax as determinants of state spending allocation (GAO 2004: 33–35).

State funding capacity and fiscal effort, which are influenced by the state's economic base and ability to raise revenues, should also determine the level of allocated funds to a community (GAO 2004: 33–35). State reaction to local goals and politics may determine not only the size of the pool of funds to be distributed but also the allocation of such funds to local communities. Fiscal effort is largely dependent on how much the local constituents support the state politicians' proposed tax impositions and initiatives. The balance between fiscal effort and capacity is a useful framework for evaluating the role and choices of the state decision makers.

Next, consider the local community context. As major stakeholders in the development and implementation of investment decisions, local constituents (community residents, businesses, and other institutions) are key actors in influencing investment decisions (GAO 2004). Demographic and other characteristics of a community should affect state-level allocation to a community.

Community size, which reflects voting potential, is a relevant factor in investment decision making. While Adelaja and Friedman's study (1999) is not related to spending on roads, the authors' finding on the significance of political clout provides a relevant insight into our understanding of the local policy decision-making process. According to Adelaja and Friedman (1999), who examined the motivations for adopting local right-to-farm (RTF) ordinances at the municipal level, the probability of adopting RTF policies increases with the size and political clout of the farm public and with incentives to promote RTF. The equivalent in road spending is that the larger community would receive more dollars.

Another local political clout–related factor is propensity to vote. City residents have been shown to have a lower propensity to vote (Hart and Atkins 2002). Also, geographic/locational attributes or contexts (that is, city versus suburban voters) should influence the probability that residents would support a proposed investment policy (Brueckner and Joo 1991). Therefore, some bond or tax levy proposals may fail or succeed at the polls depending on the relevance of the proposed outcomes to the values, tastes, and preferences of the potential voters (Brueckner and Joo 1991).

Partisanship is another factor that can affect the distribution of transportation investment. Kemmerling and Stephan (2002) show that political affiliation is a decisive factor in explaining the distribution of transportation investment grants across large cities in Germany. The likelihood of obtaining a transportation investment grant from a higher tier government unit is greater when the party affiliation of the grant receivers and grant giver is the same. The lobbying capacity of residents also provides a sound explanation for why some communities might become more successful in generating grants for infrastructure development than others (Kemmerling and Stephan 2002).

Resource allocation decisions at the state, county, or local level therefore have an inherent political component that can determine the nature and level of distribution. Road-spending allocation is particularly expected to have a political component in the way it is designed and in the way it allocates resources over time. The relationship between party affiliation and spending is well documented in the literature, and it suggests two conclusions: one party, more than the other, is likely to favor equitable distribution by race and class; and the two parties prefer to distribute resources to constituents who favor them.

The characteristics of local voters should drive political behavior at the local level. Local preferences and tastes, which are reflected by education, household size and composition,

89

and other demographic characteristics that affect population mobility, can influence voting behavior (Timpone 1988).

Drawing from the idea about the state's role in shaping investment decisions, a key a priori expectation is that communities or groups that exert more influence on the state's or a granting agency's decision would receive more grants or appropriations than communities with lesser influence. In other words, how well the competing communities or groups influence the granting agency would determine the probability that a community would receive larger grants relative to other communities in a region. The expectation is that competing groups or communities vie for the best allocation scheme that would maximize the benefits of residents in their community. These community benefits may include increasing property value through improved roads or transportation services in the community, and opportunities for attracting private investment and jobs.

The state, as the granting agency, is the ultimate decision maker. The state must then balance the interests of the competing communities in maximizing its own objectives, subject to the pressures from the electorate and from competing economic and political interest groups (Adelaja and Patel 2005). The expectation is that the granting agency is concerned about its political capital and would prefer to provide larger grants to communities that increase or maintain its stock of political capital in a particular region (Kemmerling and Stephan 2002).

From the above, it appears that local transportation infrastructure development is sensitive to complex interactions between grant giver (that is, state government) and recipients (local communities) and is subject to social, economic, political, and geographical contexts that play a role in how resources are allocated or distributed. Political affiliation and partisanship, community size and local political clout, and geographical and demographic characteristics of local communities emerge as factors that are linked to the investment decision-making process. They also are linked to the pattern of distribution of transportation grant allocation at the local community level. A conceptual framework for explaining financing and grant distribution for local road development is presented later based on a political economy framework.

The Michigan Context

It was mentioned above that Michigan is an excellent case study of road-spending allocation to local units of government. This is particularly so because the state is struggling to reposition itself, and virtually all state expenditure categories are being looked at in terms of their impacts on positive growth. Road-spending allocations to communities represent a huge expenditure category. Furthermore, the fact that over 75 percent of state residents reside in Metropolitan Statistical Areas (MSAs, or metros) that depend highly on the performance of core cities has made urban revitalization an important state policy priority, especially among urban political leaders.

Road-spending allocation in Michigan communities is such an important policy discussion simply because revenue for transportation development in the state is a limited resource. The state's transportation revenues can hardly cope with the demand for building and maintaining the existing road infrastructures at the local and regional levels. As shown

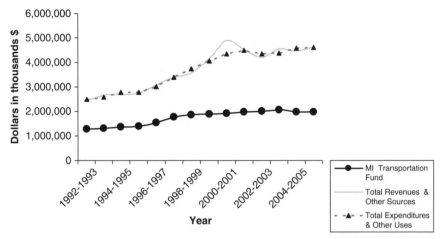

Source: SEMCOG Transportation Factbook for SE Michigan, 2000 Michigan Department of
Transportation, Finance and Administration.

FIGURE 4.1
Transportation Revenues and Expenditures, and Michigan Transportation Fund

in figure 4.1, yearly deficits were incurred as total expenditure or outflow exceeded revenue
inflow, with few exceptions (Michigan Department of Transportation Finance Division). The
Michigan Transportation Fund (MTF), which is the state's primary source of revenue for
roads, simply cannot meet budgetary needs, even with the fuel tax increase since 1997
(Welke et al. 2000). For example, between 1992 and 2006, the MTF accounted for an average
of less than half (47 percent) of the total transportation revenues in Michigan per year, which
is about $1.7 billion dollars (figure 4.1). Given the road-funding limitations in the state, cou-
pled with broader economic conditions triggering inflation and significant increases in the
cost of road-building materials, the road-funding allocation across local governments has
and will continue to impose a challenge to the state's policy makers. Furthermore, road-
funding limitations will reflect upon the economic performance in Michigan communities,
both at the local and regional levels.

The Milken Institute ranked 200 American metropolitan areas on the basis of their performance (DeVol, Wallace, and Bedroussian 2006). All Michigan metropolitan areas on the
list were in the bottom twenty, with the exception of Ann Arbor, which ranked 156th nationwide. The poor performance of the Michigan metropolitan areas has been blamed on the
continuous decline of the central cities (Vey 2007). With 75 percent of the state's population
living in or near cities, the success of Michigan is somewhat expected to be determined by
the success of the central cities. Strengthening the position of Michigan cities is an issue of
increasing policy importance because the metropolitan areas that surround them also rely
on these cities. The revitalization of Michigan cities is viewed in many circles as an important strategy for the economic reposition of a state that is having difficulty adjusting to the
"New Economy."

What is the link between road spending and state economic development? Sprawl is usually viewed as synonymous with urban decline. Therefore, policies to stem the incidence of
sprawl are increasingly attractive at the state and local levels as solutions to the problems

91

facing urban areas (Byun et al. 2005; Hughes 1975). The various causes of sprawl have been well documented in Michigan and other states (Bruegmann 2005; Squires 2002). In particular, some have argued that highway infrastructure investment causes sprawl, central-city decline, and growth in urban fringe areas (Baum-Snow 2007; Berechman et al. 2006; Voss and Chi 2006). The dramatic increase in highway spending between 1957 and 1972 is therefore viewed as a major cause of urban sprawl. The white flight and capital flight of the 1950s through the 1970s are seen as being partly connected to the rule change that allowed greater highway spending.

The Michigan Land Use Institute (MLUI) report "Follow the Money: Uncovering and Reforming Michigan's Sprawl Subsidies" argued that the state's spending patterns fueled sprawl because they tended to encourage infrastructure and other development in rural and suburban communities when such infrastructure already exists in cities and near urban areas (Schneider, McClelland, and Guy 2005). In response to some of these criticisms, in 2005 Governor Jennifer Granholm signed an executive order requiring new government facilities to be located in already built areas of the state.

A review of the origin of state allocation of funds to local units of government to support local spending on roads is appropriate at this point. Based on the user benefit principle of roads financing, the MTF was established through Public Act (PA) 51 of 1951. Since then, PA 51 has governed state appropriations for interstate and local highways and public transportation programs (Hamilton 2007).[2] Technically, the formula-based policy addressed the issues associated with the nonurban-biased scheme during the years prior to the enactment of PA 51. Prior to PA 51, the allocation scheme was a matter of political haggling (Warner 1962). Funds for road development went favorably to the rural interests as dictated by the Horton Act, which required that half of all state highway construction funds be devoted to trunk lines in the northern portions of the state (Welke et al. 2000). The inferior bargaining position of the urban interests was clearly shown, based on the fact that the only funds allocated to cities were those remaining after the counties and townships had met their debt obligations (Warner 1962). Those debt obligations were often very large, leaving no funds for allocation to cities and villages.

The enactment of PA 51 improved the road-financing strategy and created an objective-based formula, free from political factions. Road classification was introduced as a criterion for allocating revenues. The MTF is generated through the motor fuel taxation, vehicle registrations, and sales of motor vehicle parts. MTF revenues are distributed based on a two-stage approach. First, distribution is made to the Michigan Department of Transportation (MDOT), to counties, and to cities and villages. Second, the allotment to cities and villages is then distributed based on existing road stock and population as prescribed in PA 51 as amended under Michigan Compiled Laws (MCL 247.651 Section 10).

Table 4.1 shows the schedule of changes in the distribution of state funds between the MDOT, the counties, and the cities and villages of Michigan. The formula has been changed seven times since 1951, perhaps suggesting that the formula has frequently been out of sync with socioeconomic and political realities. No changes have been made since 1985, however (Welke et al. 2000). As shown in table 4.1, the percentage of funds allocated to the MDOT has declined from its high of 44 percent in 1951 to 39.1 percent today. On the other hand,

Table 4.1. Changes in the Michigan Transportation Fund Distribution Formula, 1951–1985

Year of Change	MDOT (%)	County (%)	Cities/villages (%)
1951	44.0	37.0	19.0
1957	47.0	35.0	18.0
1967	46.0	34.0	20.0
1972	44.5	35.7	19.8
1978	46.7	34.3	19.0
1982	41.9	37.4	20.7
1984	35.2	35.2	19.6
1985	39.1	39.1	21.8

SOURCE: Welke et al. 2000.

the percentage going to counties has increased from 37 percent in 1951 to 39.1 percent today. The percentage going to cities and villages has increased from 19 percent in 1951 to 21.8 percent today. The shift from the MDOT to local units of government is revealing. It might suggest a move toward decentralized spending and emphasis on local roads and away from centralized spending on trunk lines.

The distribution of the MTF to cities and villages in Michigan (see column 4 of table 4.1) is based on an "internal" formula that accounts for population and road mileage factors. In distributing the net amount available to cities and villages, PA 51 first divides the amount for major streets (75 percent) and for local streets (25 percent). Then the city and village "internal" formula apportions these two amounts to municipalities, 60 percent on the basis of population and 40 percent on the basis of major and local mileages (Welke et al. 2000). Hence, population and existing infrastructure are the two factors that presumably were chosen to drive the allocation of funds.

The literature has shown that in any public allocation process, race, class, and politics are important drivers of the ultimate decisions (Alesina, et al. 1999; Pampel 1994). Are distributions of the MTF based on the formula only driven by population and existing infrastructure, or are they sensitive to the more complex set of racial, class, and political objectives? Obviously, locational equity (urban versus rural) was a primary driver of the decision to enact PA 51 in the first place. Also, locational competition and disparity have class, race, and political implications. The fact that minorities may be less mobile is captured in the phrase "white flight." Similarly, population is not politics neutral. The literature has shown that cities tend to be more Democratic than suburban communities (Sauerzopf 1999b). Whether or not the formula is race, politics, and/or income neutral is a relevant issue for empirical analysis, as discussed above.

Given the above, the total funding allocated to the ith community (any one community from a range of communities) can be specified (assuming a linear allocation function) as indicated in equation 1 in appendix 4.1. Note that road-spending allocation to community i (RS_i) is determined by population (Pop_i), existing stock of roads ($Infra_i$), income or socioeconomic class ($Class_i$), party affiliation of community leaders ($Polit_i$), racial composition of the community ($Race_i$), and other factors ($Other_i$). Parameter estimates of equation 1 would explain the allocation process if a formula based strictly on population and existing infra-structure does not exist. The equation accounts for the first two variables, population and infrastructure, as well as others. However, if the formula is binding and the allocation is strictly a result of population and infrastructure, then parameters α_4, α_5, and α_6 from equation 1 should be statistically no different from zero. The essence of this study's analysis is to verify if α_4, α_5, and α_6 are equal to zero. By comparing the parameters of the specified function to the existing formula, the social, racial, and political equity issues related to road-spending allocation can be highlighted.

The Case Study Area

The Detroit Metropolitan Statistical Area (MSA), which includes Oakland, Macomb, and Wayne counties in Michigan, is the case study area for this research (see figure 4.2). The region comprises the most urbanized area in the state. About 40 percent of the state's total population, which is 9.94 million people, live in this region as of the year 2000. The U.S. Bureau of the Census (2000) reported that a total of 3.9 million and 4.04 million people lived in these three counties in 1990 and 2000, respectively. In terms of roadways, the Southeast

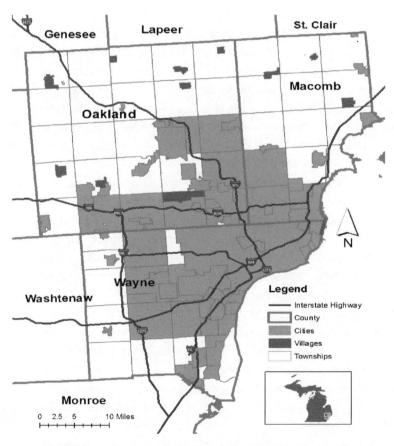

Source: Michigan Geographic Data Library, Center for Geographic Information.

FIGURE 4.2
The Study Area

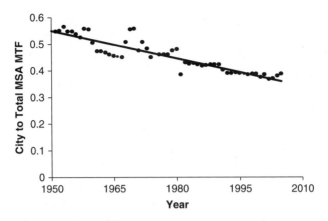

Source: Computed by the authors from MDOT Report #139.

FIGURE 4.3
MTF Allocation: Detroit City as a Share of the Metropolitan Region, 1952–2002

Michigan Council of Governments indicated that the Detroit MSA has a total of 15,416 roadway miles, 68 percent of the total roadways in the state of Michigan (SEMCOG 2000).

An examination of the pattern of distribution across the municipalities in the Detroit MSA yields interesting results. While allocation to the city of Detroit has continuously been the highest in the region, the proportion of the MTF allocation to the city of Detroit in relation to total allocation to the metropolitan region ranged from 56 percent in 1952 to 37 percent in 2002, indicating a decreasing trend of the city's share over time (see figure 4.3). As indicated above, this is expected given the nature of the formula.

Conceptual Framework

In this section, we build on previous literature in identifying the types of variables that should be included in an empirical model of state road-spending allocation. A political economy framework is used. The model theoretically characterizes the political behavior of decision makers, given local electoral preferences. Allocation of financial resources is inherently an economic decision, with underlying cross-community political competition as an interfering factor. Similar modeling framework is used in earlier works by Pelzman (1976), Hahn (1990), and Campos (1987), who explored the influence of different interest groups on political or regulatory outcomes.

To simplify the framework, consider two competing interest groups: residents in the central city of a metropolitan area, and residents of suburban or rural areas. Let α be a spending percentage parameter that is equal to zero when all spending is allocated to the central city or urban core but equal to 1 when all spending is allocated to suburban and rural communities. Central city residents desire a low level of α. On the other hand, suburban and rural residents desire a high level of α.

Under this framework, subject to a set of conditions and preference factors, suburban and rural residents will lobby the state for as high a road-spending allocation to their

95

communities as possible (that is, $\alpha = 1$). Central city residents, however, will lobby for α equal to 0 ($\alpha = 0$). The political decision makers (state government) must then endogenously consider the optimal level of α, the level that maximizes its own utility (interest). The objective of the state government is to maximize votes or accumulate political capital.[3]

We assume that those in state government behave rationally in the sense that they only decide on such measures as they believe would raise their electoral prospects (Hahn 1990). The utility function (or objective function) of the government may thus be regarded the same as the expected total vote function given by equation 2 (appendix 4.2). Equation 2 captures the objective function of the state government (u^G), which is determined in this case by the voting population of central-city residents (C), the voting population of suburban and rural residents (S), the probability that the average group (city or rural) household or individual will vote for the government (Π^i), and all other characteristics that affect the probability of voting by any group. A stakeholder's support for a winning candidate (represented by a political party) will depend on the candidate's support for policies favorable to the stakeholder's group.

The current framework is tied to the main goal of the essay, which is to test the class, location, and racial implications in existing road-spending allocation. Π^c, the probability of city residents being supportive of state politicians, is determined by α, as well as income, race, location, and other socioeconomic and demographic factors. For instance, while the preference for voting for a politician may be greater in a city, if the state enacts favorable road funding to the city, voter turnout may actually be lower in a city. Voter turnout has been shown to be determined by socioeconomic and demographic factors (Timpone 1988). Similarly, Π^s can also be argued to potentially exhibit racial, class, and location components.

The first- and second-order conditions for maximizing total votes given a decision on α are given by equations 3 and 4 in appendix 4.2. These conditions ensure the existence of a decision on α that will maximize the objective of the decision maker(s). The optimal level of spending allocation, that is, α^*, that state government will select in order to maximize votes can be defined as a function of the exogenous variables. To determine the effect of exogenous factors on optimal choice of α, one can totally differentiate equation 2 and derive comparative static results. The total differentiation is given by equation 5, and all comparative static results are given by equations 6 through 9 in appendix 4.2.

The signs on equations 6 and 7 confirm the basic political intuition that the higher the ratio of suburban to city core residents, the greater the likelihood of transportation spending outside of the central city, and vice versa. Furthermore, a change in any exogenous variable x_i that would either increase or decrease the vote-maximizing level of α^* chosen by the state government, depending on the nature of the variable, can affect transportation funding. Note that vectors $\mathbf{x}$ and $\mathbf{z}$ essentially share the same elements, in which case the total effect of that factor on α^* will be the sum of the expressions in equations 6 and 7, with the sign of the combined expression determined by the number of central-city and suburban or rural residents, and by the nature of functions $d(\mathbf{x})$ and $d(\mathbf{z})$. The notations $\mathbf{x}$ and $\mathbf{z}$ include race, class, and location, but also include social and political dynamic factors such as community size, party affiliation, community characteristics, public goods, and existing road infrastructure. The conceptual framework provides the rationale for developing an empirical model of spending allocation.

Now, consider the fact that Michigan uses an allocation formula to distribute road funds. By design, a given formula only compensates communities based on population and existing infrastructure. If the formula works strictly the way it is intended to and compensates only for the two factors, the patterns of funding allocation resulting from it would be expected to be insensitive to other factors. If, however, the distribution is sensitive to other factors, then the formula itself can be considered to be partly a conduit for the aspirations of constituents related to those factors. The fact that the formula has been revised a few times suggests that the factors not contained in the formula may be the basis for disequilibrium. The focus in this essay, therefore, is to analyze and decompose the pattern of spending allocation resulting from the given formula and to test it for race, political affiliation, income, class, and location neutrality. In other words, if race, class, income, political affiliation, or location is found to be a statistically significant causal factor, then the formula has a built-in responsiveness to these issues. Therefore, the estimate of allocated dollars against anticipated causal factors is proposed based on the conceptual model. Confirmation of conclusions from the conceptual model would suggest whether the formula is race, class, politics, and location sensitive.

Empirical Model

Road-funding allocation, as discussed earlier, is determined by a formula that includes only population and existing road infrastructure. However, there are numerous factors that can drive population and road density changes that indirectly affect road-funding allocation. For instance, population density at any time at a given location depends on such factors as the population's racial composition, the population's income, employment opportunities, natural amenities, closeness to urbanized locations, and so on. Based on a regression analysis, the relationship between allocated funds (based on existing population and road density) and hypothesized drivers of population and road density (such as race, class, location, party affiliation, and so forth) can be estimated to determine the indirect influence of these latent factors on road-funding allocation.

The conceptual framework section presented key political factors that should affect the allocation of road spending across communities if there was no formula. In the framework, in addition to population and road stocks, other factors, such as race, location, political affiliation, and class, were relevant. However, the formula seems to suggest that these factors may not be relevant. In this section, an empirical model is developed to test whether the variables of race, location, political affiliation, and class are significant determinants of what appears to be a formula based explicitly on population and road stock. Given the existence of a formula, the empirical specification must consider the structure of the formula.

Given Michigan's current road-funding allocation scheme, the framework of allocation can be specified as in equation 10 in appendix 4.3. From equation 10, road spending allocated to community i (RS_i) is determined by current population in community i (P_i), current road stock in community i (R_i), allocation weights for population and road stocks (ε_1 and ε_2, 60 percent for population and 40 percent for road stocks in the current formula), and per capita share of the total spending to community i given its existing population and roads (η_1 and η_2).

Both P_i and R_i are dynamic in the sense that they change over time. This would cause changes in the amount of funding community i receives for road spending over time vis-à-vis other communities. Current levels of population for each community are determined by the initial levels of population and by the change between the initial levels and the current population (Carlino and Mills 1987). A similar argument applies to road stocks. Thus, decomposing the components of P_i and R_i further yields equations 11 and 12 in appendix 4.3. These equations indicate that current levels of population and road stock in a given community are determined by lagged period stock of each and a change in population (ΔP) and road stock (ΔR) over time to the current period. Note that change in population between two time periods for each community itself is determined by socioeconomic conditions in a given community at a given time period, local political dynamics, the level of public goods provision, and a host of other community-specific characteristics. Hence, the change in population can further be decomposed into its determinants in community i as indicated in equation 13. Equation 13 shows that change in population itself in a given community is determined by household characteristics (income, race, education, and so forth), community characteristics (poverty rate, crime, and so forth), public good provision and taxes (police, fire, parks, property taxes, and so forth), housing characteristics (housing stock, housing price, and so forth), and other factors that determine the change in population. Whether these hypothesized factors determine population change is tested by regressing population change against these factors, and results are reported in table 4.2. Equation 13 is important because it captures the movement of population across communities over time, hence posing implications to long-term road-funding allocation equity. To the extent that population change is an integral part of the decision on road-funding allocation, factors that determine long-term population movement across communities will indirectly impact road fund receipts by communities. In this regard, equation 13 identifies crucial factors that are

Table 4.2. Estimation of Population Change against Its Hypothesized Determinants

Variable	Coefficient	t-statistic
Intercept	−2245.721	−1.361
Population 1992	−0.089*	−1.825
MTF92	1.175	0.119
Value	0.0003	0.051
Distance	82.543[†]	2.014
Tax	0.414[‡]	4.538
Fire	−0.765[‡]	−2.727
Highway	−0.137	−0.554
Parks	−0.403	−1.329
Police	0.154	0.926
Nonwhite	9.055	0.317
Income	0.009	0.428
R^2	0.92	

*significance at the 10% level

[†]significance at the 5% level

[‡]significance at the 1% level

embedded in population dynamics with potential impacts on long-term fund allocation equity. Factors such as income, race, poverty, and so forth are thus embedded in population change with indirect impacts on fund allocation.

Similarly, the change in the stock of roads can be decomposed further, as indicated in equation 14. This implies the current stocks of roads are determined both by past investment in roads in a given community and additional investment in roads between two time periods. Additional investment in roads itself is not independent of socioeconomic conditions, as indicated in equations 15 and 16. Thus, as in the case of population change, road stock change is also a dynamic element that varies based on socioeconomic conditions across communities. Through substitution and rearranging, the determinants of road spending over time are given in equation 16, which indicates that the stock of roads is determined, among other things, by initial investment in roads and by socioeconomic factors.

Based on understanding of the individual drivers of population and road stock changes over time (factors that determine road-spending allocation), the econometric model estimated is given in equation 17. Equation 17 allows for testing whether road-funding allocation is determined purely on the basis of the formula (population and road stock) or would implicitly be determined by such factors as income, race, politics, and location. Only if such variables in the model become insignificant can the road-funding allocation mechanism be viewed as insensitive to race, class, location, and political affiliation. However, if the coefficients are significant, then despite the formula, allocation is not equitable and is driven by these indicators of bias.

To operationalize the empirical model, first the change in population equation is estimated against the latent variables that are hypothesized to drive it to understand the relationship. Then, based on the model in equation 17, road-funding allocation to each community is estimated by regressing allocated road funds against the drivers of population and road stocks. This approach will enable testing for sensitivity of the current formula to race, location, and political factors.

Data and Estimation

To estimate the determinants of allocated road funds, socioeconomic, political, and spatial data are collected for 1992–2002, the study period. The 1992–2002 time frame is used in order to ensure that the effects of endogenous changes in the formula are controlled for, and to isolate the distributional impact of the given formula. Indeed, the time frame chosen is the only census decade in which the formula did not change. Data limitations also limited the ability to focus on other time periods.

Table 4.3 summarizes the definition of variables and data sources. RS_i is represented by the amount of road spending allocated to each community in the study region (MTF_i) and is used as a proxy for α. MTF_i data are collected from Report 139 of the MDOT. The empirical model posits that the transportation allocation at a community level (MTF_i) is a function of political clout (proxied by the initial level of population, P_{t-1}), the political party affiliation variable ($POLITICS_i$), and socioeconomic factors that are assumed to reveal tastes and preferences of community residents, such as income ($INCOME_i$), property values (VALUE$_i$), the

Table 4.3. The Definition of Variables and Data Sources

Variable	Description of variable	Source
Income	household median income	U.S. Bureau of the Census
Distance	distance from Detroit (miles)	Computed by one of the authors using Hawth's Tools
Highway	per capita highway expenditure	Census of Governments, U.S. Bureau of the Census
Value	Median value of owner occupied houses (2000)	U.S. Bureau of the Census
Fire	per capita fire expenditure	Census of Governments, U.S. Bureau of the Census
Library	per capita library expenditure	Census of Governments, U.S. Bureau of the Census
Parks	per capita parks expenditure	Census of Governments, U.S. Bureau of the Census
Police	per capita police expenditure	Census of Governments, U.S. Bureau of the Census
MTF	Michigan Transportation Fund (State grant)	Report #139, Michigan Dept. of Transportation
Nonwhite	% nonwhite	U.S. Bureau of the Census
Politics	1 = >50% Democrats, 0 = <50%	Census of Governments, U.S. Bureau of the Census
Tax	per capita property tax revenue	Census of Governments, U.S. Bureau of the Census

distance of the community from a central city ($DISTANCE_i$), the racial composition of the community ($\%NONWHITE_i$), and the property tax revenue of the community (TAX_i), which reveals the fiscal capacity of a particular community.

Data on each of the above variables were collected from the U.S. Census report, except for $DISTANCE_i$, which was computed using Hawth's Tools. The political affiliation variable ($POLITICS_i$) is a dummy variable that is equal to 1 when a community has above 50 percent of its population (majority) as registered Democratic voters in the 2000 legislative elections and zero otherwise. To capture the impact of public services on population dynamics, $HIGHWAY_i$, $FIRE_i$, $PARKS_i$, and $POLICE_i$ expenditure variables are included. These variables are collected from U.S. Census report. Since no data are available on the local road spending outside of state allocations, that variable was not accounted for in the model.

The econometric model is dynamic in the sense that the lagged dependent variable is included as an explanatory variable. The model is tested for potential econometric specification problems. The existence of a lag term of the dependent variable as an explanatory variable poses an econometric problem as it may potentially be correlated with model errors. Tests for robustness and potential error correlation in the model suggest that there is no serious endogeneity problem. The model is also tested for potential spatial autocorrelation, that is, the tendency of variables to be correlated across geographic areas. Numerous studies have shown the potential spatial (spillover) effects of public spending (Baicker 2005; Bloch and Zenginobuz 2006). Two common tests of spatial dependence and autocorrelation are Moran's *I* and Lagrange Multiplier tests. These tests confirm the existence of spatial correlation of a spatial lag form, that is, road-spending allocation seems to have a spatial pattern, but econometric model errors are spatially random. To account for this problem, a spatial lag specification is used. The spatial econometric specification of road-spending allocation determinants are given in equation 18 in appendix 4.3. To operationalize a spatial lag model, weight matrices are created to capture whether two communities are contiguous neighbors, hence capturing the impact of neighboring community characteristics on another community's road-spending allocation. Since Ordinary Least Squares estimation procedure are ineffective in the presence of spatial lags in econometric model, an alternative estimation procedure based on maximum likelihood estimation is utilized in estimating equation 18.

Empirical Results

Parameter estimates of the spatial autoregressive model are presented in table 4.4. Both the R-squared and adjusted R-squared were 0.99, reflecting the dynamic nature of the model and the inclusion of a lagged dependent variable as an independent variable. As seen in table 4.4, eight of the thirteen estimated coefficients were statistically significant at the 5 percent level. The coefficient of lagged population was significant at the 1 percent level, with a value of $23.30. This suggests that for each additional person in a community, the community receives an additional $23.30. This is consistent with a priori expectations that growing communities, which are typically nonurban, receive more funds over time. On the

Table 4.4. Empirical Model Results (dependent variable = MTF)

Variable	Coefficient	t-statistic
Intercept	−224,136.56[‡]	−31.67
Population 1992	23.30[‡]	3.08
MTF 1992	0.568[‡]	3.32
Value	−0.46[†]	−1.95
Distance	5730.62[‡]	3.68
Tax	12.31[†]	2.19
Fire	41.92*	2.43
Highway	2.04	0.47
Parks	7.08	1.46
Police	−6.73	−1.05
Nonwhite	192.37	0.16
Income	3.74[‡]	2.72
Politics	−73734.10*	−1.98
WMTF (neighboring communities MTF)	0.014	1.99
R^2	0.99	

*significance at the 10% level
[†]significance at the 5% level
[‡]significance at the 1% level

other hand, shrinking communities, which tend to be urban, receive less funds over time. Hence, in Michigan, where almost every metropolitan area is sprawling, the cost of sprawl to urban communities due to change in population is approximately $23.00 per person.

Lagged spending is reflective of existing road infrastructure. Recall that urban communities have high endowment of both population and roads, and therefore high lagged spending. The estimate for lagged spending is $0.57, which suggests that, ceteris paribus, the decade change in allocation is $0.57 for a community. That is, for each dollar received in the previous decade, the community receives $0.57. This suggests that the average community is receiving less over time. This is not surprising, given the relatively slow Michigan economy.

The estimated coefficient for Median Housing Value is −0.46, which suggests that communities with high median housing value have lower road-spending allocation. High median value of housing can mitigate the change in population by deterring entrance from outside the community and hence allocated road spending.

The coefficient of distance from Detroit is significant, and the estimate is $5,730.62. Therefore, for every mile of distance away from Detroit, a community will typically get $5,730.62 more. This pure distance effect suggests the erosion of the urban center road-spending allocation. For instance, a hypothetical community located ten miles away from Detroit will receive $57,306 more per year. Considering this is an independent effect from population, this result suggests a pure distance bias against cities.

The coefficient of property taxes is $12.31, which suggests for every dollar of local property tax revenue, state road funds received increases of $12.31. This may suggest that high property value communities are rewarded in the allocation process. The significant coefficient for fire expenditure ($41.92) also suggests that communities with significant allocation for fire protection are better rewarded. The coefficient of median household income, our measure of class equity, is significant, and the estimate is $3.74. This suggests that high-income communities, which are often suburban, receive a $3.74 premium per $1.00 higher median household income. This clearly reflects existing class bias in road-spending allocation.

The political affiliation dummy variable isolates the effect of being a majority Democratic registered voter community. The estimated coefficient of $73,734.10 suggests that predominantly Democratic communities have allocated funds that are significantly lower, compared with predominantly Republican communities. This large marginal effect shows the relevance of political affiliation to the receipt of resources from higher levels of government. This result confirms the existence of political bias within the road-spending allocation system.

The coefficient of percent nonwhite population was insignificant, which rejects the hypothesis of racial bias in road-spending allocation. Similarly, *HIGHWAY, PARKS,* and *POLICE* spending were insignificant at the 10 percent level.

Our spatial proximity and neighboring communities' spillover effect variable was significant at the 5 percent level. The estimated coefficient of $0.014 suggests that neighboring communities with high road spending will have a spillover influence on their neighbors to the tune of approximately 1 cent per dollar they receive. This measures the pure spillover effect of neighboring communities.

Conclusions and Implications for Metropolitan Policy

This chapter investigates road-spending allocation to local units of government by the state government. The study attempts to test the current formula-based fund allocation system for existence of sensitivities in funding by exploring biases related to class, race, location, and politics. In the case study of the Detroit metropolitan area, it is found that the formula, which is specified to reward population growth and existing infrastructure, does work to achieve its allocation objective by putting more money in the suburbs. However, the formula rewards other factors not exclusively accounted for in the formula, namely class, politics, and location. Communities with lower household income, majority Democratic voters, lower property values, limited fire protection coverage, and at closer distances to urban centers are less favored by the formula. On the other hand, the formula is rewarding suburbanites, high-income households, and Republican-dominated communities. It is, however, race neutral. By explicitly identifying these internal biases, the study suggests that future evaluations of the formula consider these biases.

The findings of this study have significant policy implications. First, road spending could be tied to sprawl and unmanaged land use patterns. The finding that more state road funds are allocated to locations away from the city may suggest a sustained pattern of sprawl in Michigan's metropolitan areas. This may have further implications in that sprawl could exacerbate the spatial distribution of and access to economic opportunities across communities over time. Therefore, the land use implications of state road-funding schemes may need to be further understood. Second, public investment in roads is a key component to encourage growth and create economic opportunities that may reduce poverty. To the extent that the current road-funding allocation scheme is negatively sensitive to income, lower income communities are disadvantaged. This could create limitations to road investment and attracting future economic opportunities in these communities. Third, urban revitalization is a pressing challenge in metropolitan areas. One component of urban revitalization is updating infrastructure and making communities attractive. The findings of this study suggest that road-funding allocation seems to compensate locations away from metropolitan areas. This may interfere to some degree with urban revitalization programs that aim to partially achieve urban competitiveness through infrastructure development.

State funding allocation schemes are in general expected to have a degree of sensitivity to equity concerns. The fact that the current formula does not explicitly address these concerns but its outcomes relate to these concerns suggests the need for caution in future revisions of the formula. To the extent to which the distributional outcomes of the current formula contradict the objectives of society, the formula may need to be respecified in future rounds to deliver more precise equity results. For example, if the formula penalizes urban communities, but society's objective is to enhance urban road infrastructure, then a simple formula locks society to a path of greater inequity. Therefore, interventions may have to be made to the existing formula to achieve the equity goals of society. In other words, while a formula might be simple and expedient, and may reduce the pressure on politicians, it may also be compromising equity goals.

Finally, the authors want to convey the potential utility of this analysis, with respect to students. It provides a procedure for undertaking a science-based analysis of a social issue with potential policy implications. The analytical approach used in our study could be used as a teaching tool for students who are interested in understanding the process of scientific research to evaluate existing policy issues, such as road-spending allocation. The study also provides useful insights that may help understand the role of political factors in shaping public policy. In our analysis, we found that despite the existence of a formula, which appears not to be sensitive to class, politics, and location factors, its outcomes have such implications. One conclusion students can draw from this is that they need to dig deeper and question political solutions that appear to be nonpolitical, and our framework gives them a tool for doing that.

Notes

1. On one hand, as connective infrastructure between communities, roads can fuel unfettered growth. On the other hand, through strategic road spending, communities can position themselves to repel growth, enhance intralocal connectivity of residential areas to shopping and employment centers, and improve quality of life for local residents. There is a difference between connecting major destinations in towns to existing neighborhoods and building major roads to connect areas with significant agriculture and vacant lands to the existing road network. Obviously, the latter is more likely to facilitate sprawl and unfettered growth.

2. The act was introduced through the House Bill 42 on January 17, 1951. It was later enacted on July 1, 1951 (Journal of the Senate, Regular Session, 8 Cong. Rec. [1951]). The MTF, formerly known as the Motor Vehicle Highway Fund (MVHF), is now a primary source of revenue for the development of roads and transportation networks at the local level. MTF funds supplement locally raised tax revenues and other funds coming from the federal or state government. The motivation for the passage of PA 51 can be traced back to the country's interest in highway transportation to aid in the defense and national development (Pohl and Brown 1997). of the legislation was informed by the Good Roads Federation Study in 1948, which indicated a need of $1.5 billion over a fifteen-year period to bring the entire highway system of Michigan (state, county, and city roads) to safe and tolerable standards (Pohl and Brown 1997).

APPENDIX 1
Basic Determinants of Road-Spending Allocation

The basic determinants of road-spending allocation can be given by:

$$RS_i = \alpha_1 Pop_i + \alpha_2 Infra_i + \alpha_3 Class_i + \alpha_4 Race_i + \alpha_5 Polit_i + \alpha_6 Other_i \qquad (1)$$

where RS_i is the road-spending allocation to community i, Pop_i is population, $Infra_i$ is existing stock of roads, $Class_i$ is a proxy for income or socioeconomic class, $Polit_i$ is party affiliation of community leaders, $Race_i$ is racial composition of the community, and $Other_i$ is other factors.

APPENDIX 2
The Political Economy of Road-Spending Allocation

The objective function of state government (vote maximization) can be given as:

$$u^G = V = C\Pi^c(\mathbf{x}, \alpha) + S\Pi^s(\mathbf{z}, \alpha), \tag{2}$$

where u^G is the utility function of the state government, C is the voting population of central city residents, S is the voting population of suburban and rural residents, c and s are superscripts for city residents and suburban or rural residents, Π^i is the probability that the average i^{th} group household or individual will vote for the government, $i = c, s$, and $\mathbf{x}$ is a vector of preference factors or other local conditions that affect Π^c, conditional on α. Similarly, $\mathbf{z}$ is a vector of preference factors or other local conditions that affect Π^s conditional on α. Stakeholder's support for a winning candidate (represented a political party) will depend on the candidate's support for policies favorable to the stakeholder's group.

The first order condition for maximizing total votes given a decision on α is:

$$\frac{dV}{d\alpha} = C\frac{\partial \Pi^c}{\partial \alpha} + C\frac{\partial \Pi^s}{\partial \alpha} = 0 \tag{3}$$

For equation (3) to define a vote maximization level of α, the second order condition must hold:

$$\frac{d^2V}{d\alpha^2} = C\Pi^c_{\alpha\alpha} + S\Pi^s_{\alpha\alpha} \tag{4}$$

The optimal level of spending allocation, that is, α^*, that state government will select in order to maximize votes can be defined as a function of the exogenous variables. To accomplish this, totally differentiate equation 2 yields:

$$dV_\alpha = \Pi^c_\alpha dC + \phi d\alpha + C\left(\sum_{i=1}^{k} \Pi^c_{\alpha x^i} dx^i\right) + S\left(\sum_{i=1}^{m} \Pi^s_{\alpha z^i} dz^i\right) + \Pi^s_\alpha dS, \tag{5}$$

where $\phi = C\Pi^c_{\alpha\alpha} + S\Pi^s_{\alpha\alpha} < 0$ and k and m are the number of exogenous variables in $\mathbf{x}$ and $\mathbf{z}$, respectively. Looking at changes in only one exogenous variable at a time, one may obtain, from equation 5, the following comparative static results:

$$\frac{d\alpha^*}{dC} = -\frac{\Pi^c_\alpha}{\phi} < 0 \tag{6}$$

$$\frac{d\alpha^*}{dS} = -\frac{\Pi^s_\alpha}{\phi} > 0 \tag{7}$$

$$\frac{d\alpha^*}{dx^i} = -\frac{C\Pi^c_{\alpha x^i}}{\phi} < 0 \tag{8}$$

$$\frac{d\alpha^*}{dz^i} = -\frac{S\Pi^s_{\alpha z^i}}{\phi} > 0 \tag{9}$$

APPENDIX 3
The Econometric Model

Road-spending allocation for a given community can be given as:

$$RS_i = \varepsilon_1 \sum RS_i\left[\frac{P_i}{\sum P_i}\right] + \varepsilon_2 \sum RS_i\left[\frac{R_i}{\sum R_i}\right] = \varepsilon_1 \gamma_i P_i + \varepsilon_2 \xi R_i = \eta_1 P_i + \eta_2 R_i \tag{10}$$

(continued)

where RS_i is road-spending allocated to community i, P_i is current population in community i, R_i is the current road stock in community i, ε_1 and ε_2 are the allocation weights for population and road stocks (60 percent for population and 40 percent for road stocks in the current formula), Υ and ξ are per capita community share of spending, and per mile community share, respectively, and η_1 and η_2 are the per capita share of the total spending to community i based on their population and roads, respectively.

Decomposing the components of P_i and R_i yields:

$$P_i = P_{i(t-1)} + \Delta P_i \text{ and} \tag{11}$$

$$R_i = R_{i(t-1)} + \Delta R_i \tag{12}$$

where $(_{t-1})$ indicates values in the lagged period, and ΔP and ΔR are changes in population and road stock, respectively. Change in population between two time periods for each community itself is determined by socioeconomic conditions in a given community at a given time period, local political dynamics, the level of public goods provision, and a host of other community-specific characteristics. Hence, the change in population can further be decomposed into its determinants in community i as:

$$\Delta P_i = \phi_i P_{i(t-1)} + \vartheta_i (R_{i(t-1)}, HHC_{i(t-1)}, CC_{i(t-1)}, PGT_{i(t-1)}, HSP_{i(t-1)}; \Omega^{\Delta P}) \tag{13}$$

where HHC is household characteristics (income, race, education, and so forth), CC is community characteristics (poverty rate, crime, and so forth), PGT is public good provision and taxes (police, fire, parks, property taxes, and so forth), HSP is housing characteristics (housing stock, housing price, and so forth), $\Omega^{\Delta P}$ is other factors that determine the change in population in community i.

Similarly, the change in the stock of roads can be decomposed as:

$$\Delta R_i = \tau_i R_{i(t-1)} + \varphi_i RS_{(t-1)}. \tag{14}$$

From equation 10, road spending of a community i at a given time is $RS_i = \eta_1 P_i + \eta_2 R_i$. By including equations 13 and 14 in the identity equations 11 and 12, inserting the resulting relationship back in equation 10, and rearranging yields:

$$RS_i = \eta_1[P_{i(t-1)} + \phi_i P_{i(t-1)} + \vartheta_i(R_{i(t-1)}, HHC_i, CC_i, PGT_i, HSP_i; \Omega^{\Delta P})] \tag{15}$$
$$+ \eta_2[R_{i(t-1)} + \tau_i R_{i(t-1)} + \varphi_i RS_{(t-1)}]$$

Rearranging equation 15 yields:

$$RS_i = \eta_1(1 + \phi_i) P_{i(t-1)} + \alpha_1 \cdot \vartheta_i(R_{i(t-1)}, HHC_i, CC_i, PGT_i, HSP_i; \Omega^{\Delta P}))] \tag{16}$$
$$+ \eta_2[1 + \tau_i)R_{i(t-1)} + \alpha_2 \cdot \varphi_i RS_{(t-1)}.$$

It can be argued that the linear parameters η, ϕ, ϑ, τ and φ are embedded in the model parameters β_i in equation 16. As a result, the empirical econometric model can be specified as:

$$RS_i = \beta_0 + \beta_1 RS_{i(t-1)} + \beta_2 P_{i(t-1)} + \beta_3 R_{i(t-1)} + \beta_4 HHC_i + \beta_5 CC_i + \beta_6 PGT_i + \beta_7 HSP_i + e_i \tag{17}$$

Equation 17 allows for testing whether road-funding allocation is determined purely on the basis of the formula (population and road stock) or would implicitly be determined by such factors as income, race, politics, and location.

Accounting for the existence of spatial dependence in road spending allocation, equation 17 can be respecified in a spatial lag form as:

$$RS_i = \beta_0 + \rho(WRS_i) + \beta_1 RS_{i(t-1)} + \beta_2 P_{i(t-1)} + \beta_3 R_{i(t-1)} + \beta_4 HHC_{i(t-1)} \tag{18}$$
$$+ \beta_5 CC_{i(t-1)} + \beta_6 PGT_{i(t-1)} + \beta_7 HSP_{i(t-1)} + e_i.$$

where ρ is the spatial autoregressive coefficient, W is the spatial weight matrix constructed based on contiguity of neighboring communities, and WRS_i is the spatial lag of road spending allocation.

REFERENCES

Adelaja, A., and K. Friedman. 1999. Political Economy of Right to Farm. *Journal of Agricultural and Applied Economics* 31(3):565–579.

Adelaja, A., and A. Patel. 2005. *Political Economy of Medical Foods Reimbursement.* East Lansing: Land Policy Institute, Michigan State University.

Alesina, A., R. Baqir, and W. Easterly. 199. Public Goods and Ethnic Divisions. *Quarterly Journal of Economics* 114(4): 1243–1284.

Baicker, K. 2005. The Spillover Effects of State Spending. *Journal of Public Economics* 89(2–3):529–544.

Baldassare, M., and W. Protash. 1982. Growth Controls, Population Growth, and Community Satisfaction. *American Sociological Review* 47(3):339–346.

Baum-Snow, N. 2007. Did highways cause suburbanization? *Quarterly Journal of Economics* 122(2):775–805.

Berechman, J., D. Ozmen, and K. Ozbay. 2006. Empirical analysis of transportation investment and economic development at state, county and municipality levels. *Transportation* 33 (6):537–551.

Bloch, F., and E. U. Zenginobuz. 2006. Tiebout Equilibria in Local Public Good Economies with Spillovers. *Journal of Public Economics* 90(8–9):1745–1763.

Brueckner, J. K., and M. Joo. 1991. Voting Behavior When Public Spending Affects Property Value. ORER Working Paper #81. Office of Real Estate Research. University of Illinois Urbana, Illinois.

Bruegmann, R. 2005. *Sprawl: A Compact History.* Chicago: University of Chicago Press.

Byun, P., B. S. Waldorf, and A. X. Esparza. 2005. Spillover and Local Growth Controls: An Alternative Perspective on Suburbanization. *Growth and Change* 36(2):196–219.

Cadot, O., L. H. Roller, and A. Stephan. 2006. Contribution to Productivity or Pork Barrel? The Two Faces of Infrastructure Investment. *Journal of Public Economics* 90(6–7):1133–1153.

Campos, R. W. 1987. Toward a Theory of Instrument Choice in the Regulation of Markets. Mimeo, California Institute of Technology.

Carlino, G. A., and E. S. Mills. 1987. The Determinants of Country Growth. *Journal of Regional Science* 27(1):39–54.

DeVol, R., L. Wallace, and A. Bedroussian. 2006. Best Performing Cities 2005: Where American Jobs Are Created and Sustained. Santa Monica, Calif.: Milken Institute.

Diamond, H. L., and P. F. Noonan. 1996. *Land Use in America.* Washington, D.C.: Island Press.

Dilworth, R. 2003. From Sewers to Suburbs: Transforming the Policy Making Context of American Cities. *Urban Affairs Review* 38(5):726–739.

GAO (General Accounting Office). 2004. Surface Transportation Spending. Report 04–744. Washington, District of Columbia. Available at http://www.gao.gov/new.items/d04744.pdf.

Hahn, R. W. 1990. The Political Economy of Environmental Regulations: Toward a Unifying Framework. *Public Choice* 65(1):21–47.

Hamilton, W. 2007. Act 51 Primer: A Guide to 1951 Public Act 51 and Michigan Transportation Funding, edited by House Fiscal Agency. Lansing, Michigan. Available at http://house.michigan.gov/hfa/PDFs/act51.pdf.

Hart, D., and R. Atkins. 2002. Civic Competence in Urban Youth. *Applied Development Science* 6(4):227–236.

Hughes, J. W. 1975. Dilemmas of Suburbanization and Growth Controls. *Annals of the American Academy of Political and Social Science* 422:61–76.

Jaret, C., L. W. Reid, and R. M. Adelman. 2003. Black-White Income Inequality and Metropolitan Socioeconomic Structure. *Journal of Urban Affairs* 25(3):305–334.

Katz, B., A. Berube, R. Prince, and H. Smith. 2003. Detroit in Focus: A Profile from Census 2000. In *Living Cities: The National Community Development Initiative.* Center on Urban Metropolitan Policy. Washington, D.C.: Brookings Institution.

Kemmerling, A., and A. Stephan. 2002. The Contribution of Local Public Infrastructure to Private Productivity and Its Political Economy: Evidence from a Panel of Large German Cities. *Public Choice* 113:403–424.

LeRoy, G., A. Lack, K. Walter, and P. Mattera. 2006. *The Geography of Incentives: Economic Development and Land Use in Michigan.* Washington, D.C.: Good Jobs First.

Lobao, L., and R. Saenz. 2002. Spatial Inequality and Diversity as an Emerging Research Arena. *Rural Sociology* 67(4):497–511.

MLULC (Michigan Leadership Land Use Council). 2003. Michigan's Land, Michigan's Future: Final Report of the Michigan's Leadership Council. Lansing: State Government of Michigan.

Molotch, H. 1976. The City as a Growth Machine: Toward a Political Economy of Place. *American Journal of Sociology* 82(2):309–322.

Molotch, H., and J. Logan. 1984. Tensions in the Growth Machine. *Social Problems* 31:483–499.

OTA (Office of the Technological Assessment). 1995. The Technological Reshaping of Metropolitan America. Washington, D.C.: U.S. Office of Technology and Assessment.

Pampel, F. C. 1994. "Population Aging, Class Context, and Age Inequality in Public Spending." *The American Journal of Sociology* 100(1): 153–195.

Pelzman, S. 1976. Toward a More General Theory of Regulation. *Journal of Law and Economics* 19(2):211–240.

Pohl, D. G., and N. E. Brown. 1997. History of Roads. Paper presented to the Association of Southern Michigan Roads Commission.

Sauerzopf, R. C. 1999a. Sprawl, Inequity, and Balkanization in Detroit: Toward Metropolitan System Balance. In *An Analysis of Sprawl, Spatial Inequity and the Context of Reform in the Detroit Region.* Detroit, Mich.: Wayne State University.

———. 1999b. The Urban Electorate in Presidential Elections, 1920–1996. *Urban Affairs Review* 35(1):72–91.

Schneider, K., M. McClelland, and A. Guy. 2005. Follow the Money: Uncovering and Reforming Michigan's Sprawl Subsidies. Beulah: Michigan Land Use Institute and United Cerebral Palsy.

Schneider, M., and P. Teske. 1993. Antigrowth Entrepreneur: Challenging the "Equilibrium" of the Growth Machine. *Journal of Politics* 55(3):720–736.

SEMCOG (Southeast Michigan Council of Governments). 2000. Transportation Factbook for Southeast Michigan: Facts and Figures on Transportation in Southeast Michigan 64. Detroit: Southeast Michigan Council of Governments.

Squires, G. D., ed. 2002. *Urban Sprawl: Causes, Consequences, and Policy Responses.* Washington, D.C.: Urban Institute Press.

Stiglitz, J. E. 2000. *Economics of the Public Sector.* 3rd ed. New York: W. W. Norton.

Timpone, R. 1988. Structure, Behavior, and Voter Turnout in the United States. *American Political Science Review* 92(1):145–158.

U.S. Bureau of the Census. 2000. Available from www.census.gov.

Vey, J. S. 2007. *Restoring Prosperity: The State Role in Revitalizing America's Older Industrial Cities.* Washington, D.C.: Brookings Institution.

Voss, P. R., and G. Q. Chi. 2006. Highways and population change. *Rural Sociology* 71 (1):33–58.

Warner, S. L. 1962. The Distribution of Highway User Taxes in Michigan. Master's thesis, Michigan State University.

Welke, R., S. Hart, R. Johnson, P. Hoffman, J. Tatter, T. Kelly, and R. White. 2000. Transportation Funding for the 21st Century. In *Michigan Act 51 Transportation Funding Study Committee* 5. Lansing: State Government of Michigan.

CHAPTER 5

Coming Together in Tough Economic Times: Workforce Development and Economic Development Move Closer in Michigan

Elsie Harper-Anderson

There has been an ongoing discussion about why those involved in workforce development (WD) and economic development (ED) cannot, or will not, work together more closely to create jobs and match them with job seekers. Previous research has documented this disconnect and the need for greater connectivity between these professional areas (Fitzgerald 1993; Giloth 2000; Harrison et al. 1995). One reason for the divide lies in the inconsistency in the geographical boundaries or service areas of public workforce agencies and ED organizations. Another point of departure relates to the goals and approach of each group. While economic development has traditionally focused on creating jobs and increasing economic activity, workforce development has focused more on placing people in jobs. Further, Fitzgerald (2004a) points out the functional separation imposed by separate funding streams and governmental departments.

In Michigan, however, recent economic hardship and policy changes have produced greater incentive for workforce agencies and economic development organizations to find common ground upon which to promote their local economies and protect their residents from economic devastation. Michigan has been hit so hard by tough economic times that workforce development and economic development have had to find innovative ways to partner for mutual survival. The economic decline of the early 2000s posed tremendous challenges for anyone in the United States involved in the creation, attraction, or retention of businesses and jobs. Regions hit particularly hard were those whose economies had high concentrations of manufacturing, technology, and financial services jobs. The economic challenge was compounded by decreased government funding for programs and initiatives that would have alleviated some of the strain. In addition, global economic forces increased the level of economic competition among regions worldwide. There was widespread call from both public and private stakeholders in local areas to strategically employ all available resources and expertise to salvage their local economies. With the national unemployment rates at a three-decade high in many areas, WD agencies charged with helping the unemployed find jobs desperately sought new approaches and strategies. ED organizations aimed at creating and retaining jobs and businesses were also under extreme pressure in a downsizing, globalizing, and skills-hungry economy.

The purpose of this research was to investigate how local workforce agencies in Michigan were dealing with the challenges presented by the economic recession of the early 2000s. Specifically, the study examines the relationships between public WD agencies and ED organizations and how those relationships affected strategies for coping with the difficult economic times.

The findings suggest that the relationship has evolved in several important ways. These transformations have resulted from a combination of economic necessity, policy changes, changes in institutional structures and networks, and changes in the attitudes and professional backgrounds of the players involved. In several local areas, the process of focusing on industry sectors and/or clusters to create jobs, train a specialized workforce, and create a competitive economy has resulted in a stronger connection between the people and organizations involved in workforce development and economic development initiatives.

Literature Review

For some time now, scholars and policy makers have called for a greater connection between WD and ED (Fitzgerald 2004a; Fitzgerald 2004b; Giloth 2000; Melendez and Harrison 1998; Harrison and Weiss 1998). The reasons the two are disconnected in the first place are extremely complicated and involve many actors and policies. Some of the most commonly cited factors have to do with organizational separations (Fitzgerald 2004b), differing performance goals and metrics (Chapple 2005; Giloth 2003), and the way each side perceives its role and the role of the other.

Both economic and social justifications support the call for greater connectivity between WD and ED efforts. The central economic argument is the equilibrium logic of a market economy, where efficiency is achieved when the labor supply produced by workforce development meets the labor demand created via economic development. Further, macroeconomic globalization trends have heightened the importance of a high-quality workforce in creating regional economic competitiveness, implying that those engaged in ED now have a greater incentive to pay attention to the development of their region's workforce (Clarke and Gaile 1998; Florida 2002). In a recent study of WD administrators, 79 percent identified the economy as a key driver in their relationship with local ED stakeholders (Harper-Anderson 2007). Social arguments, on the other hand, include the goal of economic development creating jobs for the hard-to-serve populations who are often clients of the workforce development system (Harrison et al. 1995) and focusing the spatial distribution of jobs created to match the capacity of the local labor force (Rosenfeld 2003; Ranney and Betancur 1992).

Recently, there has been some progress as businesses, nonprofits, and government agencies are beginning to collaborate more on WD and ED efforts. In a recent national survey of

WD administrators, 88 percent reported feeling more connected to their local ED partners than they felt five years earlier (Harper-Anderson 2008). Because some businesses lack the capacity to find and keep workers by themselves, they have partnered with local governments to develop the workforce, and in turn, to enhance the local economy (Giloth 1998). ED organizations are also beginning to partner proactively with WD agencies for delivery of training programs (Eberts and Erickek 2002). And firms concerned about potential labor crises in replacing skilled workers are also becoming involved in WD processes (Giloth 2003).

Additionally, changes in the labor market—including service sector growth, the collapse of internal career ladders, the growth of temporary employment, and insecurity among employers—have all encouraged ED organizations to cooperate with WD service providers to some extent (Cappetti 1997; Osterman 1999). Together, these market dynamics produced incentives to create new WD initiatives that bridge the gaps between supply and demand (Giloth 2000).

Federal workforce policy has also encouraged the link. The Workforce Investment Act (WIA) of 1998 was devised as a comprehensive mechanism to provide employment assistance and job training for those who needed it. The WIA was innovative in many ways, particularly in comparison to its legislative predecessors (Job Training Partnership Act and Comprehensive Education Training Act). The act brought together several disparate workforce and training programs under one umbrella. It also promoted a dual customer focus requiring local workforce boards to meet the needs of local businesses as well as retain their traditional focus on jobseekers. It established one-stop centers that would each serve as a local portal to all publicly funded workforce and training services both for local businesses and jobseekers. The act also stipulated that local business leaders play a greater role in workforce administration by being included on the Workforce Investment Boards(WIB). The intent of the act was that the workforce system be more demand driven and hence local administration more connected to the economies of which it was a part. All of these factors encouraged greater ties between the workforce system and those in the local economic and business arenas.

Finally, the use of sectors and/or clusters as a strategy to focus WD could provide a framework for the two sides to work together. In its simplest form, sector-based workforce development entails targeting particular high-growth industries, kinds of facilities, or companies on which to focus investment (Finkle 1999). At more advanced levels, cluster-based development focuses on identifying interdependent competitive industries in hopes of strengthening the linkages and improving the overall outcome of the economy to gain economic competitive advantage for the region (Porter 2000).

The demand-driven approach to WD is conducive to the use of sectors or clusters as a way to focus WD efforts.[1] The strategy has been well established as an ED approach for some time now. Over the last decade, workforce agencies have also started using this strategy to a greater extent. For WD agencies, the focus of sector initiatives has primarily been on creating employment opportunities for low-income people in the most promising sectors, whereas the goal for ED and business stakeholders has been to attract businesses and increase economic activity in the area regardless of the specific benefactors. Porter's (2000)

113

notion of creating competitive advantage, which emphasizes both the need for a well-trained workforce and the goal of attracting and expanding business activity, binds the two processes (WD and ED) together and makes them interdependent. The simultaneous focus of the two groups on specific sectors or clusters within a local economy could provide a common framework to link up the WD and ED.

Research Methodology

The purpose of this research was to investigate how local WD agencies in Michigan were dealing with the challenges presented by the economic recession of the early 2000s. Specifically, the study examined the relationships between public WD agencies and ED organizations in local areas and how those relationships affected strategies for coping with the difficult economic times. The intent was to develop theory about the relationship between workforce development and economic development WD and ED.

This study uses an embedded case study design wherein analysis of the Michigan case draws on the experiences of six Local Workforce Investment Areas (LWIAs) within the context of the state's economic and policy environment. Under the WIA, State Workforce Investment Boards, consisting of business leaders and public officials, are responsible for administration of WIA funds (among others) at the state level. Within each state, local Workforce Investment Boards (WIBs) are responsible for administration at the local level of designated LWIAs. This study used LWIAs as the unit of analysis for selecting participants. The group of LWIAs invited to participate were selected to capture variety on several characteristics over the study period (1999–2003), including unemployment rates, performance on Department of Labor's WIA performance measures,[2] number of clients served in WIA-funded programs, WIA funding levels, and level of urbanization. Of Michigan's twenty-five LWIAs, eight were invited to participate in the study and six participated.

The primary source of data for this research was in-depth semistructured interviews. Interviews were conducted with a total of forty-six administrators, staff, and Workforce Investment Board (WIB) members of Michigan Works! system between October 2004 and June 2005. The broad interview topics included strategies for implementing WD programs; local impacts of the economic recession; strategies for dealing with those impacts; and local relationships between WD and ED agencies and leaders. To supplement interview data, archival material either provided by the participants or found on public Web sites is included in this study. For example, WIA performance reports available for each LWIA on the U.S. Department of Labor's Web site were used to analyze WIA service levels and performance patterns. In addition, Web sites for local governments were reviewed to understand the organizational structure and relationship between public WD and ED functions in each area.

The overall approach to analysis was explanation building using the embedded cases. I conducted both individual case and cross-case analysis. Based on interview transcripts, each visit was summarized in the form of a structured case report to ensure uniform and consistent coverage of key themes. In addition, transcripts were coded based on key themes that emerged during analysis.

During the economic decline period, administrators of workforce development programs were in an extremely vulnerable position due to pressure to meet performance standards. Many of them were hesitant and some extremely reluctant to discuss these issues. In fact, my intentions in conducting the research were openly questioned on several occasions. In order to ease concerns, an assurance of the strictest confidentiality and anonymity was essential for both individual interviewees and participating local areas. To honor that assurance, limited information on the detailed characteristics of participating areas is presented here.

The Michigan Case

Michigan's Economy in the Early 2000s

As describe by Ballard (chapter 2) and Sands and Reese (chapter 3), in the early 2000s the Michigan economy was in a particularly tenuous state. The combination of macroeconomic forces (such as increased global competition for jobs, the shift to knowledge-based products and methods, and the rise in service jobs) combined to cause a national recession with particularly brutal effects in Michigan. The details of the Michigan economy have been discussed in detail earlier (chapter 2), so I will not fully recount them here. However, a few key points are worth highlighting to explain the challenges to the workforce system in Michigan.

The most basic indicator of the economic troubles in Michigan is the unemployment rate. As shown in figure 5.1, since 2001 the annual unemployment rate for Michigan has remained above that of the nation, with the gap steadily increasing. Several workforce administrators in Michigan interviewed for this research estimate the real unemployment rate in the state to be much higher. As one workforce administrator explained in reference to discouraged workers who are left out of the unemployment calculation, "They still want jobs. They just don't go to the unemployment agencies every week writing that down, and so they're not counted."

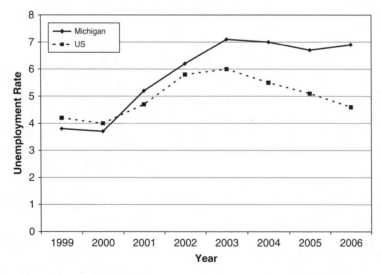

Source: U.S. Department of Labor.

FIGURE 5.1

Unemployment Rates in Michigan and United States, 1999–2006

Not only was the number of jobs shifting, but the nature of available jobs was as well. The state lost over 40,000 high-paying, low-education jobs between 1990 and 2003, and gained nearly 217,000 low-paying, low-education jobs (Glazer and Grimes 2004). According to Glazer and Grimes (2004), about 60 percent of the jobs added to the Michigan economy between 1990 and 2003 were in knowledge-based industries.[3] These knowledge-based jobs often require higher levels of education and different skills than those possessed by the laid-off manufacturing workers. This shift challenged the WD system; those seeking work needed to acquire job skills demanded in the new economy, and training providers had to find ways to provide the skills to more people with less federal funding.

Despite the job loss, in 2001 Michigan's average earnings per job were 2.5 percent above the national average (MEDC 2002). This has historically been the case in Michigan due to the prominence of the automobile industry and strong unionization. Hence, the challenge for the WD systems was to try to find employment for the dislocated workers with low-education levels who had lost unusually high-wage blue-collar jobs.

The changes taking place on the demand side of the labor market were only complicated by shifts in the nature of the labor supply. Between 1990 and 2000, the labor force in Michigan rose by 13 percent, primarily due to more women and younger people in the labor force. At the same time, the proportion of workers with a bachelor's degree or above rose by nearly 50 percent between 1991 and 2000. With more degree holders in the labor pool, naturally the education expectations and requirements of employers went up. By 2000, the workforce included a larger number of less-experienced and/or less-educated workers than it had a decade earlier and a greater number of degree holders for them to compete with.

These economic trends together created four related challenges for the WD system in Michigan:

1. The increased number of workers who entered the workforce during good economic times, but were laid off in the recession, were likely looking for jobs, and hence workforce offices had more clients than ever to serve.
2. Jobs being created were increasingly knowledge intensive, resulting in a mismatch for the skills of many of the laid-off workers and recent entrants in the labor market.
3. With the increase of bachelor's degree holders in the workforce, competition for the open jobs was much more intense and hence more challenging for the less-educated workers.
4. The high-earnings tradition made it difficult to convince laid-off blue-collar workers that low-paying service jobs were the only thing available for them without further training.

Amid all of the challenges in the economy during this time, public WD agencies had to find ways to overcome the obstacles and connect job seekers to jobs.

Public Workforce Development in Michigan
Public workforce in Michigan is administered by Michigan Works!, a statewide association of local workforce boards, local elected officials, and WD agency directors utilizing WIA and other funding sources. WIA funds are awarded to states, and states in turn disperse these

funds to LWIAs.[4] Each state and each local area is governed by a WIB. The act requires that the U.S. Department of Labor negotiate target performance levels with individual state WIBs and that state WIBs in turn negotiate performance levels with each local WIB within its boundaries.

Acting as the state WIB for Michigan, the Council for Labor and Economic Growth was created in December 2004 and given oversight authority for Michigan's workforce system. This seventy-three-member board includes key leaders from business, labor, community colleges, universities, community-based organizations, local workforce boards, the K-12 educational community, and government (Department of Labor and Economic Growth 2007).

At the beginning of this research in 2004, Michigan Works! consisted of twenty-five LWIAs (in Michigan, called Workforce Development Areas). Some of the LWIAs represent multiple jurisdictions, such as counties, whereas others in more populated areas may represent only a portion of a county or city.[5] Michigan Works! employees staff the local WIBs. Each local workforce area and its WIB are responsible for administering several federal, state, and local programs focused on employment and training. In order to provide the services required by the WIA, each local WIB contracts with local service providing agencies at various sites within its jurisdiction. The Michigan system includes 111 such sites.

Workforce development and its programs are highly susceptible to the economy's ups and downs. In Michigan, the increase in unemployment between 1999 and the early 2000s put a tremendous strain on the WD system. Participation in WIA-funded programs in Michigan increased steadily from 14,294 individuals enrolled in 2000 to 23,087 in 2003—an increase of 61 percent. As figure 5.2 illustrates, between 2001 and 2003 thirteen of the twenty-five local workforce areas in Michigan increased the number of people served by WIA funds by at least 50 percent. Nine of the twenty-five areas increased the number of people served by 100 percent or more, and one of those areas experienced an increase of 256 percent.[6] For the most part, however, resources did not increase in proportion to the demand for service. Figure 5.3 compares percentage changes in funding to percentage changes in people served under WIA in Michigan, showing that not only did funding decrease for both periods, but the number of people served under WIA increased at an even greater rate.

Thus, it is no surprise that for each of the first three years for which WIA performance data were reported, only four or five of the twenty-five workforce development areas in Michigan completely met their negotiated performance standards.[7] At the time that interviews for this research took place, many LWIAs continued struggling to reconcile DOL performance requirements with the economic reality in their areas.

Economic Development in Michigan

ED efforts occur at the state, regional, and local levels in Michigan. At the state level, the Michigan Economic Development Corporation (MEDC), a public-private organization with regional offices around the state, is charged with keeping businesses in Michigan and helping them grow; attracting new businesses; providing information on Michigan and its industries; providing assistance regarding site location, financing, employee recruitment and training, and acquiring permits; and coordinating site development, resources, and services (MEDC 2004).

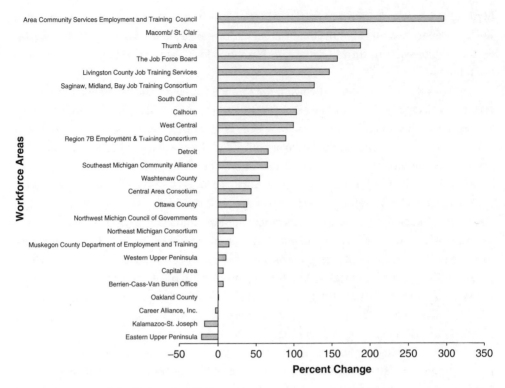

Source: U.S. Department of Labor Employment and Training.

FIGURE 5.2

Change in Participants Served by Michigan Workforce Areas

According to local workforce administrators, the MEDC's efforts vary from place to place. Some local areas' workforce staff reported during interviews that the local Chamber of Commerce or city ED office worked very closely with the MEDC; in other places, local workforce and ED leaders reported limited interaction with the state organization. One local workforce agency respondent thought it was the size of the business or development deal

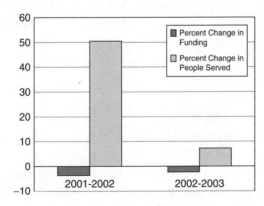

Sources: GAO Report; WIA Michigan Annual Report.

FIGURE 5.3

Percent Change in WIA Funding and People Served in Michigan, 2001/02–2002/03

under consideration that determined the level of MEDC versus local involvement. Indeed, local workforce staff tended to conceptualize ED in terms of local efforts, relationships, and traditions, including local manifestations of state and regional initiatives.

Fundamental to any discussion about the connection between WD and ED is a clarification of terms. Unlike the bureaucratic structure of the public workforce system, the haphazard nature of local economic development organizations and initiatives can make "economic development" hard to define and analyze. Much of the difficulty comes from ambiguity related to three broad categories: the process of implementing ED activity, the practices of local ED professionals, and the activities that contribute to ED goals but are undertaken by stakeholders not explicitly identified as part of the field of ED.

The American Economic Development Council uses a process-based definition of ED, which it defines as "creating wealth through the mobilization of human, financial, capital, physical and natural resources to generate marketable goods and services" (AEDC 1984: 18), while Blakely and Bradshaw (2002) focus more on the practice itself and define ED as the mechanism by which local governments or community-based organizations stimulate or maintain business activity and/or employment. On the ground, many different types of organizations and individual stakeholders undertake activities that contribute to attracting businesses, creating employment opportunities, and the enhancement of the business environment. Hence, a discussion of the connection between WD and ED necessarily includes those engaged in the broader process, the professional practice as well as the individual activities that are characterized as ED in nature.

This research suggests that the true embodiment of the ED concept is locally specific. When questioned about their partnerships with ED organizations, Michigan workforce administrators had locally developed understandings of which individuals, activities, and organizations fulfill the ED function in their areas. For example, in some areas, traditional ED offices exist within local government institutions and are responsible for administering incentives for new businesses and producing the ED plan for the area. In other, often rural, areas, ED is fully undertaken by local business owners and may consist of plans to improve the central business district in an effort to attract new businesses. In general, conceptualizations of the local administrators interviewed for this research combined local efforts with local manifestations of state and regional initiatives. The specific form of ED described in each area was embedded in local relationships, traditions regarding divisions of responsibility and protocol for undertaking these types of initiatives, and available resources.

Based on interview responses, four types or organizations stood out as common implementers of local ED in the areas studied: Chambers of Commerce, public agencies, development boards and councils, and individual business owners. However, in more rural settings often with few resources, there was often no entity specifically in charge of ED. In two such areas where interviews took place, the assumption was that if businesses needed information or assistance, the MEDC would be the most logical contact. In between the state and local levels are numerous regional initiatives, collaborations, and consortia that may link several jurisdictions together. For example, several ED organizations define their service areas as "Southwest Michigan" or "the Upper Peninsula," which suggests an area broader than a local region yet smaller than the state.

119

Research Findings: Six Ways the ED-WD Relationship Has Evolved

Two themes dominated the interviews: how workforce agency staff and their WIBs were navigating the difficult economic times and the relationship in each local area between the workforce agencies and ED agencies and stakeholders. It became clear that interview participants generally believed that a close relationship with ED agencies was crucial to addressing current economic challenges. Massive job losses in Michigan, the ailing auto industry, decreases in federal program funding, and out-migration of young, educated workers all culminated to heighten panic and urgency around consciously addressing the status of local economies. Economic challenges caused both sides to work harder to come up with meaningful and highly customized strategies to create a competitive local economy in their area. Interviews suggest that desperation to save local economies from devastation forced a great deal of innovation in partnership arrangements, strategic approaches, and resource sharing. Innovations came in the way WD and ED partnered, the roles they assumed, the way personal and business networks intersected, and the career paths of experts in the two fields. One agency director reflected on the economic crisis:

> I think that [the economic decline] has put us more in a competitive mode . . . . I can say that since there's just not enough to go around for everyone, we are working much smarter, and I think the partnerships are much more meaningful, and I think it's because of the partners themselves. I think we all come to the table now and we're very serious, we're in this together, and we're very committed to joint ownership, joint decision making, and joint sharing of resources. Anything other than that [total commitment] is just smoke in the air.

While economic challenges were at the forefront, they combined with other factors to create changes. Over the course of the research, it became clear that the relationship between ED and WD was evolving in significant ways. Some of the progress was due to direct action on the part of the actors involved; another portion is the result of broader changes in the economy, in work productivity, and in policy. The end result is that the division between WD and ED is no longer as wide, and, in fact, the connection between them has increased dramatically. From my research analysis, I am able to identify six factors that are contributing significantly to the evolution of the relationship between WD and ED in Michigan from the perspective or WD staff, administrators, and board members.

1. The Boundary between Workforce Development and Economic Development Is Less Precise

In many of Michigan's local workforce areas, the discrete division between the WD and ED functions is no longer as clear or distinct as it once was. Several changes have contributed to the blurred relationship.

First, in many areas the two functions have been brought together under one larger administrative unit. For example, Detroit's workforce development effort is now part of the Economic Development Organization (EDO), which encompasses the Employment and Training Department (workforce development), Detroit Economic Growth Corporation (economic development), and several other city agencies and outside organizations that play a role in the ED process. The goal of the EDO is to realize the "Mayor's vision of creating

120

a coordinated structure to streamline and coordinate all ED activities for Detroit" (City of Detroit Web page). The result of this innovative collaboration has been consistency, or at least common leadership, and in theory complementary goals, priorities, and vision.

Second, many organizations now serve either dual or multiple purposes, including both WD and ED. The director of one agency in a small rural workforce area asserted his team "does it all" due to limited funding and the need to multitask. He believed that "workforce and economic development are two sides of the same coin," and it is most effective to have one group of experts address the issues simultaneously. Others echoed this sentiment that ED and WD are one and the same and hence should not be separated.

Third, intermediary organizations whose sole purpose is to coordinate resources now work to create seamless systems. One administrator of an intermediary said, "Everybody plays a role in economic development, including the workforce folks, and somebody needs to fit the pieces together so that they add up to results." What is new is the recognition of the connectivity between the two functions and embodiment of "dual knowledge" in individual workers. Hence, the division between WD and ED organizations, functions, and workers is significantly less distinct.

2. The Players Are Changing

Interviews revealed the key players in the workforce development arena have changed dramatically. Local business leaders are involved, and WD agencies are attracting employees with a broader array of education and training backgrounds. In addition, the WIA mandated that business leaders become a more substantial part of workforce investment boards, with the idea that businesses would then become legitimate customers of the one-stop centers. Beyond meeting this mandate, several workforce administrators thought that business leaders have become more interested in labor force development and taken a more active role because the business leaders had realized the importance of a well-trained workforce for a competitive economy. Specifically, WD administrators identified industry leaders, business owners, Chamber of Commerce leaders, and executives at local corporations as those currently involved, in contrast to a decade ago. One administrator boasted that "my WDB [Workforce Development Board] members are all CEOs." He also made the point that those running WD agencies are no longer necessarily "social workers." The ED perception of the WD function as a social service to low-income welfare recipients was echoed by the majority of interview participants. However, one of the workforce agencies where interviews were conducted had four staff members who held Master's of Business Administration (MBAs), the degree often held by those in the corporate workforce. Several interviewees believed that this new cadre of business players on the workforce side has increased the willingness of ED organizations and other business owners to work with the entire workforce team.

3. Intersecting Networks, Shared Knowledge, and Social Capital Have Led to a Better Connection

Networks of institutions, initiatives, and professional relationships have proliferated and become more sophisticated both within and between the ED and WD domains, crossing the boundaries that historically divided the two fields. For example, there has been a tremendous

121

upsurge in the number of organizations—such as boards, collaborations, regional commissions, and so on—that network people together. To address the complex issues these groups face, stakeholders from a wide spectrum of specializations are involved. For instance, one regional commission reviewed in this research included members from the local Chamber of Commerce, K-12 education, higher education, trade organizations, local businesses, and several social service organizations. One workforce administrator who also is a member of the commission explained that a group structured in this way "brings people out of the silos" that have kept them separate. Further, several administrators explained that they continue to sit on the same boards and working groups even after their official title and/or organizational affiliations have changed. The result of more local, regional, and national networks, made up of individuals with diverse backgrounds and interests taking on workforce and ED issues simultaneously, has been a great deal more crossover and connectivity between the two fields.

Beyond increased networks, cross-fertilizing career paths of high-level experts have also created new connections between the fields. Several administrators interviewed had held positions in both WD and ED. This has led to two important changes. First, the dialogue on either side is broader when lead administrators have experience and knowledge of both sides. And second, the increased connectedness is embedded in the social capital of individuals who can access key players on both sides of the ED/WD field. For example, one agency director explained that because he had worked for decades in workforce related positions in state government, had headed an economic development organization, and was now directing a local workforce agency, people knew him and his work, and so he had access to and the attention of key decision makers on both sides. Because his reputation and past affiliations got him in the door, he could put important workforce issues in front of ED decision makers, and visa versa.

4. Customization Has Led to Collaboration

Attempts to build economies on existing local assets and to consider local traditions and relationships have led to the development of highly customized strategies that are based on local institutions, resources, and relationships already in place. Leveraging of these local assets has necessitated the formation of new partnerships and collaborations. Some of these partnerships have occurred directly between WD and ED organizations, and some circuitously by way of their partners. Several agency leaders told similar stories of being in a survival mode trying to create a plan based on the local area's assets and deciding to join forces rather than "reinvent the wheel." This sentiment is shared by many across the nation. In a recent survey on the relationship between workforce development and economic development organizations, respondents reported sharing resources quite frequently. Eighty-four percent of the workforce administrators surveyed reported sharing customers with local economic development organizations, while 79 percent share committees, 36 percent share funds, 29 percent share staff, and 19 percent share space (Harper-Anderson 2008).

One example in Michigan was a "one-stop" office combining all human and space resources between the WD and ED partners, to fill gaps in the previous system. In this office there was no differentiation in staff regardless of which agency paid the employee. Employees for this group of agencies were all located in one place, wore identical ID badges, and assisted customers, including the WIA staff, local community colleges, and a private staffing agency. The agency administrator explained that this arrangement worked in this particular area because of the unique relationship between the agencies involved and a local understanding regarding how they would combine resources.

Other examples of customization reported by several agencies included workforce training programs designed to meet the needs of specific local ED initiatives under way. One respondent explained that in his area, the only remaining manufacturing employer decided to relocate, so his agency worked with the local ED organization to design a specific training program to create a pool of skilled workers for new technologies to breathe life into the floundering plant. The new program targeted a segment of workforce clients that had been hard to place, utilizing their relationship with a nearby trade school for certain components of the program. By customizing a local strategy, this area was able to meet the immediate ED needs and utilize existing resources, including local trade schools, all while meeting the local WD agency's need to serve hard-to-place clients.

Many workforce agency leaders made it clear that integration into a larger system of service delivery based on specifics in their particular areas was necessary for successfully connecting people to jobs. Supportive services such as child care, parenting classes, nutritional support, and transportation had to be tied together with workforce programs and local ED initiatives. The interviews revealed that each local area had developed a highly customized service delivery system that required a great deal of partnering and collaboration. This collaboration was the intended spirit of the WIA, and those in local areas believed it was encouraged by the state as well. One agency director discussed her perception of the state's stance on how WD funds are used: "I think everybody takes a look at how best to implement programs in their area. They [the state] understand that each of us has to work with what we have and what will work based on other institutions and resources in our areas. So they let us design our own system to some extent."

Attempts to tailor programs to a particular area's needs have involved careful consideration of what each stakeholder can offer to make success more likely. As one director put it, "In an area like this, with long-standing relationships and traditions, you just can't get things done using the cookie-cutter approach. You have to devise strategies that will mesh with what works here." She went on to say that "trying to devise a plan that works specifically for this area requires strange bedfellows, but this is what is necessary based on our history and the politics of this area." Several of the local areas have formalized their collaboration efforts in contractual agreements. One director of a local WIB explained that formal agreements allow the WD agency and the ED council to share not only space and operating expenses but also "the whole process of planning and implementing a strategy to sustain and strengthen our economy."

5. Politics and Policy Have Dictated Connectivity

In March 2004, a floundering state economy caused the governor of Michigan to declare war on unemployment. Governor Jennifer Granholm stated that she wanted the thousands of unfilled jobs in the state to be filled in the following six months. In a press conference in early 2005, the governor stated:

> We'll combine state and federal resources and tap the tremendous potential of our community colleges. In the year ahead, we expect to match up to 30,000 Michigan residents with jobs that are going waiting today . . . . Right now, Southeast Michigan is turning to Canada to fill 3,000 positions in the health care industry . . . . Detroit Medical Center has 400 vacancies for nurses, medical technicians, and laboratory staff. Henry Ford has another 500. These are good jobs. Jobs that we can train qualified people for right here in Michigan. And, most importantly, because there's just no substitute for quality health care close to home—these jobs won't ever be out-sourced." (Granholm 2005)

From the view of several of the workforce administrators interviewed, Governor Granholm's statement meant that the MEDC and the ED leaders must start talking to and coordinating with WD leaders to make the system work better.

6. Workforce Development Is Now Acting More Like Traditional Economic Development

Perhaps the most important factor that has both complicated and strengthened the connections between WD and ED is that workforce agencies and professionals are increasingly acting more like traditional economic developers. The ways in which administrators and staff conceptualize their roles have increasingly included new functions not previously on the WD agenda, due in part to the strategies of the WIA of 1998, which are based more on business concepts than on traditional approaches of social services. Most of the administrators interviewed wanted to be regarded as important contributors to the creation of a competitive regional economy, not as social workers. This attitude, more reflective of business logic and market principles, brings new approaches to customers, business strategies, self-images, and even organization names. The result has been a fundamental redefinition of the relationship between WD and ED professionals and organizations. Fitzgerald and Green Leigh (2002) characterize this phase of WD as market driven and connect it to Porter's (2000) regional competitive approach.

One important development here is how workforce developers have increasingly begun taking the more common ED strategy of sector- and/or cluster-based approaches to their efforts. In its simplest form, sector-based workforce development targets investment in particular high-growth industries, kinds of facilities, or companies based on a local or regional competitive advantage (Finkle 1999). At more advanced levels, interdependent competitive industries may cluster to gain a competitive advantage (Porter 2000).

The WD focus in the old model was primarily on creating employment opportunities for low-income people, whereas the goal for ED has been to attract businesses and increase economic activity in general regardless of the specific benefactors. Now, creating or advancing a competitive advantage requires a well-trained workforce matched to specific new or expanded business activity, thereby binding together the WD and ED processes. While the idea of focusing on specific sectors is not new, the amalgamation of WD and ED goals created through deliberate collaboration and structured interaction is a step forward and could hold promise for how the two sides can focus their efforts more effectively in the future.

Many WD leaders in this study believed that sector-based strategies allowed them to focus on local economic strengths, including their unique labor force. As one workforce administrator put it, "We began by looking around and asking, what are we in a position to take advantage of?" When asked how they customized their programs, almost all of the administrators mentioned using sector- or cluster-based strategies, targeted not just to the needs of low-income workers but rather to building a strong economy that links newly trained low-income workers to new or expanding businesses in the area. When asked about partnerships with economic developers, many workforce administrators immediately began discussing their cluster and/or sector strategies.

The effectiveness of using sector-based approaches for bridging the gap between WD and ED appears to lie in the fact that these approaches provide a framework that incorporates the goals of and provides a role for both ED and WD. The decision to focus on a particular set of sectors or clusters seems to provide a clear mission for WD agencies on where to focus their training of workers and services to employers. On the flip side, with a unified vision, ED leaders know to focus their activities on the same industries or sectors for maximum impact on the economy. Some sort of agreement or understanding of what those targets are seems to create a point of convergence for the two sides. Based on interviews, it appears that this "convergence space"—that is, the common ground—has forged greater interaction and increased understanding of each other's roles and strategies for innovation, specifically how the two sides connect.

Another prevalent and dramatic example of how workforce developers are acting more like economic developers is seen through an increased emphasis on marketing and branding. One administrator boasted, "I spend $300,000 a year on marketing, billboards, TV, radio, and direct ad mail. . . . I target every business in the area with five or more employees." Other workforce agencies have hired professional marketing firms and paid for slick new logos. One administrator writes a weekly local newspaper column and has a talk radio show to promote his organization. Some organizations have changed their names, some have renovated their buildings, and others have invested heavily in traditional marketing, using television, billboards, and radio ads to become more appealing to their business customers and partners.

That workforce agencies struggle against the stigma of serving welfare clients and being viewed as social service organizations is not a new phenomenon. Previous research has shown that whereas economic developers are often regarded as partners with business, workforce developers are regarded as social workers (Fitzgerald 2004a). While they have tried before to escape that image, workforce developers are now trying new approaches that focus on businesses as their primary customers. One workforce administrator with an extreme view said:

> The jobseekers are not my clients. The businesses are my only clients. At the end of the day they are the ones who have the jobs that I want to fill. So, I use all of my resources and energy to market my organization and services to them. I am all over the place just like any other business making sure that they know who we are and what we have to offer them and quite frankly why we are a smarter choice than some staffing firm.

Although most interviewees' views were not quite as extreme, the spirit of these remarks was common, reflecting an increased customer-service focus on businesses in addition to job seekers.

Not only are WD offices dealing with their business customers in a more business-like manner, they are proactively pursuing businesses to use their facilities and services and to employ their job-seeking clients. In the old model, one workforce administrator explained, the workforce staff accompanied ED staff to meetings when requested, or they would wait for the ED staff to send businesses to them. Such interactions are no longer the only mode of contact, as workforce developers now often take the lead by setting up their own meetings with new or expanding businesses.

Using innovations in information technology, the aggressive pursuit of business clients has included the creation of new products and services such as customized information provision, geographic information services, and current labor market information. These innovations have been instrumental in building rapport with and confidence from potential employers.

While many of the activities described above look like ED, the underlying motivations remain true to the spirit of WD. Several interviewees stressed that their ultimate goal is to create a strong economy through attraction, retention, job creation, and innovation, in an effort not simply to boost economic indicators but also to increase the well-being of job-seekers. One emphatically said that "it's all about putting more people to work, retaining more good jobs for people . . . not just about making corporations more profitable."

The various trends described above have placed workforce development agencies and economic development organizations in a common realm. The combination of development has resulted in increased connectivity at three levels: direct connectivity, connectivity via overlap, and institutional/network connectivity. Table 5.1 divides several of the contributing factors according to types of connections. Each of the changes described above have contributed to one or multiple types of connectivity. For example, the less precise boundary between WD and ED has both created connectivity via overlapping activities and through intermediary organizations that address both ED and WD issues. At all levels, new connections have formed based on the evolving relationships between the two sides and in the transformations of attitudes and needs within each. All of these connections and intersections have created opportunities to develop and/or refine a common language and lens for framing the issues and approaches that seek to enable more productive interactions and collaborations. The shift has contributed to a more common framework from which leaders

Table 5.1. Typology of Workforce Development and Economic Development Connectivity

Direct Connections	Overlap	Institutional and Network Connections
Formal agreements	Blurred boundaries	Boards and commissions
Joint projects	Dual purpose organizations	Intermediary organizations
Shared resources	Overlapping roles	Intersecting networks
New partnerships	Shared knowledge	

and organizations in the two fields approach their work. A key theme that echoed through-out the interviews with WD personnel is that now their goal is to think strategically and work toward self-sustaining systems, whereas before the goal was geared more toward "placing individual bodies in jobs." This goal of empowerment and economic sustainability is very compatible with the ED concept of creating competitive advantage.

Despite the resounding call for stronger connectivity and the beginning of more collab-orative efforts, there is still a great deal of work to be done. Specifically, the WD administra-tors interviewed in Michigan saw a need for more consistent and systematic connectivity as compared to the sporadic and ad hoc model that they see now. They complain that while they can attest to project collaboration, the juncture between the ED system and WD sys-tem in local areas is far from seamless. The good news is that forward progress is occurring. Alongside the economic push, changes between and within WD and ED have facilitated a closer relationship between the two. The key finding of this research is that evolution in the roles that the two domains play, the relationships among institutions and individuals, and the work styles of these entities have all been instrumental in changing the nature of inter-action between WD agencies and professionals and their ED counterparts toward greater connectivity. Although the trend toward linkage is not new, understanding the dynamics of how the individual pieces and the relationship are evolving is critical for continued progress on closing the gap. The Michigan case suggests that several factors underlie both the per-ception of a decreasing gap and real progress in linking these areas together.

Conclusions and Policy Implications

The Michigan study suggests that economic necessity is driving workforce development and economic development closer together in an organic process that depends on specific local conditions and on local manifestations of macrolevel trends. However, the changes in the relationship are extremely complex. They represent the culmination of shifts in the macro-economy, policy, institutional structures, and the labor market. The specific manifestation of these combined forces in Michigan is reflected in the evolutions uncovered here. In many of Michigan's local areas, ED and WD agencies came together to get the most out of their limited resources. What began out of necessity, however, is now seen in many places as the only way to move forward.

Cluster- or sector-based strategies provide a role for both sides and focus their responses on the local manifestations of macroeconomic developments that made them vulnerable in the first place. How the cluster concept will unfold remains to be seen. One criticism of the approach is the uncertainty and risk associated with trying to pick "winners." The purpose of this report is not to promote sector-based strategies, but rather to point out their grow-ing importance as well as their usefulness for engaging and linking the two complementary functions. The key lesson to be learned from Michigan is that a unity of vision and purpose was necessary to bring WD and ED teams together to design mutually beneficial innovative strategies.

While the idea of focusing on specific sectors is not new, the amalgamation of WD and ED goals to support a jointly devised vision created through deliberate collaboration and structured interaction is definitely a step forward and could hold promise for how the two sides can focus their efforts more effectively in the future. Continuing to work in that collaborative spirit toward comprehensive, competitive, and innovative approaches to achieving WD and ED goals seems to hold a great deal of promise for building stronger, more economically and socially sustainable systems for creating jobs, creating a strong workforce, and having the two match up.

Although the conclusions drawn here are strictly from the perspective of Michigan WD administrators, the findings have been confirmed in follow-up studies both with ED administrators in Michigan and with workforce agencies across the country (see Harper-Anderson 2007, 2008). Specifically, quantitative research confirms that both WD and ED administrators believe that the two functions have become more connected over the last five years (Harper-Anderson 2007). In addition, the economy is a major reason for their collaboration (Harper-Anderson 2008). Finally, the level of connection and the use of the sector-based approach have had a positive influence on achievement of workforce- and economic-related outcomes.

Several unresolved issues and role conflicts still need to be worked out between the stakeholders and organizations in WD and those in ED. Specific processes and procedures guiding the interaction between the two domains are constantly evolving and must be customized for the multiple levels and forms of ED. In addition, as in any type of relationship, the union between WD and ED in each local context is uniquely contoured by local institutions, the traditions and politics of the area, and the specific details of that local area's economy. Despite these continuing challenges, the process thus far has produced encouraging results, suggesting that the two sides can find common ground.

From a policy perspective, these findings suggest that federal and state workforce and ED policies should acknowledge the interdependencies between the two domains. A critical factor for the success of collaboration lies in locally constructed views of the key players and objectives. A common complaint from interviewees was stringent regulations that separate funding sources and hold each side to unconnected measures of success, which limits their ability to create and implement unified strategic planning. When we use lenses and definitions that are too broad and attempt to make generalizations about relationships and phenomena that are very locally specific, we fail to see forward progress and innovation as readily. Allowing flexibility to customize the way funds get used and to determine who the most beneficial partners are in a given area is more consistent with today's economic reality and the evolving relationship between WD and ED in specific local areas. This research suggests that greater attention and flexibility for locally driven meaning and success criteria could be the key to better understanding the progress being made toward bridging the gap between economic development and workforce development.

Notes

This study was funded by the generous support of the Center for Local State and Urban Policy at the University of Michigan. An earlier version of this manuscript was published as "Coming Together in Tough Economic Times: Workforce Development and Economic

Development Move Closer in Michigan" Policy Report No. 10, Center for Local State and Urban Policy, University of Michigan, January 2008.

1. Consistent with the findings of Fitzgerald and Green Leigh (2002), most of the people in the workforce development organizations that I interviewed invariably used the terms "cluster," "sector," and "targeted industry." Henceforth I will refer to the strategies involved as sector based, with the understanding that more complex iterations including clusters are also included.

2. The WIA of 1998 established seventeen performance measures related to the implementation of the act. Each state negotiates yearly targets for performance on each measure with the U.S. Department of Labor, and the state in turn negotiates target levels with each of its LWIAs. Specific data on performance can be obtained from http://www.doleta.gov/performance/results/wia_national_performance.cfm.

3. Knowledge jobs include those in management, research and development, engineering and design, purchasing, logistics, marketing, and finance (Glazer and Grimes 2002).

4. In 2004, there were 640 workforce areas in the United States.

5. See http://www.michiganworks.org/page.cfm/14 for a map of Michigan Development Areas.

6. Based on Michigan Annual WIA Reports Program Years 2000, 2001, 2002,and 2003.

7. It is important to point out that the while many local areas in Michigan did not meet their performance standards, the state has consistently met its performance requirements by negotiating performance levels with local areas above the federal negotiated state levels and by renegotiating their requirements with the DOL when necessary.

REFERENCES

American Economic Development Council (AEDC). 1984. *Economic Development Today: A Report to the Profession*. Schiller Park, Ill.: AEDC.

Benner, C., S. Herzenberg, and K. Prince. 2003. *A Workforce Development Agenda for Pennsylvania's New Governor: Building the Infrastructure of a Learning Economy*. Harrisburg, Pa.: Keystone Research Center.

Blakely, E. J., and T. K. Bradshaw. 2002. *Planning Local Economic Development Theory and Practice*. 3rd ed. Thousand Oaks, Calif.: Sage.

Buss, T. F. 1999. The Case against Targeted Industry Strategies. *Economic Development Quarterly* 13(4):339–356.

Cappetti, P., ed. 1997. *Change at Work*. New York: Oxford University Press.

Castells, M. 1996. *The Rise of the Network Society*. Cambridge, Mass.: Blackwell.

———. 1997. *The Power of Identity*. Cambridge, Mass.: Blackwell.

Chapple, K. 2005. Wicked Problems, Local Solutions. Paper presented at the forty-seventh annual meeting of the Association of Collegiate Schools of Planning, Kansas City, Missouri.

City of Detroit Web page. Http://www.ci.detroit.mi.us/econdevel/about_the_edo.htm.

Clarke, S. E., and G. L. Gaile. 1998. *The Work of Cities*. Minneapolis: University of Minnesota Press.

Conway, M., and I. Rademacher. 2002. *SEDLP Synthesis of Findings: Working with Value: Industry Specific Approaches to Workforce Development*. Washington, D.C.: Aspen Institute.

Department of Labor and Economic Growth Web page. Http://www.mi.gov/mdcd/0,1607,7–122–1678_43625—,00.html.

Dressner, J., and W. Fleischer. 1998. Next Door: A Concept Paper for Place-Based Employment Initiatives. New York: Corporations for Supportive Housing Research.

Eberts, R. W., and G. Erickek. 2002. The Role of Partnerships in Economic Development and Labor Markets in the United States. Upjohn Institute for Employment Research, Working Paper 02–75.

Ellwood, D. T. 1999. The Plight of the Working Poor Children's. Roundtable No. 2. Washington, D.C.: Brookings Institution.

Fagan, J. H. 2000. Do Northeast Ohio's Drivers Derive Competitive Advantage from Shared Labor? *Economic Development Quarterly* 14(1):111–125.

Finkle, J. A. 1999. The Case against Targeting Might Have Been More . . . Targeted. *Economic Development Quarterly* 13(4):361–364.

Fitzgerald, J. 1993. Labor Force, Education and Work. In *Theories of Local Economic Development,* edited by R. D. Bingham and R. Mier. Newbury Park, Calif.: Sage.

———. 2004a. Moving the Workforce Intermediary Agenda Forward. *Economic Development Quarterly* 18(1):3–9.

———. 2004b. Pathways to Good Jobs: Can Career Ladders Solve the Low Wage Problem? *American Prospect* 15(1):57–59.

Fitzgerald, J., and V. Carlson. 2000. Ladders to a Better Life. *American Prospect* 11(15):54–60.

Fitzgerald, J., and N. Green Leigh. 2002. *Economic Revitalization: Cases and Strategies for City and Suburbs.* Thousand Oaks, Calif.: Sage.

Florida, R. L. 2002. *The Rise of the Creative Class and How It's Transforming Work, Leisure, Community and Everyday Life.* New York: Basic Books.

Ganzglass, E., M. Jensen, N. Ridley, M. Simon, and C. Thompson. 2001. *Transforming State Workforce Development Systems: Case Studies of Five Leading States.* Washington, D.C.: National Governor's Association Center for Best Practices.

Giloth, R. P. 1998. *Jobs and Economic Development: Strategies and Practices.* Thousand Oaks, Calif.: Sage.

———. 2000. Learning from the Field: Economic Growth and Workforce Development in the 1990s. *Economic Development Quarterly* 124(4):340–359.

———. 2003. Workforce Intermediaries: Partnerships for the Future. Economic Development Quarterly. 17(3):215–219.

Glazer, L., and D. Grimes. 2002. *Michigan Workers in the Boom Years: Employment and Employment Earnings 1991–2000.* Ann Arbor: Institute of Labor and Industrial Relations, University of Michigan.

———. 2004. *A New Path to Prosperity? Manufacturing and Knowledge-Based Industries as Drivers of Economic Growth.* Ann Arbor: Institute of Labor and Industrial Relations, University of Michigan.

Granholm, Jennifer. 2005. State of the State Address. Lansing, Michigan, February 8.

Harper-Anderson, E. 2007. He Said, She Said: Comparing the Perspectives of Economic Development and Workforce Development Administrators on Factors Affecting Local Connection. Paper presented at the forty-eighth annual meeting of the Association of Collegiate Schools of Planning, Milwaukee.

———. 2008. Measuring the Connection between Economic Development and Workforce Development: Examining the Role of Sector–Based Strategies for Local Outcomes. *Economic Development Quarterly* 22(2):119–135.

Harrison, B., et al. 1995. *Building Bridges: Community Development Corporations and the World of Employment Training.* New York: Ford Foundation.

Harrison, B., and Weiss, M. S. 1998. *Workforce Development Networks: Community-Based Organizations and Regional Alliances.* Thousand Oaks, CA: Sage Publications.

Hughes, M. A. 1996. *The Administrative Geography of Devolving Social Welfare Programs.* Washington D.C.: Brookings Institution, Center on Urban and Metropolitan Policy.

Lerman, R. I., and F. Skidmore. 1999. *Helping Low-Wage Workers: Policies for the Future.* Washington D.C.: U.S. Department of Labor.

Markusen, A. 2004. Targeting Occupations in Regional and Community Economic Development. *Journal of the American Planning Association* 70(3):253–268.

Melendez, E., ed. 2004. *Communities and Workforce Development.* Kalamazoo, Mich.: W. E. Upjohn Institute for Employment Research.

Michigan Economic Development Corporation (MEDC). 2002. *The Michigan Economy: 1989–2002.* Lansing: Michigan Economic Development Corporation.

———. 2004. Http://www.michigan.org/index.asp.

O'Shea, D., and C. T. King. 2001. *The Workforce Investment Act of 1998: Restructuring Workforce Development Initiatives in States and Localities.* Albany, N.Y.: Nelson A. Rockefeller Institute of Government.

Osterman, P. 1999. *Securing Prosperity.* New York: Century Foundation.

Parr, J. B. 2002. Agglomeration and Trade: Some Additional Aspects. *Regional Studies* 36(6):675–684.

Peters, A., and P. Fisher. 2004. The Failures of Economic Development Incentives. *Journal of the American Planning Association* 70(1):27–37.

Peters, D. J. 2005. Using Labor-Based Industry Complexes for Workforce Development in Missouri. *Economic Development Quarterly* 19(2):138–156.

Pindus, N. M., C. O'Brien, M. Conway, C. Haskins, and I. Rademacher. 2004. *Evaluation of the Sectoral Employment Demonstration Program.* Washington, D.C.: Urban Institute.

Porter, M. E. 2000. Location, Competition, and Economic Development: Local Clusters in a Global Economy. *Economic Development Quarterly* 14(1):15–34.

Riccio, J. A. 1999. *Mobilizing Public Housing Communities for Work: Origins and Early Accomplishments of the JOBS-PLUS Demonstration.* New York: Manpower Development Research Corporation.

Ranney, D. C., and J. J. Betancur 1992. Labor-Force-Based Development: A Community-Oriented Approach to Targeting Job Training and Industrial Development. *Economic Development Quarterly* 6(3):286–296.

Rosenfeld, S. A. 2003. Expanding Opportunities: Cluster Strategies That Reach More People and More Places. *European Planning Studies* 11(4):359–377.

Strawn, J., and K. Martinson. 2000. *Steady Work and Better Jobs: How to Help Low Income Parents Sustain Employment and Advance in the Workforce.* New York: Manpower Development Research Corporation.

U.S. Bureau of Labor Statistics Web site. Http://www.bls.gov/.

Wiewel, W. 1999. Policy Research in an Imperfect World: Response to Terry Buss, "The Case against Targeted Industry Strategies." *Economic Development Quarterly* 13(4):357–360.

Wilson, W. J. 1998. *When Work Disappears.* New York: Basic Books.

PART 2

Environmental Concerns

Flushing the Conflict: Wastewater Cooperation among Michigan's Local Governments?

Eric S. Zeemering

Wastewater policy debates in Michigan are characterized by both conflict and cooperation. The potential for cooperation is great. Public works and utilities are frequently the subject of interlocal service contracts, as seen in research from Michigan and other states (cf. LeRoux and Carr 2007; Marando 1968; Wood 2006; Zeemering 2007).[1] Local governments can contract for wastewater service with neighbors who already produce the service, jointly build and operate a wastewater treatment facility, or form a special district or authority for that purpose.[2] Yet local officials' discussions about wastewater policy, as portrayed in newspaper coverage, are often characterized by conflict. The conflict frequently involves tensions between older central cities that have built and control wastewater infrastructure and younger suburban neighbors who contract for the service. The extension of sewerage is interconnected with patterns of metropolitan development; therefore, citizens and policy makers should be attentive to opportunities to flush conflict and promote interlocal cooperation on wastewater treatment. Cooperative wastewater policy dialogue could be an important component of greater metropolitan cooperation in Michigan. However, evidence in this chapter shows that the topic of land use and metropolitan growth is *not* a major focus of news coverage about wastewater policy.

This study analyzes newspaper coverage of wastewater policy debates because newspaper coverage provides an important link between policy makers and the mass public. Newspaper coverage helps citizens understand the primary points of conflict in local wastewater policy. The media also provide an outlet for local elites to frame or shape public understanding about interjurisdictional negotiations. Various studies about service contracting and network management investigate the skills used by administrators to negotiate intergovernmental cooperation (Kickert, Klijn, and Koppenjan 1997; Agranoff and McGuire 2003,

2004; Goldsmith and Eggers 2004; Kamensky and Burlin 2004). Other studies investigate how demographic, financial, geographic, or social network characteristics of local governments contribute to service cooperation decisions (Friesema 1971; LeRoux and Carr 2007; Marando 1968; Morgan and Hirlinger 1991; Thurmaier and Wood 2002; Wood 2006). Yet greater attention must be given to the link between local elites' policy debates about interlocal cooperation, the information conveyed to citizens through the media, and subsequent public understanding of metropolitan cooperation and conflict. This study adds to our understanding of local government cooperation by investigating a small part of this process. How is public debate about wastewater policy framed in newspaper coverage and communicated to the public? Is wastewater cooperation conveyed as something potentially related to land use, or is citizen attention directed toward other frames? Further, do citizens read about instances of cooperation, or does coverage emphasize conflict?

To consider these questions, this chapter analyzes the case of Grand Rapids and the neighboring North Kent Sewer Authority (NKSA). Grand Rapids and the NKSA were engaged in an active wastewater policy debate beginning in the late 1990s and ending with the NKSA commitment to build a new wastewater treatment plant. The case study has implications for other regions managing wastewater conflict and cooperation. Content analysis of newspaper coverage quantifies evidence about how often citizens read particular frames or emphases in coverage of wastewater policy debate. The frames studied include land use, public finance, political control or decision making authority over wastewater infrastructure, and environmental concerns. This investigation sheds light on what citizens are being told about cooperation on wastewater treatment, and considers the implications for citizen understanding of metropolitan affairs.

Citizens and Newspaper Coverage of Wastewater Policy Debates

Why should policy makers and researchers be interested in the content of newspaper coverage about wastewater policy debates, rather than investigating actual disputes, decisions, and agreements? By analyzing the content of policy debates, we can identify issues that are present in the discussion, as well as the absence of issues that we might expect to see. In a comparison of water, sewerage, and urban growth policies in several U.S. metropolitan areas, Kenney, Downing, and Hayes (1972: 1) argue, "public policies concerning the provision of public water and sewerage services can and does [sic] have an important effect on the pattern, character, and sequence of urbanization. Unfortunately, the users of these potentially powerful tools for guiding urban growth only rarely recognize this." Analyzing newspaper coverage allows us to evaluate how conflict between Grand Rapids and the NKSA was explained to the public. At the least, this approach has the potential to alert citizens and policy makers to the absence of an integrated wastewater and metropolitan growth discussion.

As policy makers engage in the complex process of structuring mutually beneficial arrangements, reconciling the interests of individual jurisdictions and the larger metropolitan community, the logic of wastewater cooperation (or noncooperation) may be publicly explained in multiple ways. These explanations, or aspects of the wastewater policy debate, can be thought about as issue frames competing for space in newspaper coverage. "Frames highlight some bits of information about an item that is the subject of a communication, thereby elevating them in salience" (Entman 1993: 53). For the current study, the primary source or communicator of issue frames is an individual newspaper story.[3] When reading about wastewater policy debates, do citizens receive stories that emphasize particular aspects of the conflict over others? If so, which frames are relevant to advance our under-standing of metropolitan conflict and cooperation in Michigan? Newspaper coverage may consistently emphasize one aspect of the conflict over a period of time, or multiple frames may compete, offering the public more than one explanation about the challenges local policy makers face in achieving wastewater cooperation.

Interest in the link between metropolitan land use and wastewater policy may direct policy makers' attention to the presence or absence of land use discussion in wastewater policy dialogue. But several other frames may also be relevant and emphasized in newspaper coverage. Considering four different issue frames in this research allows for an exploration of competing explanations for cooperation and conflict in wastewater policy. Presence or absence of the four frames—land use, public finance, political control of infrastructure, and environmental concerns—may have different implications for the development of inter-jurisdictional cooperation on wastewater. These four frames have been deductively selected and developed, based on research in urban administration and due to this volume's normative interest in connections between public policy and the growth, governance, and vitality of Michigan's metropolitan areas.[4]

To better understand each frame, a review of existing research explicates the relationship between the frame and wastewater policy debate. Each frame may also be relevant to the development of interjurisdictional conflict and cooperation; thus the review of each frame also comments on the frame's relevance to interjurisdictional cooperation. After discussing each of the four frames, content analysis is discussed as a methodological approach to measure frames. Then, the study considers the use of each frame in the case of Grand Rapids' wastewater policy debate.

Wastewater Policy and Metropolitan Land Use

Clearly, the extension of water and sewerage has a demonstrable effect on urbanization and development patterns in metropolitan areas. Thus, we can predict that land use will be an important frame shaping wastewater policy debate. Central cities in American metropolitan areas have been large-scale producers of wastewater treatment service, and many central cities grew by annexing neighboring territory so that residents could obtain desired urban services, such as sewerage. But central cities lost their monopoly on these services early in the history of U.S. urban development. As the costs of developing infrastructure in the sub-urbs decreased, annexation to central cities became less desirable (Dilworth 2003, 2005). Suburbs capable of developing their own wastewater infrastructure could decouple from the central city and plan their own growth and development. Fragmentation pressures contin-ued over time. In response to dramatic post–World War II suburban growth, some metro-politan areas adopted cooperative regional approaches to wastewater treatment, with a strong role for central cities; yet other small and suburban communities continued to develop their own wastewater infrastructure, often with aid from the federal government (Melosi 2000: chapter 16). As suburbs developed their own sewerage, central cities lost a useful tool for directing, or at least having a say in, metropolitan growth.

Development patterns allowed by local governments through their zoning codes have implications for the cost of sewerage. Development and land use patterns impact the cost of building and maintaining sewerage. Spier and Stephenson (2002) use a simulation to test how variations in land use affect the costs of water and wastewater service. Their model suggests costs are "most sensitive" to changes in lot size. Higher housing tract dispersion and greater distance between service production facilities and housing centers also increase infrastructure costs. Officials in many jurisdictions are aware of these relationships and may discuss both land use and sewerage when talking about local policy. Burby, Kaiser, and Moreau (1988: 126) surveyed water and sewer utilities in nine states. They found that 61 percent of municipal providers and 69 percent of county utilities attempted to use extension policy to support specific land use plans. Only 41 percent of municipalities reported that land use planning was used as a source to guide water and sewer extension. Because land use patterns impact the cost of service provision, land use is expected to be a salient frame in wastewater policy debates.

Local government officials, seeking opportunities for economic development, might also integrate their discussions of wastewater policy and land use because they desire new growth, but hope to attract it without sprawl. Two studies of the central Indiana region demonstrate the interconnections between the availability of sewerage and growth. Ottensman (2003) uses a growth forecasting model to show that the presence of water and sewer infrastructure is important for understanding patterns of future development. Assessing different models and restrictions for growth, he finds that requiring new development to hook up to urban water and wastewater utilities results in the urbanization of less land and restricts development to areas that are closer to existing urban centers. Nunn (2003) finds that local public investment is positively associated with private investment, and this relationship is stronger in counties that have stronger planning capacity. In other words, controls on growth and carefully planned infrastructure extension may be important for directing and coordinating development (Warner and Molotch 2000). Local policy makers might employ a range of additional strategies to use wastewater policy to constrain or shape growth (Tabors, Shapiro, and Rogers 1976: chapter 4). For local governments in Michigan, the ability to coordinate public infrastructure needs across jurisdictional boundaries may be important to preserve environmental resources in some areas and to open opportunities for economic development in others. This offers further support for the expectation that the land use frame will be evident in newspaper coverage of interjurisdictional wastewater policy debates.

Finally, land use and wastewater dialogue may be united because growth and increased housing density places new environmental burdens on septic systems in recently rural places. The use of septic systems raises concerns for local government officials in Michigan due to the possibility of groundwater or surface water contamination, particularly as housing density increases (Michigan State University Extension 1998). While large lot zoning and density restrictions may aid environmental safety for septic users, these same developmental criteria foster sprawl patterns of exurban development. For example, in an eight-county study of on-site wastewater treatment in Wisconsin, researchers found that development using on-site wastewater treatment was characterized by dispersed land use patterns (Hanson and Jacobs 1989). The option of on-site wastewater treatment versus municipal treatment is relevant for many of Michigan's cities and townships, as they work to develop property on their common borders. Extension of wastewater service would allow more compact development and the preservation of open space. Township officials seeking wastewater service from neighboring cities are an additional source for the land use frame in newspaper coverage of interjurisdictional wastewater policy dialogue.

For these reasons and others, the land use frame is expected to be salient in coverage of wastewater policy debate. But will the land use frame be associated with interjurisdictional conflict or with cooperation? Research on metropolitan growth suggests a tension between central cities and suburbs on growth-related issues. For example, Orfield (1997: 70–72) suggests sewer rate structures and investment in new infrastructure benefit growth-oriented suburbs rather than central cities. But tension in land use cooperation may vary across jurisdictions. Jacobs (2004) notes that local governments in Southeast Michigan historically engaged in competition over auto industry investment and avoided collective discussion of metropolitan growth. But in West Michigan, Visser (2004) describes the Grand Valley Metropolitan Council as an entity contributing to constructive dialogue on land use patterns. Further, public and private sector actors in Michigan have advanced normative goals centered on farmland preservation, citizen education about land use, and smarter metropolitan growth (Jelier, Townsend, and Wills 2005; Katz 2003; Michigan Land Use Leadership Council 2003). This public interest in addressing sprawl and metropolitan growth is expected to be evident in media coverage. While tensions about growth and sprawl may still exist in Michigan, discussions of land use accompanying wastewater policy debate in newspaper coverage are expected to be cooperative rather than conflict oriented.

Public Finance

The costs associated with infrastructure development provide an important alternative or supplementary explanation for understanding the instance of conflict and cooperation in wastewater policy debates. Wastewater system finance is not unrelated to land use (Tabors, Shapiro, and Rogers 1976: chapter 3), and we may expect to see concomitant discussion of the frames in wastewater policy debates. Public officials may debate the rates for service provision billed to citizens or to customer communities. Budgeting for infrastructure development, expansion, and maintenance will also appear in wastewater policy discussions.

First, rates for sewer service are salient for residents and policy makers because they are a visible and regular reminder of the costs associated with wastewater service arrangements. Local governments in metropolitan areas engage in both cooperation and competition (Park 1997). Public-choice theorists describe metropolitan areas as competitive venues in which residents can seek out the bundle of public goods and services that most closely meets their preferences for the price (or tax payment) that the citizens-consumers are willing to pay (Tiebout 1956; Ostrom, Tiebout, and Warren 1961; McGinnis 1999). Thus, local governments within a metropolitan area have incentives to provide wastewater

services at a lower rate than other jurisdictions in the metropolitan area. Any one suburban jurisdiction alone may not be able to produce wastewater treatment more affordably
than the existing central-city system, but coalitions of suburban governments can collaborate to provide a competitive alternative to existing central-city infrastructure. When local
governments engage in such partnerships, citizens will read about both conflict and cooperation in their local newspapers—cooperation among suburban partners and conflict
between the suburban coalition and the central city.

Second, public infrastructure investment will be discussed during wastewater policy
debates because the strategies that cities use to fund infrastructure have long-term implications for the financial health of the city and the tax rates paid by residents (Pagano and
Perry 2006; Perry 1995; Dowall 2001). The cost of infrastructure maintenance is salient in
Michigan. For example, a 2001 study by the Southeast Michigan Council of Governments
(SEMCOG) indicated that Southeast Michigan would require an additional $14 billion to
$26 billion of investment in wastewater infrastructure by 2030 (SEMCOG 2001: 33). As will
be discussed below, other communities in the state, including members of the NKSA, are
investing in the construction of new wastewater treatment facilities. Some of this development comes as suburban jurisdictions attempt to escape disputes with central cities about
how the costs for infrastructure are distributed across the metropolitan area. As suburban
residents develop their own sewerage or use on-site treatment options, and as population
decreases in central cities, there are fewer taxpayers and ratepayers to support the old
urban infrastructure. Central cities experience the cost and burden of managing old infrastructure, often focusing on system maintenance, without the support from growth or
new system users and fee payers (Holst 2007). The Michigan Land Use Leadership Council
recognized this challenge by charging local policy makers to assess historic patterns of
investment in infrastructure: "When state and local leaders, under current authority, review
water and sewerage infrastructure systems and develop recommendations to ensure that
the systems are effectively planned and coordinated at a multijurisdictional level, it is imperative that they recognize the value of the historical investment the individual jurisdictions
have made in these systems" (Michigan Land Use Leadership Council 2003: 72). The council's recommendations point to the need for interjurisdictional cooperation in infrastructure
finance, and a preference for maintaining existing systems over new system development.
Yet suburban governments have the ability to form coalitions to build new wastewater
infrastructure and separate themselves from historic central city systems. In other words,
cooperation in metropolitan regions does not necessarily benefit central cities or the entire
metropolitan region evenly.[5]

Because of this tension, public finance frames in newspaper coverage can be associated
with both conflict and cooperation. When coverage emphasizes relations between central
cities and suburbs, public finance frames are likely to discuss tension in rate-setting methodology and system maintenance. These frames will be associated with conflict. When coverage emphasizes new infrastructure development among suburban partners, coverage is more
likely to emphasize cooperation, as partners are moving forward on a new public works project. Understanding the links between the public finance frame and the partners involved in
the agreement is important because interlocal cooperation research often highlights the

economic and service benefits that can be gained through service collaboration. This analysis draws our attention to the *costs* associated with interjurisdictional relationships and not just the benefits. This is a critical step in advancing our understanding about the messages conveyed to citizens about wastewater policy, as well as costs and benefits of cooperation in their metropolitan area.

Political Control

Closely associated with the distribution of costs are questions about political control over wastewater treatment systems. The state of Michigan allows local governments to use a variety of strategies to cooperate on urban services. The Citizens Research Council of Michigan (2007: 91–100) has produced a useful guide on intergovernmental cooperation, which includes discussion of water and wastewater treatment authorizing legislation. These cooperative options range from the formation of new special districts or authorities to interlocal contracts.[6] Because local officials have many options regarding how to cooperate, discussion of political control over wastewater infrastructure will be an additional frame evident in newspaper coverage of wastewater policy debates. Here, "political control" refers to the legal organization of control over the wastewater treatment system and participation in decision making about wastewater infrastructure. While state law allows for a variety of cooperative mechanisms, cooperation does not always involve "equal" partners. Public discussion about the political control of sewerage may emphasize complaints about perceived power inequities suffered by members of multijurisdictional wastewater systems.

When jurisdictions are crafting new power-sharing arrangements, coverage of the debate may emphasize how jurisdictions work to balance or share power. When local governments discuss political control of existing sewerage, controlled primarily by central cities, the public debate may focus on the desire of suburban jurisdictions to exercise greater political control over wastewater treatment. Suburban communities may lobby for a change from service contracts to governance by a metropolitan-wide authority. In locations where an authority already exists, suburban partners may lobby for greater membership on the wastewater governing board. For example, in a study of Philadelphia, Adams (2007) found special districts had increasing participation by suburban residents over time. Contract relationships for urban services may exhibit path dependence over time, making contract or governance structure unlikely to change (Joassart-Marcelli and Musso 2005; Holst 2007); however, debate about political control over infrastructure may be salient in public debate and associated with conflict.

Discussion of political control may also demonstrate cooperation. Michigan's Conditional Land Transfer Agreement (PA 425 of 1984), popularly known as the "425 agreement," allows cities and townships to cooperate on property transfer and the provision of public goods for the purpose of economic development (Taylor, Harvey, and Shields 2004). Sewerage is one of the services often included in 425 agreements. A survey of local government officials by Bassett (2006) shows that 425 agreements are often preferred to annexation, but township officials may still hold concerns about land transfer. Further, she found that ancillary cooperation in planning and zoning does not frequently occur. Thus, public debate surrounding wastewater policy and 425 agreements may emphasize cooperation on land

141

transfer, sewerage extension, and political control of the property, but this frame is unlikely to be accompanied by discussion of the land use frame.

In sum, the political control frame may be associated with cooperation in some instances, but discussion of ongoing debates about the governance of wastewater treatment systems is more likely to emphasize conflict. Political control of wastewater treatment infrastructure may bear directly on the rates paid by member communities and ratepayers; thus the public finance frame may closely accompany the political control frame in coverage of wastewater policy debates. While participants in multijurisdictional wastewater systems could theoretically explore connections between wastewater and land use, research suggests a weak link between special district governance of wastewater and interjurisdictional cooperation in policy areas like land use (Burby, Kaiser, and Moreau 1988). Discussion of the fourth and final frame allows us to explore more opportunities for interlocal cooperation.

Environmental Concerns

Environmental concerns are a final alternative frame for wastewater policy debates considered in this research. Public health was one of the original justifications given for developing municipal sewerage in densely populated areas (Melosi 2000). Wastewater treatment policies are often a component of larger concerns about water quality and watershed management. Several different research programs have focused attention on the development of cooperative institutions for watershed management and protection (e.g., Crockett and Marengo 2005; Schneider et al. 2003; Leach, Pelkey, and Sabatier 2002). While local governments may be active participants in environmental initiatives, these efforts often involve private and nonprofit sector actors (Koontz et al. 2004). The ability of local governments to cooperate on wastewater policy may be salient to the stakeholders interested in watershed quality. Consequently, environmental concerns will occupy space in local newspaper coverage.

Environmental policy questions often elicit conflicting opinions (Norton 1991). Environmental concerns can also unite local government actors in cooperative efforts. In a study of participation in New England watershed management planning, Webler et al. (2003: 116) found that "environmental ethics" was one factor or social perspective explaining project participation by local government officials. Applying this logic to wastewater policy, local officials may be more inclined to engage in cooperative intergovernmental efforts when environmental concerns are present in policy discussions. Officials may also be pressured to cooperate by environmental groups and community organizations urging sensitivity to environmental goals. The environmental frame is most likely to be accompanied by discussion of the land use frame, as both frames have implications for the physical environment of the metropolitan area. Association of environmental concerns with public finance and political control of wastewater infrastructure will be less likely. Environmental concerns are a final frame of interest in this study.

To summarize, several different frames may be apparent in the discussion of interjurisdictional dialogue about wastewater policy. Any given newspaper story may focus primarily on one frame or mention all four. Analyzing a case through newspaper coverage has potential drawbacks. Newspaper stories may focus on what the reporter deems interesting about the policy problem, rather than exhaustively documenting local officials' many points of negotiation. At the same time, studying how policy debates are conveyed to the public can provide insight into how interlocal conflict is portrayed to the public. During interlocal negotiations, policy makers may need to be attentive not only to activities at the negotiating table but also to what citizens and residents are learning about the metropolitan cooperation process.

Research Approach

A case study of the wastewater policy debate in the Grand Rapids area from the late 1990s through 2005 demonstrates how land use, public finance, political control, and environmental concerns shape policy dialogue. Development of the case relies on coverage of the policy debate from the *Grand Rapids Press*. The case demonstrates mounting conflict between Grand Rapids and the NKSA, while patterns of cooperation congeal elsewhere. Why is a study of Grand Rapids useful? Grand Rapids provides a distinct case of both cooperation and conflict in metropolitan affairs and wastewater policy. The city successfully negotiated an ongoing service contract with some of its neighboring suburbs while failing to do so with others. Out of the conflict with its northern neighbors sprang new cooperation, as the city of Rockford and several townships opted to cooperate on the development of their own wastewater treatment facility. How did media coverage portray these events to the public? Carefully tracing events and discussion of each frame allow us to understand how the dialogue evolved. In the case of Grand Rapids, no smoking gun explains the final outcome. No claim is made that the case is representative of other wastewater policy debates in the state; however, the logic of the causal process linking public debate and interlocal cooperation can be applied to evaluate other cases in the state.

Content analysis is used to quantify the instance of each frame in newspaper coverage over an eight-year period (1998–2005).[7] An electronic search was used to identify relevant newspaper stories.[8] Each article was read to determine if multijurisdictional activity was discussed. Excluded are all letters to the editor, stories about routine road closures and maintenance, and stories about political candidates and campaigns. Each article was then coded using a coding scheme to identify the presence or absence of conflict and cooperation, and each of the four frames. A second coder also coded a five-year period of newspaper coverage. The intercoder reliability rate for articles coded by both coders was 84 percent. This suggests that another researcher employing the same coding scheme should be able to replicate the study. To consider the implications of the Grand Rapids case for wastewater cooperation in other parts of Michigan, the researcher also read newspaper stories about wastewater conflict in other Michigan communities over varying periods of time. The relevance of the Grand Rapids case for other communities in Michigan will be discussed in the conclusion.

Conflict and Cooperation in Grand Rapids

The city of Grand Rapids historically led Kent County in wastewater treatment, providing service to Ada, Alpine, Cannon and Courtland townships; Cascade, Gaines, Grand Rapids, and Plainfield Charter townships; the cities of East Grand Rapids, Kentwood, Rockford, and

143

Walker; and Tallmadge Charter Township in Ottawa County. More recently, Wright Township in Ottawa County was also added as a customer community. The city of Wyoming is the primary inner-ring suburban city that took on this task separately. Grand Rapids provided wastewater treatment service to its customer communities through wholesale and direct-bill relationships.[9] Among the wholesale customers were the communities of the NKSA, who contracted with Grand Rapids through an ancillary relationship with Kent County. Their contract was established in 1976, expiring in 2008. Grand Rapids' current wastewater customers in Kent County and the NKSA communities are identified in figure 6.1.

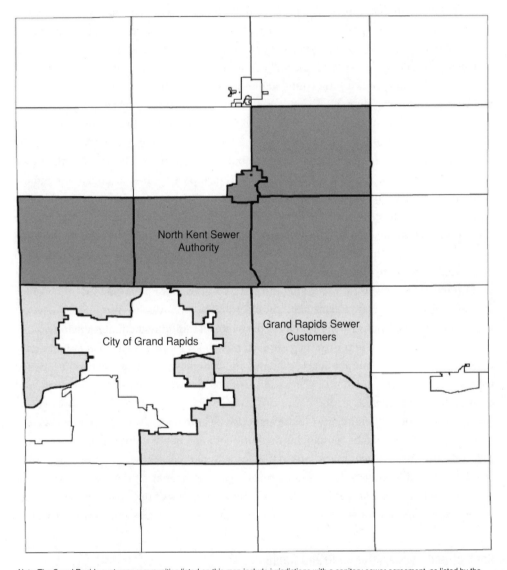

Note: The Grand Rapids customer communities listed on this map include jurisdictions with a sanitary sewer agreement, as listed by the city of Grand Rapids. Grand Rapids customer communities in Ottawa County are not shown on this map. Water and sanitary service agreements are available at http://www.ci.grand-rapids.mi.us/index.pl?page_id=6070.

FIGURE 6.1

North Kent Sewer Authority and Grand Rapids Customer Communities in Kent County

Wastewater policy was actively debated in the Grand Rapids metropolitan area during the late 1990s. Grand Rapids' wastewater customer communities neared the end of contracts initiated in the 1960s and 1970s. The expiration of the contracts provided Grand Rapids officials a window of opportunity to integrate new provisions on land use and metropolitan cooperation into the sewer contracts with suburban neighbors. Grand Rapids Township was the first jurisdiction to face an expiring contract, and township officials were not eager to embrace these new goals. Not only did the proposed agreement contain significant rate increases, but township officials expressed dissatisfaction with Grand Rapids' approach to negotiation. For example, a January 1998 letter from Grand Rapids mayor John Logie to Grand Rapids Township officials outlined significant penalties for failing to renew the sewer contract before a March deadline (Donovan and Harger 1998). Grand Rapids' initial firm stance prompted some wastewater customers to evaluate their options. Ada Township, for example, began to explore alternatives to contracting with the city of Grand Rapids, even though its sewer contract was not schedule to expire until 2012 (Lord 1998). Financial concerns expressed by the customer communities highlighted the need for extended negotiation.

Grand Rapids officials and representatives from a limited set of customer communities engaged in extended bargaining to refine the new sewer contract. When completed, the negotiations resulted in a rate methodology to advance the principle that "growth pays for growth" (Harger 1998; Donovan 2002). Hook-up fees increased, and participants agreed to an Urban Utility Boundary to limit ongoing sprawl beyond the central city (Donovan 2002; LaMore and Supanich-Goldner 2000: 60). Attached to the new wastewater treatment contract was the requirement that customer communities participate in an Urban Cooperation Agreement, which charged an additional per capita fee to develop a pool of money for regional projects. A case study of the intergovernmental leadership of Grand Rapids mayor John Logie noted that "meetings between Logie and two city commissioners on one side and the township supervisor and two customer mayors on the other have since resulted in sixty-five principal points of agreement in the master water-sewer agreement and ten major points in the Urban Cooperation Agreement" (LaMore and Supanich-Goldner 2000: 60).

In November 1998, the city of Grand Rapids invited administrators and elected officials from its customer communities to gather together for a big event to unveil the results from the negotiating team's efforts. A number of jurisdictions, such as the cities of Walker, East Grand Rapids, and Kentwood, readily embraced the new contract. Walker officials signed the new agreement before their contract expired. Walker mayor Don Knottnerus suggested that the "growth pays for growth" rate methodology would benefit more heavily developed jurisdictions like Walker, allowing them to pay for wastewater treatment without subsidizing expansion of the system in other fast-developing jurisdictions (Heibel 1998a). Succeeding in negotiations with the inner-ring customers that contributed the bulk of the wastewater flow to the system, Grand Rapids officials seemed unprepared for serious objections from the jurisdictions that would be the most burdened by the new rate methodology.

Several jurisdictions expressed concerns and attempted to delay adoption of the agreement. For example, Gaines Township officials desired an external opinion about the legality of the contract, including the Urban Cooperation Agreement. With twenty years remaining on their existing contract, Gaines officials were in no hurry to sign a new agreement. Grand

145

Rapids assistant city manager Eric DeLong responded to these complaints by contrasting the recalcitrant jurisdictions with those who signed on to the agreement quickly. He noted, "Certain communities are making good and significant progress and others aren't" (King 1999). In a newsletter article, DeLong and Hatch (2000) explained that the city of Grand Rapids and the five customer communities that had signed the agreement by early 2000 represented "80 percent of the customer base and billed volume of the system." They also described the jurisdictions that had not signed the agreement as unsupportive of regional goals: "Holdouts have challenged the new rate methodology, put forward a contrarian view of the use of economics to provide land use incentives, and argued that the agreements may have unintended consequences" (DeLong and Hatch 2000: 6).

The NKSA communities' objections to the new sewer contract posed the greatest challenge to Grand Rapids' plans for integrating wastewater treatment and land use principles. The city of Rockford and Alpine, Cannon, Courtland, and Plainfield townships began working together under the NKSA in 1997 to collectively address their concerns about how the Kent County Department of Public Works had been performing maintenance on sewerage in northern Kent County (Heibel 1999). The county had managed the communities' wastewater system since the inception of service with the city of Grand Rapids. When the NKSA communities questioned the terms proposed in Grand Rapids' new wastewater treatment contract, the NKSA served as a convenient vehicle for the members to continue working together on wastewater treatment concerns. The NKSA contracted for a financial study to determine the impact of the new rate methodology proposed by Grand Rapids. Several issues were of central concern to the NKSA. Instead of measuring the flow of material through the system and billing the flow, the new agreement factored in land area, number of hookups, and total treatment. The new formula would result in increased costs for the townships with undeveloped land. Additionally, the NKSA contested Grand Rapids' method of deriving levels of inflow/infiltration. The rainwater or runoff that enters the system from outside sources is primarily a problem in areas with older piping. Many of the suburban areas had sewer piping less than thirty years old, while some piping in the city of Grand Rapids was significantly older. Finally, the NKSA communities objected to the Urban Cooperation Agreement, arguing that regional cooperation efforts should not be tied to wastewater treatment rates.

The costs associated with the new wastewater treatment contract versus the costs associated with the construction of a new wastewater treatment plant by the NKSA were regularly discussed in newspaper coverage. For citizens reading about the debate, the implications of wastewater treatment for their monthly bills was emphasized much more frequently than concerns about conflict or cooperation on metropolitan growth and land use. Officials with the NKSA, concerned about the costs of the proposed Grand Rapids contract, began by investing in a second study to weigh the costs of signing the new Grand Rapids contract against the feasibility of building their own wastewater treatment facility (Heibel 1998b). With the study complete, the northern communities were armed with the evidence that contributed to the significant coverage of the public finance frame for the duration of the conflict. "A sewer agreement proposed by Grand Rapids for its customer communities in northern Kent County will double rates, making it 'slightly more cost effective' for the communities to build their own sewer treatment plant" (Deiters 1999). This cost differential was regularly repeated in subsequent converge.

While the NKSA kept the focus on the financial impact of Grand Rapids' new sewer rate methodology, customer communities that endorsed the new Grand Rapids contract attempted to maintain a focus on land use and metropolitan cooperation. The new contract with customer communities was praised as innovative because it encompassed concerns about metropolitan growth and land use in addition to wastewater treatment rates. Normative concerns about the links between wastewater treatment and metropolitan growth were evident in early coverage. Coverage indicated that the new contract was designed by Grand Rapids and a set of suburban jurisdictions to "use sewer service as a tool to manage how the region grows" (Naudi 2000). The land use frame was strongly invoked in regular reporting and in editorials. Walker mayor Don Knottenerus (1999) argued in one editorial that sewer cooperation was critical to address the sprawl problem in West Michigan: "If the growth pattern continues unabated, it will create problems for water and sewer systems as well as other infrastructure that will need to be built to accommodate development. This would lead to huge public capital expenditures. If the public is unwilling to pay for these expenditures it will surely pay in other ways—public health threats and environmental degradation."

Knottnerus explained that efforts to address sprawl were getting lost in the conflict with the NKSA. He noted, "We're beginning to learn who is committed to regional cooperation and who is not." His editorial also indicated the tight connection between land use and other frames in the policy debate. Proponents of the new contract had to address questions of public finance because the NKSA regularly highlighted how much the new Grand Rapids contract would cost their citizens and ratepayers. In a later editorial, NKSA concerns about the link between land use and the sewer rate methodology were recognized as legitimate. The editors wrote: "20 percent of the rates would be based on the size of the area serviced in a community. That's designed to discourage suburbs from allowing large-lot residential developments. North Kent officials persuasively argue that the provision serves mainly to punish them for decisions made in the past. A community should not have to pay extra for homes that were built years ago on large lots" (Grand Rapids Press 2000).

In some ways, the new wastewater treatment contract between Grand Rapids and its customer communities gave suburban jurisdictions greater political control of the system than before the new agreement, including participation on a utility advisory board. While this structure for political control of the wastewater system gives suburbs greater voice than a system controlled by Grand Rapids alone, the structure falls short of calls by the Grand Valley Metropolitan Council (1994) to move toward a regionally governed wastewater authority. The gap between the new contract and goals for metropolitan cooperation were highlighted by the *Grand Rapids Press* in a series of closely dated editorials in which the newspaper urged the city of Grand Rapids and the NKSA to engage in serious negotiations to maintain one metropolitan treatment system (Grand Rapids Press 1999a, 1999b, 1999c, 1999d). But the NKSA and outside observers suggested the negotiations were not productive. Jerry Felix, executive director of the Grand Valley Metropolitan Council, explained to the *Grand Rapids Press* that the city of Grand Rapids did not make significant changes during the negotiation process. "The negotiations [*sic*] (from Grand Rapids) came in with marching

147

orders from someone that they don't anticipate making any changes in the contract, so explain to them why they should sign" (Deiters 2000).

With no progress in negotiations with Grand Rapids, in early 2001 the NKSA exercised an option to purchase property on the Grand River for the construction of a new wastewater treatment plant. As the NKSA continued down the path toward building its own treatment facility, newspaper coverage also highlighted the political control the North Kent jurisdictions would gain by operating their own system. One report stated that "authority members said they do not want to be at the mercy of Grand Rapids, which controls half the votes on a utility advisory board set up to govern the treatment system" (VandeBunte 2003). North Kent officials' interest in political control of their own sewerage might also have been motivated by their negative experiences with Kent County as the intermediary in their previous contract with Grand Rapids. Controlling the wastewater system, the NKSA does not have to coordinate with the county or with Grand Rapids to address system maintenance concerns.

As the conflict between Grand Rapids and the NKSA progressed, and as the NKSA looked increasingly likely to move forward by building its own facility, the media also covered the cost implications of the new plant. Some questioned the cost estimates of the NKSA due to increased construction material costs since the NKSA's initial study. Despite the increased cost of the plant, NKSA officials were reassured by follow-up studies that building a new plant would not have a significantly different cost than signing the Grand Rapids contract (VandeBunte 2005a). As costs equalized, political control of wastewater infrastructure became a more salient justification for building a plant. A significant last-minute concession on the part of Grand Rapids, allowing the North Kent communities to not sign the Urban Cooperation Agreement, also did not change the communities' interest in building a new treatment facility (VandeBunte and Harger 2005).

By the end of 2005, the partner communities of the NKSA had negotiated how their costs would be shared for the operation of a new wastewater treatment facility. While public finance dominated coverage, land use reappeared in a different form. While early land use coverage focused on the "growth pays for growth" argument, the new coverage questioned how a new wastewater treatment facility would impact land use in northern Kent County. For example, payment of the bonds for the plant would be covered by sewer rates, as well as by hookup fees. Coverage suggested that the North Kent communities' need to meet a goal of at least 350 new sewer hookups per year would only fuel more sprawl, even though ratepayers might save on their monthly bills (VandeBunte 2005b).

With the construction of a new plant, environmental frames also entered the public dialogue. Critiques about the NKSA building its own plant often linked land use concerns with complaints about a new treatment facility discharging into the Grand River. The NKSA also had to deal with environmental challenges associated with building the new plant. Plainfield Township residents expressed concern that having a wastewater treatment plant in their "backyards" would decrease property values and pollute air quality (Heibel 2000). Finally, the NKSA was forced to address concerns about a threatened plant species, spending about $10,000 to move American beak grass away from the construction of the new treatment facility (Deiters and VandeBunte 2004). Additional concerns about the environmental impact of a new treatment facility may have been mitigated by the NKSA's use of innovative technology (VandeBunte 2004). For example, in an update on the plant's construction, Plainfield Township manager Robert Homan (2006) wrote:

> It is becoming clear that the increasing sewer rates in the NKSA member communities are necessary to pay for the [clean water plant] and its operation. Customers should remember that the "new deal" offered our communities by Grand Rapids some seven years ago raised the cost of treating our sewage to the point where this project became feasible. In a way we owe some sort of positive acknowledgement to Grand Rapids for making it possible for us to divert millions of gallons from the City's plant and treat our own sewage to a "clean water state" using the new Membrane Bio-Reactor technology.

The new treatment facility began operation in the fall of 2008. While officials communicate that the costs associated with the project are significant, NKSA communications also convey that the five North Kent County jurisdictions prefer their new partnership to the old relationship with the city of Grand Rapids.

Summarizing Frames in the Grand Rapids Case

Content analysis of coverage in the *Grand Rapids Press* demonstrates discussion of land use was present in the Grand Rapids wastewater policy dialogue, but it was overwhelmed by stories emphasizing public finance. Table 6.1 displays the total mentions of each frame in newspaper coverage from 1998 to 2005. Land use was mentioned in 36 percent of the stories during the eight-year period, but public finance appears in an overwhelming 76 percent of the coverage. The costs of the Grand Rapids contract and the construction of the NKSA "clean water plant" were regularly emphasized, even when stories mentioned other policy concerns. While Grand Rapids achieved cooperative outcomes with some of its neighboring jurisdictions, metropolitan area residents reading the *Grand Rapids Press* were more likely to read about conflict. Conflict was evident in fifty-one articles, or 42 percent of the total coverage. Both conflict and cooperation are present in the stories about land use. Of the forty-three stories that mentioned land use, twenty-one emphasize conflict and thirteen emphasize cooperation. The others are neutral.

Table 6.1. Article Frames on Grand Rapids and Interlocal Wastewater Policy, 1998–2005

Articles (N)	121
Conflict	51 (42%)
Cooperation	34 (28%)
Land Use	43 (36%)
Finance	92 (76%)
Political Control	65 (54%)
Environment	39 (32%)

NOTE: Conflict and cooperation frames do not sum to 100 percent because some articles were coded "neutral." Multiple frames may be present in the same story.

149

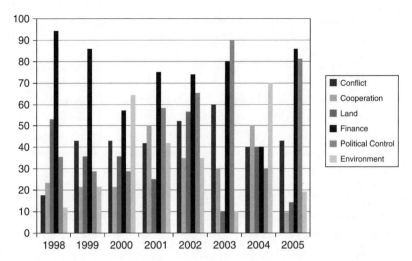

FIGURE 6.2
Article Frames as a Percentage of Total Stories by Year, 1998–2005

Concern about political control was a second prominent frame, mentioned in 54 percent of the newspaper articles. Political control was a point of tension between Grand Rapids and the NKSA, but political control was also discussed with Grand Rapids' other customer communities, as the new treatment contract gave them somewhat greater input in the governance of the system. Of the sixty-five stories mentioning political control, only twelve emphasize cooperation (18.5 percent), with forty-two highlighting conflict (65 percent). Environmental concerns were infrequently mentioned, and were more likely to have a cooperative or neutral emphasis. Thirty-two percent of the stories reporting wastewater policy dialogue mention environmental concerns. Of these, 44 percent are associated with cooperation, and only 28 percent are associated with conflict.

Over the eight-year period, the frames present in wastewater policy dialogue and the instance of conflict and cooperation did shift and change. Figure 6.2 illustrates stories containing each frame, as a percentage of total stories by year. The figure suggests conflict was emphasized most frequently during the years that the NKSA explored alternatives to the Grand Rapids contract. Environmental frames were more likely to be emphasized in the years that the NKSA was engaged in planning or construction of the new clean water plant. While early coverage emphasized the land use goals of the new Grand Rapids contract, finance clearly dominated coverage. Only in 1999 and 2002 were land use frames emphasized in over half of the newspaper coverage on wastewater policy dialogue. Taken as a whole, citizens in the Grand Rapids metropolitan area who read coverage of wastewater policy dialogue were most likely to learn about the financial implications of wastewater policy and tension between the central city and its suburban neighbors.

Implications for Michigan Citizens and Policy Makers

What lessons does this study have for local government officials and citizens in Michigan who want more opportunities to flush conflict and engage in cooperative approaches to wastewater policy? First, policy makers who hope to emphasize metropolitan cooperation cannot escape the economics of urban service provision. Grand Rapids officials had the laudable goal of linking wastewater treatment and land use policy. By working with some of their closest neighbors and largest sewer customers, they were able to come to agreement on an important list of goals to advance metropolitan cooperation. Yet even before the November 1998 announcement of the agreement formulated by the negotiating team, several of the Grand Rapids customer communities emphasized that a significant increase in the cost of wastewater treatment might force them to consider other wastewater treatment options. Suburban jurisdictions were particularly concerned that a "growth pays for growth" formula would unfairly penalize existing residents, rather than curb new construction. Although some suggested that the NKSA studies greatly underestimated the cost of constructing a new treatment plant, participants in the policy debate should have recognized that the Grand Rapids rate structure could be a stumbling block to keeping the NKSA communities as customers of the Grand Rapids system. If the cost of public infrastructure and urban services dominates media coverage, policy makers must address these concerns at the bargaining table, and explain to the public how differences on financial concerns are being resolved.

Second, when negotiating interlocal cooperation, officials should not describe cooperation as inevitable. Early in the conflict, Grand Rapids officials emphasized that the customer communities that made up the majority of the flow in the system had already signed the new contract, and that the other jurisdictions would inevitably sign the agreement (DeLong and Hatch 2000; LaMore and Supanich-Goldner 2000). While the jurisdictions making up the NKSA may not have been significant existing contributors to flow in the wastewater system, together they do control land use for a large portion of northern Kent County, as shown in figure 6.1. As such, their participation in the Grand Rapids contract was critical in order for the central city and inner suburbs to achieve their future land use goals. By seriously engaging the NKSA earlier in the dispute, and by taking threats to exit the system seriously, Grand Rapids and the other customer communities might have maintained the relationship with the NKSA and had some input into the extension of wastewater infrastructure in northern Kent County. With the understanding that cooperation is not inevitable, even when the abandonment of a multijurisdictional infrastructure project seems unlikely, local government officials can commit themselves to engaging conflict early and seriously.

Third, policy makers with the normative goal of integrating land use and wastewater policy will need to take active steps to ensure that the relationship between sewerage and metropolitan growth is communicated to the public through media coverage of the policy debate. As Grand Rapids and the NKSA dialogue focused on the rate methodology and the feasibility of constructing a new wastewater treatment plant in northern Kent County, the public was not regularly reminded that the dispute had implications for metropolitan growth. Occasionally, land use implications of the new treatment facility were mentioned in newspaper coverage, but coverage did not systematically emphasize the link between wastewater policy and land use. For the media, discussing cost estimates from financial studies is easier than discussing hypothetical future land use patterns. If local governments want to systematically link land use, metropolitan cooperation, and the control of wastewater

151

infrastructure, local officials will need to develop public relations strategies to communicate this information to the public on an ongoing basis. In the case of Grand Rapids and the NKSA, NKSA meetings about the potential benefit of a new plant were regularly covered by the media. To maintain an emphasis on land use, Grand Rapids, the Grand Valley Metropolitan Council, universities, or community organizations could have sponsored forums to provide public information about wastewater policy and land use in Kent County. In sum, local governments need active public relations campaigns to convey the implications of metropolitan conflict and cooperation.

Fourth, central-city officials should be attentive to suburban interests in the political control of important regional services. As evident in this and other studies (Adams 2007), suburban jurisdictions are interested in the services provided by core cities. The organization of special districts and authorities often allows suburban jurisdictions to participate directly in the governance of important regional programs and infrastructure. The Grand Valley Metropolitan Council (1994) has identified this as a possible path for Grand Rapids. The new contract did give customer communities some additional voice in wastewater policy, although the city of Grand Rapids maintains significant control. In the future, Grand Rapids will have to consider the potential costs and benefits of transferring control of wastewater to a regional authority. Regional or multijurisdictional authorities for wastewater treatment might be an important institutional strategy to aid other Michigan local governments in the integration of dialogue about sewerage and land use.

In conclusion, wastewater policy dialogue in the Grand Rapids metropolitan area provides useful lessons for all local governments in Michigan. This chapter specifically highlights how information about regional policy is communicated to the public. When reading about the Grand Rapids—NKSA wastewater treatment debate, citizens were most likely to read stories including a discussion of the financial implications of wastewater policy. Land use and environmental concerns were present in the coverage, but the NKSA decision to build a new wastewater treatment plant can largely be understood as the result of conflict about finances and the political control of infrastructure. Existing research points to links between wastewater treatment policy and patterns of land use. If Michigan local officials hope to expand interlocal cooperation on wastewater treatment, they must develop strategies to convey land use and sustainability values to the media and the public.

Notes

1. Local governments are more likely to contract with other local governments for services that are measurable and highly "asset specific," services that require specialized investment, like wastewater treatment (Brown and Potoski 2003: 456).
2. In this chapter, I do not discuss the mechanisms available to local governments for cooperation. Instead, I focus on the political debate that often facilitates or hinders cooperation. Readers interested in specific mechanisms for cooperation should reference helpful materials produced by the Citizen's Research Council of Michigan (2005, 2007).
3. Further details about the sources for frames within the newspaper stories are not considered here. For example, political elites from central cities and suburban neighbors

may communicate different frames when talking about sewerage. Future research on the politics of interlocal cooperation should consider how different sources make use of different frames. Also note that the source for a frame can be the newspaper story itself, as the newspaper reporter explains the interjurisdictional conflict without quoting the explanations of actors involved in the conflict.

4. An alternative approach would be to inductively construct frames by reading a sample of stories, identifying all potential frames used in that sample, and then coding the remaining data based on those frames. The deductive approach is preferred in this study because existing theory and research can help us identify relevant variables.

5. The unevenness of metropolitan partnerships has been discussed in research on state legislative politics (Gainsborough 2001; Orfield 1997), as well as in research on participation in interlocal contracting (Friesema 1971; Marando 1968; Williams et al. 1965).

6. Private sector contracting and operation are also considered by some jurisdictions (Heilman and Johnson 1992; Werkman and Westerlin 2000).

7. For those unfamiliar with content analysis, Krippendorff (1980) provides a useful discussion of the method.

8. Specific search criteria are provided so this study can be easily replicated or expanded by interested researchers. The *Grand Rapids Press* was accessed using the online database Factiva. A keyword search was conducted using the words "City of Grand Rapids" and the terms "wastewater or sewer."

9. The Grand Rapids treatment contract recognizes two types of customer communities. *Wholesale* customer communities like the NKSA are billed on metered flow of wastewater. Wholesale customers then directly bill their customers. *Retail* customers like the city of Walker receive service directly from Grand Rapids, and customers are directly billed.

REFERENCES

Adams, C. 2007. Urban Governance and the Control of Infrastructure. *Public Works Management and Policy* 11(3):164–176.

Agranoff, R., and M. McGuire. 2003. *Collaborative Public Management*. Washington, D.C.: Georgetown University Press.

———. 2004. Another Look at Bargaining and Negotiating in Intergovernmental Management. *Journal of Public Administration Research and Theory* 14(4):495–512.

Bassett, E. M. 2006. This Land is *Our* Land? An Analysis of Land-Use Planning and Cooperation under Michigan's Conditional Land Transfer Act. *State and Local Government Review* 38 (1):23–33.

Brown, T. L., and M. Potoski. 2003. Transaction Costs and Institutional Explanations for Government Service Production Decisions. *Journal of Public Administration Research and Theory* 13(4):441–468.

Burby, R. J., E. J. Kaiser, and D. H. Moreau. 1988. Coordination of Water and Sewer Extension Policy with Land Use Planning: Key Factors Influencing the State of Practice. *Journal of Urban Affairs* 10(2):119–139.

Citizens Research Council of Michigan. 2005. *Catalog of Local Government Services in Michigan*. CRC Memorandum No. 1079. Livonia, Mich.: Citizens Research Council of Michigan.

———. 2007. *Authorization for Interlocal Agreements and Intergovernmental Cooperation in Michigan.* Livonia, Mich.: Citizens Research Council of Michigan.

Crockett, C. S., and B. G. Marengo. 2005. Watershed Management Practices. In *Management Innovation in U.S. Public Water and Wastewater Systems,* edited by P. Seidenstat, M. Nadol, D. Kaplan, and S. Hakim. Hoboken, N.J.: John Wiley and Sons.

Deiters, B. 1999. Study Says Agreement Will Double Sewer Rates. *Grand Rapids Press,* December 2.

———. 2000. Sewer Pact Dumped; Leaders to Build Plant. *Grand Rapids Press,* June 1.

Deiters, B., and M. VandeBunte. 2004. Rare Grass Stalls Work on Sewer Treatment Plant. *Grand Rapids Press,* October 13.

DeLong, E., and J. Hatch. 2000. New Water and Sewer Partnership Creates a Platform for Key Regional Issues. *Getting Smart! The Newsletter of the Smart Growth Network* 3(4):5–6.

Dilworth, R. 2003. From Sewers to Suburbs: Transforming the Policy-Making Context of American Cities. *Urban Affairs Review* 38(5):726–739.

———. 2005. *The Urban Origins of Suburban Autonomy.* Cambridge, Mass.: Harvard University Press.

Donovan, B. 2002. Township Gets Tough on Runoff. *Grand Rapids Press,* March 14.

Donovan, B., and J. Harger. 1998. City Talks Tough in Negotiations with Township for Water, Sewer. *Grand Rapids Press,* February 5.

Dowall, D. E. 2001. Rethinking Statewide Infrastructure Policies: Lessons from California and Beyond. *Public Works Management and Policy* 6(1):5–17.

Entman, R. M. 1993. Framing: Toward Clarification of Fractured Paradigm. *Journal of Communication* 43(4):51–58.

Friesema, H. P. 1971. *Metropolitan Political Structure: Intergovernmental Relations and Political Integration in the Quad-Cities.* Iowa City: University of Iowa Press.

Gainsborough, J. F. 2001. Bridging the City-Suburb Divide: States and the Politics of Regional Cooperation. *Journal of Urban Affairs* 23(5):497–512.

Goldsmith, S., and W. D. Eggers. 2004. *Governing by Network: The New Shape of the Public Sector.* Washington, D.C.: Brookings Institution Press.

Grand Rapids Press. 1999a. Cooperate or Else. *Grand Rapids Press,* December 13.

———. 1999b. An Expensive Drink of Water. *Grand Rapids Press,* August 9.

———. 1999c. A Flood of Bad Feelings. *Grand Rapids Press,* October 8.

———. 1999d. Roadblock to Cooperation. *Grand Rapids Press,* November 15.

———. 2000. Get Together on Water, Sewer. *Grand Rapids Press,* June 7.

———. 2005a. License to Spill. *Grand Rapids Press,* February 3.

———. 2005b. Numbers: Big to Bigger. *Grand Rapids Press,* August 16.

Grand Valley Metropolitan Council. 1994. Metropolitan Development Blueprint Report. Grand Rapids, Mich.: Grand Valley Metropolitan Council. Http://www.gvmc.org/blueprint/bp_report.shtml.

Hanson, M. E., and H. M. Jacobs. 1989. Private Sewage System Impacts in Wisconsin: Implications for Planning and Policy. *Journal of the American Planning Association* 55(2):169–180.

Harger, J. 1998. Water-Sewer Pact Proposed to Control Sprawl. *Grand Rapids Press,* November 19.

———. 2002. U.S. Judge Tosses Communities' Suit Over Sewage Pact. *Grand Rapids Press,* February 27.

Heibel, L. R. 1998a. City OK's Water, Sewer Pact. *Grand Rapids Press,* November 26.

———. 1998b. North Kent Considers Possibility of Own Sewage Plant. *Grand Rapids Press,* September 17.

———. 1999. Communities Press County Over Control of Sewer System. *Grand Rapids Press,* September 16.

———. 2000. Waste Not, Want Not. *Grand Rapids Press,* June 24.

Heilman, J. G., and G. W. Johnson. 1992. *The Politics and Economics of Privatization: The Case of Wastewater Treatment.* Tuscaloosa: University of Alabama Press.

Holst, A. 2007. The Philadelphia Water Department and the Burden of History. *Public Works Management and Policy* 11(3):233–238.

Homan, R. C. 2006. Update on Progress in Building the New PARCCSIDE Clean Water Plant. Http://www.plainfieldchartertwp.org/pct_nksa.htm.

Jacobs, A. J. 2004. Inter-Local Relations and Divergent Growth: The Detroit and Tokai Auto Regions, 1969 to 1996. *Journal of Urban Affairs* 26(4):479–504.

Jelier, R. W., C. L. Townsend, and K. C. Wills. 2005. United Growth: Michigan State University's Rural and Urban Land Use Strategy in West Michigan. In *Partnerships for Smart Growth: University-Community Collaboration for Better Public Places,* edited by W. Wiewel and G.-J. Knapp. Armonk, N.Y.: M. E. Sharpe.

Joassart-Marcelli, P., and J. Musso. 2005. Municipal Service Provision Choices within a Metropolitan Area. *Urban Affairs Review* 40(4):492–519.

Kamensky, J. M., and T. J. Burlin. 2004. *Collaboration: Using Networks and Partnerships.* Lanham, Md.: Rowman and Littlefield.

Katz, D. 2003. *Michigan's Farmland Preservation Program: An Assessment.* Midland, Mich.: Mackinac Center for Public Policy.

Kenney, K. B., D. A. Downing, and G. G. Hayes. 1972. *Urban Water Policy as an Input in Urban Growth Policy.* Knoxville: Water Resources Research Center, University of Tennessee.

Kickert, W J. M., E.-H. Klijn, and J. F. M. Koppenjan, eds. 1997. *Managing Complex Networks: Strategies for the Public Sector.* London: Sage Publications.

King, K. 1999. Some Townships Balk at Proposed Sewer Pact. *Grand Rapids Press,* June 24.

Knottnerus, D. E. 1999. Water-Sewer Cooperation Deters Sprawl. *Grand Rapids Press,* December 31.

Koontz, T. M., T. A. Steelman, J. Carmin, K. Smith, C. Mosele, and C. W. Thomas. 2004. *Collaborative Environmental Management: What Roles for Government?* Washington, D.C.: Resources for the Future.

Krippendorff, K. 1980. *Content Analysis: An Introduction to Its Methodology.* Newbury Park, Calif.: Sage.

LaMore, R. L., and F. Supanich-Goldner. 2000. John Logie and Intergovernmental Relations in Grand Rapids, Michigan. In *Governing Middle-Sized Cities: Studies in Mayoral Leadership,* edited by J. R. Bowers and W. C. Rich. Boulder, Colo.: Lynne Rienner.

Leach, W. D., N. W. Pelkey, and P. A. Sabatier. 2002. Stakeholder Partnerships as Collaborative Policymaking: Evaluation Criteria Applied to Watershed Management in California and Washington. *Journal of Policy Analysis and Management* 21(4):645–670.

LeRoux, K., and J. B. Carr. 2007. Explaining Local Government Cooperation on Public Works: Evidence from Michigan. *Public Works Management and Policy* 12(1):344–358.

Lord, K. 1998. Township to Study Its Water and Sewer Options. *Grand Rapids Press,* February 26.

Marando, V. L. 1968. Inter-local Cooperation in a Metropolitan Area: Detroit. *Urban Affairs Quarterly* 4(2):185–200.

McGinnis, M. D. 1999. *Polycentricity and Local Public Economies: Readings from the Workshop in Political Theory and Policy Analysis.* Ann Arbor: University of Michigan Press.

Melosi, M. V. 2000. *The Sanitary City: Urban Infrastructure in America from Colonial Times to the Present.* Baltimore: Johns Hopkins University Press.

155

Michigan Land Use Leadership Council. 2003. *Michigan's Land, Michigan's Future: Final Report of the Michigan Land Use Leadership Council.* Lansing: Michigan Land Use Leadership Council.

Michigan State University Extension. 1998. *Small-Scale Septic Systems: Their Threat to Drinking Water Supplies and Options for Local Government.* East Lansing: Michigan State University Extension.

Morgan, D. R., and M. W. Hirlinger. 1991. Intergovernmental Service Contracts: A Multivariate Explanation. *Urban Affairs Quarterly* 27(1):128–144.

Naudi, J. 2000. Water Dispute Threatens Regional Planning Efforts. *Grand Rapids Press,* July 28.

Norton, B. G. 1991. *Toward Unity among Environmentalists.* New York: Oxford University Press.

Nunn, S. 2003. Public Infrastructure, Private Built Investment, and Local Planning Capacity: An Examination of Linkages in the Central Indiana Region, 1990–2000. *Public Works Management and Policy* 8(1):48–61.

Orfield, M. 1997. *Metropolitics: A Regional Agenda for Community and Stability.* Washington, D.C.: Brookings Institution Press.

Ostrom, V., C. M. Tiebout, and R. Warren. 1961. The Organization of Government in Metropolitan Areas: A Theoretical Inquiry. *American Political Science Review* 55(4):831–842.

Ottensmann, J. R. 2003. LUCI: Land Use in Central Indiana Model and the Relationships of Public Infrastructure to Urban Development. *Public Works Management and Policy* 8(1):62–76.

Pagano, M. A., and D. Perry. 2006. *Financing Infrastructure in the 21st Century City: "How Did I Get Stuck Holding the Bag?"* Chicago: Great Cities Institute, College of Urban Planning and Public Affairs, University of Illinois at Chicago.

Park, K. 1997. Friends and Competitors: Policy Interactions Between Local Governments in Metropolitan Areas. *Political Research Quarterly* 50(4):723–750.

Perry, D. L., ed. 1995. *Building the Public City: The Politics, Governance, and Finance of Public Infrastructure, Urban Affairs Annual Reviews.* Thousand Oaks, Calif.: Sage.

Schneider, M., J. Schloz, M. Lubell, D. Mindruta, and M. Edwardsen. 2003. Building Consensual Institutions: Networks and the National Estuary Program. *American Journal of Political Science* 47(1):143–158.

Southeast Michigan Council of Governments (SEMCOG). 2001. Investing in Southeast Michigan's Quality of Life: Sewer and Infrastructure Needs. Detroit: Southeast Michigan Council of Governments.

Speir, C., and K. Stephenson. 2002. Does Sprawl Cost Us All? Isolating the Effects of Housing Patterns on Public Water and Sewer Costs. *Journal of the American Planning Association* 68(1):56–70.

Tabors, R. D., M. H. Shapiro, and P. P. Rogers. 1976. *Land Use and the Pipe: Planning for Sewerage.* Lexington, Mass.: Lexington Books.

Taylor, G. D., L. R. Harvey, and W. Shields. 2004. *The Conditional Land Transfer Act: Research, Reflections and Policy Recommendations.* Detroit: Southeast Michigan Council of Governments (SEMCOG).

Thurmaier, K., and C. Wood. 2002. Interlocal Agreements as Overlapping Social Network: Picket-Fence Regionalism in Metropolitan Kansas City. *Public Administration Review* 62(5):585–598.

Tiebout, C. M. 1956. A Pure Theory of Local Expenditures. *Journal of Political Economy* 64(5):416–424.

VandeBunte, Matt. 2000. Wastewater Collection Evaluation Authorized. *Grand Rapids Press,* December 14.

———. 2002. Algoma Township Planners Give Initial Approval for Meijer Store. *Grand Rapids Press,* October 16.

———. 2003. North Kent Will Build Sewer Plant. *Grand Rapids Press,* February 13.

———. 2004. North Kent's Sewer Plant Idea Displayed. *Grand Rapids Press,* January 22.

————. 2005a. Consultant Says New Sewer Is a Toss-up. *Grand Rapids Press,* June 3.

————. 2005b. Study: Hookup Fee Key to Sewer Savings. *Grand Rapids Press,* August 2.

VandeBunte, M., and J. Harger. 2005. N. Kent Unswayed by City's Concession. *Grand Rapids Press,* February 4.

Visser, J. A. 2004. Voluntary Regional Councils and the New Regionalism: Effective Governance in the Smaller Metropolis. *Journal of Planning Education and Research* 24:51–63.

Warner, K., and H. L. Molotch. 2000. *Building Rules: How Local Controls Shape Community Environments and Economies.* Boulder, Colo.: Westview Press.

Webler, T., S. Tuler, I. Shockey, P. Stern, and R. Beattie. 2003. Participation by Local Government Officials in Watershed Management Planning. *Society and Natural Resources* 16(2):105–121.

Werkman, J., and D. L. Westerlin. 2000. Privatizing Municipal Water and Wastewater Systems: Promises and Pitfalls. *Public Works Management and Policy* 5(1):52–68.

White, E. 2004. Witness Cites Lag in Action on Spill. *Grand Rapids Press,* October 16.

Williams, O. P., H. Herman, C. S. Liebman, and T. R. Dye. 1965. *Suburban Differences and Metropolitan Policies: A Philadelphia Story.* Philadelphia: University of Pennsylvania Press.

Wood, C. 2006. Scope and Patterns of Metropolitan Governance in Urban America: Probing the Complexities in the Kansas City Region. *American Review of Public Administration* 36(3):337–353.

Zeemering, E. S. 2007. Who Collaborates? Local Decisions about Intergovernmental Relations. Ph.D. diss., Indiana University.

CHAPTER 7

Best Practices in Protecting Green Infrastructure: Benchmarking County Park Systems

Betty Gajewski

Our village life would stagnate if it were not for the unexplored forests and meadows which surround it. We need the tonic of wildness.

—Henry D. Thoreau, *Walden or Life in the Woods*

The nature of county parks, in Michigan and elsewhere, continues to change. For well over 100 years, county park systems have strived to meet the leisure and recreation needs of the surrounding metropolitan areas by setting aside green spaces as relief from congested urban conditions. After World War II, county parks evolved from pleasant picnic grounds to more diverse recreational opportunities that address shifting demands of growing urban populations. Today, these traditional functions remain increasingly valuable for Michigan's metropolitan areas; but the mission of county parks is again being reworked to include the restoration and preservation of green infrastructure.

The quickening pace of sprawl in many metropolitan areas of Michigan has compromised the functioning of natural systems. The well-being of these metropolitan areas is intimately tied to how well their green infrastructure is being preserved. For example, drinking water for Michigan's metropolitan areas cycles through green infrastructure, rising urban temperatures are moderated by green infrastructure, and damages from flooding are tempered by green infrastructure.

Despite its importance, green infrastructure is not always well maintained or preserved. A recent study found that the quantity and quality of green infrastructure in the nine counties within the urbanizing southeast corner of Michigan declined from 1991 to 2002, open space diminished by 10 percent, and pavement increased by 21 percent (American Forests 2006). Although tree cover increased by 2 percent within the studied area, tree canopies in the three watersheds decreased. As a result, the quantity of storm water runoff increased, while air and water quality decreased. Over the next thirty years, researchers estimate that the regional cost for handling increased storm water runoff and improving water quality will be between $14 billion and $26 billion (American Forests 2006).

Ottawa County, a major agricultural county in Michigan, lies in the midst of an urbanizing triangle containing one of the fastest growing metropolitan areas in Michigan. The county is experiencing sprawl rising not only from its own communities but also from development flowing from the Muskegon area and a significant portion of Grand Rapids' suburban expansion. Ottawa County, Michigan's tenth most populous county, has experienced the third fastest rate of population growth among the state's eighty-three counties (U.S. Census Bureau 2000). As development advances toward and along the Lake Michigan shoreline, there is concern that Ottawa County could someday resemble the vast uninterrupted expanses of urbanization characteristic of the Los Angeles region, as well as the Chicago and Detroit metropolitan areas (WMSA 2002). This scenario has increased awareness of the community qualities that would be lost to such development patterns, not just in Ottawa County but also throughout the West Michigan region. One regional attribute recognized as being vulnerable to unchecked development was West Michigan's green infrastructure. For Ottawa County, green infrastructure is represented by coastal sand dunes, wooded ravines, river bayous, and remnant wetlands, as well as open spaces preserved in farm fields and woodlots.

The diminution of the county's green landscape has not gone unnoticed by county residents. In 1996, Ottawa County voters—a fiscally conservative electorate—voted to tax themselves over ten years so that some green space would be preserved, specifically within their county park system. Then, in 2006 county voters approved the renewal of this millage. Ottawa County voters recognized the necessity of compensating for the loss of green spaces through the acquisition of additional parklands.

Regional efforts are also under way in West Michigan and other parts of Michigan to address the loss of green infrastructure. Although the Ottawa County park system has been highlighted here, it is not the only county to intentionally preserve natural features and manage green infrastructure within the county park system. Other metropolitan counties in Michigan and across the country are sustaining the natural features of their communities by preserving green infrastructure within their park systems as growth consumes more land and fragments natural systems.

County park systems can be key to assembling regional green infrastructure around Michigan's metropolitan areas. Although all park systems have been identified as critical in preserving West Michigan's green infrastructure, the integral role that county park systems can play as hubs within a connected green infrastructure network has not been evaluated. Some counties are particularly outstanding in these efforts. This chapter examines these efforts to identify best practices that may provide benchmarks for Ottawa County's green infrastructure efforts.

Green Infrastructure Variously Defined

"Green infrastructure" is a relatively new term, currently without a universally accepted definition. Mark Benedict and Edward McMahon are credited with creating the term, which they have defined as "an interconnected network of green space that conserves natural ecosystem values and functions and provides associated benefits to human populations," describing green infrastructure as a community's natural "life support system" (Benedict and McMahon 2002). In creating this term, Benedict and McMahon have noted that, just as communities need to manage their "gray infrastructure"—their network of roads, sewers, utilities, and other constructed systems—they should also be compelled to purposefully manage their green infrastructure—their network of natural systems that sustain clean air, water, and natural resources and enriches the quality of life in the community (Benedict and McMahon 2006).

Since the first use of the term, "green infrastructure" has come to represent a myriad of "green" components at various landscape scales: from national forests to urban street trees, from watersheds to rain gardens, from migratory flyways to backyard bird feeders. "Green infrastructure" has become an umbrella term covering many natural and cultural initiatives, encompassing elements of storm water management, wilderness and agricultural preservation, and alternative transportation networks, such as greenways and bikeways. Bennedict and McMahon, in defining "green infrastructure," have also conceived a new framework for land use planning.

Among the various definitions currently in use, there are several worth noting. The U.S. Environmental Protection Agency (EPA), for example, focuses on the role of green infrastructure in managing water quality, defining it as "an array of products, technologies, and practices that use natural systems—or engineered systems that mimic natural processes—to enhance overall environmental quality and provide utility services" (USEPA 2007). A definition used by the state of Maine suggests that green infrastructure consists of natural capital and its sustainable management; physical capital associated with its efficient use and management; and private property rights and civic traditions surrounding human access to it (MSPO 2006). In its green infrastructure planning, Montgomery County in Maryland explains green infrastructure as "a network of natural areas" of countywide significance that maintains natural ecological processes and contribute to health and quality of life, with its value greater then the sum of its individual resources (MNCPPC 2006). The Green Infrastructure Vision for Chicago Wilderness considers green infrastructure to be "the interconnected network of land and water that supports biodiversity and provides habitat for diverse communities of native flora and fauna at the regional scale" (Chicago Wilderness 2004).

This broad scope in defining green infrastructure and using its concepts for different purposes is similarly represented in Michigan. In its park planning guidelines, the Michigan Department of Natural Resources notes that green infrastructure, in contrast to traditional conservation, "provides for conservation in anticipation of land development, growth management, and traditional gray infrastructure" (MDNR 2006). The Michigan Council for Arts and Cultural Affairs emphasizes the connectivity role of green infrastructure—for example, by managing a building's storm water with rain gardens, green roofs, and pervious parking lots, and connecting these projects to green spaces. The council further notes that these practices not only serve environmental protection but can also enhance the artistic and aesthetic value of a project (MCACA 2006).

161

Many regional initiatives in Michigan have articulated various perspectives on the meaning of green infrastructure in their region. The "Growing Greener" initiative of the Southwest Michigan Planning Commission pursues green infrastructure as a "planned and managed network" of wilderness, parks, greenways, conservation easements, and working lands with conservation value (SMPC 2006). GLS GreenLinks describes green infrastructure as "those land-based resource assets vital to community well being" elevated to being equal with economic and community assets (GreenLinks 2006). The green infrastructure vision of the Washtenaw Metro Alliance is represented by an "interconnected system of open space . . . that supports ecological function, biodiversity, water quality, productive farmland, recreational opportunity and scenic character" (WMA 2007). The Saginaw Bay Greenways Collaborative sees green infrastructure as the new relationship between smart growth and smart conservation (SBGC 2005). The "Green Infrastructure Initiative" of the West Michigan Strategic Alliance modifies the Benedict and McMahon definition to include "other environmental assets that conserve the functions of natural ecosystems," further categorizing the region's green infrastructure into critical areas of biodiversity, trails and greenways, regional watersheds, shorelines and dunes, urban green areas, and farmland (WMSA 2002).

Individual Michigan communities have similarly offered a multitude of green infrastructure perspectives. Oakland County's "Green Infrastructure Visioning Project" envisions green infrastructure as "an interconnected network of open spaces, natural areas and waterways" focused "on conservation values and the services provided by natural systems in concert with, not in opposition to, land development" (Oakland County 2008). With its urban ecosystem analysis of the Detroit area, American Forests developed a digital model of green infrastructure as "the vegetative land cover along with its ecological interactions with soil, air, and water" best represented by the community's tree canopy, the largest component of green infrastructure, as a measurable barometer of how well green infrastructure is doing (American Forests 2006). Within the context of increasing foreclosures and land vacancies in the city of Flint, community advocates view this trend as an opportunity to repurpose the land and restore green infrastructure through parks, natural areas, urban farms, community gardens, greenways, and other greening efforts that bio-remediate contaminated land, protect sites prone to flooding, preserve headwaters of local watersheds, provide alternative transportation links, and create economic opportunities through entrepreneurial agriculture (Gillotti 2007).

As reflected in this collection of definitions, what "green infrastructure" represents will continue to be tailored to satisfy different community or organizational needs, highlighting the term's versatility in the scale, shape, and location of green infrastructure plus its multiple natural and social benefits. However, as a review of these and other definitions might suggest, green infrastructure basically uses or mimics ecological processes, whether in natural landscapes or engineered green spaces that stand in for compromised ecosystems. Like gray infrastructure, green infrastructure is also about strategically connecting essential components and preserving critical services that allow systems to function as intended. For many organizations, defining green infrastructure might be the easier task. Putting that definition to work can be more challenging.

The Evolution of County Park Systems and Green Infrastructure

"Green infrastructure" is a new term, but it has historic roots. One way to put green infrastructure in a historical perspective is to review why the present system of county parks was
created—reasons that still resonate with contemporary concerns—and how the ideals of
green infrastructure have come full circle. As Benedict and McMahon acknowledge,
although green infrastructure may be recently popularized in conservation literature and
discussions about land use planning, it is not a new concept (Benedict and McMahon 2002).
Its origins can be found in conservation efforts started more than 150 years ago, specifically
in connection with the creation of parks, including county parks, as a response to the growth
of metropolitan areas and the concomitant loss of natural landscapes. Green infrastructure,
as embodied in many parks, reflects the ongoing evolution of land conservation strategies
(Benedict and McMahon 2003).

Late in the nineteenth century, city residents sought to escape increasing urban conges-
tion by relocating to undeveloped lands outside of crowded cities. At about the same time,
community leaders noticed the continuing loss of natural landscapes and its impact on the
desire of urban populations to have access to natural beauty. A movement to establish parks
to preserve this natural beauty for the benefit of urban residents was initiated (Benedict and
McMahon 2003).

Frederick Law Olmsted, the visionary landscape architect of New York City's Central Park
in 1858, anticipated that green spaces outside of metropolitan areas might be destroyed and
that by the time urban expansion reached these outlying areas, green spaces would be badly
needed (Jacobs 1961). In addition, Olmsted promoted the linkage of parks with other green
spaces rather than leaving parks as isolated parcels.

This movement came to Michigan's most populated city. After Detroit's acquisition of
Belle Isle, citizens petitioned the city in 1879 to develop the island as a public park that
would emulate the parks and tree-lined boulevards of Paris. In 1883, the city secured the
services of Olmsted to design the park (NPS 1938). In the 1893 metropolitan parks plan for
Kansas City, Missouri, George Kessler similarly proposed linear parks to serve future neighborhoods as the city expanded, connecting significant sites with the countryside (Benedict
and McMahon 2003).

Today's concerns about the loss of green infrastructure from the expansion of urban areas
can be traced back to 1895, when the first county park was established in Essex County, New
Jersey, the county that includes the city of Newark (NPS 1938). At this time, Essex County had
a population exceeding 300,000 and was destined for rapid growth due to its proximity to
New York City. As described by one of the first county park commissioners, community leaders grew concerned that the county was in danger of becoming completely urbanized, losing
the natural benefits of its mountain ridges, fertile valleys, and wooded slopes. In addition,
Essex County was "made up of thickly settled cities and towns whose people are without
opportunity to get near Nature or Larger parks outside of cities" or "enjoy any open air recreation, except on the public highways or by trespassing upon private properties" (Kelsey 1905).

So began the movement for a county park system. Members of the local Board of Trade
observed that in nearly every large city in Europe and the United States—including Detroit, it

163

was specifically noted—a movement for larger parks and park systems was taking form. The city of Newark had approved a park plan but had taken no action. The county's townships were reluctant to establish and care for parks at their own expense. It was concluded that the only way a suitable system of parks and parkways could be established was by the county. Wasn't the entire county "parkable," supporters inquired? No one questioned the need for a system of county parks. Influential newspapers of the time supported the movement. Although there was novelty in the control of parks by the county, there were greater advantages, it was said at the time, from unifying all interests in the county for civic betterment (Kelsey 1905).

The momentum for county parks escalated. As residences rapidly occupied vacant lands, the county was urged not to delay in organizing a park system, since attractive lands were being removed from possible use as public parks. Concerns were expressed about how public sidewalks were disfigured by trolley, telegraph, and telephone poles and how these corridors could be improved with trees and other landscaping. Anticipating the continued expansion of electricity to power transportation as people moved between cities and the suburbs, the use of landscaping along designated parkways to dampen the impact of this traffic and noise was promoted (Kelsey 1905).

These parks and parkways would make Essex County more attractive, it was suggested. Every home near parks and parkways would become more appealing and valuable. The entire cost of park projects would eventually be realized through tax revenues from increased property values. "Every piece of property would share in the improvement and the cost be largely or fully compensated in this way. . . . People would not be purchasing just land. They would also be purchasing the ambiance of a metropolitan area made beautiful by the parks" (Kelsey 1905).

As Olmstead advocated, park supporters in Essex County envisioned a connective system of parks rather than separate, isolated sites. Smaller parks, it was proposed, would be under the purview of municipalities. Acquisition of parklands would connect features of the county park system, such as linking county parks together with parkways. Without this connection, it was noted, the county park system would be like a "pearl necklace minus the string" (Kelsey 1905).

Essex County citizens were quick to bless this plan. Civic organizations passed resolutions commending it, and citizens and conservation groups in other parts of the country wrote letters favoring its adoption. Essex County voters approved a $2.5 million bond referendum for the purchase of parkland (Kelsey 1905). The experience provided model legislation that created impetus for creating other county park systems.

By 1915, the county park concept spread to DuPage and Cook counties within the Chicago metropolitan area (Burke 1999). Serving the Detroit metropolitan area, Elizabeth Park became Michigan's first county park in the state's first county park system, the Wayne County park system in 1919 (Darga 1999). The first Ottawa County park was established in 1929 on Lake Michigan (Deur 1977). By 1930, just twelve counties within ten metropolitan regions controlled over 76 percent of the total county park acreage in the United States (NPS 1938).

The first county parks were often located along public transit lines, offering easy access and nearby respite to urban residents. Early in the history of county park systems, parkways—a 200-to-500-foot-wide stretch of landscaping on either side of a road—was also a popular form of park, often intended to follow river corridors and connect other county parks. As Essex County demonstrated, the county, as a political unit with access to sufficiently large acreage and adequate financial resources, was able to acquire and develop green spaces that municipal entities were finding difficult to provide. Although nature was preserved for its own sake in most county parks, many existed for the purpose of leisure and recreation for urban populations (NPS 1938).

Following World War II, the demand by increasingly urban populations for leisure and recreation experiences exploded (ORRRC 1962). The postwar growth of cities, the availability of more leisure time, and convenient transportation heightened the desire for recreational lands (Burke 1999). Providing leisure and recreation became a key purpose for most county parks rather than preserving natural features, an objective many county park systems today continue to pursue exclusively.

The trend since the 1990s is toward a renewed appreciation of the parks, which have become instrumental in defining key community amenities. Today, parks at all levels are deeply entwined with other functions. They often serve multiple purposes—recreational pursuits, exercise for health and fitness, economic development, and community centers that foster social networks and family relationships. To this list of park functions can be added preservation of threatened landscapes—woodlands, wetlands, and wildlife corridors—and maintenance of the natural functions or ecosystem services, such as storm water management, flood control, and air-quality improvements. This multifunctionality is one of the basic characteristics of green infrastructure, as well as parks (Benedict and McMahon 2002).

Assessing County Park Systems and Green Infrastructure

The number and size of county park systems have increased steadily over the last century. It is estimated that there are now thousands of county parks in hundreds of county park systems throughout the United States, most located in metropolitan areas where 80 percent of the population now lives (Harnik et al. 2006). Michigan has thirty-five county park systems that are members of the Michigan Association of County Parks and Recreation Officials. Individual county parks in the state typically range from a few acres of habitat preservation to more sizable holdings with features that are comparable to state parks. The total acreage in these county park systems range from fewer than 100 acres to over 11,000 acres with offerings that include golf courses, dog parks, swimming centers, playgrounds, disc golf, parkways, and camps and campgrounds. County parks with fewer acres tend to have areas for picnicking, playgrounds, ball fields, winter sports, nature study, boating, and swimming. Those county parks larger than 500 acres are big enough to preserve more expansive areas of the natural landscape, and, consequently, less of the park is set aside for recreational activities.

Since World War II, the expansion of both urban and county park systems has slowed considerably. As the public's interest in conserving natural landscapes in parks weakened, many parks began to deteriorate from both overuse and underuse as well as from neglect and vandalism (Harnik et al. 2006). This slowdown and ensuing deterioration have been attributed not only to declining park budgets but also to the continued growth of suburban areas and the perception that the role of parks in these low-density suburbs had become superfluous (Harnik et al. 2006).

Few studies have considered the contributions of county parks in managing the green infrastructure of a region. Despite this renewed interest in how parks contribute to the green infrastructure of metropolitan areas, benchmarks have not been established to present best practices. No authoritative protocol for assessing the green infrastructure of a park or accepted benchmark for establishing best practices in county park systems is available. There are, however, a few examples of evaluation strategies for national and urban parks, plus an award program for all levels of parks, that offer some insight. These efforts are summarized below.

The National Parks Conservation Association (NPCA) evaluates the health of national parks by using specific metrics to assess various aspects of the parks. These metrics indirectly include green infrastructure elements ranging from biodiversity to air quality (NPCA 2002). Report cards are issued by the NPCA on the condition of key natural and cultural resources in specific national parks. The overall objectives of the program are to determine patterns of preservation and degradation of natural and cultural resources across the national park system, illustrate the trends of resource condition in the national park system, and suggest approaches for measuring and monitoring indicators in the parks. Experts in related fields perform the assessment, including a review of management documents and programming activities in research, monitoring, and education. The criteria used in this report card focus much more on evaluating discrete ecological and cultural elements than on identifying any specific best practices in managing the park systems for these elements.

Another example of a process for evaluating park systems is the National Gold Medal Awards for Excellence in Park and Recreation Management, presented every year by the American Academy of Park and Recreation Management and the National Recreation and Park Association (NRPA). According to the NRPA website, the award process focuses on the achievements of park systems within different population categories, including county park systems. Although the award program started in 1965, there is no summary that benchmarks the types of best practices utilized by award winners in managing the natural features of the park system. The award process requires the applicants to self-examine and assesses their goals and accomplishments. A panel of professionals with expertise in park and recreation management selects the finalists, based on their entry forms, a twelve-minute video presentation, and a copy of their five-year plan. The award gives national recognition to park systems based on the following criteria:

1. Excellence in long-range planning
2. Fiscal resource management
3. Citizen support systems
4. Environmental stewardship
5. Preservation
6. Technological integration
7. Program planning and assessment
8. Professional development
9. Agency recognition
10. Services for special populations

For several years beginning in the 1990s, the Trust for Public Lands (TPL) collected and published data on the nation's city park systems (Harnik et al. 2006). Initially, the focus was on comparing urban park acreage and funding levels in the largest cities. These indicators were found to be inadequate to define the fundamental elements that constitute an excellent city park system. To answer that question, the TPL convened a group of urban and park experts in 2001. This workshop subsequently yielded a list of broad measures that could be used to define a successful city park system. Data on key indicators for these measures were collected through a mail survey of park and recreation systems in major cities. The resulting report was a first step in benchmarking city park systems with data showing how fifty-five U.S. city park systems compared. The report also provided examples of best practices in the cities studied. The report became known as "The Seven Habits of Highly Effective Park Systems" (Harnik et al. 2006). The seven indicators of park excellence or best practices include:

1. Mission statements with a clear expression of purpose
2. Ongoing planning and community involvement
3. Sufficient resources to meet the system's goals
4. Equitable park access
5. User satisfaction
6. Safety from physical hazards and crime
7. Benefits to the city beyond park boundaries

Since there were no benchmarks discovered for comparing the best practices identified specifically in county park systems, let alone for preserving green infrastructure, it was decided to adapt the TPL "Seven Habits" indicators, particularly using four of the seven indicators as relevant to county park systems. The specific indicators are used as points for comparison among selected county park systems; the benchmarks are not intended to correspond to any ideal condition, a particular standard, or a goal to be achieved. As the "Seven Habits" suggest, a best practice represents an exceptional practice that appears to be most successful at attaining beneficial results for the park system. Additionally, the term "park system" includes more than the physical characteristics of the parks, such as park acreage or trail miles. Park system also refers to the functional details that make parks possible, notably insightful leadership and relevant policies as well as the procedures established for planning, budgeting, and managing the day-to-day operations of the parks.

In order to create a county peer group, several counties were selected based on a similar population size (between 230,000 and 300,000) with Ottawa County. Since Ottawa County has experienced significant population growth in recent decades, choosing four counties with even larger populations may provide a glimpse into how highly populated metropolitan areas sustain green infrastructure within county park systems. Three additional Michigan counties were also included. Two counties—Ingham and Kalamazoo—had a population size comparable to Ottawa County, and one, Oakland, represented a more intensely populated Michigan county. In selecting these counties, another objective was to include geographic diversity. All of the benchmarked counties were associated with metropolitan

167

areas. The county park systems, including Ottawa County, selected for this exploratory comparison included:

- Du Page County Forest Preserve District, Illinois
- Gwinnett County Parks and Recreation Department, Georgia
- Howard County Department of Recreation and Parks, Maryland
- Ingham County Parks and Recreation Commission, Michigan
- Marin County Department of Parks and Open Space, California
- Lancaster County Department of Parks and Recreation, Pennsylvania
- Leon County Division of Parks and Recreation, Florida
- Kalamazoo County Parks and Fairgrounds, Michigan
- Kitsap County Department of Facilities, Parks and Recreation, Washington
- Oakland County Parks and Recreation Commission, Michigan
- Ottawa County Parks and Recreation Commission, Michigan
- Springfield-Greene County Park Board, Missouri

Demographic data were compiled for the selected counties to compare the similarities and differences in the communities as well as the implications for the county park system. For example, the income and educational profiles of both Howard County in Maryland and Marin County in California, with over 50 percent of the population with bachelor's degrees or higher and the highest incomes for the selected counties, suggest greater recreation demand and therefore the most potential for a greater level of interest in green infrastructure issues. Dramatic population increases, such as over 66 percent for Gwinnett County in Georgia between 1990 and 2000, implies a challenge for securing parkland fast enough to meet rising demand. Longer commutes for residents, especially over thirty minutes, suggest less time to visit and become familiar with the county parks of Kitsap County in Washington, Marin County in California, and Gwinnett County in Georgia. Other metrics were also used, where available, for comparing county park systems. The number of county parks, total park acreage, and park acreage per 1,000 residents are often used for comparing park systems with established national recreational standards (table 7.1). Each of the twelve county park websites was screened to ascertain which practices were apparent and reflected the four TPL "habits of highly effective park systems."

Parks do not just happen, and green infrastructure does not automatically protect itself (Harnik et al. 2006). As one of the "seven habits" of effective park systems, a clear expression of purpose, as reflected in a mission statement, declares the intentions of the park organization for its park system and guides its decisions and actions toward a desired outcome (Harnik et al. 2006). Although the term "green infrastructure" was not specifically utilized in any of the mission statements, other phrases, such as "natural resources," "environmental stewardship," and similar wording, suggest these concepts could include green infrastructure. For example, the mission statement for the Howard County park system promotes "opportunities for all residents to pursue safe and enjoyable leisure activities in balance with the protection and conservation of natural resources." Similarly, Kitsap County intends to develop and manage "open space and natural areas acquired and provided for beautification, urban growth buffers, passive recreational use, habitat preservation, storm water

Table 7.1. Comparison of County Park System Metrics and 2000 U.S. Census Data on Benchmarked Counties

County, State	2000 Pop.	Number of Parks and Acreage	Park Acres per 1,000 Residents	Total Land Acreage	Percent of Land Area in County Parks	Percent Population Change 1990–2000	Persons per Square Mile	Median Household Income	Percent Population with Bachelor's Degree or Higher	Mean Work Commute in Minutes
Oakland, Michigan	1,194,156	11 6,000+	5.0	558,729	1.0	10.2	1,369	$61,907	38.2	26.5
Du Page, Illinois	904,161	60 25,000+	26.6	213,760	11.7	15.7	2,710	$67,887	41.7	29.0
Gwinnett, Georgia	588,448	28 8,000+	1.4	277,120	2.9	66.7	1,360	$60,537	34.1	32.2
Lancaster, Penn.	490,562	8 2,000+	0.4	607,360	0.3	11.3	496	$47,380	20.5	21.7
Howard, Maryland	247,842	46 8,211	3.2	161,280	5.1	32.3	983	$74,167	52.9	30.2
Ingham, Michigan	279,320	12 1,400	0.5	358,400	0.4	<0.9>	500	$41,540	33.0	20.1
Marin, California	247,289	49 15,175	6.1	387,840	3.9	7.5	476	$71,306	51.3	32.3
Greene, Missouri	240,391	80 2,700+	1.1	432,000	0.6	15.6	356	$34,157	24.2	19.2
Leon, Florida	239,452	11 2,800	1.2	426,880	0.7	24.4	359	$37,517	49.9	21.7
Kalamazoo, Michigan	238,603	5 1,191	0.5	359,680	0.3	6.9	425	$44,667	21.8	24.1
Ottawa, Michigan	238,314	25 4,680	2.0	362,240	1.3	26.9	421	$52,347	26.0	19.4
Kitsap, Wash.	231,969	74 5,694	2.5	253,440	2.3	22.3	586	$51,042	25.3	32.5

SOURCE. Individual County Park Web sites and U.S. Census Bureau, http://quickfacts.census.gov/qfd/index.html.

169

control, trails and land banked for future opportunities"—all concepts associated with green infrastructure. Another example is provided by the mission for the Kalamazoo County park system to "provide responsible stewardship and preservation of our green spaces and historic resources with recreation, relaxation, and learning opportunities for everyone."

Ongoing planning combined with community involvement, another indicator of effective park systems, builds on a process that "demonstrates a path of achievement" and "expresses a final outcome" (Harnik et al. 2006). An inventory that periodically assesses the environmental challenges faced in the park system and the types of ecosystems at risk and in need of additional attention needs to be part of an ongoing planning process related specifically to preserving green infrastructure. Both Marin and DuPage counties have defined what system-wide natural features should be protected and then determined what has in fact been protected. Kitsap County notes that it has more marine habitat than any other county in the lower forty-eight states, and the county is regularly visited by more than 200 species of birds, with 115 species that nest there. Most of the county park systems surveyed noted the challenges of managing invasive species but did not specify how nonnative species were displacing native species or contributing to their decline. Very few identified whether the park system contained habitat for endangered or threatened species. DuPage County, however, has been active in improving habitat for the endangered Blanding turtle and has identified habitat locations.

The ability to build community support and involvement, outside of required public hearings, along with cultivating an informed constituency, has also become an indicator of successful park systems (Harnik et al. 2006). All of the benchmarked counties used a website to educate and engage their stakeholders in programs or projects that highlight the preservation of green infrastructure. In addition to the websites, most county park systems either mailed hard-copy newsletters or made electronic newsletters available, along with other relevant publications, such as brochures on selected issues or the results of completed studies. Similarly, most county park systems have utilized programs involving naturalist-led hikes or have promoted presentations on nature-related topics. DuPage County has created a tree identification trail that teaches interested groups how to identify their local trees. Another technique for cultivating a constituency is the organization of volunteers or "friends" groups, which were found in most of the selected park systems.

For most park systems, the strength of their partnerships with the private sector, other nonprofit organizations, or other governmental entities expanded community wisdom and improved the effectiveness of their efforts in preserving green infrastructure. DuPage County is a member of Chicago Wilderness, a consortium of over 200 public and private organizations that shares green infrastructure expertise and insights with the larger conservation community. Greene County Parks has partnered with several organizations, such as the Watershed Center, Ozark Greenways, Audubon Society, and the Missouri Department of Natural Resources and Conservation, on a variety of projects. Leon County has accessed some of the most knowledgeable expertise for green infrastructure through the Nature Conservancy, particularly for the unique Red Hills region and Woodville Karst Plain of northern Florida.

Another habit of effective urban park systems is securing sufficient resources to meet the park system's goals, including reliable funding dedicated to park acquisition and development

(Harnik et al. 2006). Seven of the twelve county park systems, in addition to Ottawa County, were funded in part by voter-approved taxation that established dedicated revenue structures. Greene and Leon counties both increased the sales tax to fund the park system, while Marin, DuPage, and Ottawa counties relied on additional property taxes. Other county park systems were supported by a combination of general funds, fees, and grants without any additional support from voter referendums. According to the Trust for Public Land LandVote website, 151 counties since 1996 have prioritized land conservation with new or reconsidered conservation programs. The TPL website further states that county voters have passed 260 ballot measures in this period, generating $14.3 billion for open space, parks, watersheds, recreational lands, and wildlife preserves. Over 77 percent of all county conservation ballot measures in the last decade have won voter approval, as highlighted on the TPL website, illustrating how willing and supportive voters are to sustain conservation in their communities.

Many of these reviewed county park systems utilized best practices. They presented strong mission statements for land conservation, participated in ongoing planning, promoted active public involvement, and brought diverse interests together to create partnerships and generate community support and funding for the county park system. Additionally, these county park systems and their green infrastructure created benefits for community vitality and ecosystem services, benefits that extended beyond park boundaries. Benedict and McMahon (2006) note that green infrastructure provides a new framework that offers a strategic approach to land conservation. Despite these identified best practices, the use of green infrastructure to strategically frame conservation, to shape the patterns of development, and to combine conservation with other community goals, such as watershed management or economic development, were much less common.

Green Infrastructure in Ottawa County Parks: A Case Study

The Ottawa County park system was selected as a case study of how green infrastructure can be positively managed within a county park system affected by metropolitan expansion. Between 1990 and 2000, the county's population increased nearly 27 percent compared to its neighboring counties with 15 percent in Kent County, 17 percent in Allegan County, and 7 percent in Muskegon County (U.S. Census Bureau 2000).

With a location that allows access to urban areas for jobs, shopping, and entertainment, as well as bordering the appealing Lake Michigan shoreline, Ottawa County will likely continue to attract growth and become more densely populated in the years ahead. Additionally, the county will continue to experience pressure on converting its green spaces to more intense urban development. Its population of over 255,000 people in 2005 is projected to approach 400,000 by 2020 (WMRPC 2001).

The history of Ottawa County is familiar. Like much of Michigan, the county was predominantly forested before European exploration and settlement. With the escalating demand for lumber, massive areas of forests were rapidly eliminated during a short period of commercial logging in the nineteenth century. Following logging, these cleared lands were converted to agricultural uses, a major economic engine for the county that remains vital today. Over the past fifty years, many of the natural areas in the county that were once

171

forested or farmed have been converted to urban uses to meet the needs of growing populations.

In surveys of its natural features, it has been noted that very little of Ottawa County's native landscape remains (MDNR 1988). The combination of logging, farming, and urban sprawl has severely fractured the county's natural landscape. The woodlands, wetlands, and other natural areas—those areas where much of the county's green infrastructure has persisted—have become much smaller pieces, physically unconnected to each other and increasingly isolated. Streams and their corridors contain the highest percentage of these wetlands and woodlands in the county, reflecting areas that were too steep or too wet to log, farm, or develop.

Park System Developments and Plans

The loss of green spaces and the fragmentation of the county's landscape did not go unnoticed. The Ottawa County Road Commission, as provided by a 1913 state law, was designated as park trustees (Deur 1977). In 1929, the seventeen-acre Tunnel Park on Lake Michigan became Ottawa County's first county park. It was not until 1941 that North Beach Park, the county's second shoreline park, was developed. The decision to enlarge the county park system was made in the late 1950s with the purchase of Riverside Park and Deer Creek Park on the Grand River and the acquisition of Grose Park on Crockery Lake in 1962. At nearly the same time, the trustees took over a township park, now known as Spring Grove Park. Hager Hardwood Forest and Arboretum was subsequently established, and a large parcel of tax-reverted land bordering the Pigeon River was purchased from the federal government. In 1973, Kirk Park, the ninth county park and third one on Lake Michigan, was developed (WSRDC 1983).

Several community leaders expressed concern that the pace of population growth in the county was not being matched by similar growth in the county park system and that the opportunities for securing additional parkland were diminishing. After discussions were initiated on how best to revitalize the county park system, the Ottawa County Board of Commissioners reviewed the advantages and disadvantages of various options provided under state law. In 1987, the Ottawa County Parks and Recreation Commission (OCPRC) was formerly organized (Ottawa County Parks Staff 1995).

The Ottawa County park system was originally created to provide a traditional source of recreation to county residents (WMSRDC 1975). With the organization of the OCPRC, another purpose was established for the county park system—preserving natural elements of the county's landscape that were gradually slipping away. Since then, the OCPRC has aggressively pursued a resource-based system of county parks, focused on identifying and acquiring lands that contain high concentrations of natural resources and green infrastructure. Those properties identified as containing critical environmental assets were prioritized for preservation by the OCPRC (Ottawa County Parks Staff 1995). When the OCPRC took over the county park system, there were nine county parks totaling about 620 acres. After nearly eighty years of existence, the Ottawa County park system has grown to more than 5,200 acres in twenty-two natural resource-based parks and ten open-space properties, with much of that growth occurring in the past ten years (Parks Commission 2008).

Further growth of the Ottawa County park system required anticipating future needs and assuring a source of stable funds to realize these needs. The Ottawa County park system has been the subject of a series of park plans, beginning with a preliminary plan prepared for the Ottawa County Road Commission in 1970. Following this preliminary plan, updates were prepared for the Road Commission in 1975 and 1983. The first plan developed by the OCPRC was completed in 1989, and it was this plan that first suggested pursuing a millage for financing park system improvements through land acquisition and development (Ottawa County Parks Staff 2006).

In 1996, the approval of the county parks millage by nearly 54 percent of county voters substantially changed the course of the county park system. The Land Legacy Program has been funded by a 0.33 mil property tax on all taxable properties in the county. These funds have been dedicated to the acquisition and development of open space and parklands. Between 1997 and 2007, nearly 3,000 acres were added to the county park system. In addition to offering recreational opportunities, park acquisitions have included property on each major lake and river system in the county, plus sites that will protect and preserve wildlife habitat, diminishing woodlands, and sensitive shore lands. With millage funds used as match, the OCPRC has been able to leverage more than $14 million in grants and private donations to further secure green infrastructure (Ottawa County Parks Staff 2008).

The OCPRC, in defining green infrastructure, has referenced the work of the Conservation Fund and the U.S. Forest Service, where the definition refers to "our nation's life support system" and "an interconnected network . . . that contributes to the health and quality of life for America's communities and people" (Ottawa County Parks Staff 2006). The green infrastructure contained in the Ottawa County park system consists of the Lake Michigan shoreline, globally unique sand dunes, river and stream valleys, ravines, woodlands, bayous, wildlife habitat, historic sites, rural and open space vistas, and corridors that accommodate the movement needs of people and wildlife. Many in Ottawa County, including its electorate, have recognized that the window for securing major pieces of its green infrastructure was closing.

The most recent county park plan was adopted in February 2006. This comprehensive plan identified the OCPRC's priorities for the next five to ten years and outlined the future direction for the county park system, including, specifically for the first time, the development of green infrastructure in the county park system (Ottawa County Parks Staff 2006). During the August 2006 election, 67 percent of Ottawa County voters renewed the parks millage for another ten-year period, providing funds for the park system through 2017. This renewal will allow the OCPRC to continue with land acquisition along major river corridors and the Lake Michigan shoreline. Funds will also be used for improvements to both new and existing park properties as well as for parks operations.

Green Infrastructure Stakeholders

The efforts to preserve and restore elements of the Ottawa County park system's green infrastructure represent a long-term commitment. This commitment can only be achieved with the support and involvement of many public and private organizations, including local units of government, private landowners, state and federal agencies, nonprofit groups, county voters, volunteer citizens, county staff, and the general public. A few of these organizations are described in the following paragraphs.

The Ottawa County park system is administered by the OCPRC. As provided under state law (Act 261 of the Public Acts of 1965), the Ottawa County Board of Commissioners appoints seven members of the ten-member OCPRC. Those members not directly appointed include the chairs of the Ottawa County Road Commission and the Ottawa County Planning Commission, along with the Ottawa County Drain Commissioner (Ottawa County Parks Staff 2006). All actions of the OCPRC are subject to the approval of the Board of Commissioners. The OCPRC is authorized to acquire land for the county park system and to develop and maintain such land and establish rules for its protection. In addition, the OCPRC establishes policies, develops plans, approves grant applications, establishes a budget, and recommends fee increases. The mission of the OCPRC is to "provide residents and visitors to Ottawa County with the highest quality of leisure opportunities and promote high standards for environmental quality and land use planning through a resource-based system of parks, open space lands, programs, and other services" (Ottawa County Parks Staff 2006).

The staff of the OCPRC are also essential to guiding the park system and represent critical players in the success of the county park system. The Ottawa County Parks staff assist the OCPRC in planning, developing, and managing the county park system. The Ottawa County Parks director, who reports to the OCPRC and the Board of Commissioners, advises and carries out the directives of the OCPRC and has day-to day management responsibility for the county park system.

In its efforts to preserve and restore the green infrastructure in the county park system, the OCPRC has partnered with a variety of organizations. Over the years, the Michigan Department of Natural Resources (MDNR), which manages the state parks and other natural areas in the county, has reviewed the plans of the OCPRC and financed, through the Michigan Natural Resources Trust Fund and county matching funds, the acquisition and development of several county parks. Similarly, the Michigan Department of Environmental Quality and the Michigan Department of Transportation have collaborated and financed several important aspects of green infrastructure improvements in Ottawa County.

Several nonprofit organizations have also been key partners in the OCPRC's activities. The Land Conservancy of West Michigan has worked to protect natural lands along the Grand River and elsewhere in Ottawa County using a variety of methods, such as setting up conservation easements or securing additional funds for acquisition. The Macatawa Greenway Partnership has been critical to the success of projects along the Macatawa River. As a member of the Green Infrastructure Leadership Council of the West Michigan Strategic Alliance, the OCPRC through the Ottawa County Parks director has shared experiences as well as gained insights into the role of green infrastructure in this larger region.

According to their website, the Friends of Ottawa County Parks, a group of park supporters that was organized in 2005, is dedicated to "connecting people with nature, recreation and the community at large by partnering with the Ottawa County Parks & Recreation Commission." The group sponsors programs and hosts events to build awareness of the Ottawa County park system.

The Ottawa County voters have played the crucial role in supporting the county park system and defining how resolutely the county park system can pursue the preservation of green infrastructure. A survey conducted in 2006 asked a random sample of Ottawa County registered voters what they liked most about living in Ottawa County. The top two answers to this open-ended question, nearly one out of three responses, were related to the county's green infrastructure, specifically "green space" by 17 percent of respondents and "Lake Michigan" by 15 percent of respondents (EPIC-MRA 2006).

In the past planning efforts, improvements to the Ottawa County park system often meant the expansion of a park to accommodate increased park use or the construction of recreational and support facilities, such as creating more parking spaces, building a boat launch, lengthening a hiking trail, or adding picnic tables (WMSRDC 1975, 1983). These types of improvements will continue to remain an integral part of operating the county park system. However, there has been a subtle transformation over the years in how the Ottawa County park system is directed and managed. For example, while preserving natural features remains one of the tenets for acquiring parkland, a county park can also be used to restore ecosystem services and secure regional green infrastructure. The following projects highlight some of the efforts that have been undertaken by the OCPRC to restore ecosystem services and secure green infrastructure in the Ottawa County park system.

In 1995, the "Parks, Recreation and Open Space Plan" first proposed establishing a greenway along the county's forty-mile Grand River corridor. The Grand River corridor, with its ecological significance and historical influence in the county, could not be effectively protected as a series of isolated parks (Ottawa County Parks Staff 1995). Following the completion of the 1995 plan, the OCPRC met with various stakeholders to introduce the concept of establishing a greenway along the Grand River. Subsequently, an inventory of natural features along the Grand River and a greenway master plan were prepared for the Grand River corridor. The inventory provided a more in-depth review and assessment of the river corridor's existing natural lands, historic sites, and other significant resources than previous studies. The study also noted that much of what remains of the county's native landscape lies along the Grand River within its riparian forests, ravines, wetlands, and bayous (Day & Associates 1997).

When the 1995 plan was being prepared, before the stakeholder meetings and the natural features inventory, the OCPRC envisioned the Grand River greenway as a nontraditional, linear open space that could connect the undeveloped, natural areas of river's corridor. There was initial trepidation in pursuing this type of strategy, suggesting that a greenway might appear as "extreme environmentalism" (Ottawa County Parks Staff 1995). After a series of stakeholder meetings, there was a much stronger position on the promotion of a greenway strategy in the county. In fact, the 2006 plan strongly emphasized the role of greenways along all three of the county's major river corridors and included a proposal for a Lake Michigan coastal greenway. This plan further highlighted the attributes of these river corridors in containing some of the county's green infrastructure and noted that these greenways also offer a natural amenity to county residents and visitors (Ottawa County Parks Staff 2006). With the completion of the 2006 plan, existing parks and new park projects were organized on the basis of designated county greenways, reflecting the plan's greenway initiatives and green infrastructure objectives. Following the adoption of this greenway strategy, acquisition of additional key lands along the Grand River and other rivers, as well as the Lake Michigan shoreline, was under way.

Green Infrastructure Projects

In 1999, Ottawa County acquired Grand River Park from Georgetown Township. At the time of this transfer, about thirty acres of farmland existed, providing little in the way of wildlife habitat. Restoring this habitat and creating a more diverse natural area were the objectives for improving this particular greenway park. During the spring of 2000, native warm-season grasses and a variety of wildflower seeds were planted in the former farm fields to create a twenty-four-acre native grassland. This native grassland created travel corridors for wildlife, provided nesting sites, offered a food source, and established winter cover that allowed animals to survive cold temperatures and winds. By creating this grassland, the diversity of the existing natural communities within the park, such as the floodplain forest, beech-maple forest, and shrub-scrub wetlands, were improved (Bauer-Ford Reclamation Design 2000).

Near to the Grand River corridor, the natural features of Hager Park, a 104-acre county park known for its mature hardwood forest and spectacular spring wildflower displays, were in danger of ongoing deterioration. Severe stream bank erosion along Hager Creek, which flows through the park, was intensifying from unlimited access to the stream by park users and by flash floods resulting upstream in a rapidly urbanizing watershed. Large amounts of soil were eroding away, undercutting large trees, exposing their roots, and destabilizing their foothold. If this erosion continued, Hager Park would lose a vital portion of its trees, wildflowers, habitat, and the hydrologic and other green infrastructure services of Hager Creek (Ottawa County Parks Staff 2006).

The OCRPC's goal was to restore Hager Creek, its stream bank, and watershed to a more natural condition. To achieve this goal, a watershed management plan was prepared to address not just the creek's segment in the park but also to consider the Hager Creek watershed beyond the park. Input from park users and watershed residents, in addition to technical experts, was obtained in preparing the watershed management plan. The full Hager Creek watershed was also studied, with its hydrologic problems and causes identified and possible solutions recommended. The declining conditions of Hager Creek were corrected by diverting a majority of the storm water runoff to infiltrate in an area of Hager Park planted with native vegetation. Other techniques for restoring the stream bank and preventing further erosion included the placement of rock riffles, live staking, and vegetated grids (Ottawa County Parks Staff 2006).

The Macatawa River Greenway was proposed under the 2006 plan. Historically, the Macatawa River wandered around its floodplain on its way to Lake Macatawa. Periodic flooding created a rich wetland habitat. Eventually, these meanderings were straightened and drainage tiles installed to improve farming. Decades after channelization, the river's floodplain and wetland habitats were severely disrupted, and flooding became more frequent as rain failed to seep into the ground. Over time, runoff into the river carried sediment, agricultural chemicals, and nutrients. These pollutants contributed to the watershed's worsening water quality, including the decline of water quality in Lake Macatawa, a lake with high recreational value in the heart of the Holland metropolitan area (Ottawa County Parks Staff 2006).

The possibility of restoring the ecological integrity of the Macatawa River's ecosystem was first envisioned in the late 1990s. Since then, beginning in 2000, nearly 600 acres of previously farmed floodplain with forested uplands were acquired within the upper Macatawa River watershed near the Holland-Zeeland metropolitan area. With the acquisition of these lands and the establishment of the Upper Macatawa Conservation Area (UMCA), the OCPRC undertook its largest and most ambitious restoration project. This project sought to fulfill four primary objectives: water quality improvement, flood reduction, wildlife habitat creation, and the development of resource-based recreational opportunities (Ottawa County Parks Staff 2006).

Since its inception, portions of the Macatawa River in the UMCA have been realigned and meanders put back into place. The river's corridor has been revegetated with thousands of tree plantings and native vegetative buffers installed to filter sediment and phosphorus from runoff. A series of shallow-water ponds, wet meadows, and other wetlands have been re-created to ease flooding by storing runoff. It has been estimated that over 16,000 pounds of phosphorous per year will be removed with full-scale restoration (MACC 2005). The restored wetlands, wooded ravines, and grasslands of the UMCA also provide habitat for a diversity of wildlife, anchoring green infrastructure that will be linked to an expanding green corridor in a rapidly urbanizing area. In addition to restoring important habitat along a unique segment of the river corridor, the UMCA provides a wide range of outdoor recreational opportunities. For example, a trail extending from the Kent County trail system will run 2.5 miles through the conservation area and on through to the city of Holland (Ottawa County Parks Staff 2006).

As the OCPRC continues to gain experience in restoring ecosystem services and securing green infrastructure in the county park systems, more ambitious projects are being planned. For example, the restoration of a gravel and sand mining complex, complete with oil wells, in an area along the Grand River, referred to as the "Bend" area, has been imagined for several years. The OCPRC identified the Bend area, an active mining operation with four operators, as the future location for a new 500-acre county park with one-and-a-half-mile river frontage once mining is completed within the next decade (Ottawa County Parks Staff 2006). In 2000, the OCPRC developed a master plan for this area. This plan also serves as the reclamation plan required as part of the permit for these four operators and was adopted by the Georgetown Township Mineral Mining Board. As mining operations wind down, the plan calls for the OCPRC to purchase key parcels and eventually develop an existing lake for recreational use and reclaim wetlands for habitat and hydrologic storage. Trails would be built along the river to connect with trails in the west from county properties and in the east from Kent County (Bauer-Ford Reclamation Design 2000).

Implications for Policy in Michigan Metropolitan Affairs

County park systems within and outside of Michigan have taken various actions to maintain the natural character of the landscape surrounding metropolitan areas. Ottawa County illustrates how a county experiencing a rapid pace of development from expanding metropolitan areas sustains a park system focused on capturing larger pieces of green infrastructure before the county's natural values are further diminished. With the support of its voters, who also recognized that this was a race against time, Ottawa County has taken steps to preserve and restore green infrastructure within county parks. The county is stringing together as much of those remaining pieces of green infrastructure as possible, especially along Lake Michigan and the county's rivers and streams. In reviewing the efforts of Ottawa County in addressing green infrastructure in its park system, the following critical lessons were learned.

Parks are embedded in a larger landscape. They do not simply contain green infrastructure; they represent infrastructure that is living, changing, and moving beyond artificial limits. Some might view green infrastructure as being contained only in a community's system of public parks and open space; that it stops at the boundary of the park or at the border of the community. When standing on the edge of a county park, it should be apparent that green infrastructure does not end at the park border or at the county line. What happens to green infrastructure on one side of the park boundary should not be any different than what is happening on the other side. The impacts of development and the influence of green infrastructure spill into and out of parks that are next door, downwind, or downstream. Borders reflect political convenience rather than ecological necessity.

Parks are intentional; they provide a sense of permanence. Thus, public officials must intentionally identify lands that are key to protecting green infrastructure and plan to permanently protect these key lands in the park system or in another venue. Green infrastructure should be used as one of the criteria in acquiring land, designing parks, and operating parks. More examples of where the concepts of green infrastructure have been intentionally addressed in park projects need to be promoted. Parks can be used as real models of how green infrastructure can be protected in other developments.

Park planners are beginning to recognize the need to transition their efforts toward contributing to a more sustainable park system. More planners are ceasing to act only as groundskeepers and are intentionally performing as stewards of the park, the natural environment, and green infrastructure. According to Benedict and McMahon (2002), successful green infrastructure initiatives have to be:

- More proactive and less reactive
- More systematic and less haphazard
- Multifunctional, not single purpose
- Large scale, not small scale, and
- Better integrated with other efforts to manage growth and development

A stable configuration of parklands that will remain permanently in public ownership is essential. Sometimes easements may be insufficient and land must be bought to keep it free of development. In a growing community, where all land may have some development value, the only workable solution for intentionally preserving critical green infrastructure might be public ownership, such as in a park. Some landowners might leave their land untouched for years, but such undeveloped land in private ownership is temporary. The next owner or generation may bring in the bulldozers.

Large protected and connected natural habitats are the foundation for any green infrastructure network. One of the most difficult and ineffective strategies in park development is to buy small parcels of land and try to reassemble fragmented properties into a park. It is a much better strategy to buy land before it is broken up. In Ottawa County, much of this land lies along river corridors where it has been difficult to farm and develop.

The rapid development in Ottawa County of the past few decades is likely to continue. Much of this development will take advantage of opportunities to live in or near natural amenities. For example, the county's position along Lake Michigan makes it a destination for recreation and a magnet for development. There will continue to be a decreasing opportunity to preserve open space. There will be lots of small green areas here and there for county parks, but the larger green areas where linkages are critical will disappear much sooner.

County park systems can play a key role in providing a robust venue for green infrastructure. They allow a broader, regional perspective on landscapes without losing the intimacy of green infrastructure associated with an individual park. Most county parks are often located within a short driving distance of metropolitan areas. They can also be part of trail networks or located along public transportation routes. County park systems can be more nimble in responding to opportunities to acquire a property in comparison to state park agencies or local communities. With the number of county park systems in Michigan that neighbor metropolitan areas, collaboration and cooperation on preserving green infrastructure throughout the state can easily be accommodated.

Although county parks make up a very small fraction of the landscape—in Ottawa County, the county parks occupy slightly over 1 percent of the county's land area—these parks are disproportionately more valuable for weaving regional green infrastructure together and anchoring the green infrastructure network for Michigan's metropolitan areas. Metropolitan areas, in considering green infrastructure initiatives, should be encouraged to vigorously support and leverage what preserved green infrastructure might already exist in the county park systems found in their own backyards.

Future efforts that could build on this initial work might include a more quantitative analysis of the relationships between metropolitan areas, county park systems, and green infrastructure. These efforts might involve surveys of county park administrators to measure familiarity with the green infrastructure concepts, acreage of green infrastructure that has been preserved or restored within county park systems, attempts at connecting county parks with other green infrastructure networks, the nature of partnerships in making these connections, and other approaches to preserving green infrastructure by county park systems in metropolitan areas.

REFERENCES

American Forests. 2006. Urban Ecosystem Analysis SE Michigan and City of Detroit: Calculating the Value of Nature. Https://www.americanforests.org/downloads/rea/AF_Detroit.pdf.

Bauer-Ford Reclamation Design. 2000. Bend Area Master Plan. Ottawa County Parks Commission.

Benedict, M., and E. T. McMahon. 2002. Green Infrastructure: Smart Conservation for the 21st Century. Http://www.conservationfund.org/sites/default/files/GI_SC21C.pdf.

———. 2003. How Cities Use Parks for Green Infrastructure. American Planning Association. Http://www.planning.org/cpf/webuser/pdf/greeninfrastructure.pdf.

———. 2006. *Green Infrastructure: Linking Landscapes and Communities.* Washington, D.C.: Island Press.

Burke, V. 1999. Feasibility of Establishing a Rural County Park System in Saline County Missouri. University of Missouri. Http://saline.missouri.edu/documents/ParksStudy/parks.htm.

Chicago Wilderness. 2004. Chicago Wilderness Green Infrastructure Vision: Final Report. Http://www.cmap.illinois.gov/uploadedFiles/archives/nipc/environment/sustainable/Green_Infrastructure_Vision_Final_Report.pdf.

Darga, N. 1999. Historic Summary of Wayne County Parks. Http://www.waynecounty.com/parks/history.htm.

Day & Associates. 1997. A Natural and Cultural Features Inventory of the Grand River Greenway Corridor in Ottawa County, Michigan. Ottawa County Parks Commission.

Deur, Lynn. 1977. Sixty-five Years: A History of the Ottawa County Road Commission 1911–1976. Ottawa County Road Commission.

EPIC-MRA. 2006. Ottawa County Citizen Survey: Executive Summary and Demographic Analysis. Ottawa County Board of Commissioners.

Gillotti, T., and D. Kildee. 2007. Land Banks as Revitalization Tools: The example of Genesee County and the City of Flint, Michigan. Http://www.geneseeinstitute.org/downloads/Revitalization_Tools.pdf.

GreenLinks (Genesee, Lapeer, and Shiawassee Counties). 2006. Conservation Needs Assessment: A Community-Based Assessment of Conservation and Recreation Needs. Http://www.flintriver.org/greenlinks/assets/PDFs/CNA_Book.pdf.

Harnik, P., R. L. Ryan, M. C. Houck, A. C. Lusk, W. D. Solecki, and C. Rosenzweig. 2006. *The Humane Metropolis: People and Nature in the 21st-Century City. Part Two: From City Parks to Regional Green Infrastructure.* Amherst: University of Massachusetts Press. Http://scholarworks.umass.edu/cgi/viewcontent.cgi?article=1003&context=umpress_thm.

Jacobs, J. 1961. *The Death and Life of Great American Cities.* New York: Random House.

Kelsey, F. W. 1905. *The First Essex County Park System.* Washington, D.C.: McGrath Publishing Company.

MACC (Macatawa Area Coordinating Council). 2005. The Macatawa Watershed Project. Http://www.the-macc.org/watershed/Macatawa%20Watershed%20Phosphorus%20Reduction%20Implementation%20Plan.pdf.

MCACA (Michigan Council for Arts and Cultural Affairs). 2006. Capital Improvements Program Guide-lines. Http://www.michigan.gov/documents/hal/mcaca_CI_Guidelines_09_225256_7.pdf.

MDNR (Michigan Department of Natural Resources). 1988. Michigan Natural Features Inventory Pro-gram: Review of Special Sites in Ottawa County. Lansing: Michigan Department of Natural Resources.

———. 2006. Guidelines for the Development of Community Park, Recreation, Open Space and Green-way Plans. Http://www.michigan.gov/documents/IC1924_149265_7.pdf.

MNCPPC (Maryland—National Capital Park and Planning Commission). 2006. Countywide Green Infrastructure Plan. Http://www.mc-mncppc.org/green_infrastructure/index.shtm.

MSPO (Maine State Planning Office). 2006. Sustaining Maine's Green Infrastructure. Http://www.maine.gov/spo/natural/gov/docs/final_white_paper061206.pdf.

NPCA (National Parks Conservation Association). (2002). State of the Parks: Natural Resources Assess-ment and Ratings Methodology. Http://www.npca.org/stateoftheparks/methodology1.pdf.

NPS (National Park Service). 1938. Recreational Use of Land in the United States: Part XI of the Report on Land Planning. Http://www.cr.nps.gov/history/online_books/recreation_use/index.htm.

Oakland County Green Infrastructure Visioning Project. 2008. Https://www.co.oakland.mi.us/peds/program_service/es_prgm/green_infras/gi_def.html.

ORRRC (Outdoor Recreation Resources Review Commission). 1962. *Outdoor Recreation for America: A Report to the President and to the Congress.* Washington, D.C.: Bureau of Outdoor Recreation, Department of the Interior.

Ottawa County Parks Staff. 1995. Ottawa County Parks, Recreation and Open Space Plan. Ottawa County Parks and Recreation Commission.

———. 2006. Ottawa County Parks, Recreation and Open Space Plan. Ottawa County Parks and Recreation Commission. Http://miottawa.org/ParksVI/Parks/plan.htm.

Parks Commission Releases New Brochure. February 20, 2008. *Grand Haven Tribune.* Http://www.grandhaventribune.com/paid/298383582636722.bsp.

SBGC (Saginaw Bay Greenways Collaborative). 2005. A Vision of Green for Michigan's Bay, Midland and Saginaw Counties: A Science- and Community-Based Process. Http://www.saginawbaywin.org/uploads/vision_green.pdf.

SMPC (Southwest Michigan Planning Commission). 2006. Low Impact Development News. Http://www.swmpc.org/downloads/LID_NEWS_2.pdf.

U.S. Census Bureau. 2000. Http://quickfacts.census.gov/qfd/index.html.

USEPA (U.S. Environmental Protection Agency). 2007. Http://cfpub.epa.gov/npdes/greeninfrastructure.cfm.

Wayne County Parks. 1999. Historic Summary of Wayne County Parks. Http://www.waynecounty.com/parks/history.htm.

WMA (Washtenaw Metro Alliance). 2007. Green Places: Open Spaces—A Plan for Coordinated Parkland and Open Space. http://wma.ewashtenaw.org.

WMRPC (West Michigan Regional Planning Commission). 2001. Ottawa County Demographic Profile. Http://www.wmrpc.org/county%20profiles/Ottawa_County_Profile.html.

WMSA (West Michigan Strategic Alliance).2002. The Common Framework: West Michigan A Region in Transition. Http://www.wm-alliance.org/documents/publications/The_Common_Framework.pdf.

WMSRDC (West Michigan Shoreline Regional Development Commission). 1975. An Update: Recreation Plan for Ottawa County. Muskegon: West Michigan Shoreline Regional Development Commission.

———. 1983. A Plan for Park and Recreation Resources in Ottawa County, Michigan. Muskegon: West Michigan Shoreline Regional Development Commission.

COUNTY PARK SYSTEM WEB SITES

Du Page County, Illinois (Forest Preserve District). Http://www.dupageforest.com.

Greene County, Missouri (Springfield–Greene County Park Board). Http://www.parkboard.org/information/about_us.htm.

Gwinnett County, Georgia (Parks and Recreation Department). Http://www.co.gwinnett.ga.us/cgi-bin/gwincty/egov/ep/gcbrowse.do?channelId=−536881904&pageTypeId=536880236.

Howard County, Maryland (Department of Recreation and Parks). Http://www.co.ho.md.us/RAP/RAP_HoCoParks.htm.

Ingham County, Michigan (Parks and Recreation Commission). Http://www.ingham.org/PK/Home.htm.

Kalamazoo County, Michigan (Parks and Fairgrounds). Http://www.kalcounty.com/parks/.

Kitsap County, Washington (Department of Facilities, Parks and Recreation). Http://www.kitsapgov.com/parks/default.htm.

Lancaster County, Pennsylvania (Department of Parks and Recreation). Http://www.co.lancaster.pa.us/parks/cwp/view.asp?a=3&q=516085&parksNav=|.

Leon County, Florida (Division of Parks and Recreation). Http://www.leoncountyfl.gov/parks/.

Marin County, California (Department of Parks and Open Space). Http://www.co.marin.ca.us/depts/PK/main/.

Oakland County, Michigan (Parks and Recreation Commission). Http://www.oakgov.com/parksrec/about/.

Ottawa County, Michigan (Parks and Recreation Commission). Http://www.co.ottawa.mi.us/ParksVI/Parks/default.htm.

CHAPTER 8

The Impact of Policy Change in Local and State Environmental Policy: Brownfield Redevelopment in Michigan

Richard Hula

B rownfield redevelopment has become an important theme in environmental policy as both federal and state governments implement programs to redevelop land parcels that are "abandoned, idled, or underused industrial and commercial facilities where expansion or redevelopment is complicated by a real or perceived environment contamination."[1] A number of characteristics of these efforts are intriguing. Perhaps most interesting is the diverse coalition supporting brownfield redevelopment. It is a coalition that often cuts across traditional divisions of political party, ideology, and region. The problem set that brownfield redevelopment is thought to address is equally diverse, capturing many elements of what Jelier and Sands (this volume) refer to as the "triple bottom line." This includes traditional environmental goals of site remediation, but now also incorporates other important policy goals. For urban policy makers, the reclamation of contaminated sites for industrial and commercial use transforms brownfield redevelopment into an important economic development tool. Some see brownfield redevelopment as a way to reduce development pressure on rural and agricultural land, and thus reduce urban sprawl. Indeed, brownfields are seen by some as a means to achieve key elements of comprehensive land use policy without the need to actually impose direct regulation.[2]

Collectively, brownfield programs reflect not only a policy shift from simple site remediation to more complex policy goals but also demonstrate a refocusing of political authority. Through brownfield redevelopment, a number of states have successfully challenged a long-established federal dominance in environmental policy. This chapter explores efforts by the state of Michigan to craft one such brownfield initiative. Although the primary focus here is the experience of a single state, the lessons to be learned from this case have national implications. Michigan is a leader in brownfield programs, but it is hardly unique. Many states are designing and implementing aggressive brownfield programs that challenge traditional federal policy (Consumers Renaissance Redevelopment Corporation 1998b). The impact of such programs will almost certainly have a profound effect on both environmental and economic policy in the coming years.

A Short Background: Federal Toxic Waste Cleanup Policy

More than two dozen pieces of federal legislation regulate toxic materials in the United States. Of these, three define the broad regulatory framework that has controlled toxic substances for the past twenty years. They are the Toxic Substance Control Act of 1976 (TSCA), the Resource Conservation and Recovery Act of 1976 (RCRA), and the Comprehensive Response, Compensation and Liability Act of 1980 (CERCLA). Each is targeted to a different period in the life cycle of hazardous material. TSCA attempts to set out rules for the review and analysis of new chemicals. The goal is to identify dangerous chemicals as they are developed so that appropriate control strategies can be devised before such chemicals cause human harm. RCRA charges the Environmental Protection Agency (EPA) to develop standards for current waste management. CERCLA is targeted to cleaning the nation's worst toxic waste sites. Together, these laws create a complex network of regulations that attempt to control toxic materials from inception to disposal.[3]

The largest and most controversial of these efforts is CERCLA. Generally known as Superfund, CERCLA (and its 1986 reauthorization, Superfund Amendments and Reauthorization Act [SARA]) sets the general parameters of toxic waste cleanup policy in the United States for nearly twenty years.[4] Table 8.1 summarizes five important structural characteristics of CERCLA. Key to understanding this legislation is its almost exclusive policy focus on public health, the dominant role of federal actors in the identification of sites and the design of remedies, the direct implementation of site remediation plans by federal authorities or their agents, the assumption that those responsible for pollution are responsible for all costs associated with cleanups, and that remediation and cleanup standards would be imposed on responsible parties by the EPA.[5] As noted, CERCLA was targeted to only the most dangerous contaminated sites. Thousands of additional contaminated sites that did not qualify for CERCLA jurisdiction were left to state action. Many states responded to this policy challenge by creating legislative frameworks very similar to CERCLA (Environmental Law Institute 1989).

CERCLA has been mired in controversy since its creation. Critics have long claimed the program is too expensive, operates with inflexible and often unrealistic standards, and, most important, simply has not led to the cleaning of many contaminated sites (Mazmanian and Morell 1992). Political support for the program has clearly waned. For example, the original taxing authority that financed the Superfund expired in 1995, and cleanups are now funded by much smaller general appropriations and payments from responsible parties. Recently, policy entrepreneurs within the EPA have sought to mute public criticism through a number of administrative reforms and public relations initiatives. Independent of legislative mandates, the EPA has sought to soften some elements of the rigid CERCLA liability standards. Other efforts have been made to increase the participation of responsible parties in the design and implementation of remediation efforts (Kettl 2002).

Table 8.1. Key Administrative Characteristics of CERCLA

Goals	CERCLA incorporated a relatively straightforward set of policy goals. The policy problem was defined in terms of public health risks of land-based toxic contamination. The preferred solution was the removal of that contamination. Although sometimes not achievable in practice, the implicit goal of CERCLA was total restoration of contaminated areas. The same standards were to be applied to all land parcels, with little thought given to the proposed use of the land after the cleaning had been accomplished. Indeed, future usage was not seen as a relevant variable in defining either general cleanup standards or site-specific remediation plans.
Responsibility	CERCLA left little question that federal authorities would be taking the lead on efforts to clean toxic waste sites. Indeed, CERCLA created what was often an explicitly antagonistic pattern of intergovernmental relations. Local governments (municipalities and counties) and, less often, state governments were more often seen as parties responsible for hazardous waste than as partners in remediation efforts. Cities, counties, states, and even other federal agencies have been declared as responsible parties in EPA actions. For state and local governments, this liability was particularly frustrating when the liability was acquired as a result of taking title to abandoned industrial properties or contaminated landfills
Response Model	CERCLA was based on the experience of federal authorities in dealing with oil spills and other marine environmental crises. Marine contamination typically requires a quick response to minimize long-term ecological damage. As a result, the typical federal response to an oil spill is the immediate implementation of a publicly financed cleanup. Once this initial effort is completed, federal agencies seek out responsible parties liable for the costs of the completed cleanup. CERCLA gave a similar authority to the EPA to act quickly in cases where the public health was threatened. In such cases, the initial cleanup could draw on interim public funding. However, as noted below, the ultimate responsibility for these costs were not public authorities.
Liability	CERCLA places responsibility for paying cleanup costs squarely on those who caused the contamination. This liability is in fact quite severe. It is retroactive, strict, joint, and several. Parties found responsible for contributing to the contamination of a site are technically liable for the full cost of cleaning that site, regardless of their overall contribution to the site contamination. Liability for site contamination is not reduced even if the responsible party clearly acted within the legal standards at the time the contamination occurred
Bureaucratic Organization	CERCLA followed a pattern established in a number of early environmental laws in which general environmental regulation was framed within a traditional command and control structure. Regulators were charged with establishing and implementing standards. Often issues of cost and the future use of the target site were explicitly excluded from the calculation of new regulations. Once regulations and/or standards were developed, polluters were simply commanded to comply

The EPA has also implemented a policy shift toward the cleaning of contaminated sites by initiating a number of pilot efforts to encourage the redevelopment of less contaminated sites that do not qualify for CERCLA intervention (that is, brownfields). Federal brownfield initiatives contrast to CERCLA in a number of important ways. Unlike Superfund sites, brownfields are seen in much more instrumental terms. That is, decisions to invest in a brownfield cleanup are driven not simply by the level of on-site contamination but also by the economic potential of the site. Thus, the estimated economic viability of the redevelopment plan is a key factor in evaluating applications for EPA brownfield pilot programs. Unlike much of the history of Superfund, the design of the EPA brownfield initiative is based on cooperation, consensus, and self-interest. The command-control logic that drives Superfund cleanups has largely been replaced in the brownfield initiative by voluntary agreements backed by grants and tax credits. Funding is based on incentives rather than a punitive liability scheme.[6] A striking aspect of the federal brownfield effort is the explicit acknowledgment of the leading role of state and local officials in cleanup efforts. Some regional EPA offices have been particularly aggressive in allowing state authorities to take a leading role on specific sites. This increased federal flexibility has been instrumental in promoting state-level innovation in brownfield policy.

In spite of announced EPA policy changes, many state and local policy makers remain skeptical of federal efforts. They see federal programs as continuing to be too rigid and overly adversarial. They remain critical of CERCLA's history of huge administrative and legal costs and its modest record of completed cleanups. Not surprisingly, many state and local policy makers see federal initiatives as ineffective and half-hearted efforts targeted to the margins of toxic cleanup policy. As a result, many state policy makers have begun to advocate a new state-based approach to brownfield cleanup.

Michigan Reforms

Over the past decade Michigan has implemented a number of environmental policy reforms, both through legislative action and executive order, to promote brownfield redevelopment. In part, these changes were seen as a traditional environmental stewardship effort to improve the cleanup capacity of the state. However, there is little doubt that the changes also reflect a new and significantly expanded political agenda that included economic development. No longer would cleanups be the unitary variable driving environmental policy. The connection of environmental and economic development goals was made quite explicit by then Michigan governor John Engler: "The cornerstone of any urban revitalization strategy must be an aggressive brownfield redevelopment program. We have made brownfields attractive by reforming the cleanup laws and offering tax credits and low interest loans to our communities. More than anything, our success comes from making brownfield redevelopment a top economic and environmental priority in the state of Michigan" (Consumers Renaissance Redevelopment Corporation, 1998a). The emphasis on the redevelopment aspects of the program became even clearer in 2000 when the state legislature expanded the scope of the program by altering the legal definition of a brownfield to include "functionally obsolete" buildings in a set of Michigan core cities. This legislation led to the possibility that a site might be treated as a brownfield even in the absence of toxic contamination.[7]

Although the changes in Michigan environmental policy are broadly consistent with federal brownfield initiatives, the magnitude of the state changes is much greater. The five most important policy innovations contained in Michigan's brownfield policy are summarized in table 8.2.[8]

Each of these policy innovations can be seen as a fairly direct effort to respond to long-standing criticisms of site reclamation based on the CERCLA model. The most fundamental contrast between Michigan policy and federal policy is that of liability. Basically, the state has incorporated the key features of past covenants not to sue into a relatively automatic framework. If a landowner is not responsible for site contamination, then he or she is not liable for the cleanup.[9] For parties responsible for the original contamination, liability remains in force. Indeed, current law has created a new affirmative responsibility of landowners to identify and remediate contaminated sites. The Michigan Department of Environmental Quality (MDEQ) is empowered to seek penalties and fines of up to $10,000 a day from responsible parties if they have not "diligently pursued" the cleanup of contaminated sites that they own.[10]

To avoid liability, new owners of potentially contaminated property are required to perform a Baseline Environmental Assessment (BEA) on their property. The BEA measures

Table 8.2. Major Policy Innovations in Michigan Brownfield Policy

Innovation	Description
Increased flexibility in cleanup standards	Brownfield redevelopment rests on the assumption that contaminated properties ought to be cleaned to levels appropriate for future use. Industrial properties need not be cleaned to residential levels. This introduction of differential cleanup standards represents a significant departure from earlier environmental regulations, which demanded a total removal of all contaminants.
Limited owner liability	Prior to the 1996 NREPA amendments, Michigan statutes followed the federal lead in imposing a strict liability framework for site contamination. This essentially held that ownership of a property carried with it the liability for cleaning that site. Changes in the law now allow purchasers to escape liability for contamination for which they are not directly responsible.
Increased reliance on private/voluntary action	New owners of potentially contaminated property can secure exemption from cleanup liability by filing a Baseline Environment Assessment (BEA) with the Michigan Department of Environmental Quality. This baseline data is to serve as a basis from which to evaluate state claims against the landowner. The completion of the BEA is largely a private action, with limited state oversight.
Increased public funding	The Brownfield Financing Act (1996) permits municipalities to create Brownfield Redevelopment Authorities. These authorities are allowed to dedicate state and local taxes generated by the redevelopment into financing remedial cleanup action on the site. Developers are also granted a tax credit on their single business tax. Direct support for cleanup activity was financed through state funds.

existing contamination levels on the property. The result of this assessment must be filed with the MDEQ within forty-five days of the purchase, occupancy, or foreclosure, whichever comes first. The new owners assume full liability for contamination beyond that reported in the BEA.[11] Owners have the option of filing a petition with the MDEQ requesting written documentation that they qualify for the liability exemption. This petition may also request a determination that the owners' proposed use of the facility is consistent with statuary demands that land use not exacerbate contamination at the site.[12]

An expected benefit of the BEA process was the identification of sites where contamination was actually less than had been anticipated. It is assumed that these sites would simply revert to the private market, and could be redeveloped without further public assistance. Indeed, a number of scholars have suggested that this discovery process is likely to be the most important outcome of state brownfield programs that seek to encourage private economic investment through a modification of liability law (Meyer and Lyons 2000). While such an argument is plausible, there is currently little empirical evidence to support or contradict such claims.

The state also reconfigured cleanup standards. Single standards were replaced by multiple criteria based on ultimate land use. Thus, the MDEQ created separate standards for residential, commercial, or industrial properties (Kummler and Card 1999). Not surprisingly, the commercial and industrial standards are less demanding than those for residential development. State law requires that a legally enforceable restrictive covenant must be in place for a property to qualify for use of specific cleanup standards. In an effort to simplify the requirements for redevelopment, the new standards are general for the state, rather than being tied to a site-specific risk analysis. As part of the reconfiguration, overall risk standards were reduced. For example, the cleanup levels for known carcinogens have been set at a risk level creating an additional cancer of 10^{-5} rather than the earlier standard of 10^{-6}.[13] Groundwater cleanup standards have also been revised to what are generally less stringent levels. Finally, the state has recognized a number of alternatives to cleaning a site to the highest possible standard. These include, among other things, exposure barriers, such as a parking lot, which limit access to contamination. A variety of institutional controls such as easements, covenants, and zoning restrictions have been used (Pendergrass and Probst 2005).[14] The state has also developed a number of alternative sources of financing. Typically, this funding is not based on general funds; rather, specific revenue streams have been directed to redevelopment efforts. Two revenue sources are of particular importance: brownfield redevelopment authorities, and the Clean Michigan bond issue. Michigan law permits municipalities to create a brownfield redevelopment authority (BRA). These authorities create a specialized institutional structure to promote local planning and implementation of brownfield redevelopment. The Brownfield Redevelopment Financing Act grants authorities a number of fiduciary powers, including paying or reimbursing private or public parties for cleanup activities; leasing, purchasing, or conveying property; accepting grants, donations of property, labor, or "other things of value" from public or private sources; investing the authorities' money; borrowing money; and engaging in lending and mortgage activities associated with property they acquire (Davis and Margolis 1997). Authorities may also create revolving loan funds to finance projects.

Each authority must develop a plan that identifies eligible properties within its jurisdiction. Elements of this plan include the identification of specific target parcels in the district, a comprehensive financial plan, and strategies for dealing with possible citizen displacement resulting from redevelopment efforts. The brownfield plan must be approved by the chartering municipality before tax increment financing is available to the authority. School tax increments become available only after the MDEQ has approved the plan.[15]

Brownfield redevelopment authorities have the legal capacity to raise revenue in several ways. They are permitted to capture increases in state and local (including school) taxes that result from the redevelopment of a brownfield. These funds can be used for evaluation and feasibility studies of specific sites, on-site demolition of buildings, necessary on-site construction, and the combining of contaminated property with adjacent parcels. The existence of an authority allows a developer/taxpayer a tax credit on Michigan's single business tax (limited to 10 percent of capital investment or an absolute cap of $1 million).[16]

A state bond issue has provided a second important funding source for brownfield work. In 1998, Michigan voters approved a $675 million environmental bond issue, Clean Michigan. The bond issued included $335 million that was targeted directly to brownfield remediation.

- $243 million to $263 million were designated to clean up contaminated sites that will promote redevelopment;
- $20 million were designated for grants to local units of government for response activities at known or suspected contaminated properties that have redevelopment potential;
- $12 million were for grants to local units of government to assist with remedial costs at municipal solid waste landfills they owned or operated that are on, or nominated for, the federal National Priorities List (that is, the Superfund list).

Local authorities are able to access these funds in a number of ways. Some projects were directly funded by the state. These sites were selected from a set of sites nominated by local authorities.[17] Other funds were allocated through remediation and assessment programs administered by the MDEQ.[18] The MDEQ reports funding nearly 800 specific projects with Clean Michigan funding (MDEQ 2008).

Program Outcomes

Public authorities in Michigan have consistently argued that the state's approach to brownfield reclamation has spurred both the cleaning of sites and new economic activity on those sites. For example, in 1996 the MDEQ published a short evaluation report based on a mailed questionnaire that had been sent to the state's 115 brownfield redevelopment authorities. In that survey, twenty-three authorities reported that their brownfield efforts had attracted private investment of $93.1 million for industrial development, $149.6 million for commercial development, and $106.75 million for residential investment (MDEQ 1999). This optimistic evaluation of the program was reinforced in a set of reports that were issued by the Consumers Renaissance Development Corporation (CRDC) in 1998 (Consumers Renaissance Redevelopment Corporation 1998a, 1998b). In fact, the state has used the brownfield

189

program in a number of aggressive marketing campaigns. For example, the Michigan Economic Development Corporation argues:

> Michigan's brownfield redevelopment efforts are considered the premier model for the country. Properties that in the not-so-distant past were considered lost forever are now being actively pursued for revitalization. The success of Michigan's brownfield efforts are due in part to liability protection and reduced remediation costs. Title may be taken to environmentally impaired property without assuming liability for existing contamination, provided the buyer conducts a BEA and discloses it to the state. Lenders may also conduct a BEA to avoid potential liability upon taking title in lieu of foreclosure. Cleanup costs are now 50 percent lower for industrial and commercial properties (Michigan Economic Development Corporation 2008).

Given the widespread sense that the brownfield program is having a positive impact in the state, it is interesting how little empirical evidence about the effects of the program exists. The evaluation work published by the MDEQ and the CRDC is, at best, anecdotal. Jurisdictions reported "estimates" of investment and job creation, with no mention of how those estimates were determined. Other published sources cite examples of specific projects as indicators of overall program success. In principle, however, it is possible to track the fate of properties identified as brownfields. The MDEQ maintains an active database listing all properties for which a BEA has been filed. Unfortunately, the state collects no systematic follow-up information as to what happens to the properties after the BEA has been filed.[19] To test whether such monitoring was feasible, a small pilot study was conducted in the summer of 2000. A stratified random sample was drawn from a list of BEA reports filed in six Michigan counties. At each site, digital photographs of the BEA properties and their surrounding neighborhoods were taken. In addition, each field assistant completed a set of coder judgments on land use, development activity, and neighborhood quality.[20] Finally, the field assistants were required to provide a narrative description of the site and neighborhood.[21]

The success of the pilot study led to a full data collection effort beginning in the summer of 2001. Data were collected each summer through the end of 2005. As in the pilot study, individual BEA sites to be observed were selected by drawing a random stratified sample from the pool of all BEAs filed in a set of target counties. A separate random sample was drawn for each county in the study, and this sample was augmented each year by an additional random sample of new BEA statements filed in the target county during the previous year. The total number of sites selected in each target county varied, with a range of 15 to 274. The number of sites selected was largely driven by the practical constraints of data collection. The final *n* in each county became a function of the number of sites that could be visited during a three-to-four-day effort. As a result, the percentage of total sites in each sample varies significantly across targeted regions. Data reported in this chapter are limited to ten Michigan counties first surveyed in 2001 and then again in 2005. A brief demographic overview of the ten counties in the sample is provided in appendix 8.1. Taken together, these counties account for approximately 25 percent of the state's population. While it is not possible to make a formal claim that these counties statistically represent the state, they were selected to capture a good deal of the state's diversity.

Initial fieldwork revealed two somewhat surprising characteristics of the MDEQ data. First is the failure of published address information to provide sufficient direction to find many of the referenced properties. Although the MDEQ provides location information on all BEA filings, many of these listings do not provide sufficient information to actually locate the sites in the field. In the early years of the project, on average only 70 percent of the random sample drawn for each target county could be located. Of those that were not located, a significant number appear to have had incorrect addresses listed. Numerous BEA addresses are close to a functional address, but fail to directly correspond to it.[22]

A second characteristic of the MDEQ database is the frequency of multiple BEA filings for the same property. Some sites had as many as four separate BEA statements. There are a number of explanations for these multiple filings. Sometimes replacement statements were filed by new owners. Other statements were updates to older filings. Finally, in some cases multiple BEAs were filed with different divisions of the MDEQ. For example, there were several instances of sites on file with both the MDEQ divisions of Environmental Response and Storage Tanks.

Substantive Findings

Figure 8.1 reports an overview of BEA filings in the entire state between 1995 and 2005. Given that the BEA filing is the primary mechanism to protect new owners from cleanup liability associated with past contamination, the relatively high rate of filing gives evidence that, at a minimum, the Michigan brownfield initiative has created a viable market in such properties. This is itself an important policy goal. However, these data do not tell us anything about the current or future use of the property. Ultimately, the use of the property is the key to whether the economic development component of the effort has been successful. To address this question, one must consider on-site change.

As noted above, judgments were made concerning specific aspects of each observed site. Specific codes include:

- Overall conditions of buildings
- General condition of neighborhood

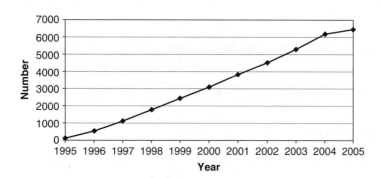

FIGURE 8.1

Total Baseline Environmental Assessments Files 1995–2005

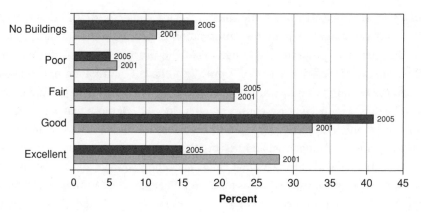

FIGURE 8.2
Condition of Buildings

- Whether the property was fenced
- Evidence of current renovation
- Whether new buildings were under construction
- Whether on-site buildings were being renovated
- Whether there was recent demolition
- Other observable construction or renovation

If the program to redevelop the sites is effective, some redevelopment activity should be observable in each sample. Assuming that there is a lag between the filing of the BEA and site redevelopment, evidence of redevelopment activity should be most apparent in the 2005 sample. Figure 8.2 compares the overall condition of buildings on sample sites observed in 2001 and 2005.[23] The data presented in figure 8.2 reveal no clear pattern. A modest "improvement" across the categories of poor, fair, and good is largely canceled out by a drop in sites rated excellent. This pattern is repeated in figure 8.3, which compares the overall condition of neighborhoods in which sample sites were observed in 2001 and 2005. Once again, an apparent improvement in sites rated poor, fair, and good is balanced by a decline in the proportion of neighborhoods reported as being in excellent condition. Figure 8.4

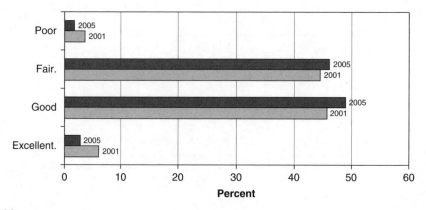

FIGURE 8.3
Condition of Neighborhood

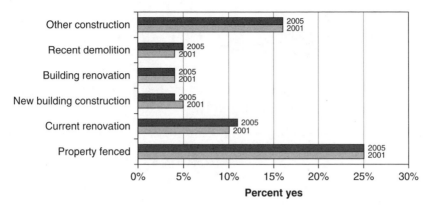

FIGURE 8.4
Miscellaneous Site Assessment Measures

compares 2001 and 2005 sites on a number of indicators, measuring whether certain types of activities were occurring on the site. While there were obviously minor variations between the 2001 and 2005 samples, once again there is little to suggest any systematic improvement between 2001 and 2005.

Cautions

Taken as a whole, the analysis presented here offers little support to claims by Michigan policy makers of widespread success in redeveloping brownfield sites. Overall activity on sample sites is, at best, modest, and, more important, there seems to be no discernable trend over time for increasing rates of redevelopment. Such results are, of course, far from definitive. Two issues deserve specific mention: the need to measure change at the site level, and the need to identify factors other than state programs and incentives that affect the probability of site redevelopment.

Figures 8.2–8.4 are based on cross-sectional analysis in which changes at the individual (site) level must be inferred from the average change within a larger population. There is no direct measurement of change at the site level. It is well recognized that the use of cross-sectional data to test for change at the unit level can seriously hide or even distort actual causal linkages.[24] However, for a subset of the 2001 and 2005 sample sites where direct observations were made for both years, it is possible to directly assess change at the site level. There is actually a very modest decline in building and neighborhood conditions. These differences are tiny (.17 for building conditions and .09 for neighborhood conditions) and fall far short of statistical significance. Figure 8.5 summarizes overall site and neighborhood change by reporting the percentage of sites and site neighborhoods that improved or deteriorated between 2001 and 2005.[25] Figure 8.5 shows that sites are more likely to deteriorate than improve. Twenty-one percent of all sites improved, whereas 36 percent deteriorated. Eighteen percent of all site neighborhoods improved, with 22 percent of site neighborhoods deteriorating. A similar pattern emerges in figure 8.6, which reports other redevelopment indicators. Although some shifting did occur, these changes did not show any consistent pattern toward improvement or redevelopment.

193

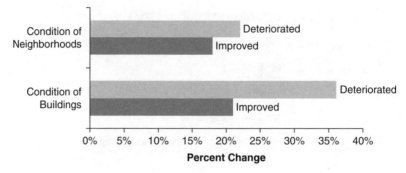

FIGURE 8.5
Site and Neighborhood Change, 2001–2005

A second methodological issue is the need to consider factors other than the brownfield initiative which might promote redevelopment. There exist at least two separate and important dimensions to such factors. The first relates to variations in site characteristics. Some sites, by the nature of their geographic location, such a those on a waterfront, may have large redevelopment potential. Other sites may have little attraction to developers. Of course, the degree and form of contamination on a site are also critical variables in defining the potential for redevelopment. Such site factors are not randomly distributed, and thus patterns of successful redevelopment are unlikely to occur randomly across the state, but rather will take on clear geographical patterns.

Local innovation and leadership are also important factors in local redevelopment. Although the broad legislative framework discussed in this chapter is state policy, major efforts to identify and redevelop sites typically occur at the county and municipal levels. It is clearly unrealistic to assume that all BEA sites somehow received the same level of "treatment" from the state and local authorities. Some county and municipal governments are much more active than others in seeking brownfield redevelopment opportunities. Moreover, there is little doubt that some officials are simply better at identifying and exploiting redevelopment opportunities.

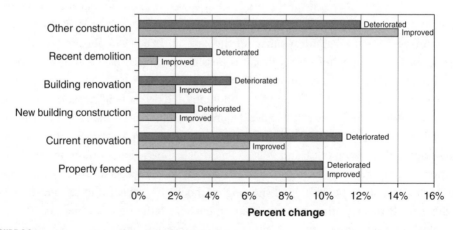

FIGURE 8.6
Changes in Nominal Indicators, 2001–2005

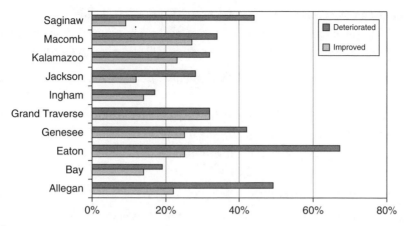

FIGURE 8.7
Change in Quality of Building on Site 2001–2005 by County

Given variations in site desirability and local capacity, it is at least plausible that program impact would be better measured using smaller geographic and political units. Figure 8.7 explores this possibility by breaking down the percentage of observed units that improved and those that deteriorated between 2001 and 2005 by individual county. Figure 8.7 suggests that scale may, in fact, be important in the evaluation of program impact. While the overall impact on building quality across the state is near zero, county-level analysis shows a good deal more variance. Some counties report significantly more success and less relative decline than others. While county variation might represent random noise in the policy process, local variables may also be driving this variance. For example, the county that reports the highest proportion of improved sites, Grand Traverse, is an important recreation and tourist center and is experiencing strong overall development pressures. Macomb County, which reports the second highest improvement rate in the sample, has the highest average county income in the state. This would certainly suggest that developers would find property in the county desirable.[26] To be sure, these examples are merely suggestive, but they do demonstrate the utility of further analysis.

Conclusion

The MDEQ data on BEA filings provides compelling evidence that the Michigan brownfield initiative has, at a minimum, created a viable real estate market for potentially contaminated land. The relatively large number of BEA statements filed with the state convincingly shows that contaminated properties are, in fact, being bought and sold. An important benefit of this market is that it creates a private development path for sites found to have less contamination than expected. Once identified, such sites no longer face the prospect of significant liability, extensive cleanups, or public oversight.

Obviously, state policy has sought to support a private market for contaminated properties, but it also aims to promote the twin goals of environmental reclamation and economic redevelopment. Michigan's long-term success in meeting these goals is more problematic. Analyses of cross-sectional and paired observation data failed to detect any clear trend in accelerated site redevelopment. However, several important questions need to be addressed

195

before rejecting policy makers' claims of success. As noted above, future analysis will need to identify both site factors and characteristics of local redevelopment programs that inhibit or promote site redevelopment. Several other issues will also need to be addressed:

- The impact and effectiveness of specific elements within the overall bundle of state and local initiatives targeted to brownfields.
- The impact of targeted state funding to directly support cleanups. This includes not only the reduction of contamination but also site redevelopment.
- The long-term sustainability of both environmental reclamation and associated redevelopment.
- The effect of efforts to engage local community residents in site redevelopment planning.

The issue of engagement, of course, refers to the "third leg" of the triple bottom line, equity. This element is less prominent in Michigan brownfield debates since across state policy there is little formal role for communities affected by redevelopment decisions. However, some local jurisdictions have attempted to mandate such engagement as a means to ensure that site development reflects neighborhood and community preferences as well as those of developers. While the evidence on the impact of. such engagement is impressionistic and incomplete, it defines a critical focus of future evaluation work.

While the empirical data reviewed in this chapter cast doubt on the many positive claims advanced for the Michigan brownfield initiative, the political success of the program is undeniable. There can be little doubt that the initiative has had a profound impact on the substance of state environmental policy. No longer is environmental policy focused almost completely on public health. Economic development has now become a key policy priority. The initiative has also demonstrated a remarkable level of political support. The effort was created by a very conservative Republican governor with the active support of Democratic core city mayors and has been able to maintain this broad nonpartisan support. In a political environment in which aid to urban areas is unpopular, brownfield redevelopment is one of the few mechanisms by which public funds continue to be directed to urban redevelopment efforts. This political strength is reflected in the legislature's decision to broaden the legal definition of brownfields in Michigan to include property with obsolete structures, and thus allow municipalities and counties to seek brownfield redevelopment funding on sites having little or no actual contamination.

There is a final observation to be made. Evidence that aggregate program outcomes are limited does not deny impressive successes by individual jurisdictions. Although evidence of such successes is largely anecdotal, they are common. The key issue for future policy is a better understanding of the circumstances in which such success occurs, and how it might be replicated.

Notes

1. This is the definition of brownfields commonly cited by the federal Environmental Protection Agency (EPA). See Kaiser (1998).
2. The third element of the triple bottom line—social equity—has played a less important role in brownfield redevelopment. Much is left to market actors in the state initiative, and there is little formal role for community actors. Although some jurisdictions have

been more aggressive than others in seeking community input into development decisions, such efforts are somewhat sporadic and certainly not required under state law or policy. See Hula (1999).

3. For a more complete discussion of RCRA and TSCA, see Rosenbaum (2005).

4. The original CERCLA legislation created a "Superfund" from a tax on polluting industries.

5. For a more complete discussion of the evolution of CERCLA, see Hays (2000) and Hula (2001).

6. Congress has observed this shifting set of goals with some ambivalence. On the one hand, there is wide support for the overall concept and direction the EPA has taken. However, some concern has been expressed that the EPA has moved beyond its statutory authority in using CERCLA trust funds to implement certain aspects of the brownfield effort. See Reisch (1998) and U.S. General Accounting Office (1997)

7. For a more complete discussion of the Michigan plan, see Hula (1999) and Szymecko and Voice (2002).

8. For an excellent overview of the changes in Michigan law, see Woodruff, Denton, and Wyngarten (1998).

9. Michigan actors note that there are two major elements of liability that continue to retard redevelopment of brownfield sites. Both are associated with CERCLA liability. Obviously, the state cannot grant immunity from federal action against property owners. As noted above, the EPA has reduced these concerns by entering a set of agreements not to sue based on a lack of responsibility for on-site contamination. A second concern is the potential of responsible parties to bring suit against new owners under CERCLA liability. While this concern is widely cited as a block to redevelopment, there seems to be no reported instance of such suits actually being filed. See Environmental Financial Advisory Board (1998).

10. Such penalties can also be assessed to new landowners if the new owners do not takes steps to identify and report current levels of site contamination. See Woodruff, Denton, and Wyngarten (1998).

11. The BEA filing essentially replaces a much more complex process in which a developer might escape liability. Prior to the amendments to Part 201, the only way to relieve a developer/purchaser from liability from existing contamination was a "covenant not to sue." This was almost always a very slow and complicated process. For example, between 1991 and 1995 only thirty-seven such covenants were implemented. See Michigan Department of Environmental Quality (1996).

12. While new owners are no longer responsible for site cleanup, they are required to meet the due care requirements that the public be protected from contamination. Indeed, such due care requirements have been extended to all owners of contaminated sites. This actually represents an extension of past liability in that potentially responsible parties now have an affirmative responsibility to show due care whether or not the site has been identified as a potential public health threat by some public agency.

13. Maximum levels for specific contaminants were set using available toxicological and chemical-specific data. Typically, these data were reviewed for individual chemicals by external panels of experts, who then recommended specific standards to the MDEQ (Kummler and Card 1999).

14. The potential health risks of these new standards are uncertain. While allowing greater human exposure to contamination seems likely to generate some absolute increase in risk, current science does not present reliable estimates of the magnitude of that increase. Particularly problematic is the interactive effects of multiple contaminants in the same site. See Hofrichter (2000).

15. Unfortunately, these plans often reveal less than might be expected. A number of jurisdictions have adopted a strategy of including a parcel in their brownfield plan only after they have identified a developer interested in the property.

16. Woodruff, Denton, and Wyngarten (1998) suggest that even if the municipality is unable or does not want to capture tax increments, the single business tax credit is cause enough for the municipality to form a BRA. Field interviews show that some BRAs have been formed primarily to have local business qualify for the single business tax rebate.

17. The MDEQ accepts local nominations, develops a ranking, and submits a priority list to the state legislature. The legislature can either modify or accept the MDEQ recommendations. Respondents at the MDEQ report that they could not remember when the legislature had not followed departmental recommendations under an earlier bond issue. Some concern was expressed that this pattern might change since the brownfield initiative has significantly expanded the criteria for project selection, and thus created a basis for political disputes.

18. As of early 2008, these bond funds were nearly exhausted.

19. It is particularly noteworthy that there is also no tracking of institutional controls or other "nonremoval" strategies of controlling on-site contamination.

20. See appendix 8.2 for a complete listing of site coding.

21. Efforts to establish and maintain reliability included intensive training sessions before commencing fieldwork. These sessions involved evaluating multiple sites (from photographs), discussing results, and identifying sources of disagreement. After training, each field observer was assigned a "practice county," and observation codes were required to achieve a .8 correlation with a set of base observations before the field observer was assigned further counties.

22. Data quality improved over the period of the research, but incorrect or incomplete addresses continue to be common in the public MDEQ data.

23. County estimates have been weighted to correct for the differences in the sample size. See appendix 8.3 for the variance in sample size across the sample counties.

24. This does not mean, however, that the central tendency measures reported are meaningless. Given that they are means computed from random samples, any substantive shift in value of a property indicator should be reflected in these means. However, such changes might occur by shifts in the quality of property being identified rather than actual site-level changes.

25. In cases where there were no observation data available for 2005, 2004 observations were used.

26. Although there is no systematic evidence on the quality of local programs, past observation shows that such variation certainly exists. See Hula (1999).

APPENDIX 1

Overview of Sample Counties

	Allegan County	Bay County	Eaton County	Genesee County	Grand Traverse County	Ingham County	Jackson County	Kalamazoo County	Macomb County	Saginaw County	Michigan
Population, 2005 estimate	113,174	109,029	107,394	443,883	83,971	278,592	163,629	240,536	829,453	208,356	10,120,860
Percent Michigan population	1.12%	1.08%	1.06%	4.39%	0.83%	2.75%	1.62%	2.38%	8.20%	2.06%	
Population, percent change, April 1, 2000 to July 1, 2005	7.10%	−1.00%	3.60%	1.80%	8.10%	−0.30%	3.30%	0.80%	5.20%	−0.80%	1.80%
Population, 2000	105,665	110,157	103,655	436,141	77,654	279,320	158,422	238,603	788,149	210,039	9,938,444
African Americans, percent, 2005	1.50%	1.40%	6.30%	20.00%	0.80%	11.00%	7.90%	9.90%	5.60%	19.30%	14.30%
Persons of Hispanic or Latino origin, percent, 2005	6.30%	4.10%	3.80%	2.40%	1.80%	5.90%	2.60%	3.00%	1.90%	7.10%	3.80%
Housing units, 2005	47,349	47,897	45,112	195,545	38,942	120,041	66,883	106,084	346,503	88,392	4,478,507
Median household income, 2003	$46,626	$39,151	$50,983	$40,262	$43,817	$40,994	$42,556	$42,179	$51,742	$37,843	$46,291
Persons below poverty, percent, 2003	8.40%	10.60%	7.80%	13.30%	7.80%	12.70%	10.90%	12.00%	7.40%	13.40%	11.00%
Private nonfarm employment, 2004	35,349	33,008	27,887	143,474	43,406	129,849	50,674	112,858	308,750	85,375	3,895,914

(continued)

APPENDIX 1

Overview of Sample Counties (*continued*)

	Allegan County	Bay County	Eaton County	Genesee County	Grand Traverse County	Ingham County	Jackson County	Kalamazoo County	Macomb County	Saginaw County	Michigan
Private nonfarm employment, percent change 2000-2004	-2.30%	-6.60%	-10.80%	-5.40%	-0.20%	1.60%	-7.40%	1.80%	-7.90%	-7.80%	-4.30%
Manufacturers' shipments, 2002 ($1000)	4,322,906	1,113,549	NA	9,269,929	1,015,515	NA	2,541,850	5,893,488	25,485,976	5,026,134	221,433,262
Building permits, 2005	713	300	498	1,854	1,163	1,023	897	1,156	4,343	582	45,328
Land area, 2000 (square miles)	827.00	444.00	576.00	639.00	465.00	559.00	706.00	561.00	480.00	808.00	56,803
Persons per square mile, 2000	127.80	248.10	180.00	681.50	167.00	499.70	224.10	424.60	1,642.0	259.60	175.0

APPENDIX 2
Site Inspection Codes

Land Use
>   1 = Residential
>   2 = Commercial
>   3 = Industrial
>   4 = Mixed use (make note of uses observed)
>   5 = Vacant
>   9 = Not Found
>   Blank = Not in sample

Overall Conditions of Buildings
>   1 = Excellent
>   2 = Good
>   3 = Fair
>   4 = Poor
>   5 = No buildings
>   9 = Not found
>   Blank = Not in sample

Fenced
>   1 = Yes
>   2 = No
>   9 = Not found
>   Blank = Not in sample

Stages of Development
>   1 = Fully redeveloped
>   Clear evidence of recently completed physical redevelopment.
>   2 = Somewhat redeveloped
>   Clear evidence of some completed physical redevelopment.
>   3 = Initial stages of redevelopment
>   Clear evidence of beginning efforts at physical redevelopment.
>   4 = No redevelopment activity
>   No evidence of any recent physical redevelopment.
>   5 = Abandoned or vacant
>   No evidence of any recent physical redevelopment or economic activity.
>   9 = Not found
>   Blank = Not in sample

Evidence of Current Renovation
>   1 = Yes
>   2 = No
>   9 = Not found
>   Blank = Not in sample

New Building Under Construction
>   1 = Yes
>   2 = No
>   9 = Not found
>   Blank = Not in sample

Building Being Renovated
>   1 = Yes
>   2 = No

(continued)

APPENDIX 2
Site Inspection Codes (*continued*)

9 = Not found
Blank = Not in sample

Recent Demolition
1 = Yes
2 = No
9 = Not found
Blank = Not in sample

General Condition of Neighborhood
1 = Excellent
Many buildings in area are new or recently renovated.
2 = Good
Buildings are older, but maintained reasonably well. Scattered redevelopment and no obvious abandoned buildings.
3 = Fair
Occasional abandoned buildings observed. Not much activity.
4 = Poor
Serious deterioration in neighborhood. Abandoned buildings are common.
No Buildings
Blank = Not in sample

Other Construction or Renovation Observable
1 = Yes
2 = No
9 = Not found
Blank = Not in sample

Type of Neighborhood Renovation
1 = None observed
2 = Residential
3 = Commercial
4 = Industrial
5 = Mixed use
6 = Vacant
9 = Not found
Blank = Not in sample

APPENDIX 3
Description of Sample 2001 and 2005

County Name	Total Number of BEAs Filed		Number of BEAs in Sample		Number of BEAs Observed	
	2001	2005	2001	2005	2001	2005
Allegan	50	93	50	93	49	0
Bay	83	149	53	97	37	78
Eaton	28	61	23	61	16	42
Genesee	331	331	153	183	83	80

APPENDIX 3

Description of Sample 2001 and 2005 (*continued*)

County Name	Total Number of BEAs Filed		Number of BEAs in Sample		Number of BEAs Observed	
	2001	2005	2001	2005	2001	2005
Grand Traverse	77	149	69	79	38	65
Ingham	266	266	126	145	50	104
Jackson	93	184	60	129	57	118
Kalamazoo	236	476	178	238	166	208
Macomb	246	444	134	284	121	226
Saginaw	161	283	115	172	92	100
Total	1,571	2,436	961	1,481	709	1,021

REFERENCES

Consumers Renaissance Redevelopment Corporation. 1998a. *Michigan's Brownfield Redevelopment Program: First in the Nation.* Jackson, Mich.: Consumers Renaissance Redevelopment Corporation.

———. 1998b. *National Comparative Analysis of Brownfield Redevelopment Programs.* Jackson, Mich.: Consumers Renaissance Redevelopment Corporation.

Davis, T. S., and K. D. Margolis. 1997. *Brownfields: A Comprehensive Guide to Redeveloping Contaminated Property.* Chicago: American Bar Association.

Environmental Financial Advisory Board. 1998. *Expediting Clean-up and Redevelopment of Brownfields: Addressing Major Barriers to Private Sector Involvement—Real or Perceived.* Washington, D.C.: U.S. Environmental Protection Agency.

Environmental Law Institute. 1989. *An Analysis of State Superfund Programs: 50-State Study.* Washington, D.C.: U.S. Environmental Protection Agency Office of Emergency and Remedial Response Hazardous Site Control Division.

Hays, S. P. 2000. *A History of Environmental Politics since 1945.* Pittsburgh: University of Pittsburgh Press.

Hofrichter, R. 2000. *Reclaiming the Environmental Debate: The Politics of Health in a Toxic Culture.* Cambridge, Mass.: MIT Press.

Hula, R. C. 1999. *An Assessment of Brownfield Redevelopment Policies.* Washington D.C.: PricewaterhouseCoppers Endowment for the Business of Government.

———. 2001. Changing Priorities and Programs in Toxic Waste Policy: The Emergence of Economic Development as a Policy Goal. *Economic Development Quarterly* 15(2):181–199.

Kaiser, S.-E. 1998. Brownfields National Partnership: The Federal Role in Brownfield Redevelopment. *Public Works Management and Policy* 2(3):196–201.

Kettl, D. F. 2002. *Environmental Governance: A Report on the Next Generation of Environmental Policy.* Washington, D.C.: Brookings Institution Press.

Kummler, R. H., and D. S. Card. 1999. *Brownfield Redevelopment: The Michigan Strategy.* Detroit: College of Urban, Labor and Metropolitan Affairs, Wayne State University.

Mazmanian, D., and D. Morell. 1992. *Beyond Superfailure: America's Toxics Policy for the 1990s.* San Francisco: Westview Press.

MDEQ (Michigan Department of Environmental Quality). 1996. *The Part 201 Amendments: One Year Later.*

———. 1999. *Brownfield Redeveloping Financing Acts: Three Years Later.*

———. 2008. Clean Michigan Initiative (CMI) Brownfield Program. Http://www.michigan.gov/deq/ 0,1607,7–135–3311_4110_23243–59428—,00.html.

Meyer, P. B., and T. S. Lyons. 2000. Lessons from Private Sector Brownfield Redevelopers: Planning Public Support for Urban Regeneration. *Journal of the American Planning Association* 66(1):46–57.

Michigan Economic Development Corporation. 2008. CATeam Programs: Brownfield Redevelopment. Http://ref.michigan.org/medc/services/general/cat/brownfield/.

Pendergrass, J., and K. N. Probst. 2005. *Estimating the Cost of Institutional Controls.* Washington, D.C.: Environmental Law Institute.

Reisch, M. 1998. *Superfund Reauthorization Issues in the 105th Congress.* Washington, D.C.: Congressional Research Service.

Rosenbaum, W. A. 2005. *Environmental Politics and Policy.* 6th ed. Washington, D.C.: CQ Press.

Szymecko, L. A., and T. C. Voice. 2002. *Brownfield Redevelopment: Guidebook for Michigan.* Chicago: Brownfield News.

U.S. General Accounting Office. 1997. *Superfund: State Voluntary Programs Provide Incentives to Encourage Cleanups.* No. GAO/RCE-97–66. Washington, D.C.: U.S. General Accounting Office.

Woodruff, F. M., C. M. Denton, and S. M. Wyngarten. 1998. *Michigan's Brownfield Redevelopment Initiative: A Primer on How to Make the Most of It.* Grand Rapids, Mich.: Varun, Riddering, Schmidt and Howlett.

PART 3

Social/Political
Dynamics

CHAPTER 9

Explaining Horizontal and Vertical Cooperation in Michigan

Jered B. Carr, Elisabeth R. Gerber, and Eric W. Lupher

M ichigan's local governments face an increasingly difficult environment for providing high-quality municipal services to their residents: they are feeling the effects of a deep national recession, legislative policies that limit their ability to capitalize on their own-source revenues, and cost pressures from various sources. Michigan's weak economy, as explained by Ballard (chapter 1), has led to reduced state tax revenues and to cuts in funding for state revenue-sharing programs that support local government operations. At the same time, constitutional and statutory policies have created property tax limitations that hamper the ability of local governments to benefit from year-to-year growth in the value of property. The cost of providing local government services is also increasing. Health care expenses, legacy costs, and the price of some common inputs like motor fuel continue to escalate. In the face of these pressures, local government officials have three primary options: increase taxes to raise more revenue, reduce spending to alter the menu of services provided to their residents, and/or find alternative methods of providing services at current levels while reducing costs.

Interlocal collaboration for the provision of governmental services is one alternative method. Despite the state's strong home rule traditions and lack of mandates or incentives for engaging in collaborative service arrangements, significant numbers of local governments currently cooperate to provide such services as public safety, libraries, water and sewer, emergency dispatch, public transit, and watershed management, as well as many others (CRC 2005). Examples abound. For instance, the city of Northville and Northville Township contract for shared dispatch and lock-up services; the Monroe County Sheriff's Office provides jailing and secondary road patrol services to all communities in the county; and the Oakland County Sheriff's Office provides street patrol services by contract to

Rochester Hills and ten township governments in the county (Martindale and Feighan 2007; SEMCOG 2006). Yet in spite of the frequency of this collaboration, our understanding of the factors affecting intergovernmental cooperation remains fairly rudimentary. Previous studies have attempted, with only limited success, to develop models illustrating the political, economic, and demographic factors affecting levels of interlocal cooperation (LeRoux 2006; Krueger 2005; Post 2002; Rawlings 2003; Wood 2004; Zeemering 2007). Consistent patterns have yet to emerge from this research literature. Likewise, even as local government officials have long recognized the important role that intergovernmental cooperation can play in providing low-cost, high-quality services, it is often not clear to them which services are the strongest candidates for collaboration and which other governmental units are the best candidates for partnerships.

We propose that a key reason for the lack of consensus in past studies, and for a lack of clarity among local officials, is that local governments pursue different types of cooperation for different reasons. In particular, we propose that a fundamentally different calculation underlies the choice between horizontal and vertical cooperation on public services for many municipal governments. By "horizontal cooperation," we mean joint activities involving governmental units at the same level of government. Common examples of horizontal cooperation in Michigan include joint police/fire dispatch and library districts between cities, villages, and townships. Many Michigan cities, villages, and townships engage in horizontal cooperation. For instance, the West Bloomfield Township Fire Department provides all fire protection and emergency medical services (EMS) for the three neighboring communities of Keego Harbor, Orchard Lake, and Sylvan Lake (SEMCOG 2006). The Chelsea District Library provides library services to some or all of the residents of four (Lyndon, Sylvan, Dexter, and Lima) nearby townships (Chelsea District Library 2008). We view these forms of horizontal cooperation as voluntary exchange relationships between two or more local governments in which each sees benefits to the cooperation, net of its costs.

In contrast, by "vertical cooperation," we refer to cooperation between units at different levels of government. Vertical cooperation includes townships, villages, or cities contracting for services with county or state government or joint provision of services by municipal governments and the county or state. Common examples of vertical cooperation include county-local emergency planning, animal control, and environmental initiatives. In Michigan, examples of vertical cooperation abound. For instance, Oakland County provides rescue training at airport facilities for first responders and law enforcement, fire, and EMS agencies from cities and townships within the county (Oakland County 2007). In some cases, vertical cooperation may involve county or state provision of core municipal services to cities, villages, or townships. For example, from 2003 until 2006, the Wayne County Sheriff's Office provided primary police services to the city of Highland Park (Wayne County 2008). In another example, the Michigan State Police currently provides overnight street patrol and emergency response to Royal Oak Township, a community in southeastern Oakland County (Martindale and Feighan 2007). The township has relied on a mix of county deputies and state troopers since it eliminated its own police force due to financial problems in 1999. We view these forms of vertical cooperation as dependency relationships in which the costs and benefits of cooperation are highly asymmetric to actors at different levels of government.

This chapter seeks to improve the understanding of intergovernmental collaboration by explaining existing patterns of both horizontal and vertical cooperation in Michigan. We focus most directly on the effects of local fiscal capacity in these decisions, as measured by a jurisdiction's total taxable property value and the basic taxing authority permitted by the types of municipal government used by the community. Next, we describe our unique data set and report descriptive statistics about patterns of service delivery arrangements in Michigan. We follow with multivariate analyses for each mode of service provision. We find that variations in fiscal capacity, both in terms of fiscal powers permitted to the unit and the amount of property wealth in the jurisdiction, affect the likelihood of intergovernmental cooperation. We conclude by summarizing our findings and discussing the policy implications of this work.

Local Fiscal Capacity and Intergovernmental Contracting

We begin with the assumption that municipal governments are inclined to self-provide services. Maintaining autonomy over service decisions is highly valued in many communities in Michigan, and local government policy makers can be expected to prefer to construct facilities, purchase equipment, and employ the municipal staff required to provide services on their own. Direct provision of services contributes to the community's identity, character, and quality of life, and enables elected officials to provide personalized service to residents (Visser 2004). The attraction of these benefits to residents and local government officials in Michigan is strong (Zeemering 2007). However, direct provision of certain services can be prohibitively costly to many local governments.

When direct service provision becomes cost prohibitive, local government policy makers consider the relative costs and benefits of alternative approaches to service delivery, such as using interlocal agreements to cooperate with potential partners. We conceptualize a local government's decision to cooperate on service provision with other governments as resulting from a consideration of the relative costs and benefits of four different options: self-providing the service, cooperating with one or more peer governments (that is, horizontal cooperation); cooperating with the state or county (that is, vertical cooperation); and not providing the service.[1] These choices are driven by a combination of internal and external factors to the local government. In terms of internal factors, we are primarily concerned with the effect of local government fiscal capacity. Low fiscal capacity may result from several factors: low property values in rural or aging urban settings; a relative lack of aggregate property wealth in poor or sparsely populated communities; or constraints on the ability of local units to raise revenues from their tax base arising from limits imposed by the state constitution, state laws, or their own charters. External factors include the number and concentration of other local governments in the immediate area.

We propose that fiscal capacity considerations lead local government officials to think about the opportunities and challenges associated with each mode of service provision in different ways. Local governments with extremely low fiscal capacity have difficulty in meeting residents' demands for public services within their budgets and may turn to other governments for services they cannot afford to provide alone. Their ability to find suitable partners, however, is likely to be quite limited. Two poor or fiscally constrained local governments may be no better suited to provide services jointly than they are to provide those services individually. From the perspective of other local governments, the prospect of cooperating with a poor or fiscally constrained neighbor is likely to be seen negatively, since that partner has limited resources to contribute to the cooperative effort (Lackey, Freshwater, and Rupasingha 2002). County or state governments, by contrast, already provide some of the same services as their constituent local governments and may be willing and able to offer support to those units. From the state's or county's perspective, a local government unable to provide basic services may lead to disinvestment, which ultimately affects not only the city or township tax base but the state and county tax bases as well. County or state governments may thus be motivated to partner with local governments, regardless of the local government's resource base. Indeed, county and state governments may view their poorest or most fiscally constrained local units to be most worthy of support from their limited resources.

For other communities, fiscal necessity will be less desperate, yet they may still choose voluntary cooperation when the perceived benefits of cooperation outweigh the political costs of ceding authority over service provision through functional or governmental consolidation. Such cooperation may be especially attractive to communities in the midrange of fiscal capacity: they are not so fiscally constrained as to view the cost of service provision as prohibitive, but they are sufficiently constrained to need to take advantage of opportunities for efficiency in service provision. For example, it may make sense for moderately constrained cities to jointly undertake substantial capital investments, either because they lack the ability to borrow enough funds individually or because they cannot fully exploit the economies of scale present in a particular investment by working alone. In these cases, local governments may choose to partner with their neighbors, particularly if those neighbors face similar circumstances. We suggest that in these cases of horizontal cooperation, it is not the lack of fiscal capacity that brings local governments into collaborative relationships. Rather, it is the possibility of leveraging opportunities that are not available or are not as attractive to local governments operating alone. The dynamics for communities in the midrange of fiscal capacity are quite different with respect to their need for county and state services. We expect that, when compared to their poorest counterparts, local governments with moderate fiscal capacity will feel less need for assistance from the state or county governments. Communities with the greatest fiscal capacity, by contrast, may prefer to retain authority over the provision of government services and provide them directly. These wealthy communities are not driven to cooperation by fiscal necessity. When they do choose joint service provision, the decision to cooperate will be more voluntary and based on cost containment rather than an inability to provide services individually.

Other Internal and External Factors

In addition to fiscal capacity, other internal factors are expected to affect local governments' choices of service provision. One set of factors is the jurisdiction's population size and the geographic dispersion of this population within the unit. Populous communities may face more complex demands for services, as their populations comprise numerous interests with diverse service needs (Oakerson 2004). Demands for expanded services may be even greater when the population is densely packed or the area covered by the government is relatively small, since the close and intense interactions of a dense population require greater government intervention to mitigate externalities (Frederickson 1999; Post 2002). Additional factors, such as the racial/ethnic composition and age distribution of the local population, may also affect the unit's service delivery choices. Older populations have been found to prefer direct service provision (Morgan and Hirlinger 1991), and units with heterogeneous populations are thought to be less attractive to potential collaborators because they have greater trouble achieving consensus on decisions about service levels and quality (Oakerson 2004). The number and spatial density of local governments in the region also affect opportunities for cooperation. "The geographic density of metropolitan area governments influences the ability of residents to live, work, and recreate in multiple communities, the likelihood that local officials will have personal as well as professional relationships, and the likelihood that policy spillovers will affect multiple communities" (Post 2002: 124).

The cost characteristics of each particular service are expected to affect the opportunity for and value of cooperation. There is less to be gained financially from collaborating on labor-intensive services such as police patrol than on services that are highly capital intensive, like public utilities. Increasing the geographic area, the number of parcels, or the population to be served requires a commensurate increase in the staffing needed to provide the service, thereby increasing costs. For other services, however, there are economies to be gained through collaboration. Local governments can benefit from economies of scale inherent in capital-intensive services, such as those requiring new facilities or equipment. Once the capital items are in place, the marginal cost to the governmental unit of providing services to an additional resident is small, and cooperation may allow participating governments to provide the service at a more efficient scale, allowing them to capture unit-cost savings (LeRoux and Carr 2007; Post 2002). Finally, local governments can benefit from economies in services that require personnel with high levels of technical skills, such as environmental management or specialized legal services. These services, which can often be provided without regard to geographic connectedness, depend on the service provider employing personnel who have obtained specialized academic training or have been recognized in their fields through a professional certification program. Once those specialists are employed, the marginal cost to the governmental unit of providing services to additional residents is small. County or state governments may be well suited to employ these personnel and provide these services, since they can offer them to local units spread over a wide area.

Horizontal and Vertical Cooperation among Michigan Municipal Governments

We examine patterns of horizontal and vertical cooperation in Michigan with data from a survey of municipal governments conducted by the Citizens Research Council of Michigan in 2005. A survey was mailed to the senior administrator in each city, village, and township government in twenty-five Michigan counties. Responses were received from 70 percent (460 units) of the governments surveyed and were evenly distributed across the three types

211

of jurisdictions.[2] Survey respondents were asked to report the delivery mechanism for 116 services provided by the jurisdiction, grouped into twenty-six functional categories. For each service, the respondents were asked to indicate if their jurisdiction directly provides the service; provides to, has provided by, or jointly provides with another unit of government; provides through a special district; contracts with a private provider; or does not provide at all (CRC 2005).[3]

We began our analysis by coding each of these services and functions according to the degree of labor or capital intensiveness, the need for technical expertise or training, and whether the service area is considered a basic service. Each function was coded in terms of the expected financial and technical burdens placed on local governments initiating provision of the service. The capital intensiveness of each service area was judged based on the cost of constructing, building, or acquiring the land, buildings, vehicles, or equipment needed to provide each service. The need for technical expertise or training was based on the need for the government to employ personnel with college degrees or professional certification to provide that service or function. Finally, basic services were defined as those services that citizens initiating a new government entity would expect that government to provide at a minimum. The coding of the services and functions is reported in appendix 9.1.

Each of the 460 responding cities, villages, and townships reported which services were provided to their residents and, if provided, the mode of service provision used. For our analyses, we collapsed each local government's responses for each service area into four variables indicating whether the service was: provided alone; provided via horizontal relationships; provided via vertical relationships; or not provided.[4] These indicator variables serve as the dependent variables in our analyses. Appendix 9.2 lists all 116 services and reports the number of municipalities reporting each provision mode.

Table 9.1 reports the twenty most frequent services/functions reported for each service provision mode. Direct provision is reported most often for basic labor-intensive functions such as purchasing, tax collection, accounting, elections, payroll, records, zoning, planning, and building code enforcement/inspection/permits, as hypothesized. Horizontal cooperation is reported most frequently for fire, library, utilities (water and sewer), emergency, and public transportation services. These are capital-intensive services or functions for which significant scale economies are likely to be present. Vertical cooperation is reported most frequently on criminal justice/courts, roads, animal control, emergency, environmental, and building regulation services. Some of these services, especially criminal justice/courts and roads, reflect legislative or constitutional provisions that require high degrees of county involvement.[5] Other services, such as crime lab, emergency planning, and environmental services, require relatively high levels of technical expertise or training.

Two additional patterns emerge from table 9.1. First, very little overlap exists between the three lists of services. Only four services appear on two top-twenty lists; none appear on all three. This suggests that different economic logics derive from each type of service, and these logics in part dictate decisions to engage in direct provision, horizontal cooperation, or vertical cooperation. Second, comparing the two forms of cooperation, there are only a few services where horizontal collaboration occurs frequently, whereas vertical cooperation is reported both at much higher rates and in many more service areas. Indeed, horizontal

Table 9.1. Most Frequently Reported Services/Functions by Mode of Provision

Self-Provision	Percent	Horizontal	Percent	Vertical	Percent
Purchasing	96.30	Fire Fighting	47.39	Jail(s)	77.17
Tax Collection	95.87	Fire Training	41.96	Animal Control	72.17
Treasury	94.09	Library	39.78	Road Signs	70.87
Accounting	93.90	Hazmat	38.04	Detention Center(s)	69.13
Election Records	90.43	Water Treatment	35.65	Crime Lab	68.04
Zoning	88.48	Sewer Treatment	34.35	Road Building	65.43
Payroll	88.02	Ambulance	33.70	Emergency Planning	64.78
Records	86.27	Fire Inspection	32.17	Animal Licenses	64.57
Election Administration	85.00	Fire Investigation	31.74	Well Permitting	63.91
Document Destruction	77.14	Water Distribution	27.39	District Court	63.70
Bldg Code Enforcement	74.57	Sewer Collection	25.87	Road Winter Maintenance	63.70
Printing	73.90	Fire Hydrants	23.04	Road Maintenance	63.48
Community Planning	68.48	Police-911/Radio	17.83	Septic Permitting	62.17
Building Permits	67.61	Emergency Planning	17.17	Police-911/Radio	62.17
Building Janitors	66.74	Dial-a-Ride	16.30	Restaurant Licensing	61.52
Parks	66.16	Watershed Mgmt	15.43	Water Quality	57.39
Fleet Purchasing	65.28	Gas Metering	15.43	Erosion Control	55.00
Fleet Garage	64.63	Bus Service	14.57	Watershed Management	53.48
Property Assessing	63.91	Senior Center	13.91	Air Quality	52.83
Building Inspection	63.48	Elections Admin	13.04	Police - Canine Unit	51.30

NOTE: *Percent* indicates the percentage of 460 municipal governments (cities, villages, and townships) reporting each mode of service delivery in 2005.

cooperation is reported by more than 20 percent of responding units for just 12 of the 116 service areas. In contrast, vertical cooperation is reported by more than 20 percent of responding units in 42 service areas.

Analysis and Results

Examining our fiscal capacity hypotheses requires that we control for important differences in the institutional structure of municipal governments in Michigan. In general, cities have a greater ability to fund the services demanded by their residents than villages or townships because city governments are allowed, by state law and/or their city charter, to levy higher property taxes than townships and villages, and to collect additional revenues not available to these other governments. To account for these differences, each model includes a dichotomous variable indicating if the municipal government is a city. Also, Michigan law permits township governments to adopt charter township status, which substantially enhances the fiscal resources available to them. Given the authority to raise additional funds, charter townships may act more like cities than general law townships in their decisions about service delivery arrangements. We account for this possibility by including a dichotomous variable indicating if the unit is a charter township.

To test our hypotheses, we merged a suite of additional variables into this service provision data set. The additional variables include several community-level fiscal, demographic,

Table 9.2. Descriptive Statistics, Independent Variables

Variable	Mean	Min	Max	Source
City	.25	0	1	Michigan Municipal League (MML)
TV/Capita	33,013	3,869	198,316	MI Dept of Treasury
TV/Capita^2	1.58e+09	1.50e+07	3.93e+10	MI Dept of Treasury
Pop 2000	13,258	130	951,270	U.S. Census of Population
Pct Ch Pop 1990–2000	13.22	−51.08	387.24	U.S. Census of Population
Land Area (Miles^2)	24.35	.10	175.20	U.S. Census of Population
Income/Cap 2000	23,325	11,394	110,683	U.S. Census of Population
Pct Afr Am 2000	3.51	0	81.55	U.S. Census of Population
Pct Elderly 2000	11.83	4.14	33.41	U.S. Census of Population
Charter Twp	.14	0	1	MML
Cities/County	12.83	1	39	MML

and political indicators, as well as regional characteristics such as the number of potential collaborators in the immediate area. We conducted separate analyses for the three modes of service provision examined. For each service provision mode, we report findings from two sets of logistic regression models. The first set of models focuses on the subset of three independent variables that operationalize our fiscal capacity hypotheses: a dichotomous variable indicating if the unit is a city (scored one for cities and zero for villages or townships), and the size of the unit's tax base (measured as taxable value per capita and taxable value per capita squared) available to support public services.[6] The second set of regression models adds several independent variables to fully operationalize our theoretical model and to test hypotheses about factors beyond fiscal capacity. Having identified where fiscal capacity is strong in the first set of regressions, the second set of models focuses on those service areas where the fiscal capacity effects are strongest. These additional regressions therefore permit us to evaluate the impact of the additional factors while at the same time assessing the robustness of our fiscal capacity hypothesis. Table 9.2 presents descriptive statistics and data sources for each of the independent variables.

Direct Provision

We begin by examining the factors explaining self-provision of government services. We propose that local governments with higher levels of fiscal capacity are more likely to self-provide government services; more populous local governments are more likely to provide services directly; and those with larger nonwhite and older populations are more likely to provide services directly. We first report limited logistic regressions for the twenty services for which local governments most frequently reported self-provision. We then estimate the more fully specified models on a subset of ten services.

Table 9.3 reports the logistic regression estimates for the models of direct provision of services. The dependent variable in each model is whether a given community reports directly providing the service in question. We use logistic regression because the dependent variable is dichotomous. Each row corresponds to the results of a separate logistic regression. The first results column reports the estimated coefficient for the variable measuring

Table 9.3. Local Fiscal Capacity and the Likelihood of Direct Provision of Services in 460 Michigan Local Governments

Service	City	TV/Capita	Population 2000
Purchasing	.86	7.20e−06	3.45e−06
Tax Collection	−.33	.000041*	.000019
Treasury	1.057*	.000042[†]	−5.39e−06
Accounting	.46	−5.79e−07	.000026
Election Records	.93*	.000035[†]	.000036
Zoning	1.28[†]	.000031[†]	.000097[†]
Payroll	1.25[†]	−7.24e−06	5.13e−06
Records	1.72[†]	2.00e−06	.000039*
Election Administration	1.26[†]	.000013	.000032*
Document Destruction	.34	−6.66e−06	7.37e−06
Bldg Code Enforcement	1.41[†]	9.25e−06	.00011[‡]
Printing	.21	6.41e−06	9.14e−06
Community Planning	1.076[†]	−8.32e−06*	.000044[†]
Building Permits	.53*	8.89e−06*	.000085[‡]
Building Janitors	−.19	−3.63e−06	−3.28e−06
Parks	2.65[‡]	−.000013[†]	.000045[†]
Fleet Purchasing	2.15[‡]	−5.37e−06	.000067[‡]
Fleet Garage	2.83[‡]	−1.56e−06	.000050[†]
Property Assessing	−.21	8.26e−06	.000062[‡]
Building Inspection	.49*	5.51e−06	.00014[‡]

NOTE: Values reported in cells are coefficients from logistic regression.

*p < .10

[†]p < .05

[‡]p < .01

the type of municipal government. Positive coefficients indicate that cities are more likely than the other types of local governments (villages and townships) to self-provide the particular service. The findings show that cities are, indeed, more likely than townships and villages to directly provide all but three of the twenty services. City governments face demands for more services and are empowered with greater authority to raise funds to support direct service provision than are the other types of municipal governments. Given access to greater resources, cities tend to do more than other types of local governments.

The coefficients reported in the second column of table 9.3 reveal the relationship between the unit's taxable value per capita (TV/Capita) and the likelihood of direct provision of the service. Positive coefficients indicate that the likelihood of direct provision is higher in communities with greater per capita property wealth. The findings show that when local fiscal capacity is measured in terms of TV/Capita, no consistent relationship with direct provision is seen for these twenty services. This suggests that, for this set of basic government services, differences in property wealth across jurisdictions are not important considerations in their decision to self-provide.

The third variable in the models shown in table 9.3 is the unit's population in 2000. As hypothesized, more populous municipal governments are more likely to directly provide all but two of the listed services, and the effect is significant for 55 percent (eleven of twenty) of the services. The estimated effects tend to become more consistently significant as the proportion of local governments self-providing the service falls (that is, as one moves down the list). We suspect that this is simply an artifact of the data. Given the high proportions of governments reporting self-provision of the first several services on the list, there is little variance to be explained by the variables in the model.

To assess the robustness of these preliminary results, and to test our additional hypotheses, we estimate more fully specified models for ten of these services. To account for the high proportion of governments reporting direct provision for several of the services in table 9.3, we estimate the fully specified models for the ten services from table 9.1 with the lowest rates of self-provision (items 11–20 on the list). The services examined are record keeping, election administration, building code enforcement, community planning, building permits, parks, fleet purchasing, fleet garage, property assessing, and building inspection.

Table 9.4 reports the findings from these ten logistic regressions. Bold-faced entries highlight the preliminary hypotheses explored in table 9.2. As hypothesized, cities and charter townships are more likely than general law townships and villages to self-provide all of the ten services, as evidenced by the positive and often statistically significant estimates on the city and charter township variables. The findings also reveal that size affects the direct provision choice in two different ways. First, more populous units are more likely to self-provide each service, and this effect is statistically significant for eight of the ten services. Second, the geographical scale of the unit is statistically related to reliance on direct provision in 60 percent (six of ten) of the services. For three services (election administration, building permits, and property assessing), greater land area increases the likelihood of direct provision. For three others (parks, fleet purchasing, and fleet garage), more land area decreases the likelihood that the municipal government directly provides the service. None of the other variables show consistent patterns across the ten services.

Horizontal Cooperation

Next, we examine our hypotheses about the effect of local fiscal capacity on horizontal cooperation. We propose that cities will be more likely to engage in higher levels of horizontal cooperation than township or village governments; communities in the midrange of fiscal capacity (TV/Capita) will be more likely to engage in horizontal cooperation, but those at the highest levels of fiscal capacity (TV/Capita^2) will be less constrained and therefore less likely to cooperate in providing municipal services; and larger numbers of potential local government partners will increase the likelihood of horizontal cooperation.

Table 9.5 reports our analysis of the relationship between fiscal capacity and horizontal cooperation for the twenty service areas where the highest levels of horizontal cooperation were reported in table 9.1. The dependent variable in each model is whether a given community reports any incidence of horizontal cooperation for the service in question.[7] The first column of results reports the estimated coefficient for the variable measuring the type of municipal government. The findings are largely consistent with our expectations about municipal structure. The city dummy variable is positive for 70 percent (fourteen of twenty) of the services examined, and is positive and statistically significant in 60 percent (twelve of

Table 9.4. Likelihood of Direct Provision of Services in 460 Michigan Local Governments—Full Model

Variable	Records	Election Admin	Bldg Code Enforcement	Community Planning	Building Permits
City	**1.98**†	**2.73**‡	**.85***	**1.39**†	**.54**
TV/Capita	**−.000017**	**−.000019**	**8.33e−06**	**2.70e−06**	**−.000018**
TV/Capita^2	3.66e−11	1.25e−10	4.43e−11	−1.57e−10*	1.43e−10
Pop 2000	**.000028**	**1.92e−06**	**.000097**†	**.000028***	**.000056**†
Pct Ch Pop	.020*	.00075	−.00056	−.0031	.0037
Land Area	.0070	.047‡	−.0050	−.0043	.012*
Income/Cap	.000036	.000045	−.000029	.000043†	6.38e−06
Pct Afr Am	−.0057	.011	.020	.0071	.0030
Pct Elderly	.032	.0017	.063*	−.022	.043
Charter Twp	.072	1.33†	.26	.81†	.72*
Cities/County	.00025	−.023	.059†	−.023*	.048†
Constant	.27	−.28	−.53	.00044	−1.00
R^2	.09	.15	.17	.10	.13

Variable	Parks	Fleet Purchasing	Fleet Garage	Property Assessing	Building Inspection
City	**2.31**‡	**2.010**‡	**2.50**‡	**2.61**‡	**.64***
TV/Capita	**8.00e−06**	**−.000024**	**−2.89e−06**	**−.000012**	**−7.32e−06**
TV/Capita^2	−1.03e−10	7.03e−11	3.00e−11	1.56e−10	7.03e−11
Pop 2000	**.000036**†	**.000046**†	**.000052**†	**.000086**‡	**.000012**‡
Pct Ch Pop	.0031	.013*	−.0066	.0039	.0027
Land Area	−.022†	−.017†	−.025†	.077‡	.0079
Income/Cap	−.000023	1.82e−06	−.000016	.000031	−6.62e−06
Pct Afr Am	.012	−.0090	−.014	−.014	−.0051
Pct Elderly	.035	.089†	.053	−.019	.021
Charter Twp	.35	1.44†	.93†	.57	.83*
Cities/County	.0022	−.0047	−.014	−.086‡	.022
Constant	.54	−.26	.50	−1.79†	−.84
R^2	.19	.21	.22	.28	.17

NOTE: Values reported in cells are coefficients from logistic regression.

*$p < .10$

†$p < .05$

‡$p < .01$

twenty) of them.[8] However, these findings reveal that municipal structure affects the likelihood of cooperation on fire services differently than on other services. Only six services display a negative sign for the city dummy variable, and all are services related to fire protection and EMS. Four of the models have city coefficients that are negative and statistically significant, indicating that townships and villages are more likely to engage in horizontal cooperation on fire fighting, fire inspection, fire hydrant maintenance, and EMS than are cities. We note that this finding is independent of the level of property wealth in the jurisdiction (since we control for TV/Capita). Townships and villages are more likely to cooperate horizontally on these fire services than are cities, regardless of the per capita tax base in the community.

Table 9.5. Local Fiscal Capacity and the Likelihood of Horizontal Service Arrangements in 460 Michigan Local Governments

Service	City	TV/Capita	TV/Capita^2
Fire Fighting	−.78[†]	−.000011	6.28e−11
Fire Training	−.14	−5.31e−06	3.63e−11
Library	.47[†]	.000023*	−1.15e−10*
Hazmat	.47[†]	7.98e−06	−2.53e−11
Water Treatment	1.47[‡]	.000045[‡]	−2.38e−10[†]
Sewer Treatment	1.11[‡]	.000057[‡]	−2.95e−10[†]
Ambulance	−.67[†]	−.000013	9.34e−11
Fire Inspection	−.87[†]	−6.70e−06	9.56e−11
Fire Investigation	−.37	−7.65e−06	6.68e−11
Water Distribution	.73[†]	.000037[†]	−1.79e−10[†]
Sewer Collection	.45*	.000036[†]	−1.72e−10[†]
Fire Hydrants	−1.52[‡]	8.49e−06	−3.44e−11
Police-911/Radio	1.24[‡]	.000021	−8.79e−11
Emergency Planning	.60[†]	.000032[†]	−1.85e−10*
Dial-a-Ride	1.57[‡]	.000075[†]	−5.32e−10[†]
Watershed Mgmt.	1.21[‡]	.000026*	−1.26e−10
Gas Metering	.29	.000019	−8.43e−11
Bus Service	2.00[‡]	.000073[†]	−6.68e−10*
Senior Center	.82[†]	.000048[†]	−2.35e−10[†]
Elections Admin.	.15	−1.52e−06	−5.48e−11

NOTE: Values reported in cells are coefficients from logistic regression.

*p < .10

[†]p < .05

[‡]p < .01

The coefficients reported in the second column of table 9.5 reveal the relationship between the unit's TV/Capita and the likelihood of horizontal cooperation. For many of the services examined, the coefficients indicate that horizontal cooperation is more likely in communities with greater fiscal capacity. The coefficient for this variable is positive in 70 percent (fourteen of twenty) of the services examined, and is positive and significant in 50 percent (ten of twenty) of them.[9] Most of the services that are positive and significant are capital intensive to varying degrees, and include water and sewer utilities, transit, and library services. Once again, the relationship between fiscal capacity and horizontal cooperation is different for fire services. Five of the six fire services examined have negative coefficients on TV/Capita, although none are statistically significant.

The third results column reports the estimated coefficient for the third measure of local fiscal capacity, TV/Capita^2. The findings largely confirm our expectations about the behavior of high-capacity jurisdictions. The coefficient shows a negative relationship in 75 percent (fifteen of twenty) of the services, which is significant in 45 percent (nine of twenty) of them.[10] Municipal governments with the greatest fiscal capacity, as measured by the value of their property tax base, are less likely to engage in horizontal cooperation. Again, the major exception to this conclusion is for the group of fire services. One explanation for this finding is that the nature of fire protection services as a basic service may mean that communities feel compelled to provide fire protection and will enter into cooperative ventures with neighbors regardless of their fiscal capacity.

To assess the robustness of these preliminary results, and to test our additional hypotheses, we estimate more fully specified models for the ten capital-intensive services with the highest levels of horizontal cooperation, excluding services related to fire fighting and fire protection. The services examined are library, water treatment, sewer treatment, water distribution, sewer collection, emergency dispatch, dial-a-ride, gas metering, bus, and senior center. Table 9.6 reports the results of these ten logistic regression analyses.

Table 9.6. Likelihood of Horizontal Service Arrangements in 460 Michigan Local Governments—Full Model

Variable	Library	Water Treatment	Sewer Treatment	Water Distribution	Sewer Collection
City	.29	1.36‡	1.15†	1.15†	1.04†
TV/Capita	.000027*	.000036†	.000046†	.000030*	.000027*
TV/Capita²	−2.05e−10†	−2.52e−10†	−3.00e−10†	−1.41e−10	−1.23e−10
Pop 2000	−9.33e−07	7.09e−06	.000011	.000012*	.000012*
Pct Ch Pop	−.010*	−.0057	−.0073	−.0025	−.0026
Land Area	−.015†	−.011	.0019	−.0013	.012
Income/Cap	.000046†	.000031	.000034*	.000018	.000013
Pct Afr Am	−.0070	.021	.0082	.0052	−.0028
Pct Elderly	−.058*	−.015	.013	−.063*	−.025
Charter Twp	−.53	1.41‡	1.26‡	1.34‡	1.31‡
Cities/County	−.019	−.0060	−.0092	−.028†	−.023*
Constant	−.60	−2.33‡	−3.19‡	−1.73†	−2.40‡
R²	.049	.16	.14	.11	.09

Variable	Police-911/ Radio	Dial-a-Ride	Gas Metering	Bus Service	Senior Center
City	.28	2.040‡	.71*	2.73‡	1.089†
TV/Capita	.000038†	.00011†	.000033	.000079*	.000048†
TV/Capita²	−2.09e−10†	−7.27e−10†	−1.47e−10	−8.22e−10*	−2.63e−10†
Pop 2000	3.16e−06	6.85e−08	6.16e−06	−7.09e−07	−.000018
Pct Ch Pop	−.021†	−.0093	−.0069	−.0062	−.0015
Land Area	−.042‡	−.00088	−.012	.00094	.00018
Income/Cap	.000016	−.000020	4.92e−06	.000027	6.41e−06
Pct Afr Am	.017	.022	.013	.027*	−.043
Pct Elderly	−.076*	−.027	−.0063	−.027	.021
Charter Twp	−.014	1.25†	1.60‡	1.92‡	.22
Cities/County	.0064	−.017	−.059‡	−.011	.0012
Constant	−1.16*	−4.099‡	−2.19†	−4.97‡	−3.55‡
R²	.13	.16	.10	.23	.07

NOTE: Values reported in cells are coefficients from logistic regression.

*p < .10

†p < .05

‡p < .01

The effects of government type and property wealth on horizontal cooperation are robust to the inclusion of our other independent variables. In no case does the relationship of the three fiscal capacity measures with horizontal cooperation change when the additional variables are included. In several service areas, one or more of the measures become statistically insignificant, but many significant effects remain in the full models. As expected, the charter township variable is positive in eight of the equations and strongly significant in seven. This indicates that charter townships are more likely than general law townships and villages to engage in horizontal cooperation on these services. Given that the full model also includes a measure of the unit's population, this finding is independent of the population of the township. This finding strongly supports our propositions about fiscal capacity and horizontal cooperation. The enhanced resources available to charter townships appear to make these governments more attractive partners in horizontal collaborations.

The findings provide little evidence that greater numbers of potential collaborators stimulate horizontal cooperation. In fact, the limited evidence for a relationship points in the other direction: horizontal cooperation is less likely in highly fragmented areas. The number of cities in a unit's county is negatively related to the likelihood of horizontal cooperation, with negative signs in all but two service areas, but significant effects in only three. This may indicate that scale economies are more easily reached within a single local government jurisdiction in densely populated regions. It also may reflect the intensity of competition for tax base created when many small cities are incorporated in close proximity to one another. Krueger (2005) argues that the best candidates for joint service provision are often the same governments the local unit most directly competes against for residents and economic development.

The findings provide little evidence that population size, population change, land area, or the population characteristics we examined affect horizontal cooperation; none of the coefficients show consistently signed or significant effects across the ten service areas.

Vertical Cooperation

Finally, we test our hypotheses about the factors explaining vertical cooperation between municipal governments and county and/or state governments. We propose that townships and villages are more likely to partner with county or state government to provide services; local governments with lower fiscal capacity are more likely to engage in vertical cooperation; and communities at the highest levels of taxable value are less likely to cooperate on service provision with the county or state governments.

Table 9.7 reports our analysis of the relationship between fiscal capacity and vertical cooperation for the twenty service areas in table 9.1 with the highest levels of vertical cooperation, with several important exceptions. It is likely that the high rates of vertical cooperation on road construction and maintenance and the operation of district courts are due to legislative and constitutional requirements for county involvement and not necessarily the choices of local decision makers to work cooperatively with counties. We therefore exclude the six services from these two areas from the analyses that follow. The next six most frequently reported areas of vertical cooperation shown in table 9.1—detective/crime investigation units, curbside mowing, police officer training, environmental education, hazardous

Table 9.7. Local Fiscal Capacity and the Likelihood of Vertical Service Arrangements in 460 Michigan Local Governments

Service	City	TV/Capita	TV/Capita^2
Animal Control	−.91†	3.73e−06	−7.59e−11
Detention Center	−.44*	3.17e−06	−4.18e−11
Crime Lab	.54†	.000016	−6.40e−11
Emergency Planning	.19	−1.15e−06	−2.90e−11
Animal Licenses	−.95†	−9.86e−06	−5.09e−12
Well Permitting	−1.95‡	.000028†	−1.02e−10
Septic Permitting	−2.035‡	.000028†	−1.34e−11
Police-911/Radio	−1.60‡	−.000026†	1.53e−10
Restaurant Licenses	1.13‡	.000013	−1.02e−10
Water Quality	−.54†	.000028†	−1.27e−10
Erosion Control	−.31	.000011	−4.82e−11
Watershed Mgmt	−.57†	8.65e−06	−4.06e−11
Air Quality	−.0037	.000015	−6.55e−11
Police—Canine Unit	−1.065‡	−.000010	9.49e−11
Detective/Investigation	−1.73‡	−5.15e−06	3.09e−11
Curbside Mowing	−2.64‡	.000047†	−3.57e−10†
Police Officer Training	−.34	−.000011	5.19e−11
Environ Education	−.44†	3.36e−06	−3.26e−11
Hazmat	−.27	4.30e−06	−4.40e−11
Police—Street Patrol	−2.93‡	6.16e−06	−1.53e−11

NOTE: Values reported in cells are coefficients from logistic regression.

*p < .10

†p < .05

‡p < .01

material handling, and police street patrols—replace the excluded services. As with the analysis of the first two service provision modes, we begin our analysis of vertical cooperation with a series of limited models that focus on our fiscal capacity hypotheses. We later add the same set of additional variables used in the previous analyses of direct provision and horizontal cooperation to test our other hypotheses on this subset of services.

Table 9.7 shows that cities are less likely than townships or villages to engage in vertical cooperation for 85 percent (seventeen of twenty) of the services, and are significantly less likely for 70 percent (fourteen of twenty) of them. These findings are consistent with our predictions for the effect of municipal structure on the likelihood of vertical cooperation. However, property wealth is a much less important determinant of vertical cooperation, as indicated by the statistically insignificant effect of TV/Capita in 75 percent (fifteen of twenty) of the services examined. Indeed, in the few instances where the coefficient on TV/Capita is significant, it is positive in four cases and negative in only one. Similarly, TV/Capita^2 is significant only once, indicating little evidence of a drop-off in vertical cooperation for communities with the greatest fiscal capacity. Together, these findings suggest that local fiscal capacity, when measured in terms of taxable property wealth, is not an important factor in local units' decisions to cooperate with the county or state governments to provide services.

221

Instead, it is the legal and constitutional capacity of the local government to generate the resources to pay for public services that is central to this decision. The limited fiscal capacity of township and village governments created by their limited tax authority is strongly related to the decision to cooperate with the county or state governments on this set of services.

Table 9.8 reports the findings from our more fully specified models. We proposed that vertical cooperation is strongly motivated by the ability of counties and the state government to serve as providers of services that require technical training or expertise. To test this hypothesis, we limit the analysis to the ten services from table 9.7 that demand high levels of technical training or expertise, and therefore present the greatest opportunities for exploiting

Table 9.8. Likelihood of Vertical Service Arrangements in 460 Michigan Local Governments – Full Model

Variable	Animal Control	Detention Center	Animal Licenses	Well Permitting	Septic Permitting
City	**.071**	**.063**	**−.11**	**−.94†**	**−.78†**
TV/Capita	**.000031**	**.000030***	**6.49e−06**	**9.92e−06**	**.000011**
TV/Capita^2	−8.94e−11	−9.47e−11	−3.19e−11	7.25e−12	1.76e−11
Pop 2000	−6.77e−06	−.000019†	−7.68e−06	−4.27e−06	−3.54e−06
Pct Ch Pop	.011	.00088	.0045	.012	.0097
Land Area	−.011	−.012	−.0037	.021†	.029†
Income/Cap	−.000044*	−.000036*	−.000017	.000010	−5.83e−06
Pct Afr Am	−.012	.022	−.0022	−.011	−.027
Pct Elderly	−.055	−.045	−.046	−.049	−.057*
Charter Twp	**.72***	**.45**	**.51**	**.53**	**.76†**
Cities/County	−.065‡	−.024†	−.056‡	−.027†	−.030†
Constant	2.84‡	2.032‡	2.20‡	.61	.79
R^2	.15	.06	.11	.17	.21

Variable	Police–911/ Radio	Water Quality	Watershed Management	Detective/ Investigation	Environ Education
City	**−.26**	**.33**	**.20**	**−.73†**	**.31**
TV/Capita	**−.000015**	**.000030†**	**3.30e−06**	**−.000013**	**3.69e−06**
TV/Capita^2	1.61e−10*	−1.15e−10	2.92e−11	5.29e−11	−1.58e−11
Pop 2000	−.000037†	−.000020†	−6.61e−06	−.000055‡	−.000019†
Pct Ch Pop	.0041	−.0011	−.000063	.016†	.0016
Land Area	.0063	.0013	.0053	.0058	−.00020
Income/Cap	−.000016	−2.28e−06	−7.94e−06	.000019	−6.54e−06
Pct Afr Am	−.016	−.012	−.22*	−.0095	−.011
Pct Elderly	−.035	−.062†	−.082†	−.056*	−.034
Charter Twp	**1.31†**	**.98†**	**.69†**	**.46**	**.97†**
Cities/County	−.052‡	−.017	−.012	−.019	−.016
Constant	2.33‡	.55	1.18†	.99*	.47
R^2	.18	.06	.04	.16	.04

NOTE: Values reported in cells are coefficients from logistic regression.

*$p < .10$

†$p < .05$

‡$p < .01$

"economies of skill." Beginning with the two measures of municipal fiscal authority, the findings show that cities are more likely than general law townships and villages to undertake vertical cooperation on half of the services and are less likely on the other half. More consistently, charter townships are more likely to cooperate vertically on each and every service area, and are significantly more likely to report vertical cooperation on six of the services. Charter townships tend to be more fiscally constrained than cities because they have fewer mills available to levy, but often have service demands on par with cities. They may need to seek out opportunities to cooperate on these technical services to a greater degree than cities.

The other major fiscal capacity variable—TV/Capita—is consistently positive, but rarely statistically significant. This finding confirms and extends the major conclusion of the reduced model. Fiscal capacity in terms of per capita taxable value is not instrumental to the decisions to cooperate on service provision with the county or state governments for this set of services, even when jurisdictional differences in population, land area, and demographic characteristics are considered. These latter factors are also largely unimportant to this decision in most communities, as indicated by the general lack of statistically significant coefficients for these factors in the ten models. We had proposed that local governments with lower fiscal capacity, whether measured in terms of tax base or municipal powers, are more likely to engage in vertical cooperation. However, these findings provide little support for our contention about the effect of TV/Capita on vertical cooperation for this set of services. It is not the ability of the community to afford service provision that determines whether local governments cooperate vertically to provide these services, but rather the extent to which they can raise own-source revenues to fund direct provision without asking residents to authorize the assessment of a special millage to support the service.

Finally, the findings in table 9.8 show that the number of cities per county is negative in all ten models and statistically significant in six, indicating that units in counties with many municipal governments are less likely to engage in vertical cooperation. This finding follows the negative relationship found for this factor in the models of horizontal cooperation, providing an even stronger case for the cooperation-depressing effects of municipal fragmentation. Fewer municipal governments in an area often translate into greater interlocal cooperation, whether the potential partners are other cities, villages, townships, the county, or state government. An unexpected finding is that the negative effect of other municipal governments on cooperation is stronger for vertical than for horizontal relationships.

Discussion

Analysis of the Citizens Research Council of Michigan's survey of local government services shows clear patterns in the methods used to deliver local government services. The direct provision of services is the method used most frequently, especially for labor-intensive services and functions basic to local government such as purchasing, tax collection, accounting, elections, payroll, and records, as well as zoning, planning, and building code enforcement/inspection/permits, as hypothesized. When measured in terms of taxable value per capita, a governmental unit's fiscal capacity is not useful for predicting whether a particular service will be directly provided. Instead, it is the institutional measure of fiscal capacity—the type

223

of municipal government—that explains the direct-provision choice. As the population within a local jurisdiction increases, the number of services provided expands, and the new services are likely to remain self-provided. Cities and charter townships (which tend to act more like cities than general law townships in the methods used to provide services) provide more services and are more likely to self-provide services than general law townships or villages.

At some point in the expansion of services, local governments are confronted with demands for capital-intensive services and services that require personnel with technical expertise or training that impose significant costs on the provider. Our analysis shows that the nature of the services plays an important role in local governments' decisions to look among their neighbors for partners (horizontal cooperation) or seek to benefit from the capacity of the state or county governments (vertical cooperation). Horizontal cooperation occurs most frequently for the provision of services that require significant capital invest-ment. Fire prevention, libraries, water and sewer, public transit, and senior centers all require investment for the construction of buildings and infrastructure or the purchase of vehicles and equipment. These costs can often act as significant deterrents for local gov-ernments to engage in the activity alone, but economies of scale can be gained by cooper-ating with other units confronting the same costs. Vertical cooperation occurs more often for the provision of services that require significant labor investment in professionals with technical expertise or training. Common examples include county-local emergency plan-ning, animal control, and environmental initiatives. The costs of employing individuals who warrant higher pay scales due to their levels of expertise or training can act as deterrents for local governments to provide those services individually, but economies of skill can be gained by piggybacking on the employment of those individuals at higher levels of govern-ment. A decision to join with other relatively small local governments does not create the economies needed to fund some services and functions; it is by engaging in vertical coop-eration that these services and functions can often be provided.

Policy Implications

These differences suggest a strategy for local officials hoping to benefit from intergovern-mental cooperation and for state policy makers hoping to promote collaboration among local governments. The patterns of cooperation we observe—including the types of local governments that engage in collaborative service provision, the partners they choose, the forms of cooperation they undertake, and the kinds of joint services they deliver—are largely consistent with the logic of cooperation laid out in our theory and hypotheses. While our analysis does not contain explicit cost data that would allow us to determine whether these arrangements are enhancing economic efficiency, the fact that a great many Michigan local governments are behaving as the theory suggests indicates, to us at least, that these forms of cooperation make sense to decision makers on the ground. By learning from and build-ing upon the experiences of local governments across the state, and by working to promote similar forms of cooperation in other localities, we believe that state and local policy makers stand the greatest chances of success in promoting viable cooperation.

Local Actions

A necessary first step for local government officials hoping to promote intergovernmental cooperation is to examine the nature of the services considered for collaboration. Services should be classified according to whether they are primarily capital intensive, labor intensive, or technically intensive. Within broad service provision categories, individual functions should also be examined to consider whether opportunities for cooperation exist for a subset of services within a broad category. For example, police protection tends to be fairly labor intensive and hence not especially conducive to collaboration, but more specific functions such as detective work and crime scene investigation tend to be technically intensive, and detention facilities are capital intensive. While joint provision of police protection might not create significant opportunities for cost savings, joint crime scene units or detention facilities may offer greater saving opportunities. County governments should also assess the services they provide to identify opportunities for new or expanded vertical collaborations.

A second step is to identify potential partners for collaboration. By understanding that capital-intensive services are especially sensitive to geographic characteristics, local government officials can begin by building horizontal relationships with neighboring communities. Similarly, by understanding that technically intensive services are not geographically based but can be provided on an as-needed basis across counties and local units, efforts to collaborate can begin by investigating state and county governments' ability to provide those services on behalf of local governments through vertical cooperation.

Identification of a suitable partner for horizontal and/or vertical cooperation requires consideration of different factors. We find that cities and charter townships are more likely than general law townships or villages to engage in horizontal cooperation. As hypothesized, the likelihood of horizontal cooperation increases in communities with greater fiscal capacity, but local governments with the greatest fiscal capacity are less likely to engage in horizontal cooperation. These findings suggest that communities with midrange fiscal capacity should seek out neighbors in similar fiscal circumstances for cooperative ventures. Notwithstanding the cooperative ventures that currently exist among local governments—especially in fire protection and library services—those governmental units with severely limited fiscal capacity are unlikely to find promising opportunities for horizontal cooperation, since neither they nor their resource-poor neighbors are able to provide capital-intensive services, either individually or jointly.

Our analysis of trends in vertical cooperation shows that a local government's fiscal conditions are not the driving factor behind the decision to engage in vertical cooperation with the county or the state. Property-rich communities are just as likely as poor or midrange communities to use vertical cooperation.

These findings suggest that opportunities exist for expansion of vertical cooperation between counties and their constituent cities, villages, and townships, regardless of the fiscal capacity of those local governments. Officials representing local governments of all size and fiscal capacity should consider their county governments as potential service providers, either by piggybacking on existing county services or through interlocal contracts to have the county provide functions and services that are currently self-provided.

225

A third step is for local governments to acknowledge that horizontal collaboration represents mutual exchange relationships between local units that seek to jointly provide services neither would or could individually provide as efficiently. Each participant expects the other(s) to contribute its "fair share" to the financing of the governmental service, and in return, both are made better off through cost savings and perhaps improved service provision. To achieve these benefits, a successful cooperative relationship requires participants to put aside their instincts toward competition for tax base in the mutual interest of improved, more economical service provision.

Competition for tax base is less salient as local governments seek partners for vertical collaboration. Because city and township residents are simultaneously state and county residents, vertical collaboration may be in the interest of all participating units. Indeed, by acting to improve the service provision capabilities of a county's weakest units, county officials can make the county as a whole a more attractive place in which to live or locate a business.

State Policies

State programs can be designed to promote greater horizontal and vertical collaboration. The state should not attempt to mold a uniform policy to promote cooperation—such programs should recognize the underlying differences in logic and motivations behind vertical and horizontal cooperation.

State policies designed to promote and facilitate horizontal cooperation should emphasize the capital-intensive nature of the services best suited for horizontal cooperation and the need for local government officials to find nearby municipalities interested in cooperating. Our analysis finds that local governments most often engage in horizontal cooperation to provide capital-intensive services. Once the capital-intensive good is purchased, acquired, or constructed, the marginal cost of providing services to additional residents, such as those in a neighboring community, is relatively small.

Given the benefits of horizontal cooperation in the provision of capital-intensive services, the state can best promote cooperation by reducing the cost of capital items for those local governments cooperating in the provision of services. One method for accomplishing this would be for the state to create a loan fund or sinking fund from which cooperating local governments could borrow or bond to acquire, purchase, or construct the capital-intensive items at lower cost than if they were to do so on their own.

The second part of the state's efforts to facilitate horizontal cooperation should concentrate on helping local governments identify and create agreements with willing partners. The state could provide consultation to those local officials seeking to initiate cooperative ventures; collect and disseminate information about research and best practices on intergovernmental cooperation; offer arbitration and/or training to local government officials; advocate for additional resources to local governments within and outside state government; administer grant and incentive programs; and maintain a moderated Web site where local governments can identify potential service-sharing partners and learn from others' experiences. The state government can work to remove barriers to cooperation by helping with the cost of negotiating, planning, and implementing a cooperative agreement. And it could do more to standardize the financial reporting requirements for local governments so that such negotiations and planning begin with all parties in agreement about the finances of such a cooperative venture.

State policies to promote vertical cooperation should recognize that cities, villages, and townships of all sizes and fiscal capacity can benefit by working with the state or their county governments to provide services. The potential role of the state in providing incentives for vertical cooperation is far different than the potential role for horizontal cooperation. The state need not help with the process of identifying potential partners, since information about the services that state and county governments can provide is more readily accessible to local governments. Also, because the state and counties are already actively engaged in the provision of services to local units, contracting may be more routinized, and negotiation over vertical cooperation tends to be limited to the level of services and the cost. Unlike horizontal cooperation, there is little need for the state to provide resources to help with planning, negotiating, or implementing cooperative agreements. And there is little need for the state to help with the cost of acquiring, purchasing, or constructing items as is the case for horizontal cooperation.

Instead, the state could provide financial incentives for local governments to work with the state or county governments for the provision of services. Incentives could be directed to cities, villages, and townships to motivate contracting with county governments for the provision of specific services, or to counties to defray the cost of providing specific services, and thus reducing their costs below what most municipalities would pay to self-provide the same services. Vertical relationships could also be created through legislative reassignment of technically intensive services from the local to the county levels.

Conclusion

Intergovernmental cooperation is increasingly seen as a tool for local governments to deal with the operational and fiscal pressures created by Michigan's continued economic troubles and by state actions to fund its services using dollars that would otherwise be passed on to local governments through state revenue sharing. The analyses in this chapter provide policy makers with insights regarding what sorts of intergovernmental cooperation can and should be facilitated through legislation and policy, and offer guidance to practitioners for assessing the potential for cooperation in their communities. We believe our examination of horizontal and vertical cooperation and direct provision will provide analysts with tools for better understanding and evaluating the incidence of intergovernmental cooperation in Michigan and elsewhere.

Notes

1. A fifth option is contracting for the service with a nongovernmental provider. The decision to use a private or nonprofit provider is beyond the scope of the current analysis.
2. The surveys were mailed in winter 2005 to every city, village, and township government in twenty-five Michigan counties. These 646 units of government represent 36 percent of the 1,776 general-purpose local governments in Michigan and contain 78 percent of

the state's population. Responses were received from 460 of the 646 governments surveyed, for a response rate of 71 percent. Response rates for each type of government were: 71 percent for cities (113 of 160); 70 percent for villages (58 of 83); and 72 percent for townships (289 of 403). For additional information, see www.crcmich.org/PUBLI-CAT/2000s/2005/catalog.html.

3. For each service, respondents were provided twelve options and were asked to choose the one that best described their unit's service-delivery arrangements. Respondents were asked to choose multiple responses only when necessary. Responses were then combined into four clusters for analysis, as described in the text. The survey response options were: (1) Does not provide or contract for this service—this service is not the responsibility of, and therefore is not provided by, your city/village/township. (2) Directly provides this service—your unit is providing this service using municipal employees. (3) Also provides this service by contract *to* residents of another community— your city/village/township is providing this service, through some sort of contract or agreement, to another community. This would usually be in addition to providing the service within your own city/village/township. (4) Jointly provides this service with another municipality—your city/village/township has entered into an agreement with a neighboring city/village/township to cooperatively provide this service. (5) Jointly provides this service with a school district—your city/village/township has entered into an agreement with a school district to jointly provide this service. (6) Jointly provides this service with the county—your city/village/township has entered into an agreement with the county to jointly provide this service. (7) Has this service provided by the state—your city/village/township contracts with the state to provide this service. (8) Has this service provided by the county—your county provides this service on a countywide basis. (9) Has the service provided by another municipality—your city/village/township has some sort of agreement or contract with another city/village/township to have that unit deliver this service. (10) Has this service provided by a special authority or special district—your city/village/township has joined a special authority with other units of local government to provide this service. (11) Has this service provided by a private provider—your city/village/township has hired, or contracted with, or has a franchise agreement with, a nongovernmental private firm—for-profit or nonprofit—to provide this service. (12) Do not know how this service is provided—you are unaware if this service is being provided by another governmental entity, but your city/village/township is not currently providing this service.

4. This coding again ignores service delivery via nongovernmental providers as an option. We consider joint provision with, and service provision by, special authorities or districts as instances of horizontal cooperation.

5. When the Great Depression in the 1930s left many townships unable to fund road maintenance, the role of county road commissions was expanded to include care of township roads. Only one township has since returned to the role of caring for its own roads (see CRC 1997). Also, adoption of the 1963 Michigan Constitution mandated certain changes in the structure of the state judiciary. Specifically, Article VI, Section 26, required that the offices of circuit court commissioner and justice of the peace be abolished and

a court or courts of limited jurisdiction be created by the legislature. Public Act 154 of 1968 carried out that mandate and vested control of court districts with the legislature. These services were excluded from the analysis.

6. In our initial analyses of direct provision (table 9.2), we include population size rather than TV/Capita[2].

7. If a community reports one or more forms of horizontal cooperation on a given service, it is coded "one" on the dependent variable. Given the structure of the data, when a community reports more than one instance of horizontal cooperation on a given service, we cannot differentiate between collaborations on a single service delivery with multiple partners, versus multiple distinct instances of service delivery with different partners. The measures used for vertical cooperation and direct provision are constructed in a similar manner.

8. Table 9.5 reports models estimated for the twenty service areas where the greatest incidence of horizontal cooperation was reported. We also estimated the same models for the remaining ninety-five service areas where the incidence of horizontal cooperation was lower. In these additional models, the coefficient on city is positive and significant in only 28 percent (twenty-seven out of ninety-five) of the service areas.

9. In the additional models estimated for services with horizontal cooperation (see note 8), the TV/Capita coefficient is significant in only 12 percent (eleven of ninety-five) of the remaining services.

10. In the additional models (see note 8), the TV/Capita[2] coefficient is negative and significant in just 2 percent (two of ninety-five) of the other services for which horizontal cooperation was reported.

APPENDIX 1
Coding of Services in CRC Survey, 2005

Service	Basic Service?	Capital Intensive?	Technical Expertise?
Printing of Municipal Documents	3	1	1
Records/Archives	3	1	1
Document Destruction	1	1	1
Training/Professional Development	1	1	2
Payroll/Benefits	3	1	2
Property Assessing	3	1	3
Treasury Functions	3	1	3
Tax Collection	3	1	3
Accounting	3	1	3
Purchasing	3	1	2
Management Information Systems	1	1	3
Geographic Information Systems	1	2	2/3
Web Site Development/Management	1	1	2
Elections Administration	3	1	2
Election Records and Reporting	3	1	1
Building Security	1	1	1
Janitorial Services	1	1	1
Cemetery Services	1	1	1

(continued)

APPENDIX 1
Coding of Services in CRC Survey, 2005 (*continued*)

Service	Basic Service?	Capital Intensive?	Technical Expertise?
Mosquito/Moth/Insect Control	1	1	1
Fleet Purchasing	1	2	2
Vehicle Maintenance	1	1	3
Vehicle Garage/Storage	1	2	1
Solid Waste Residential	1	1	1
Solid Waste Non-Residential	1	1	1
Recycling	1	2	1
Landfill/Resource Recovery	1	3	1/2
Building Permits	2	1	2
Building Inspection	2	1	3
Code Enforcement	2	1	3
Well Permitting	2	1	3
Septic Permitting	2	1	3
911/Radio Communications	3	2/3	1/2
Police Officer Training	1	1	3
Police Street Patrol	3	2	2
Police Bike Patrol	1	1	2
Police Foot Patrol	1	1	2
Police Horse Patrol	1	2	2
Police Marine Patrol	1	3	2
Police Helicopter Patrol	1	3	2
Detectives/Crime Investigations	1	1	3
Police Canine Unit	1	2	2
Emergency & Disaster Response	2	1	3
Crime Laboratory	1	2/3	3
Jail(s)	1	3	1
Detention Center(s)	2	3	1
Animal Licenses	1	1	2
Animal Control	1	2	2
Fire Inspection	1	1	3
Fire Training	1	1	3
Fire Hydrant Maintenance	1	1	1/2
Fire Investigations	1	1	3
Fire Fighting/Rescue	2	3	2
Ambulance/EMS	2	3	3
Hazmat Handling and Response	1	2/3	3
Zoning Administration/Enforcement	2	1	2
Engineering	1	1	3
Surveying	1	1/2	3
Community Planning/Development	1	1	2
Business Retention/Expansion	1	1	2
Business Licensing	1	1	2
Restaurant/Food Regulation	1	1	3
Public Convention Center	1	3	1
Promotion/Tourism	1	2	1
Attorney/Legal Services	3	1	3
District Court	1	2	3
Mediation or Dispute Resolution	1	1	3
Road Construction/Improvement	1	3	1

APPENDIX 1
Coding of Services in CRC Survey, 2005 (*continued*)

Service	Basic Service?	Capital Intensive?	Technical Expertise?
Road Maintenance	1	3	1
Winter Road Maintenance	1	3	1
Road Signs and Signals	1	2	1
Street Lights	1	2	1
Sidewalk Construction/Maintenance	1	2/3	1
Roadside Mowing	1	2	1
Sidewalk Beautification	1	2	1
Water Treatment	1	3	2/3
Water Distribution	1	3	1
Sanitary Sewer Collection	1	3	1
Sanitary Sewer Treatment	1	3	2/3
Storm Water Management	2	2	2/3
Storm Water Collection	2	3	1
Storm Water Treatment	2	3	2/3
Water Metering and Billing	1	2	1
Gas Metering and Billing	1	3	1
Electric Metering and Billing	1	3	1
Cable Service	1	3	1
Parking Lots and Structures	1	3	1
Parking Meters	1	1/2	1
Internet Broadband	1	2/3	2
Wireless Internet (Wi-Fi)	1	2/3	2
Public Bus System	1	3	1
Dial-a-Ride	1	2	1
Airport	1	3	3
Soil Quality and Conservation	1	2	3
Water Quality and Conservation	1	2	3
Watershed Management	1	2	3
Air Quality Regulation	1	2	3
Erosion Control Structures	1	2	3
Environmental Education	1	1	2
Hospitals/Clinics	1	3	3
Parks	1	2/3	1
Playgrounds	1	2	1
Community/Recreation Center	1	3	1
Senior Center	1	3	1
Forestry Services	1	2	1
Golf Course	1	3	1
Community Pool	1	3	1
Trails	1	2/3	1
Beach Facilities	1	3	1
Marina/Port Facilities	1	3	1
Museum/Art Gallery	1	3	2
Library	1	3	2
Zoo	1	3	2/3
Community Theater	1	3	1
Stadium/Arena	1	3	1
Entertainment Facilities	1	2/3	1

NOTE: 1 = low; 2 = medium; 3 = high.

APPENDIX 2
Percentage of Local Governments Reporting Each Provision Mode by Service or Function, CRC Survey, 2005

Service	Direct Provision	Horizontal Cooperation	Vertical Cooperation	Does Not Provide/Contract
Printing of Municipal Documents	73.9%	2.8%	8.5%	9.2%
Records/Archives	86.3%	0.9%	6.19%	8.1%
Document Destruction	77.1%	0.2%	2.0%	10.4%
Training/Professional Development	51.7%	9.1%	19.1%	22.5%
Payroll/Benefits	88.0%	0.7%	0.9%	5.9%
Property Assessing	63.9%	11.7%	14.1%	1.8%
Treasury Functions	94.1%	1.1%	9.1%	1.4%
Tax Collection	95.9%	4.1%	12.8%	.7%
Accounting	93.9%	0.4%	0.4%	1.6%
Purchasing	96.3%	1.7%	5.7%	2.5%
Management Information Systems	41.2%	1.7%	10.0%	27.0%
Geographic Information Systems	24.1%	6.1%	38.7%	28.8%
Web Site Development/Management	41.5%	1.1%	6.7%	34.5%
Elections Administration	85.0%	13.0%	29.8%	1.8%
Election Records and Reporting	90.4%	8.3%	19.8%	1.4%
Building Security	55.9%	1.1%	3.9%	33.1%
Janitorial Services	66.7%	1.3%	0.2%	8.3%
Cemetery Services	55.7%	5.7%	0.2%	29.3%
Mosquito/Moth/Insect Control	19.7%	0.9%	22.6%	48.2%
Fleet Purchasing	65.3%	2.6%	8.3%	29.5%
Vehicle Maintenance	50.7%	2.8%	1.1%	29.3%
Vehicle Garage/Storage	64.6%	2.2%	0.4%	30.2%
Solid Waste Residential	13.9%	5.9%	2.8%	35.8%
Solid Waste Non-Residential	7.0%	3.0%	2.4%	51.8%
Recycling	16.5%	9.8%	13.3%	30.0%
Landfill/Resource Recovery	5.7%	7.8%	10.7%	50.7%
Building Permits	67.6%	7.4%	15.4%	4.1%
Building Inspection	63.5%	9.6%	16.5%	4.3%
Code Enforcement	74.6%	4.8%	14.8%	3.6%
Well Permitting	9.2%	3.9%	63.9%	26.8%
Septic Permitting	8.30%	3.91%	62.2%	27.9%
911/Radio Communications	17.6%	17.8%	62.2%	12.8%
Police Officer Training	34.0%	10.0%	46.5%	24.8%
Police Street Patrol	40.3%	6.1%	39.4%	20.9%
Police Bike Patrol	27.8%	3.0%	20.2%	47.7%
Police Foot Patrol	23.6%	2.8%	18.0%	52.9%
Police Horse Patrol	0.9%	2.0%	20.7%	73.9%
Police Marine Patrol	1.8%	1.1%	31.3%	65.1%
Police Helicopter Patrol	0.0%	1.3%	27.0%	67.6%
Detectives/Crime Investigations	32.7%	5.4%	49.1%	20.5%
Police Canine Unit	14.3%	9.6%	51.3%	31.1%
Emergency & Disaster Response	30.9%	17.2%	64.8%	13.5%
Crime Laboratory	5.7%	3.3%	68.0%	23.0%
Jail(s)	5.2%	3.0%	77.2%	24.1%
Detention Center(s)	8.6%	3.3%	69.1%	25.5%
Animal Licenses	38.7%	4.8%	64.6%	9.7%
Animal Control	13.8%	4.1%	72.2%	15.8%

APPENDIX 2
Percentage of Local Governments Reporting Each Provision Mode by Service or Function, CRC Survey, 2005 (*continued*)

Service	Direct Provision	Horizontal Cooperation	Vertical Cooperation	Does Not Provide/Contract
Fire Inspection	48.6%	32.1%	14.1%	9.0%
Fire Training	53.2%	42.0%	15.2%	6.5%
Fire Hydrant Maintenance	50.2%	23.0%	6.7%	19.4%
Fire Investigations	38.0%	31.7%	33.7%	9.7%
Fire Fighting/Rescue	60.9%	47.4%	3.9%	2.7%
Ambulance/EMS	31.8%	33.7%	18.5%	10.4%
Hazmat Handling and Response	34.9%	38.0%	43.0%	10.1%
Zoning Administration/Enforcement	88.5%	1.5%	7.2%	3.6%
Engineering	18.0%	0.9%	8.0%	18.0%
Surveying	9.9%	0.7%	10.2%	29.7%
Community Planning/Development	68.5%	4.1%	17.0%	7.7%
Business Retention/Expansion	35.4%	5.4%	17.8%	39.0%
Business Licensing	30.8%	1.1%	31.1%	36.9%
Restaurant/Food Regulation	3.3%	1.5%	61.5%	32.2%
Public Convention Center	3.1%	2.8%	12.0%	73.9%
Promotion/Tourism	11.6%	6.1%	18.0%	59.0%
Attorney/Legal Services	N/A	1.3%	7.4%	14.0%
District Court	8.7%	7.2%	63.7%	19.6%
Mediation or Dispute Resolution	6.6%	2.4%	34.8%	35.4%
Road Construction/Improvement	24.9%	1.1%	65.4%	7.9%
Road Maintenance	38.9%	1.5%	63.5%	7.0%
Winter Road Maintenance	36.2%	1.3%	63.7%	8.1%
Road Signs and Signals	31.4%	3.5%	70.9%	7.7%
Street Lights	33.2%	5.0%	30.7%	11.0%
Sidewalk Construction/Maintenance	34.9%	1.7%	23.7%	32.7%
Roadside Mowing	38.6%	0.9%	46.7%	15.8%
Sidewalk Beautification	42.1%	2.06%	18.5%	35.1%
Water Treatment	22.8%	35.7%	8.3%	36.7%
Water Distribution	37.8%	27.4%	7.4%	35.1%
Sanitary Sewer Collection	39.4%	25.9%	9.8%	32.2%
Sanitary Sewer Treatment	23.8%	34.4%	13.3%	32.7%
Storm Water Management	38.0%	11.1%	23.9%	34.5%
Storm Water Collection	36.9%	8.3%	20.9%	36.9%
Storm Water Treatment	15.9%	9.1%	17.2%	52.9%
Water Metering and Billing	43.8%	15.4%	7.2%	35.8%
Gas Metering and Billing	1.3%	2.4%	1.1%	46.4%
Electric Metering and Billing	3.3%	3.0%	1.1%	44.1%
Cable Service	2.0%	2.6%	0.7%	39.2%
Parking Lots and Structures	26.4%	1.3%	1.1%	67.8%
Parking Meters	5.3%	0.2%	0.7%	90.3%
Internet Broadband	2.4%	0.9%	0.9%	62.2%
Wireless Internet (Wi-Fi)	2.2%	1.3%	1.1%	67.3%
Public Bus System	2.8%	14.6%	17.0%	68.6%
Dial-a-Ride	8.8%	16.3%	23.0%	53.2%
Airport	2.6%	5.0%	13.3%	78.6%
Soil Quality and Conservation	8.3%	5.9%	N/A	29.5%

(*continued*)

APPENDIX 2
Percentage of Local Governments Reporting Each Provision Mode by Service or Function, CRC Survey, 2005 (*continued*)

Service	Direct Provision	Horizontal Cooperation	Vertical Cooperation	Does Not Provide/Contract
Water Quality and Conservation	12.3%	8.3%	58.0%	26.4%
Watershed Management	15.1%	15.4%	53.5%	25.5%
Air Quality Regulation	1.8%	3.5%	52.8%	36.0%
Erosion Control Structures	9.9%	4.8%	55.0%	28.4%
Environmental Education	14.5%	8.7%	45.2%	32.2%
Hospitals/Clinics	2.2%	5.0%	10.7%	65.3%
Parks	66.2%	10.4%	17.0%	18.9%
Playgrounds	61.8%	12.2%	9.4%	26.1%
Community/Recreation Center	29.6%	9.8%	8.3%	56.1%
Senior Center	25.5%	13.9%	14.1%	45.9%
Forestry Services	17.1%	1.7%	15.2%	64.9%
Golf Course	5.7%	3.7%	4.6%	73.2%
Community Pool	10.6%	8.9%	5.0%	73.4%
Trails	34.2%	7.2%	19.4%	48.4%
Beach Facilities	9.9%	3.9%	9.8%	76.4%
Marina/Port Facilities	5.5%	2.4%	4.1%	84.9%
Museum/Art Gallery	8.5%	6.7%	5.7%	71.6%
Library	23.6%	39.8%	19.4%	26.8%
Zoo	0.7%	1.7%	2.8%	91.2%
Community Theater	4.4%	6.1%	2.8%	81.8%
Stadium/Arena	3.3%	5.7%	4.8%	83.6%
Entertainment Facilities	4.2%	3.3%	3.3%	83.3%

NOTE: Row totals do not sum to 100 percent because "provision through a nongovernmental provider" and "unknown" are omitted.

REFERENCES

Chelsea District Library. 2008. Library District. Http://www.chelsea.lib.mi.us/librarydistrict.html.

CRC (Citizens Research Council of Michigan). 1997. *Michigan Highway Finance and Governance.* CRC Report No. 321. Livonia, Mich.: Citizens Research Council of Michigan.

———. 2005. *Catalog of Local Government Services in Michigan.* CRC Memorandum 1079. Livonia, Mich.: Citizens Research Council of Michigan.

Frederickson, H. G. 1999. The Repositioning of American Public Administration. *PS: Political Science and Politics* 32:701–711.

Krueger, E. 2005. A Transaction Costs Explanation of Inter-Local Government Collaboration. Ph.D. diss., University of North Texas.

Lackey, S., D. Freshwater, and A. Rupasingha. 2002. Factors Influencing Local Government Cooperation in Rural Areas: Evidence from the Tennessee Valley. *Economic Development Quarterly* 16(2):138–154.

LeRoux, K. 2006. The Role of Structure, Function, and Networks in Explaining Interlocal Services Delivery: A Study of Institutional Cooperation in Michigan. Ph.D. diss., Wayne State University.

LeRoux, K., and J. Carr. 2007. Explaining Local Government Cooperation on Public Works: Evidence from Michigan. *Public Works Management and Policy* 12(1):344–358.

Martindale, M., and M. Feighan. 2007. Wounded, Two Wait Close to Half-Hour for Police. *Detroit News,* July 17.

Morgan, D., and M. Hirlinger. 1991. Intergovernmental Service Contracts: A Multivariate Explanation. *Urban Affairs Quarterly* 27(1):128–144.

Oakerson, R. 2004. The Study of Metropolitan Governance. In *Metropolitan Governance: Conflict, Competition, and Cooperation,* edited by R. Feiock. Washington, D.C.: Georgetown University Press.

Oakland County. 2007. *Regional Cross-Boundary Initiatives: Oakland County, Michigan.* Pontiac, Mich.

Post, S. 2002. Cities and their Suburbs: "Go Along to Get Along." Ph.D. diss., Rice University.

Rawlings, L. 2003. The Determinants of Cooperation among Local Governments in Metropolitan Areas. Ph.D. diss., George Washington University.

SEMCOG (Southeast Michigan Council of Governments). 2006. Joint Public Services. Detroit, Mich.

Visser, J. 2004. Townships and Nested Governance: Spoilers or Collaborators in Metropolitan Services Delivery. *Public Performance and Management Review* 27(3):80–101.

Wayne County. 2008. Sheriff's Office, Wayne County, Michigan. Http://www.waynecounty.com/sheriff/divsions/divisons.html.

Wood, C. 2004. Metropolitan Governance in Urban America: A Study of the Kansas City Region. Ph.D. diss., University of Kansas.

Zeemering, E. 2007. Who Collaborates? Local Decisions about Intergovernmental Relations. Ph.D. diss., Indiana University.

CHAPTER 10

Regional Housing Policy: Can Crisis Spawn Collaboration?

Dale E. Thomson

A s the dominant form of land use in urban metropolitan areas, housing interacts with a multitude of issues—economic development, transportation, tax policies, public services, environmental quality, race relations, migration, and so forth—that collectively determine a region's quality of life. Housing policy is one of the more critical areas for regional cooperation because the availability of decent, safe, and affordable housing throughout a region is essential to ensuring equality of access to economic, educational, recreational, and social opportunities available throughout metropolitan areas. Although they operate through submarkets that are often confined to neighborhood boundaries, housing markets tend to be regional, with consumers choosing among substitutable submarkets across jurisdictions within a given economic region. The regional dimension of the housing market means that government intervention in one part of the region can have significant spillover effects in other parts of the region, so much so that spillover effects may overcome the benefits expected from the initial intervention. These factors create a strong intuitive appeal for regional cooperation in planning and developing housing. Yet of all the metropolitan issues addressed in this book, housing may be the most vexing to advocates of regional cooperation.

This chapter uses a policy analysis framework to explore the potential for increasing regional cooperation on housing in Michigan. It synthesizes key insights from the public policy literature to outline the policy factors affecting the adoption of regional approaches to housing problems. Using housing affordability data for Michigan metropolitan areas and a detailed analysis of demographic, institutional, and housing market data for Southeast Michigan, it assesses the extent to which impediments to regional cooperation have altered the probability of attaining regional cooperation on housing. The analysis concludes that significant changes in the scale and scope of housing affordability and the housing needs of the elderly have created new opportunities for regional cooperation. However, the significant impediments in the political/organizational environment that remain create substantial obstacles for those seeking to capitalize on these opportunities. Modest cooperation on components of these broad issues, particularly housing for the elderly, may be the best hope for regional cooperation in the near term.

Policy Factors Affecting Regional Cooperation on Housing

The lackluster history of success in promoting regional government, governance, or cooperation has prompted several studies documenting reasons for failure (Basolo and Hastings

Table 10.1. Factors Affecting Policy Definition and Adoption

Factor	Scholarly Source
Characteristics of the Problem	
• *Scope and Scale*	• Rochefort & Cobb 1993
• Frequency	
• Immediacy	
• Number of People Affected	
• Severity of Consequences	
• Proximity to Policy Makers	
• *Problem Population*	• Rochefort & Cobb 1993; Schneider
• Worthiness of Policy Action	& Ingram 1993.
• Familiarity to Policy Makers	
• Sympathetic vs. Threatening	
• *Cause of the Problem*	• Cobb & Elder 1971; Rochefort &
• Avoidable vs. Unavoidable	Cobb 1993
• Personal	
• Complexity	
• *Awareness of the Problem*	• Birkland 1997, 2004; Cobb & Elder
• Indicators	1971, 1983; Cobb, Ross, and Ross
• Labels	1976; Kingdon 1995; Nelson 1971;
• Triggering or Focusing Events	Rochefort & Cobb 1993.
• Media and Public Attention	
Characteristics of the Policy Solution	
• *Availability, Technical Feasibility*	• Cobb and Elder 1971; Kingdon
• *Acceptability*	1995; Pressman & Wildavsky 1984;
• *Affordability*	Rochefort & Cobb 1993
• *Categorical Precedence*	
• *Complexity of Implementation*	
• Multiplicity of Decision Points	
• Multiplicity of Intervention Targets	
Characteristics of the Political/Organizational Environment	
• *Multiplicity of Participants*	• Allison 1971; Hamm 1983;
• *Multiplicity of Interests and Values*	Heclo 1978; Kingdon 1995; Lipsky
• *Multiplicity of Intensities*	1968; Lindblom 1950; Lowi 1972;
• *Multiplicity of Resources*	Pressman & Wildavsky 1984;
• *Issue Networks, Policy Subsystems,*	Sabatier 1988; Steinberger 1980;
Iron Triangles, Policy Coalitions	Truman 1971.

2003; Gainsborough 2001; Norris 2001; Swanstrom 2001). The work of public policy scholars provides a useful basis for integrating the insights of such studies into a cohesive framework for clarifying and assessing impediments to regionalism for a given policy issue.

Policy scholars have adopted myriad approaches for analyzing the policy-making process to understand the factors that determine what policies get adopted and why. Those approaching the topic from a policy process model have identified determinants of whether an issue will make it to decision makers' agendas, what alternatives will be considered to address a given issue, and whether the adopted alternative is likely to be implemented successfully (Birkland, 1997, 2004; Cobb and Elder, 1971, 1983; Cobb, Ross, and Ross 1971; Kingdon 1995; Nelson 1984; Pressman and Wildavsky 1984; Rochefort and Cobb 1993; Schneider and Ingram 1993). Those seeking to craft policy typologies or explain the role of issue networks or subsystems have supplied critical insights into the political and organizational factors that often determine policy success (Hamm 1983; Heclo 1978; Lipsky 1968; Lowi 1972; Sabatier 1988; Steinberger 1980; Truman 1971). Scholars outlining models of decision making have added important concepts (Allison 1971; Lindblom 1950; Simon 1947). Table 10.1 highlights some of the more relevant studies in these areas.

Key factors influencing the adoption of policies are rooted in the characteristics of the policy problem, the characteristics of the solution to the problem, and the characteristics of the political and organizational environment in which policy action must occur. Changes in the characteristics of the "regional housing problem" may increase the potential for regional cooperation in metro areas across the state, but the nature of the solutions and political/organizational environment present considerable impediments, particularly in Southeast Michigan.

Policy Factors Related to Characteristics of the Problem

"Policy problems are not simply givens, . . . they are matters of interpretation and social definition" (Cobb and Elder 1983: 172). The scale and scope of the problem are critical determinants of whether policy makers deem an issue worthy of government action. Although no heuristic applies universally, the more frequent the problem, the more people it affects, the more severe the consequences, and the closer the impact to the policy maker, the more likely the problem is to see action from decision makers (Rochefort and Cobb 1993). Problems that are viewed as crises or emergencies (that is, the stranded mountain climber metaphor) tend to receive attention more readily than routine problems (Birkland 1997, 2004).

Scale of Housing Problems in Michigan's Metropolitan Housing Markets
For some time, housing market indicators have shown that many households in Michigan's metropolitan areas suffer from unaffordable or poor-quality housing and that significant differences exist in the health of housing submarkets within metropolitan areas. Yet only modest resources[1], originating mainly from federal sources, have been dedicated to addressing these problems. Interjurisdictional collaborations to address housing issues on

239

a metropolitan level have been lacking. This is due, in part, to the scale of the problems. While many households have experienced housing problems, their numbers have not been substantial enough to stimulate regional approaches. Recent housing affordability data show that the scale of housing problems has increased dramatically across Michigan's metropolitan areas. The potential for collaborative approaches may increase as a result.

The standard definition of an affordability problem is when a household pays more than 30 percent of its income on housing (excessive cost burden). Table 10.2 shows the extent of housing cost burden by county for Michigan's metropolitan areas.[2] The trends are clear. The 1990s brought little change in the proportion of households with excessive cost burden.[3]

Table 10.2. Excessive Housing Cost Burden by County for Michigan Metropolitan Areas

County	% Hoseholds Paying 30% or More of Income on Housing		
	1989	1999	2005
Benton Harbor			
Berrien	23%	23%	28%
Detroit-Ann Arbor-Flint			
Genessee	26%	23%	35%
Lapeer	21%	21%	33%
Lenawee	20%	20%	32%
Livingston	19%	20%	32%
Macomb	20%	20%	33%
Monroe	19%	20%	30%
Oakland	22%	23%	33%
St. Clair	25%	23%	34%
Washtenaw	30%	29%	39%
Wayne	29%	26%	41%
Grand Rapids-Muskegon-Holland			
Allegan	19%	20%	29%
Kent	21%	21%	33%
Muskegon	23%	22%	33%
Ottawa	16%	18%	28%
Jackson			
Jackson	20%	20%	34%
Kalamazoo-Battle Creek			
Calhoun	23%	22%	32%
Kalamazoo	25%	24%	33%
Van Buren	25%	21%	34%
Lansing-East Lansing			
Clinton	17%	16%	29%
Eaton	19%	20%	29%
Ingham	27%	28%	35%
Saginaw-Bay City-Midland			
Bay	22%	20%	29%
Midland	19%	20%	28%
Saginaw	26%	23%	34%

SOURCES: (1989) 1990 Census (SF3) Tables H051 & H058, (1999) 2000 Census (SF3) Tables H69 & H94 (2005) 2006 American Community Survey Tables B25070 & C25093.

In some counties, however, since 1999, cost burden has increased dramatically. Eighteen out of the twenty-five counties saw their totals increase by at least 10 percentage points.[4] The average increase for all counties was 11 points. By 2005, at least 28 percent of each county's households were experiencing housing affordability problems. In most counties, at least one-third of the households had problems. If we look at the increase in the number of households, rather than the percent of households, the increases are even more dramatic— 90 percent, on average. By 2005, an estimated 1,098,000 households in these counties had affordability problems.

Housing affordability problems have numerous negative effects, including reductions in disposable income, deferred maintenance, restricted access to regional opportunities, problems with resale, and foreclosure, and negatively affect the social equity component of the triple bottom line. A comparison of foreclosure data from the Register of Deeds in two of the counties included in table 10.2—Oakland and Wayne—demonstrates how the changes in affordability have created shared concerns even for counties experiencing significantly different trends coming into the 1990s. From 1993 to 2002, foreclosures rose 232 percent in Wayne County—from 2,089 to 6,935. Oakland County experienced a 210 percent increase over the same period—from 561 to 1,740 (Thomson 2006).[5] Oakland's foreclosures grew another 9 percent from 2002 to 2004. The median dollar amount of foreclosures in Oakland County rose 271 percent from 1999 to 2004—from $36,680 in 1990 to $137,045 in 2004. Amounts also grew in Wayne County—from $32,433 in 1999 to $57,427 in 2002—though the median value still remained lower than in Oakland.[6] Oakland's total foreclosures were still much lower than Wayne's due to the large number of foreclosures in Detroit, but when Detroit's properties are excluded, Oakland County's trend in and number of foreclosures are virtually identical to Wayne's (figure 10.1), with both counties experiencing dramatic increases since 2000.

The foreclosure problem has continued to escalate throughout the region. Oakland County reported 4,855 new home foreclosures in 2006 (Gray and Brasier 2007) and expected to have about 7,800 foreclosures in the county in 2007 (Askari, Guest, and Turk 2007). In 2007, Michigan had the third highest total in the nation of homes in some state of foreclosure.[7] In January 2008, Michigan had the fifth highest total, and the twenty-five counties reported above accounted for 98 percent of the homes that proceeded to foreclosure during the month.[8] The ten counties in the Detroit–Ann Arbor–Flint metropolitan area accounted for 63 percent of these foreclosures. Yet Ingham, Kent, Muskegon, and Ottawa counties all had at least ninety-five properties foreclosed during the month, and in thirteen counties the number of foreclosure-related filings per household was higher than the national average.

The foreclosure problem is forecast to escalate in the near term as a result of increases in the interest rates of many adjustable rate mortgages in the coming year. The increase in foreclosures nationwide, particularly for subprime loans, has clearly created problems for global financial institutions, and the resulting credit crunch is making it more difficult to sell homes in the state. Moreover, the increase in foreclosures poses considerable problems for the communities where the foreclosures occur. Michigan's foreclosure laws, the sluggish sales market, and the large number of homes added to the sales market as lenders try to

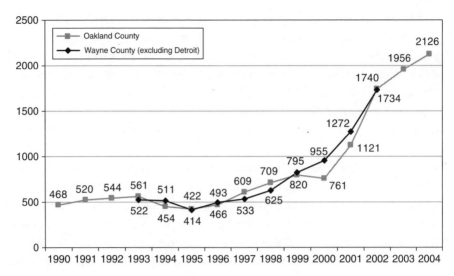

Source: Oakland and Wayne County Register of Deeds.

FIGURE 10.1
Residential Mortgage Foreclosures in Oakland and Wayne Counties, 1990–2004

recoup their losses through resale cause many foreclosed homes to sit vacant or unmarketable for at least six months, and often much longer. Maintenance on these homes is often ignored, and the blighting effect on neighborhoods can be great. The high number of foreclosures also dampens sale values of other homes on the market.

The trend in sales and property values in Oakland County, one of the nation's wealthiest counties, is illustrative of the potential outcomes when affordability problems, foreclosures, and a stagnant economy mix. In the 1990s, the county led the state in housing unit growth, adding almost 60,000 units to its existing stock, and its pace of development remained similar through 2004. Housing sales, however, did not keep pace. After peaking at about 22,000 in 1998, annual sales dropped continuously through 2004, the latest period for which data are available. The first two-thirds of 2004 brought the slowest pace of sales in ten years and put the county on track to experiencing the largest year-to-year decline in sales volume in more than ten years.[9] The decline in sales of existing homes was even greater than suggested by these numbers, as new homes accounted for a growing share of sales over the period (Thomson 2006). For 2006, Oakland County reported its slowest growth in assessed value for property in almost forty years—a decline that began in 2000 (Gray and Brasier 2007). For 2008, assessed values were expected to decrease (Angel 2008).

Similar trends were reported in other counties. Despite some gains in early 2007, home sales across Southeast Michigan continue to lag far behind prior years' totals (Gallagher 2007). Macomb and Wayne counties projected declines in assessed values of 5 percent or more (Angel 2008). After steady increases in sales prices from 1991 through 2005, sales prices of homes began declining throughout the Detroit metropolitan region in January 2006. In January 2008, they were just slightly higher than their January 2000 value—21 percent lower than the December 2005 peak.[10] Similar data show that the Grand Rapids and Lansing regions have also seen sales values decline since 2005.[11]

It is clear that the scale of problems related to housing affordability, sales volume, and foreclosures has grown tremendously in terms of both households and counties affected in metropolitan areas across the state. It is unclear how long these trends and their effects will persist, but most forecasts suggest little change in the coming years. While decreases in housing prices resulting from a declining sales market may improve affordability for some households, they will have little effect on households that are unable to sell or otherwise leave their present homes. Moreover, the damage that the foreclosure crisis can cause seems too great of a cost to pay for many communities. The public policy literature suggests that the increased scale of housing problems offers the potential for adoption of regional approaches to addressing these problems as more communities recognize that they are not immune from the problems.

Scope of Housing Problems in Michigan's Metropolitan Housing Markets

The changing scope of housing problems should enhance the potential for regional solutions. Specifically, the expansion of affordability problems to middle-income households, the increasing complexity of accommodating the affordability and special housing needs of a rapidly increasing elderly population, and the pending expansion of need for housing for people with disabilities create a broader range of housing concerns than those historically associated with addressing the affordability needs of low-income households. As with overall affordability and foreclosures, these market dynamics will be affecting counties across metropolitan areas throughout the state. As a broader range of interrelated issues need to be addressed, the ability of any one community to address them successfully will diminish, and the need to collaborate on solutions may become more evident.

Expansion of Income Groups Affected

Historically, affordability problems, declining home sales and values, and foreclosures have been perceived to be predominantly an issue for lower-income residents in older cities, such as Detroit, Pontiac, Flint, or Benton Harbor, and isolated older, inner-ring suburban communities that surround such cities. While the number of residents suffering from these problems has been significant, their numbers have been small relative to the total population of their region. Although the consequences of the problems have sometimes been severe, they have generally been geographically contained.

The data reported above demonstrate that housing problems are affecting counties of varying socioeconomic characteristics. Further analysis confirms that middle- and upper-income households account for a growing share of those households experiencing problems.

In 2004, an average of about one-third of households earning $35,000 to $49,999 had housing affordability problems. Totals were higher in metro Detroit, where 40 percent or more of households in Lapeer, Livingston, Oakland, and St. Clair counties had affordability problems (table 10.3). On average, almost one-fifth of households earning $50,000 to $74,999 had problems, with higher proportions in metro Detroit. The prevalence of affordability problems for households earning $35,000 or more has grown dramatically in recent years. On average, the percentage of households earning $35,000 to $49,000 with affordability problems grew by 17 points from 1999 to 2005. The increase for households earning $50,000

Table 10.3. Affordability Problems by County and Income Group

	% of Households in Income Group with Affordability Problems (2005)				
County	"Less than $20, 000"	"$20, 000 to $34, 999"	"$35,000 to $49,999"	"$50,000 to $74,999"	"$75,000 "to more"
Benton Harbor					
Berrien	72%	38%	22%	9%	3%
Detroit-Ann Arbor-Flint					
Genessee	88%	44%	30%	16%	6%
Lapeer	78%	48%	48%	27%	5%
Lenawee	81%	46%	27%	19%	6%
Livingston	81%	73%	47%	33%	10%
Macomb	86%	53%	38%	23%	6%
Monroe	74%	48%	29%	24%	9%
Oakland	87%	63%	44%	30%	11%
St. Clair	81%	49%	40%	20%	5%
Washtenaw	94%	71%	39%	30%	12%
Wayne	88%	59%	36%	21%	8%
Grand Rapids-Muskegon-Holland					
Allegan	79%	39%	28%	23%	4%
Kent	85%	52%	28%	16%	5%
Muskegon	81%	43%	25%	10%	3%
Ottawa	81%	46%	37%	20%	5%
Jackson					
Jackson	75%	52%	32%	15%	5%
Kalamazoo-Battle Creek					
Calhoun	80%	43%	22%	12%	3%
Kalamazoo	81%	47%	31%	15%	3%
Van Buren	76%	44%	34%	17%	5%
Lansing-East Lansing					
Clinton	88%	58%	31%	25%	6%
Eaton	85%	39%	36%	22%	5%
Ingham	88%	53%	32%	15%	4%
Saginaw-Bay City-Midland					
Bay	76%	40%	20%	15%	4%
Midland	79%	44%	14%	13%	2%
Saginaw	83%	47%	26%	10%	2%

SOURCES: 2008 Americancommunity Survey, Table B25106.

to $74,999 was 12 points. To put this in perspective, the November 2004 mean annual wage for all occupations in the metro area was $43,590.[12]

Housing for the Elderly

Affordability holds particular relevance for elderly households. With fixed incomes and housing costs that may increase as rents, property taxes, or interest rates increase, affordability problems tend to be more common among this population than for younger households. On average, one-third of households sixty-five years or older in each county had affordability problems in 2005 (table 10.4). The average countywide increase of 9 percent

Table 10.4. Housing Affordability Problems for Elderly Households

County	% Elderly (65 or older) Households Paying 30% or More of Income on Housing		
	1989	1999	2005
Benton Harbor			
Berrien	26%	22%	31%
Detroit-Ann Arbor-Flint			
Genessee	28%	24%	32%
Lapeer	29%	25%	36%
Lenawee	27%	22%	33%
Livingston	28%	26%	32%
Macomb	31%	24%	36%
Monroe	27%	22%	31%
Oakland	31%	29%	37%
St. Clair	29%	26%	32%
Washtenaw	29%	26%	32%
Wayne	30%	27%	39%
Grand Rapids-Muskegon-Holland			
Allegan	24%	22%	31%
Kent	27%	24%	35%
Muskegon	27%	22%	35%
Ottawa	23%	22%	36%
Jackson			
Jackson	25%	22%	30%
Kalamazoo-Battle Creek			
Calhoun	25%	22%	31%
Kalamazoo	28%	24%	28%
Van Buren	27%	28%	37%
Lansing-East Lansing			
Clinton	29%	18%	NA
Eaton	27%	25%	28%
Ingham	24%	25%	34%
Saginaw-Bay City-Midland			
Bay	26%	21%	30%
Midland	21%	23%	30%
Saginaw	27%	24%	33%

SOURCES: (1989) 1990 Census (SF3) Tables H051 & H060, (1999) 2000 Census (SF3) Tables H71 & H96 (2005) 2006 American Community Survey Tables B25070 & C25093.

was a reversal of the trend experienced in the 1990s, when affordability problems for the elderly decreased in most counties.

The affordability trend for the elderly is consistent with the overall patterns for affordability, but particularly troubling given the vast expansion in the region's elderly population that is expected to occur over the next few decades. The Southeast Michigan Council of Governments (SEMCOG) estimates that the sixty-five or older population in Southeast Michigan—excluding Genesee, Lapeer, and Lenawee counties—will almost double by 2030 (table 10.5). Growth estimates run from a low of 69 percent in Wayne County to a high of

Table 10.5. Estimated Growth in Elderly Population

County	Estimated Population Age 65 or Older				
	2000	2010	2020	2030	% Change 2000–2030
Livingston County	13,035	17,446	28,180	42,825	229%
Macomb County	107,651	126,546	175,961	232,534	116%
Monroe County	16,225	20,552	30,600	41,829	158%
Oakland County	134,959	154,395	213,555	275,469	104%
St. Clair County	20,087	22,617	32,031	42,235	110%
Washtenaw County	26,274	33,634	51,529	72,631	176%
Wayne County	248,981	265,142	342,031	421,463	69%
Total	567,212	640,332	873,887	1,128,986	99%

SOURCE: Southeast Michigan Council of Governments Regional Development Forecast.

229 percent in Livingston County. The explosion of the elderly population will occur at a time when the region's total population grows by a modest 12 percent. Consequently, the elderly, who accounted for a little more than 10 percent of the region's population in 2000, will account for more than 20 percent in 2030. Their share of households will be even greater.

What will this expansion mean for the region's housing market? The answer is far from certain, but change is inevitable. The elderly population in the coming decades is likely to exhibit significantly different traits than in the past. The future elderly are expected to live longer, have more active lives, and be wealthier. Yet increased life expectancy will eventually translate into more disabilities, higher medical costs, and a need for greater wealth to ensure financial sustainability over a longer period of time. Historically, aging households have tended to downsize to homes that require less maintenance and have greater accessibility. Many retirees move to regions of the country with warmer weather. Active living retirement communities are increasingly popular. Nonetheless, the United States has also seen evidence of a growing desire among elderly households to "age in place." Housing has served as a primary asset base as households age. Recently, however, that asset base has eroded for many households in Michigan. How much will that change in the coming years? Will a large number of homes currently owned by forty-five-to-sixty-four-year-olds come on the market en masse? Will the sluggish housing market, declining property values, growing affordability problems among the elderly, and vast increase in foreclosures significantly diminish the asset base of the elderly? How will the combination of factors impact the housing market? Data from Oakland County where the elderly currently account for a smaller share of households than in most counties inform such inquiries.

Oakland County's elderly population is expected to grow by 104 percent, accounting for about 21 percent of the county's population by 2030. Table 10.6 shows the estimated number of elderly households by decade, assuming that the living arrangements for the elderly in 2000 hold constant over the next three decades.[13] By 2030, the elderly would account for approximately 31 percent of Oakland County's households.

Table 10.6. Oakland County's Estimated Elderly Households, 2000–2030

2000	2010	2020	2030
87,610	100,227	138,631	178,823

SOURCE: Authors' manipulation of SEMCOG and Census data.

The elderly account for a disproportionate share of households with affordability problems in Oakland County. If the prevalence of affordability problems among the elderly stayed at the 1999 level, an estimated 53,000 elderly households would have affordability problems by 2030. If the 2005 percentages prevailed, the total would rise to 66,000.

Among special needs groups, elderly households are the best served by government-subsidized housing in Oakland County. Still, the supply is inadequate to meet the current demand, let alone the growth in demand that is likely to occur. Michigan State Housing Development Authority (MSHDA) data on housing units with project-based subsidies indicate that at least 7,862 units in subsidized housing developments are set aside for elderly residents in Oakland County.[14] While the future demand for subsidized units for the elderly is uncertain, the total number of units would need to grow by 42 percent (about 3,300 units) by 2020 in order to serve the same percentage of elderly households (8.4 percent) as currently served. It would need to grow by another 3,200 units by 2030 (Thomson, 2007).

These estimates relate solely to the elderly population that will remain in Oakland County. Yet the growth in elderly households masks a trend that will hold special importance for the county in the coming decades—the out-migration of elderly households. Since the mid-1990s, Oakland County has experienced a net loss of population through domestic migration. The largest cohort moving out of the county has been people fifty-five or older—mostly moving out of the state (Thomson 2007). A comparison of SEMCOG and 2000 census data suggests that the county could lose about 106,000 households currently headed by thirty-five-to-sixty-four-year-olds. This loss would have various impacts; an immediate one would be homes being placed on the market. About 5,700 sales per year, an amount equal to 25 percent of the average annual sales volume from 1995 to 2003, would need to occur to accommodate this out-migration. To put this in perspective, an estimated 3,600 homes were sold annually to accommodate the out-migration of older homeowners in the 1990s. This equates to 18 percent of the average annual sales volume from 1995 to 2003. The number of homes sold annually by elderly homeowners likely will be even larger, as many elderly homeowners who remain in Oakland County will elect to move to smaller and/or newer owner or rental units.

People with Disabilities

The growth in the number of elderly households will also increase the need for housing and support services for people with disabilities. This will occur in two ways. First, as the population of the region ages, the number of people with disabilities in that population will increase. Second, children with disabilities that currently live with their parents or other relatives—a large share of the existing nonelderly disabled population—will need to find

247

alternative housing. These trends will compound the tremendous existing pressures for housing for people with disabilities.

Census data indicate that in 2000, at least 18,300 Oakland County residents sixty-five or older (14 percent of all elderly, 36 percent of all elderly with disabilities) had a disability that necessitated special housing or support services.[15] If the 2000 percentages of the elderly with disabilities held constant for the next few decades, the number of elderly persons needing special housing or support services would grow to 21,000 in 2010, 29,000 in 2020, and 37,000 in 2030. Based on census data, an estimated 53,100 Oakland County residents aged twenty-one to sixty-four years had disabilities in 2000 that necessitated special housing or support services.[16] Presently, most of this population lives with parents or other family members. As these family members age, much of this population will need new housing arrangements.

While this discussion of elderly households has focused on Oakland County, counties throughout the state are expected to see a growth in elderly households as baby boomers age. Given the current level of affordability problems among the elderly, the anticipated growth in the number of people with disabilities in search of housing, the housing preferences of the elderly, the shortage of housing alternatives for the elderly, and the sheer growth in the elderly population, changes in housing stock and elderly services are likely to be necessary to accommodate this demographic change across the state. The extent and type of changes are unclear, but change seems inevitable. Regional approaches to increase the supply of both traditional housing for the elderly and new, alternative housing arrangements to enable this population to age in place could prove beneficial. Collaboration on support services to enhance the quality of life for those elderly who choose to remain in their existing housing could also help. Collaborative efforts to forecast how metropolitan housing markets will be affected as elderly homeowners leave the region or sell their homes for smaller, more manageable units also seem warranted.

Characteristics of the Population with Problems in Michigan's Metropolitan Housing Markets

The changes in scope outlined above point to another facet of current and future housing issues that may further the potential for regional collaboration—the changing characteristics of the population experiencing housing problems. Public policy scholars have clearly demonstrated that policy makers are more prone to enact policy responses to social problems when they are familiar with, and feel an affinity for, the population suffering from those problems.

Clearly, the population suffering from housing affordability problems is changing. Increasingly, suburban residents, many of them white, are experiencing such problems. This could be important for advocates of policy change, as political power in metropolitan regions shifted from the city to the suburbs many years ago, and relatively few minorities serve as elected officials in these communities. The population experiencing problems is now more familiar to the policy makers that wield power across metropolitan areas and at the state level. It is closer to them in distance and characteristics and, therefore, likely to garner greater empathy.

The projected growth in the elderly population, overall and as a share of households experiencing housing problems, may also prompt policy action. While the elderly have not benefited disproportionately from policy changes of late, the elderly have long had a favored status among policy makers. Housing policy is no exception; several programs directly target elderly households. In Oakland County, for example, more than 50 percent of units with project-based subsidies are set aside for the elderly (Thomson 2006). Many communities have home repair programs targeted to the elderly. The federal government targets a portion of its increasingly scarce housing construction subsidies to the Section 202 program, which exclusively builds units for the elderly, one of the few groups for which public housing units can be set aside. Many policy makers have elderly family members, are elderly themselves, or will soon become elderly. The elderly are also politically active, which enables them to prompt action from policy makers even when empathy does not exist. The status of the elderly as "deserving" of policy interventions is likely to grow as the elderly account for a greater share of the state's and country's population.

Causes of Housing Problems in Michigan's Metropolitan Housing Markets

The extent to which groups are deemed worthy of policy action is often intertwined with the cause of the problem. Problems that result from an individual's actions and are avoidable if a person alters behavior tend to receive less attention than those that people suffer through no fault of their own (Rochefort and Cobb 1993). Also, problems with simple causes are easier to understand and address than those for which causes are complex; therefore, they are more likely to receive attention from policy makers.

Housing affordability problems have always been caused by a variety of factors related to both the cost of housing and household income. Some of these causes are linked to individual choices, such as buying or renting housing that is too expensive when cheaper housing is available, incurring unnecessary or high-cost home equity loans, or avoiding work. Other causes are linked to broader forces, such as unequal access to educational and economic opportunities; an insufficient supply of safe, decent, and affordable housing; exclusionary zoning and other regulatory practices that prevent affordable housing from being built; or economic downturn. While there is no uniform regional or statewide perspective on the causes of affordability problems, the lack of substantial policy actions to address these problems and the history of racial and city-suburbs animosity suggest that past affordability problems have commonly been attributed to the actions of either the households experiencing the problems or the governmental leaders of the communities where these households lived. Changes in the scope of the housing problems and the characteristics of the population suffering from those problems, combined with the obvious changes in the economy of the state, create the potential for an enhanced understanding of the causes of affordability problems.

The contrasting conditions in Detroit and Oakland County illustrate the differences in causal factors. In Detroit, low household income has played a larger role in creating affordability problems than has housing cost (Thomson 2004a). As such, the housing problems of low-income Detroiters are dismissed by many as resulting from poor individual choices related to education, work, housing, child rearing, or deviant social behavior. Although usually incorrect, such attributions were convenient and easy when problems were geographically isolated and suffered by a population with little political power. As problems have

249

expanded to wealthier communities, attribution of causes has become more complex. In Oakland County, for example, high housing costs play a more significant role. From 1995 through August 2004, less than half of all homes sold in the county (46 percent) were sold at prices affordable to households earning the median income for the region at the time of sale (Thomson 2006). Moreover, more than half of the affordable sales (55 percent) were concentrated in just eight of the county's sixty-one cities, villages, and townships. Affordable rental housing is also highly concentrated, especially subsidized units. For at least half of the region's households, it is tough to find affordable housing in Oakland County.

Individual households cannot control the supply of housing. Thus, where an inadequate supply of affordable housing exists, it is more difficult to lay the blame for affordability on individuals. Both market forces and land use and zoning decisions by local policy makers have played a significant role in causing affordability problems. Economic changes since the late 1990s, detailed elsewhere in this text, have further complicated matters, lowering incomes of households, many of whom purchased homes during a period of inflated housing prices.

These dynamics have been compounded by increased flexibility of financing options. The 1990s brought a wave of increasingly risky behavior by lenders and borrowers. Lenders sought to capture a growing share of the housing market by loosening underwriting criteria to qualify more people for loans. Some borrowers were able to purchase homes for which they previously could not qualify. The seemingly unlimited growth in home values led many people to pull equity out of their house through refinancing of home equity loans, often with adjustable interest rates, balloon payments, interest-only payments, and other options that lowered the short-term costs of the loan, but exposed the borrowers to risk of significant cost increases. As the economy has declined and interest rates have risen, many borrowers now find their mortgages unaffordable. They are also unable to sell their homes for the amount necessary to cover their loan, and they have difficulty refinancing loans given their lower incomes and decreased housing values.

This combination of factors has created what might be dubbed a perfect storm for a housing market decline. Just as we tend to avoid placing blame for natural disasters on the victims who suffer them, we are less inclined to blame those who are suffering from this storm for causing it. Market dynamics that have increased housing costs, governmental actions that have constrained the supply of affordable housing, economic forces that have driven down incomes, and institutional forces that have created unnecessary and unwise financing vehicles are increasingly recognized as contributing to the situation. Although individual choices are an important contributor, the scale of affordability problems and their growing impact on households that have previously not experienced problems have made many people willing to attribute at least some responsibility to broader forces.

Housing market problems associated with the growth in the elderly population add yet another dimension to the causal inquiry. Partly because the full impact of the aging population has yet to be felt, and partly because the aging of the population is a demographic force that is impossible to control, there is simply little blame to go around.

The bottom line is that the causes of problems related to affordability, foreclosure, and housing for the elderly and people with disabilities have grown in number and complexity.

Although policy scholars indicate that the complexity diminishes the likelihood of action, the increased difficulty in attributing the problems to avoidable actions of individual households may be more important in influencing policy action given the significance that this factor has played in inhibiting action in the past.

Characteristics of Regional Policy Solutions to Housing Problems in Southeast Michigan

Even when there is agreement that a particular issue is a problem, policy action will be contingent upon the alternatives for addressing the problem. Of primary concern is whether a solution is available, affordable, and acceptable. Rochefort and Cobb (1993) refer to these characteristics collectively as the nature of the solution. Availability refers to whether the technology exists to solve the problem. Affordability refers to the absolute and relative costs of solving the problem, one factor affecting a policy alternative's likely acceptability among the public and elected leaders. Political, economic, religious, and other deeply held ideologies are other critical dimensions of acceptability. Policy makers will assess the extent to which the available alternatives are consistent with their values or those of significant constituent groups. This assessment will often trump questions of availability and affordability.

Pressman and Wildavsky (1984) remind us that even when there is agreement that a solution is available, affordable, and acceptable, the complexity of implementation, including the multiplicity of decisions points and intervention targets, may render a solution infeasible. These various dimensions of the solution to a proposed problem embody an ends-means dimension of policy choices, where the means of addressing the problem become more important than the problem itself (Lindblom 1950; Rochefort and Cobb 1993).

Availability

The technology is readily available to address housing affordability problems. Although the effectiveness of the specific mechanisms varies, policies that provide financial assistance to builders, buyers, owners, or renters generally make housing more affordable for recipients or occupants of the subsidized units. Public subsidies to finance repairs to homes of low-income owners and renters tend to improve the condition of those homes at an affordable cost and sometimes reduce monthly housing costs, via increased energy efficiency, for example. Regulatory approaches have also been used to reduce costs or ensure provision of affordable housing. When such interventions are targeted to the special needs of the elderly and people with disabilities, they have proven effective at addressing affordability for these specific groups, particularly when combined with support services. The technology for addressing problems associated with the increase in the number of elderly households is less certain, mainly because the scale and nature of the specific effects of this increase are so uncertain.

In spite of the regional nature of housing markets and the availability of technology for addressing affordability problems locally, the technology of addressing housing needs on a regional scale is less certain. The most substantial regional approaches involve fair-share allocation plans, such as those in New Jersey and California (Listokin 1971; Meck, Retzlaff, and Schwab 2003). While such strategies have achieved a greater dispersion of affordable housing in some regions, they tend to focus on planning, rather than actual provision of

251

housing, and provide few tools for enforcing adherence to plans. Regional housing trust funds that dedicate funding from specific regional or state revenue sources to be used only for housing purposes in the participating communities are an increasingly popular approach for addressing housing needs across jurisdictions (Meck, Retzlaff, and Schwab 2003). Yet, overall, few regional plans exist. Where they do, it is difficult to quantify their impact. Where it has been quantified, results are mixed (Meck, Retzlaff, and Schwab 2003).

Affordability

The affordability of solutions to housing problems is one of the greatest obstacles to their adoption. For example, it costs an average of more than $17,000 per unit to provide construction or rehabilitation assistance through the federal government's HOME Investment Partnerships program.[17] For rental housing, the cost exceeds $23,000 per unit. These totals represent only the portion funded by HOME. Typically, projects are funded through multiple public and private sources. Even programs that seek to make existing units more affordable are expensive. The federal government's American Dream Downpayment Initiative, which helps buyers purchase homes, provides up to $10,000 per household assisted. Programs that provide temporary utility payment assistance cost much less, but even these are expensive when the number of households needing help is large. Even if it cost only $1,000 per household to eliminate housing affordability problems, it would cost more than $380,550,000 to eliminate problems for just half of the households estimated to have affordability problems in 2005 in metropolitan Detroit. Given the great fiscal constraints facing local and state government in Michigan, expensive policy options are unlikely, even if the problem is obvious and severe. Indeed, given the general absence of major local initiatives to address recent housing trends, it may be that local leaders simply find the solutions too costly and are deferring to national leaders for solutions to what has become a nationwide problem.

Acceptability

Affordability clearly limits the acceptability of regional solutions to housing issues. Various other values of policy makers and their constituents, which are often grounded in ideology, also influence acceptability. For example, while housing advocates, developers, and social service advocates may support public subsidies for housing, free-market and public-choice advocates often oppose them on the grounds that they create aberrations in the private market. Political conservatives often consider direct financial assistance to individual households an inappropriate use of government resources, particularly when it results in a redistribution of revenue across income groups.

As important as deeply rooted cultural, political, and economic ideologies are to the acceptability of housing interventions generally, they are far more important to the acceptability of housing interventions implemented on a regional scale (Norris 2001). Most regulatory and financial policies related to housing are controlled locally. Regional approaches to housing policy require local governments to coordinate, share, or relinquish control of regulatory policies or financial resources. Inevitably, some local autonomy is sacrificed. Public-choice advocates and conservatives tend to consider implementing policies through regional bodies to be more prone to excessive government regulation and to inhibition of freedoms than those implemented locally. Minority and low-income groups in central cities sometimes oppose regional initiatives out of concern that their political power will be diminished and their voices lost. Politicians and the public alike, regardless of political affiliation, race, or income, are often inherently opposed to relinquishing local control, even when such a position reduces the potential for solving problems. Very few examples of regional approaches to housing exist nationwide, largely because of a lack of political support for interjurisdictional action (Basolo and Hastings 2003; Meck, Retzlaff, and Schwab 2003).

These ideological impediments are typical of those that impede regionalism in policy areas that focus on lifestyle issues (Norris 2001). They are particularly pertinent for regional approaches to housing when the policy solution enables low- or moderate-income households to live in a community that was previously inaccessible due to cost. In fact, many communities have adopted regulatory policies specifically to prevent the construction of affordable housing in their communities (Advisory Commission on Regulatory Barriers to Affordable Housing 1991; Schill 2004). Some community members will oppose regional approaches on the grounds that they will lower property values and tax revenues, although studies increasingly challenge the premise of this argument (Galster 2003). Often, opposition is rooted in more nefarious rationale, such as racial or class bigotry.

Policy Factors Related to the Political/Organizational Environment

It is clear that the characteristics of the problem and solution overlap. These determinants of policy action are deeply intertwined with the political and organizational environment of the policy issue. Various multiplicities—participants, interests, ideologies, intensities, and resource bases—evident in the political/organizational environment of a given policy issue are what make the characteristics of the problem and solution so important. It is within this environment that the varying perspectives on policy acceptability and affordability and the characteristics of the problem intersect. The primary determinant of whether regional approaches will be adopted to address Michigan's metropolitan housing issues will be whether the political/organizational environment will change in response to housing market changes. An examination of the political/organizational environment in Southeast Michigan illustrates the challenges inherent in realizing this outcome.

Characteristics of Political/Organizational Environment of Southeast Michigan's Housing Market

Participants in housing delivery systems include those involved in planning, financing, constructing, maintaining, marketing, and improving physical structures or providing support services to occupants. Organizations that regulate each of these activities are important as well. Housing delivery systems include representatives from the private sector (financial institutions, builders, developers, realtors, utilities, and so forth), government (planners, inspectors, elected officials, housing finance agencies, public housing commissions, and so forth), and the nonprofit sector (affordable housing developers, special needs service providers, and so forth). Each can be classified into one of six organizational components—builders/developers, financers, regulators, owners/managers/marketers, postconstruction service providers, and occupants. The specific organizations that are relevant for each component vary by the type of housing being provided, but most will be affected by any government intervention in the housing market. Each will bring its own interests, intensity of interest, and resources to bear on policy decisions.

A quick look at market activity shows there were a vast number of transactions and participants in Southeast Michigan's housing market. In 2005, approximately 634,000 applications for home purchase, refinance, or home improvement loans were submitted in the nine-county region. About 321,000 loans were originated.[18] In that same year, the seven counties included in the SEMCOG region issued permits to construct over 18,700 units and demolish more than 3,400 units.[19] From 2000 to 2003, the city of Detroit alone issued almost 32,000 permits for housing construction and repair activities (Thomson 2004b). In Oakland County, over 20,000 residential sales occurred annually from 1995 to 2003 (Thomson 2006).

At least one consumer was involved in each of these activities. Most sales involved realtors and financial institutions. In St. Clair, Macomb, Oakland, Lapeer, and Livingston counties in 2005, 815 financial institutions reported lending activity.[20] In Wayne County alone, 712 institutions were active. Construction, demolition, and repairs involved builders, developers, and financial entities.

Government agencies were also involved in each transaction, be it through assessing fees or taxes in the case of sales and loans; determining whether the activity can occur, regulating aspects of the activity, and inspecting the resulting product in the case of construction and repairs/improvements; providing financial assistance in the case of some sales or repairs; or simply recording that the activity took place. Although the government is involved in each of these activities, the government's ability to significantly alter these activities without creating unintended consequences is limited. Even with a smaller number of transactions, the sheer number of governmental units involved makes coordination or agreement on policy alternatives difficult. The 2002 Census of Governments identified 300 city, village, township, and county governments in the nine counties of Southeast Michigan.[21] Each could have been involved in at least one of the transactions identified above. Many control zoning and permitting within their jurisdiction. Separate units within these communities tend to get involved in development and maintenance of housing-related infrastructure (for example, sewers, water, roads). About thirty communities within the region operate programs funded by the federal Community Development Block Grant, which provides funding for housing activities, adding another layer of governmental involvement. Add to this list about forty public housing agencies, some of which operate as autonomous public entities. Of course, federal and state agencies, such as the U.S. Department of Housing and Urban Development, the Michigan State Housing Development Authority, and the Michigan Department of Human Services, also play roles in housing activity in the region. Various nonprofit agencies develop and operate housing or provide housing-related services in the region.

These private sector, nonprofit, and governmental participants bring a variety of political, cultural, and economic interests, as well as personal interests, to the table. Many of these interests are tied to the values discussed earlier, and they often conflict. Sellers and landlords want to maximize profit, while buyers and renters want to minimize cost and maximize value. A similar conflict is evident for developers and builders. Financing entities want to minimize governmental involvement in their lending activity, while consumer, civil, and housing rights advocates often seek greater regulation.

Even within groups interests will differ (Truman 1971). Some elderly consumers will want institutions to focus on providing active-living retirement communities. Some will want efforts to focus on services to enable them to stay in their current homes. Still others will want direct financial assistance to lower costs. Even the same entity may have conflicting interests. For example, while seeking to maximize its tax base, the city of Detroit will also have a clear interest in accommodating the housing needs of low-income households by ensuring an adequate supply of low-income housing. While trying to ensure affordability, it will also want to maximize revenue for its water utility, an entity whose bills are a component of housing cost.

Each group will bring different resources to the table to influence policy decisions. Home builders may be able to ensure policies comply with their preferences by contributing to political campaigns, whereas low-income households are dependent upon convincing reference groups with greater resources to push for their cause (Lipsky 1968).

Of all the entities involved in the regional housing market, agreement among many of the 300 units of county and municipal government is most critical to the adoption of regional policies to address housing problems. In spite of the indicators that show the shared problems among these communities, the interest in regional solutions may not be great. Local governments in Oakland County may support efforts to improve affordability within the county since the prevalence of problems among every income group is higher than in most counties throughout the region. Governments within Macomb County may also be interested in policies to ensure affordability within the county. However, since many households have moved from Oakland County to Macomb County in the past decade, often in pursuit of more affordable housing (Thomson 2006), governmental units in Macomb County might not support regional policies if they improve affordability in Oakland County.

So, has anything changed in the political/organizational environment to make regional cooperation on housing more likely? There are some hopeful signs. In 2002, the Michigan Suburbs Alliance was formed to bring together leaders throughout the region to improve regional cooperation and address the shared interests of the region's mature suburbs. As of May 2007, twenty municipal and county governments were charter or affiliate members, and participation in its activities is strong. In 2007, One D: Transforming Regional Detroit was created by six major business, civic, and social service organizations—Cultural Alliance of Southeastern Michigan, Detroit Metro Convention and Visitors Bureau, Detroit Regional Chamber of Commerce, Detroit Renaissance, New Detroit, and United Way for Southeastern Michigan— to unify efforts to promote economic prosperity, educational preparedness, regional transit, race relations, and quality of life throughout the tricounty region. At the state level, Governor Jennifer Granholm is pushing local governments and school districts to share services and is encouraging such behavior by tying it to funding sources. Media attention to the affordability issue as it has affected home sales and foreclosures has also been high.

255

While such changes are welcome to advocates of regional approaches, little has changed in the political environment, and none of these organizations has focused directly on housing issues. Indeed, recent exchanges over attempts to alter control of Detroit's water and sewer system, consolidate city and suburban public transit systems, and create regional financing sources for expanding Cobo Hall and funding cultural institutions suggest that little has changed.

Conclusion

Public policy scholars have shown that policy action is highly dependent upon the characteristics of the problem to be addressed, the characteristics of the proposed policy solution, and the political/organizational environment surrounding the policy deliberations. Housing market indicators show that the scale of affordability problems has increased dramatically in most counties across Michigan's metropolitan areas. Foreclosures, stagnant housing sales, and declining home values are increasingly shared concerns. The scope of problems has also grown to include many more middle-income and elderly households. The increase in elderly households expected in the coming decades further complicates housing issues throughout Michigan's metropolitan areas. Specifically, how it will impact metropolitan markets is unclear, but change is inevitable and warrants exploration, particularly in terms of the potential growth in housing needs for people with disabilities. These housing issues affect more people (both directly and indirectly) in more communities more frequently, in more ways, and with greater severity than in the past. The regional nature of housing markets and the complexity of these issues call for regional approaches to addressing them. The public policy literature suggests that the characteristics of these housing problems—expanded scale and scope, changes in the population suffering, and changes in the causes—make regional approaches more likely than in the past.

Unfortunately, the policy literature also suggests that the nature of potential regional solutions, particularly in terms of affordability and acceptability, still pose great barriers to their adoption. Most important, the multiplicity of participants, interests, ideologies, intensities, and resource bases evident in the political/organizational environment of Southeast Michigan create substantial obstacles to regional solutions to housing affordability and the housing needs of the elderly. These obstacles stem from deeply rooted political, cultural, and economic ideologies that have stymied regional cooperation in Southeast Michigan for decades. The extent to which the political/organizational environments in Michigan's other metropolitan exhibit these characteristics varies, but the presence of multiplicities will surely pose difficulties in all metropolitan areas.

These forces are only likely to change if the scale and scope of the problems continue to escalate to a point where cooperation is considered critical to regional survival, and resources from federal sources are insufficient to address the need. In the meantime, regional governance of housing policy will not occur. Advocates of regional cooperation are most likely to see success in efforts that are nominally regional, but involve little in terms of sharing or relinquishing power. Such efforts may include joint advocacy to state and federal governments for financial assistance or other macropolicy solutions, regional study groups to explore the impact of and possible solutions to housing problems, and region-wide information or educational campaigns, all of which are consistent with what Meck, Retzlaff, and Schwab (2003) refer to as "second-best approaches," which are more probable than higher level solutions in most parts of the country.

Notes

1. The $263 million to be provided to Michigan communities through the U.S. Department of Housing and Urban Development's Neighborhood Stabilization Program and the refinancing of mortgages through the Hope for Homeowners initiative in 2009 are notable departures from previous modest levels of federal support.
2. The metropolitan areas used here are the Metropolitan Statistical Areas and Consolidated Metropolitan Statistical Areas identified by the U.S. Census Bureau.
3. The Comprehensive Housing Assessment System (CHAS) of the U.S. Department of Housing and Urban Development (HUD) provides special tabulations of decennial census data that provide precise measures of cost burden for 1989 and 1999. The 1989 data report cost burden only for households earning 95 percent or less of the HUD-adjusted area median income (HAMI). The 1999 data report cost burden for all households. No CHAS data are available for 2005. To enable comparisons of cost in 1989, 1999, and 2005, this chapter reports census data from the SF3 file (1989 and 1999) and the American Community Survey (2005). These totals include households paying exactly 30 percent of their income on housing. On average, the 1999 percentages from the census and reported in this table were 1 percentage point higher than the cost burden figures reported in CHAS data.
4. Some of the difference may be attributable to differences in sampling and estimation techniques used for decennial census and annual American Community Survey data, but the overall trend that is evident would not be different.
5. Here, foreclosures are defined as those homes for which a sheriff's sale occurred—the final stage of foreclosure. These numbers are lower than the totals commonly reported in the popular press. Press accounts typically refer to RealtyTrac, Inc. data that report all homes in any stage of foreclosure—from notice of default to sheriff's sale. Many of these homes are sold or refinanced before an actual foreclosure occurs.
6. During the same period (1999–2002), the median value of Oakland County's foreclosures rose 50 percent—from $72,122 to $107,943.
7. Data Source: RealtyTrac's U.S. Foreclosure Market Statistics by State—2007 totals, http://www.realtytrac.com/ContentManagement/pressrelease.aspx?ChannelID=9&ItemID=4303&accnt=64847. This includes preforeclosure (for example, notice of default, trustee sales) through sheriff's sale (that is, final foreclosure). Properties that progressed from one stage to another during the year would be included in this count more than once.
8. Data Source: RealtyTrac's Michigan Foreclosure Market Statistics by County—January 2008 totals, http://www.realtytrac.com/ContentManagement/pressrelease.aspx?ChannelID=9&ItemID=4301&accnt=64847. This reports only the REO Property totals reported by RealtyTrac, Inc. These are the homes that were actually repurchased by the lenders (that is, foreclosed).

9. It was the largest year-to-year decline since at least 1995, the first year of sales data available for this analysis.

10. Data source: Standard and Poor's/Case-Shiller Home Price Index January 2008 data, http://www2.standardandpoors.com/portal/site/sp/en/us/page.topic/indices_csmahp/0,0,0,0,0,0,0,0,0,3,1,0,0,0,0,0.html.

11. Data source: National Association of Realtors' Median Sales Price of Existing Single-Family Homes for Metropolitan Areas report for the fourth quarter of 2007, http://www.realtor.org/Research.nsf/Pages/MetroPrice.

12. These wage data were derived from the U.S. Bureau of Labor Statistic's May 2004 Metropolitan Area Occupational Employment and Wage Estimates, http://www.bls.gov/oes/2004/november/oes_2160.htm. They do not include workers in Washtenaw or Genesee County.

13. These totals do not include elderly people living in group quarters.

14. I use the term "at least" because some of the subsidized developments listed in the MSHDA database do not have information on unit type for all of the units included in the development. Some of the units included in the unit count are market-rate (that is, not subsidized) units. The overwhelming majority of units in this count are subsidized.

15. This is a conservative estimate that includes only those with a self-care disability and a disability that inhibits their ability to go outside the home. It does not include any of the elderly who report only a physical disability, mental disability, or hearing/vision disability that might justify special housing or support services.

16. This estimate includes the disability categories found in the elderly estimate, plus those with employment disabilities. Such disabilities would likely necessitate financial assistance to make housing affordable.

17. HOME Program National Production Report as of July 31, 2007: Home Cost per Unit by Activity Type and Tenure (Based on Completions), http://www.hud.gov/offices/cpd/affordablehousing/reports/production/073107.pdf.

18. 2005 Home Mortgage Disclosure Act Aggregate Reports for MSA/MD's in Southeast Michigan, http://www.ffiec.gov/hmdaadwebreport/AggTableList.aspx.

19. 2005 building permit data from SEMCOGs permit database, http://www.semcog.org/Data/BuildingPermits/index.htm.

20. 2005 Home Mortgage Disclosure Act List of Reporting Institutions for MSA/MDs in Southeast Michigan, http://www.ffiec.gov/hmdaadwebreport/AggTableList.aspx.

21. 2002 Census of Governments—State of Michigan data, http://www.census.gov/govs/www/cog2002.html.

REFERENCES

Advisory Commission on Regulatory Barriers to Affordable Housing. 1991. "Not in My Back Yard": Removing Barriers to Affordable Housing. Report to President Bush and Secretary Kemp by the Advisory Commission on Regulatory Barriers to Affordable Housing. Washington, D.C.: U.S. Department of Housing and Urban Development.

Allison, G. 1971. *Essence of Decision: Explaining the Cuban Missile Crisis.* Boston: Little, Brown.

Angel, C. 2008. Taxes Rise, Home Values Fall, Owners Say, "Huh?"—Proposal A to Blame. *Detroit Free Press,* March 14.

Askari, E., G. Guest, and V. Turk. 2007. More in Danger of Losing Homes. *Detroit Free Press,* August 15.

Basolo, V., and D. Hastings. 2003. Obstacles to Regional Housing Solutions: A Comparison of Four Metropolitan Areas. *Journal of Urban Affairs* 25(4):449–472.

Birkland, T. 1997. *After Disaster: Agenda-Setting, Public Policy, and Focusing Events.* Washington, D.C.: Georgetown University Press.

———. 2004. The World Changed Today: Agenda-Setting and Policy Change in the Wake of September 11 Terrorist Attacks. *Review of Policy Research* 21(2):179–200.

Cobb, R., and C. Elder. 1971. The Politics of Agenda Building. *Journal of Politics* 33:892–915.

———. 1983. *Participation in American Politics: The Dynamics of Agenda-Building.* 2nd ed. Baltimore: Johns Hopkins University Press.

Cobb, R., J. Ross, and M. Ross. 1971. Agenda Building as a Comparative Political Process. *American Political Science Review* 70:126–138.

Gainsborough, J. 2001. Bridging the City-Suburb Divide: States and the Politics of Regional Cooperation. *Journal of Urban Affairs* 23(5):497–512.

Gallagher, J. 2007. Region's Housing Sales on the Rise. *Detroit News,* March 24.

Galster, G. 2003. Review of the Literature on Impacts of Affordable and Multifamily Housing on Market Values of Nearby Single-Family Homes. Paper prepared for the Brookings Institution Symposium on the Relationships Between Affordable Housing and Growth Management, Washington, D.C.

Gray, K., and L. Brasier. 2007. Oakland Co. Growth Hits 40-Year Low. *Detroit Free Press,* April 20.

Hamm, K. 1983. Patterns of Influence among Committees, Agencies, and Interest Groups. *Legislative Studies Quarterly* 7 (August):379–426.

Heclo, H. 1978. Issue Networks and the Executive Establishment. In *The New American Political System,* edited by Anthony King. Washington, D.C.: American Enterprise Institute.

Kingdon, J. 1995. *Agendas, Alternatives and Public Policies.* 2nd ed. New York: HarperCollins.

Lindblom, C. 1950. The Science of Muddling Through. *Public Administration Review* 19 (Spring):79–88.

Lipsky, M. 1968. Protest as a Political Resource. *American Political Science Review* 62:144–158.

Listokin. D. 1976. Fair Share Housing Allocation. New Brunswick, NJ: Center for Urban Policy Research, Rutgers University.

Lowi, T. 1972. Four Systems of Policy, Politics, and Choice. *Public Administration Review* 33 (July–August):298–310.

Meck, S., R. Retzlaff, and J. Schwab. 2003. Regional Approaches to Affordable Housing. Planning Advisory Service Report No. 513/514. Chicago: American Planning Association.

Nelson, B. 1984. *Making an Issue of Child Abuse.* Chicago: University of Chicago Press.

Norris, D. 2001. Prospects for Regional Governance under the New Regionalism: Economic Imperatives versus Political Impediments. *Journal of Urban Affairs* 23(5):557–571.

Pressman, J., and A. Wildavsky. 1984. *Implementation.* 3rd ed. Berkeley: University of California Press.

Rochefort, C., and R. Cobb. 1993. Problem Definition, Agenda Access, and Policy Choice. *Policy Studies Journal* 21(1):56–71.

Sabatier, P. 1988. An Advocacy Coalition Framework for Policy Change and the Role of Policy-Oriented Learning Therein. *Policy Sciences* 21:129–168.

259

Schill, M. 2004. Regulations and Housing Development: What We Know and What We Need to Know. Paper prepared for the U.S. Department of Housing and Urban Development's Conference on Regulatory Barriers to Affordable Housing, Washington, D.C.

Schneider, A., and H. Ingram. 1993. Social Construction of Target Populations: Implications for Policy and Politics. *American Political Science Review* 87:34–47.

Simon, H. 1947. *Administrative Behavior.* New York: MacMillan.

Steinberger, P. 1980. Typologies of Public Policy: Meaning Construction and Their Policy Process. *Social Science Quarterly* 61 (September):185–197.

Swanstrom, T. 2001. What We Argue About When We Argue About Regionalism. *Journal of Urban Affairs* 23(5):479–496.

Thomson, D. 2004a. At What Cost? An Analysis of Housing Affordability in Detroit. Report prepared for City of Detroit Planning Commission.

———. 2004b. Detroit Residential Building Permit Activity from 2000–2003 (First Draft of Findings from Preliminary Analysis). Report prepared for City of Detroit Planning Commission.

———. 2006. *Comprehensive Housing Needs Assessment for Oakland County, Michigan.* Detroit: Wayne State University Center for Urban Studies.

Truman, D. 1971. *The Governmental Process: Political Interests and Public Opinion.* New York: Knopf.

CHAPTER 11

Michigan's Urban Policies in an Era of Land Use Reform and Creative-Class Cities

June Manning Thomas

Two conceptual themes have influenced Michigan's efforts to enhance the revitalization of its cities in the early years of the twenty-first century. The first is the urban redevelopment component of the land use reform movement, associated with efforts to reduce urban sprawl, promote smart growth, develop more compact urban patterns, and spur redevelopment of older central cities. The second is the creative-class cities concept, which suggests that enhanced central-city amenities and attraction of certain "creative" classes of workers lead to greater metropolitan economic growth and central-city vitality.

The land use reform movement has generated very specific policy activities in Michigan. In 2003, Governor Jennifer Granholm created the Michigan Land Use Leadership Council (MLULC), charged with assembling knowledge related to the relationship between land use and state policy and developing specific recommendations for improving Michigan's governmental policies. The MLULC, in a bipartisan effort headed by a Republican former governor and a Democratic former attorney general, identified a number of areas for investigation and policy recommendation. They labeled one "urban revitalization," which later documents referred to as "urban redevelopment." The MLULC final report, issued in August 2003, called for the need to reduce concentrated poverty; create pedestrian-friendly, mixed-income, diverse urban cores; and create a safe living environment for all residents, among a number of other key principles (MLULC 2003). The resulting recommendations generated several important legislative initiatives and agency actions. A comprehensive update posted in early 2007 indicated specific state actions carrying out the various recommendations (MLULC 2007).[1]

The creative-class cities movement has also contributed to specific policy initiatives in Michigan during the early 2000s. Many of these relate to the Cool Cities initiative, which

Granholm promoted. As one of the major strategies that the MLULC targeted for action under urban redevelopment, Cool Cities consists of a set of programs designed to support nominated redevelopment projects in large and small Michigan cities. In a series of funding rounds, the state provided supplemental financial support for projects ranging from building renovation in promising commercial districts to urban park development. In associated background materials, the state referenced conceptual underpinnings that drew heavily from the creative-class cities movement, with a strong focus on promoting talent, innovation, diversity, and urban environment, a combination that closely echoed urban economist Richard Florida's widely publicized recommended strategies for metropolitan economic development: talent, technology, tolerance, and urban amenities (Florida 2004). (A companion chapter in this book, Hoffman and Pyne's "The Brain Drain Wars," focuses on "talent," by examining the state's supposed "brain drain.")

Both of these initiatives relied on specific underlying theories to justify their programs, but sometimes these theories have problems of conception or implementation that severely weaken their effectiveness as guides to state policy. This chapter will briefly review several possible alternative approaches to urban revitalization, with a focus on policies aimed toward distressed cities and promulgated at the state level. After a cursory description of the state's recent urban policies, I briefly summarize the Myron Orfield and Jennifer Vey approaches to urban revitalization, and then consider the broad outlines of land use reform and creative-class cities approaches, the two dominant theories now governing state action. As we will see, a number of key ideas from Orfield and Vey could expand current thinking about how contemporary state urban policy can help revitalize Michigan's cities.

Urban Policies in Michigan

The last previous publicly visible attempt to make recommendations concerning Michigan's urban policies may date back thirty years, to the Republican administration of Governor William Milliken, who organized an "action group" charged with offering recommendations for state policies and programs designed to assist cities.[2] The resulting hallmark report, "Cities in Transition: Report of the Urban Action Group to Michigan Governor William G. Milliken," offered a set of guiding principles and specific recommendations for reform (Michigan 1977). Some of the recommendations were similar to those in more recent times—such as the 1977 report's suggestion that the state expedite foreclosure on tax delinquent properties, and that the state improve job development capabilities—although it is not clear which recommendations were actually implemented. This report followed a period of heightened federal and state governmental efforts to turn around trends of depopulation and disinvestment clearly visible in the 1960s and 1970s (Mollenkopf 1983).

Short papers posted on the state of Michigan's Web page offer summaries of accomplishments for two "centerpiece" program areas: "Cities of Promise" and "Cool Cities" (Michigan's Urban Agenda n.d.; Michigan Office of the Governor 2008) Cities of Promise, an inter-agency effort which focused on targeting state agency resources on eight core cities, began a five-year initiative in 2005 in Saginaw, Flint, Detroit, Pontiac, Hamtramck, Highland Park, Benton Harbor, and Muskegon Heights. Related programs focus on affordable housing, poverty reduction, and neighborhood improvements. Cool Cities began in 2003 with catalyst grants designed to support selected projects, and by 2006 the initiative included four programs— Neighborhoods in Progress (formerly "catalyst grants"), Michigan Main Street, Blueprints for Michigan's Downtowns, and Blueprints for Michigan's Neighborhood—as well as supportive resources such as conferences and resource toolkits. Possibly because of fiscal problems, in 2007 the governor announced winners only for Michigan Main Street and Blueprints for Michigan's Downtowns, and in 2008 the state reorganized its efforts with a strong focus on its Main Street programs (Michigan CCI 2008).

As reported by the Senate Fiscal Agency, two Cool Cities programs, Main Streets and Blueprints for Michigan's Downtowns, actually date from Governor John Engler's administration, which ended in 2003, and the total amount of state dollars invested in all Cool Cities programs during the Granholm administration has been extremely modest (Pratt and Tyszkiewicz 2007). Cool Cities grants were available to cities large and small, and were not targeted to distressed cities. A grant to a project site (such as a commercial or business incubator building, or a park or streetscape project) under the neighborhood "catalyst grant" program typically was for a maximum of $100,000, far too little to serve as anything other than a catalyst. Nevertheless, the Cool Cities initiative has other important nongrant attributes, such as support for local community-based planning and encouragement of state agencies to collaborate in project areas, and in some ways it is very popular throughout the state.[3] The state commissioned a private consultant firm to carry out a series of evaluation studies, although the firm has not issued the results of its findings (Public Policy Associates 2008).

State leaders have apparently given some thought as well to related strategies concerning revenue sharing, schools, safety, health care, minority businesses, and transportation (Michigan's Urban Agenda n.d.). The urban redevelopment component of the MLULC document offers basic principles for action in land use. Otherwise, however, it is difficult to discern the scope of the state's urban policies.

One of the conceptual difficulties of creating a sweeping statement of contemporary state urban policies is the problem of definition posed by the existence of powerful "nonurban urban policies." In an article published in 1987, urban economist Edwin Mills listed several "nonurban" urban federal policies that were of far more importance in affecting urban space than any "urban policies," which the United States did (and still does) not seem to have in any cohesive fashion. Examples of such nonurban policies are the location of government offices and their employees, affecting in particular national and state capital cities and places with large military bases; home rule legislation, provisions of which have led to numerous autonomous suburban governments within a metropolis; transportation policies, housing programs, tax policies, and antipoverty or welfare programs; and, finally, the relatively weak and poorly funded "urban development programs" (Mills 1987). "Urban redevelopment" policies must of necessity attempt to make incremental changes in the face of powerful public policies and market-driven forces supporting and promoting decentralization and central-city decline.

The same conceptual framework for understanding the relative standing of reputed federal "urban policies" must apply to contemporary state efforts as well. Michigan's policies in areas as diverse as education, revenue sharing, corrections, and transportation affect

Michigan's cities. As Ballard attests in chapter 1 in this volume, the loss of state revenue sharing, the large increases in funding for corrections, and the real decline in funding for environmental areas have had dramatic impacts on local governments. The extent to which the state considers these as interconnected, however, is not clear (Michigan's Urban Agenda n.d.; Michigan Office of the Governor 2008).

One approach of Michigan's state government has been to issue "catalogs" of various state programs of benefit to urban areas. In 1990, the governor's office issued "Working with Our Cities," a resource directory of then-existing state programs with either substantive or tangential relevance to central cities, a directory that this chapter's author helped create (Michigan Office of the Governor ca. 1990). As part of the Cool Cities initiative, Granholm's administration gave designated Cool Cities recipients priority access to state programs, which they could tap in order to provide financial resources and technical assistance for various efforts. These are listed in a "toolbox," a weighty, Web-based compendium of existing state programs accessible to nongrantees as well as Cool Cities grantees. Listing more predictable programs such as neighborhood improvement and low-income housing subsidies, this resource also includes information about applying for funding from over 170 other state programs, ranging from economic and workforce development to traffic safety, coastal zone management, and library support. Rather than a cohesive statement of policy, connected with a comprehensive set of associated programs of proven effectiveness in revitalizing urban areas, however, this is—as it claims to be—a toolbox of program or grant possibilities, large and small, of major and minor importance.[4]

The MLULC document (2003) and related policies are therefore of critical importance in understanding the overall framework for the state's urban policies during the first decade of the 2000s. The urban redevelopment section of that document focuses on "urban" issues, and other sections give some insight into possibilities for other land use–related "nonurban" urban policies. The MLULC offered specific examples of potential changes in legislation, but it created recommendations largely by proposing incremental changes in existing initiatives, rather than by creating new ones. As an example, the state already had several programs related to geographic areas targeted for investment incentive, such as enterprise zones or historic district tax credits. The MLULC recommendations concerned how to enhance these programs' ability to improve urban areas, with existing programs as a baseline, and no evidence exists that it assessed the effectiveness of current efforts in order to determine logical next steps or to suggest replacements for them.

The MLULC section on urban revitalization suggested policy changes that fell into three broad areas: siting of public buildings and facilities, state and local assistance in attracting private investment, and public/private support for livable communities. The first category focused on locating new and relocated public offices in existing urban areas, as well as on encouraging investment in existing urbanized areas by state universities and local school districts. The second category included encouraging private investment in existing urbanized areas; enhancing technical assistance for such programs as enterprise zones, historic district tax credits, and downtown development authorities; supporting brownfield reuse; and consolidating tax-reverted property. The third category included such efforts as improving urban green space, encouraging blight control, creating affordable housing, and

enhancing employees' ability to gain access to the workplace without sole reliance on auto-
mobiles and surface parking lots. This section also referenced efforts to retain and attract
diverse residents to Michigan cities through such means as the Cool Cities programs. The
resulting list of recommendations numbered just over fifty for "urban redevelopment"
alone (MLULC 2007).

Getting Michigan legislators to cooperate on creative legislation has proven to be particularly challenging in recent years, in part because of the high turnover and constant focus
on political campaigns that term limits have encouraged (Tothero 2003). Although the fact
that the state implemented any of the MLULC recommendations is commendable, especially given the turnover, partisanship, and ongoing budget crises that have faced the
Michigan legislature in recent years, it is nevertheless true that much more could have been
done. Of the fifty redevelopment recommendations, table 11.1 indicates those few that, four
years later, appeared to be "fully addressed," according to the consultant group funded by
the Kellogg Foundation's People and Land initiative. Although the consultants are not clear
about the definition of "fully addressed," those recommendations listed in table 11.1 had
associated laws put in place as well as related agency action. In some cases, however, action
has been modest; for "site additional public offices in already-urbanized areas," for example, a law to this effect has been signed, but few state government agencies have been in a
financial position to move or build offices and other facilities. The follow-up report lists only
two new public agency offices, set up by the Department of Environmental Quality (MLULC
2007: 1), that were located under these guidelines.

The "Safe Routes to School" initiative may have important and laudable effects as the
state taps into federal dollars designed to enable students to walk to a selected number of
schools, urban, suburban, and rural (MDOT 2008), but given its typical distribution pattern
this seems quite modest as a program targeted to urban areas, as is the initiative to discourage fraud against immigrants.[5] Of those listed in table 11.1, perhaps the four indicated

---

Table 11.1. Summary of 2003 Michigan Land Use Leadership Council (MLULC) Recommendations for "Urban Redevelopment" That Were Addressed "Fully" within Four Years

Original Michigan Land Use Leadership Council Recommendation	Passage of Related Laws
Site additional public offices in already-urbanized areas	Yes
Support reuse of brownfields via redirection of funding under Clean Michigan Initiative	Yes
Adopt Land Bank Fast Track Authority and allow similar local authorities	Yes
Help local governments expedite adjudication of code violations (blight elimination)	Yes
Build "livable" urban areas by supporting local "Safe Routes to School" programs	Yes
Retain and attract a diverse population by supporting Cool Cities	Yes
Retain and attract immigrants by enforcing consumer protection laws to prevent fraud against immigrants	Yes

SOURCE: As reported in MLULC, "MLULC Recommendations and Related Responses," a People and Land document, prepared by Public Sector
Consultants, accessible at http://www.peopleandland.org/MLULC_Recommendations/index.cfm. January 16, 2007, version. Italicized initiatives are
particularly noteworthy according to this chapter's author.

Table 11.2. Summary of 2003 Michigan Land Use Leadership Council (MLULC) Recommendations for "Urban Redevelopment" That Were Addressed "Partially" within Four Years

Original Michigan Land Use Leadership Council Recommendation	Passage of Related Laws
Require school district compliance with local plans	Yes
Maintain state grants and loans for redevelopment	Yes
Promote reuse of existing and historic buildings	Yes
Promote livable areas through various means such as access to urban waterfronts	Yes
Establish trust fund for mixed-use housing	Yes
Expand Michigan IDA program re: home ownership	Yes

SOURCE: As reported in MLULC, "MLULC Recommendations and Related Responses," a People and Land document, prepared by Public Sector Consultants, January 16, 2007 version accessible at http://www.peopleandland.org/MLULC_Recommendations/index.cfm.

by italics have the greatest potential to offer substantive development assistance to central cities. Brownfield cleanup is a major impediment for urban redevelopment in the state, and the land bank authority and blight elimination bills that have been passed help address commonly recognized problems of vacant properties with code violations and overabundant tax-delinquent or tax-reverted properties.

The People and Land initiative also indicated that six of the fifty urban redevelopment recommendations were "partially addressed" (these are listed in table 11.2). While all of these recommendations benefited from passage of related laws, actions were more modest than recommended by the MLULC. For example, the state funded at least one urban waterfront initiative, Tricentennial Park in Detroit, but this was the only such project listed. State government succeeded in passing legislation that required school districts to notify zoning authorities of planned expansion plans in townships, but efforts to require new school construction to comply with local zoning laws failed.

The need for effective action is clear. Several sources have monitored the status of Michigan's cities. One Michigan-based source is Michigan Higher Education Land Policy (MIHELP), a consortium of scholars based in Michigan universities and funded by the Kellogg Foundation. In "State of Michigan Cities: An Index of Urban Prosperity," the authors provided summary information particularly for the period 2000–2005 for several Michigan cities, including Ann Arbor, Battle Creek, Detroit, Flint, Grand Rapids, and eight more.[6] Their index of prosperity assessed such factors as crime rate, property value changes, median household income, and employment rate. They determined that for these and other key measures, these thirteen Michigan cities lagged below the state as a whole for every criterion except presence of young adults in 2000, and every criterion except employment change and young adults for 2005. For example, with property value change, the average increase in property values (State Equalized Value) between 2000 and 2005 in urban areas fell well below the percentage increase in the state as a whole, although a few cities experienced increases (MIHELP 2007, p. 25). This report, by its nature, refrained from making policy recommendations, but other scholars have undertaken both data analysis and policy recommendations.[7] The next section of this chapter reviews some of the concepts that might inform future action based on our review, above, of Michigan's current urban policies.

Before leaving this section, however, it is important to note that the context of the economy makes assertive urban-centered action on the part of state government particularly difficult in the state of Michigan. Its economy has suffered enormously from the loss of manufacturing jobs over the past few decades. The state's Senate Fiscal Agency best presents the repercussions of declining revenue. During the period from Fiscal Year 1994–1995 to Fiscal Year 2003–2004, for example, the state lost 20.2 percent of its manufacturing jobs, most of this in 2000–2004. State revenue grew during the first portion of that nine-year period but experienced increased volatility during the period from 2000 to 2004 (Olson and Mangla 2005). A similar report issued in 2007 found that economic problems had caused significant stress for the state budget over the previous six years, even though state government cut its workforce drastically, by 14.8 percent; employee costs nevertheless rose by 16.6 percent, and expenditures for health care, transportation, and corrections continued to grow (Olson and Kleidon 2007). The state, therefore, operates under several budgetary constraints described fully by Ballard (chapter 1, this volume), and key expenditures are rising even though revenues are falling. One possible response to such a situation, however, is to find more creative and cost-effective ways to support cities, which have served as engines of economic growth in the past and could yet again, according to certain theorists (Glaeser 1998).

The Orfield/Vey Approach

Myron Orfield, author of *American Metropolitics: The New Suburban Reality,* and Jennifer Vey, the lead author of a Brookings Institution report on state governments' role in revitalizing older industrial cities, offer key recommendations that are worthy of consideration. Both look particularly at matters of economic and workforce development, human services, social equity, and regional cooperation.

Orfield's publications have examined American metropolitan areas throughout the country, starting with Minnesota, where he once served as state legislator (Orfield 1997, 2002). His coauthored "Michigan Metropatterns" analyzed Michigan's key metropolitan areas, particularly the Detroit, Grand Rapids, Lansing, Flint, Kalamazoo, Saginaw, and Traverse City areas (Orfield and Luce 2003). When combined with Orfield's other texts, these sources examine key performance measures for Michigan cities and their suburbs as well as promote certain policy approaches. The key variables that Orfield and Luce explored and mapped for Michigan metropolitan areas measure fiscal, economic, and social health. The authors argued that some older and semirural suburban areas are suffering from declining growth and increasing costs, as are central cities, and they strongly recommended that government leaders and residents from these disparate places cooperate, strengthen regional entities, and fight for state policies that better address their needs. They also recommended several policies designed to counter deficits in municipal and family economic well-being.

Indicators for each municipality include its share of regional households, property tax base, median income, percent of students eligible for free lunch, percent of minority students, and percent of affordable housing units. They use such social, economic, and municipal fiscal indicators to classify municipalities into seven categories, ranging from central cities and stressed suburbs to low-stress suburbs and industrial towns.[8] According to their data for the most distressed of two of their seven classifications, the central city and stressed suburbs, a high percentage of Michigan citizens from the seven metropolitan areas listed in the preceding paragraph live in one of these two categories of communities (Orfield and Luce 2003). For example, in the Lansing area 38 percent of metropolitan households live either in the central city or in "stressed" suburbs, the latter characterized by growing social needs, tax bases below regional averages, and high rates of student poverty. For Kalamazoo, 38 percent of households are in the same position.

Considering the next two of their seven categories—the at-risk low-density suburbs and at-risk established suburbs, both with below-average median incomes, older housing and infrastructure, and tax rates rising faster than in other communities—we see even more metropolitan-area households in jeopardy. For Lansing, 27 percent additional households in the metropolitan area as a whole live in such municipalities, as do 31 percent in Kalamazoo. In fact, for the seven metropolitan areas studied, Orfield and Luce found that each had more than half of its households living in one of these four types of central-city, stressed, or at-risk municipalities (for example, 65 percent of Lansing-area households, 69 percent of Kalamazoo-area households).

They recommended regional reform in three major areas:

- Tax reforms, such as protecting revenue sharing, implementing tax-base sharing, and other policies, such as shifting tax burdens from improvements to the land itself, none of which are strong features of the MLULC recommendations;
- Regional land use planning, with a few recommendations that are similar to the MLULC approach, such as enhancing "smart growth" and reusing urban land; and
- Metropolitan partnerships, such as encouraging local governments to cooperate concerning services, a theme also evident in the MLULC report, and strengthening regional entities, an approach less evident in the MLULC recommendations.

The Vey report, published by the Brookings Institution, and influenced by other Brookings scholars such as Bruce Katz, did not focus specifically on Michigan, but it included data on 302 U.S. cities, including Michigan's cities, from 1990 to 2000.[9] It determined that sixty-five "older industrial cities" placed in the bottom fifth of cities ranked by economic prosperity. This was measured by 1990–2000 changes in "city economic condition indicators" (such as employment, annual payroll, and number of establishments), and 2000 status of "residential economic well-being indicators" (such as median household income, unemployment rate, poverty rate, labor force participation rate, and per capita income). This approach favors economic growth, which is probably why cities such as Los Angeles fell within the ranks of "older industrial cities," as did Miami, Baltimore, Cleveland, and Milwaukee, with strong over-representation in the Midwest and Northeast. The four Michigan cities that fell within this group of sixty-five lowest economic performers, as defined by the author, were Detroit, Flint, Kalamazoo, and Saginaw (Vey 2007).

While the quantitative analysis in this report is somewhat limited by its strong focus on the ten-year change of "city economic condition indicators," the policy suggestions for state governments are excellent. Taking up the bulk of the report, the potential state strategies revolve around five key areas:

- Help older industrial cities address basic issues such as neighborhood schools, safe streets, and a competitive cost climate for businesses and residents (tax policies);
- Build on basic economic strengths such as downtown revitalization, focus on competitive niches, and connect with other cities and regions;
- Transform the physical landscape by fixing urban infrastructure (sewer, water, transportation, and road systems), investing in catalytic projects, and creating marketable sites;
- Grow the middle class by building residents' skills, supporting low-income workers, and reducing the costs of being poor (such as mortgage and retail rates);
- Build "neighborhoods of choice" characterized by mixed-income housing, strong inner-city markets, historic preservation, and code enforcement.

Both Orfield and Vey, then, value the economic health of municipalities, as well as the need to enhance family economic well-being, and both focus in particular on the poor. Vey also specifically mentions the need to support downtowns, promote marketable projects, and transform the physical landscape. Glimmers of these suggested approaches are apparent in the MLULC recommendations (which predated the Vey report), particularly the third and fifth bullet points listed above for Vey. The land use approach exemplified by the MLULC, however, is not one that is commonly associated with several of the factors listed above. It may be useful to consider, briefly, why this is the case.

The Land Use Approach

The conceptual orientation of the land use approach is connected with the concept of environmental stewardship presented in other chapters of this book. In the "sustainability lens" figure used in this book's introduction, then, land use would fall into the bottom left of the triangle. However, this approach extends beyond environmentalism; it is also firmly grounded in the view that reform of land use is the most important way to develop and redevelop central cities and other urbanized areas, and therefore is linked to the economic prosperity component of the triple bottom line. This approach has greatly influenced the MLULC's recommendations for reforming Michigan's urban policies. Hence we see, particularly in the urban redevelopment section but also in the original MLULC report in its entirety, a great deal of attention paid to discouraging government support of sprawl and increasing the effectiveness of government support of central-city redevelopment.

Referring yet again to the themes of this book summarized in the introduction, sustainability relates as well to the other two corners of the triangle: economic vitality and social good. Unfortunately, the land use approach traditionally does not make explicit the economic linkages to promoting and advancing social good such as alleviating poverty, improving schools or workforce development, creating safe streets, or encouraging inner-city commerce. Although some observers may associate the land use approach with specific offshoots that do mention these kind of concerns, such as some aspects of the "new urbanism" movement, this approach to urban revitalization is really more closely associated with land use planning, as practiced in particular by urban planners specializing in land use. The classic texts in urban land use planning deal largely with the analysis and regulation of land use and the proper placement and provision of municipal services, often assuming that market-driven development is a given, to be regulated rather than requiring stimulation (Berke et al. 2006). Only very recently have professional and academic reference materials provided guidance concerning how the land use approach can help alleviate conditions associated with urban distress, short of simply bulldozing and rebuilding. I will not attempt to review these trends here, but recent examples of contemporary thinking could include Belmont's and Garvin's strategies for central-city revitalization (Belmont 2002; Garvin 2002). These authors focus on traditional neighborhood and business district redevelopment. The extensive literature on brownfields has also provided excellent guidance concerning the specific challenge of finding new uses for abandoned or environmentally distressed land parcels.

It is true that some linkage exists between urban containment land use issues and urban revitalization. A recent article (Nelson et al. 2004) reports on one of the few studies designed to determine, based on empirical evidence, whether enhanced metropolitan land use helps revitalize central cities. Nelson and coauthors were interested in examining whether control of urban sprawl was associated with enhanced private construction in central cities, as a proxy for "urban revitalization." In a study that examined U.S. metropolitan areas in which some sort of containment policy—growth boundaries, service extension limits, or greenbelts—had been in place since at least 1985, they found a distinctive difference in 1985–1995 construction activity taking place in those areas that had strong containment policies as opposed to those areas with weak ones. In terms of inner-city investment, that is, controlling growth at the fringes did appear to enhance development in central cities and inner-ring suburbs. Although suburban areas in both contained and relatively uncontained metropolitan areas grew during the period of study, it appeared that containment shifted development from rural and exurban areas inward, toward suburban and urban areas (Nelson et al. 2004).

Apparently, central-city redevelopment, as measured by construction activity, is much less effective in the absence of urban containment. This suggests that urban land use policies that aim to redevelop cities may work best linked with land use control of outer-rim areas. A related concept is that central cities may fare best under conditions of regional governance, cooperation, or tax base sharing (Orfield 1997, 2002, Orfield and Luce 2003; Rusk 1995).[10] These theories suggest the need to examine the MLULC recommendations concerning control of sprawl and governmental cooperation or consolidation, as well as urban redevelopment.

The Creative-Class Cities Approach

To the more traditional land use approach to urban redevelopment, personified by the MLULC and its urban initiatives, the state of Michigan has added the more modern creative-class cities approach. As noted previously, one of the major "fully addressed" issues under the urban redevelopment component of the MLULC recommendations has been the state of Michigan's Cool Cities initiative. A pilot Cool Cities program offered for the first few years provided catalyst grants for urban development projects, with subsequent revisions in program descriptions and resources. The broader initiative's attempts to attract and retain "talent"—members of the "creative class"—have included scholarships for college students, investment in technology, and support for workforce training for key industries.

The four basic Cool Cities concepts of talent, innovation, diversity, and environment are, in essence, a very slight revision of Richard Florida's model for improving metropolitan economic development. Particularly in his books, but also in his articles, on his Web page, and in his consultative activities with local and state governments in the United States and elsewhere in the world, Florida reported that the U.S. metropolitan areas that are growing demonstrate that economic growth is associated with four major factors: talent, technology, tolerance, and amenities. More specifically, Florida claimed that his extensive regression analysis of key economic and demographic variables, coupled with his own focus groups assembled in order to provide qualitative feedback, demonstrated that those metropolitan areas that grew in terms of their relative advancement in high-technology employment had four characteristics. They contained certain talent, measured by the relative presence of key "creative-class" professionals (listed in Hoffman and Pyne, chapter 12 in this volume); innovation, variously defined but largely measured by patent activity; and tolerance of diversity, measured first (Florida 2002) by a male couples–only Gay Index and then later (Florida 2004) by a more extensive Diversity Index, which included immigrants, racial integration, and the presence of artists and related professions ("bohemians"). Florida also assessed urban amenities, as determined by aesthetic qualities, urbanity, and entertainment, and measured by various popular indices. He then moved from simple reporting of these findings to policy recommendations, urging state and local governments to seek to attract creative-class residents in order to spur economic growth, and to view the presence of "bohemians" and gays, for example, as a leading indicator of the tolerance necessary for high-technology economic growth (Florida 2002, 2004, 2005).

The close parallel between Richard Florida's concepts and Michigan's four Cool Cities principles is apparent. Michigan's Cool Cities initiative owes much conceptually to the creative-class cities concept, as evidenced by its Web page's reference to key principles and recommended readings (Michigan CCI 2008), by at least one high-profile urban policy study that informed the MLULC (Michigan Future Inc. 2003), as well as by urban amenities programs for downtowns and neighborhoods. Analysis of Florida's concepts is important because many states and localities are patterning their urban economic development strategies on these concepts. The problem with a theoretical reliance on Florida is twofold: first, other analysts have challenged some flawed analysis and erroneous conclusions in some of his work; and second, no independent evidence yet exists that following his prescriptions leads to central-city or metropolitan economic growth (Rausch and Negrey 2006; Thomas and Darnton 2006; Donegan et al. 2008).

One of the key ingredients of both editions of Florida's book *The Rise of the Creative Class* is a series of lengthy tables ranking various U.S. cities according to how well they fit his model of forward-moving metropolitan economies. All Michigan metropolitan areas listed ranked fairly low in several of the characteristics that he tagged as important for economic growth; according to his "Creativity Index," for regions over 1,000,000 in size, Detroit ranked

271

Table 11.3. Richard Florida's Rankings of Components of Michigan Cities' Tolerance Index, Compared to High-Tech Index, for Forty-nine U.S. Metropolitan Regions over One Million in Size

Large Region Located in Michigan	High-Tech Index Rank*	Melting Pot Index Rank[†]	Gay Index Rank 2000[‡]	Bohemian Index Rank[§]
Detroit	49	22	45	24
Grand Rapids	43	36	38	31

SOURCE: Florida 2004: 254–262.

*High-Tech Index rank is measured by the Milken Institute's measures of relative presence of high-technology firms in a metropolitan area.

[†]Melting Pot Index rank is determined by the relative presence of foreign-born people in an area's population.

[‡]Gay Index rank is determined in this section of Richard Florida's book (2004) by the relative presence of male homosexual couples in an area's population, using Year 2000 census data. (Tables in the appendix use males plus females in the definition.)

[§]Bohemian Index rank is determined by the relative presence of certain creative professions, such as those associated with the fine arts.

113th and Grand Rapids 131st. For regions 500,000 to 1,000,000 in size, Saginaw ranked 249th, and Benton Harbor (184th) and Jackson (214th) fared little better for their size categories. Table 11.3 shows Florida's data for a key set of variables for forty-nine large regions, again indicating relatively low rankings for Michigan's two large regions. It has become apparent that great caution is necessary in interpreting these data, however (Thomas, Darnton, and Supanich-Goldner 2005). Other empirical studies, designed to assess the relationship between creativity and economic development and testing the "creativity index," have found many conceptual and methodological difficulties (Rausch and Negrey 2006, Donegan et al. 2008).

Here is a very brief overview of concerns, more fully dealt with in other sources. First, the High-Tech Index of employment may be biased against older industries, such as the automobile industry, whose jobs may not ostensibly appear to be "high tech" and yet may include high-technology productivity (Chapple et al. 2004). The Gay Index has numerous difficulties in multivariate analysis (even when female couples are added), chief among them being the possibility that this index actually measures an area's educational levels, with which it is highly correlated, suggesting that educational levels (talent) should be substituted as a more valid measure to use in regression models. Several attempts to replicate the analytical connection between the presence of gay couples or "bohemian" artists and economic development have not succeeded (Clark 2004a; Rausch and Negrey 2006), and research is still being carried out on the role of artistic populations in economic growth (Markusen and King 2003). Rausch and Negrey (2006) have done extensive examination of Florida's "creative-class cities" methodology, and their more sophisticated regression analyses found the following: a higher proportion of the creative class does not necessarily translate into better regional economic performance as measured by gross metropolitan product (GMP), and metropolitan populations with larger creative-class presence actually experienced a decline in GMP, suggesting that merely adding such individuals to the population does not help enhance economic development. This last point had already been persuasively argued by Scott (2006). Rausch and Negrey (2006) also found that a rise in GMP was indeed connected with two key variables, but that these were the relative concentration of foreign-born population and tolerance in the form of the lack of *racial* segregation, as measured by Gini coefficients (one of several methodological ways to measure inequality). Furthermore, it is not clear that urban amenities programs can change location decisions, or that people will go anywhere unless the prospects for jobs are very good (Scott 2006). These findings call into question much of Florida's analysis, and hence his policy recommendations.

Looking again at table 11.3, it appears that the presence of immigrants, the "Melting Pot Index," is the most reliable variable listed, and possibly also the High-Tech Index, tempered with knowledge of the potential problems of definition noted above. One important fact about the High-Tech Index is that this is very fluid, because such firms open and close, grow or downsize, or move, quite frequently. It could be, for example, that Grand Rapids could change very fast in its technology rankings with the presence of the new campus of the Michigan State University Medical School and related research facilities.

Finally, the "creative-class cities" model is somewhat different from the "creative-cities" label. Creative-class strategies refer in particular to attracting certain categories of professional and technical workers. A more general label, "creative cities," however, could refer to "entertainment cities," characterized by strong artistic and tourist sectors (Clark ed. 2004), or to other, more creative forms of redevelopment. Landry (2000), for example, presents case studies that offer strategies from improved signage to educating slum children in Delhi, suggesting that cities be "creative." The state has helped sponsor an annual conference that is focused on many aspects of art, entertainment, culture, and urban development, with much less focus on the "creative class" than some of its other programs, and with much more credibility.

This brief review should lead us to look critically at those aspects of Michigan's urban policies that rely too heavily on the creative-class cities model, as well as to consider other complementary strategies not yet implemented fully. An excellent example would be the policies related to immigrants. Much of the available literature confirms the importance of attracting foreign-born populations as a strategy for economic growth (Thomas and Darnton 2006). As we can see from table 11.3, the Detroit and Grand Rapids regions fare pretty well in terms of their relative percentages of immigrants. Table 11.1 shows that the one MLULC strategy related to immigrants was rather weak, addressing only consumer protection laws affecting immigrants. Further attracting this particular population may be very difficult for states, as immigrant presence is based in large part on federal legislation regulating admission to the country as a whole, but considering other possible mechanisms to support their presence in specific urban localities may be important. Sources suggest that both highly educated and not-so-educated immigrants have great economic value; highly educated immigrants bring technological skills, while less tech-savvy immigrants bring a strong work ethic and a willingness to invest in housing and commercial establishments (Thomas and Darnton 2006). Looking at another key variable identified by Rausch and Negrey (2006), enhancing racial tolerance (or its proxy, relative lack of racial segregation) may also hold great promise. While in Michigan the problem of racial segregation, particularly in the Detroit metropolitan area, seems fairly difficult to address (Thomas 1997), some recent private initiatives have been made to overcome this, and greater attention from the state could be useful.

273

Much of the Cool Cities initiative is based on the "urban amenities" component of the creative-class model, which is also connected with the movement among other parties to enhance arts and entertainment, attractive downtowns, and pedestrianism (Clark ed. 2004). Florida's measures for this fourth dimension of his model were very poor, and very few of the analysts mentioned above have been able to include reliable measures of amenities in their models. At least one recent study, however, shows that urban planners see a strong association between urban amenities such as pedestrianism, historic preservation, entertainment, and the presence of useable mass transit, with downtown vitality in small metropolitan areas (Filion et al. 2004). Furthermore, Clark (2004b) has found that artistic and other amenities are associated with attractiveness of certain cities to surveyed populations, but he warns that different age groups are attracted by very different kinds of amenities. In general, experiential accounts of certain high-profile projects suggest that improving urban amenities in key project areas can be very helpful as an urban redevelopment strategy, if carried out with a coherent program in mind (Clark ed. 2004, Clark 2004b; Garvin 2002), but how to ensure that such strategies manage to triumph over major factors of decline and decentralization is not yet known.

Summary and Recommendations

Michigan has made some strides in passing legislation designed to assist its cities. Not for thirty years had a major initiative organized by a sitting Michigan governor sought to look comprehensively at several areas of concern related to urban areas and their central cities. Although only a small portion of the fifty MLULC recommendations related to urban redevelopment in land use actually became viable programs or led to agency action within four years, a few actions emerged. Given the extreme budget constraints and structural deficit facing the state, and other challenges as well, it is not surprising that only a limited amount of action was taken to advance Michigan's urban policies.

Looking at the future, it is important to examine how the programs that have been put in place match what is known about successful urban redevelopment. This chapter's brief review of several approaches shows that not all analysts agree, but that many have suggestions that may be important to consider concerning ways of revitalizing Michigan's cities.

Orfield's work reminds us to consider the relationship between municipalities within a region. As he notes, several kinds of municipalities suffer from the fragmentation and extremes of wealth and poverty that characterize Michigan's metropolitan areas. Not central cities alone but also certain stressed suburbs need focused consideration if they are to survive. His is a constant voice for regional land use planning, as well as for tax reforms and for keeping attention focused on households and children living in conditions of economic stress.

Vey is also a strong voice for the role of the state in helping to address the economic vitality of workers and families and well as of municipalities. Additional policies informed by Vey (and her colleagues at the Brookings Institution) would aim to address land use issues such as downtown revitalization, investment in urban infrastructure, and mixed-income housing, as well as tax policies that affect the competitive cost climate for business and residents, workforce development, and the costs of mortgages and retail goods. She also reminds us of the essential importance of safe streets and good schools. As does Orfield, she looks at support of low-income families as an important requirement for urban redevelopment.

This chapter characterized Michigan's urban policies as revolving around two approaches, the land use and creative-class cities approaches. The land use perspective to urban development is well represented in the current MLULC initiative, but many of the related recommendations have not been implemented. Much attention is given to the need to build livable communities that have the capacity to attract and retain residents. In addition, this chapter suggests that it is very important to consider the linkage between urban redevelopment strategies and urban containment. The recommendations contained in other portions of the MLULC's 2003 report go far in their call for regional cooperation, but not very far in this direction; urban containment is still a relatively foreign concept in Michigan. Drawing from Orfield and Vey, I might suggest a more focused initiative to look at the potential for cooperation between distressed central cities and stressed, inner-ring suburbs. In addition, as they noted, tax reforms will continue to offer opportunities for improvement concerning cooperation between cities and suburbs.

In terms of creative-class cities, it may be important to examine current state programs to determine if they fully encourage factors proven to be effective attractors of urban revitalization. Current attempts to enhance urban amenities for promising projects in various cities, for example, may indeed prove effective routes to urban revitalization, but this is not a scientific process, and the specific conditions under which this is true are not fully known. (For one approach, see Garvin 2002.) Rather than rely too much on such a strategy, other complementary efforts would be important. As for efforts to attract creative-class workers or future workers (students), such efforts may also need careful examination. Scott (2006) and Rausch and Negrey (2006) suggest that people go where jobs are and where solid conditions exist for business development, and it is not yet clear that urban amenities can change people's location decisions. What is known is that certain conditions are not favorable to urban vitality, such as rampant racial segregation, and this suggests a possible direction for action. As for immigrants, encouraging their presence may become a very important strategy for older industrial cities and states. It may also be important to develop the human resources that already exist in a place rather than to depend on the importation of new ones.

The issues of reformed land use, economic development, and improved cities are inextricably linked. Although Michigan suffers great economic hardships, the state also has the ability to target funds and reshape priorities, as it did in some ways with the Cool Cities and MLULC initiatives. And yet this approach could be considerably broader and more closely linked with basic service provision, education, and human resource development than is the typical creative-class cities approach, such as promoted by Richard Florida. Reviewing again the Brookings Institution's (Vey 2007) list of proposals for state action, we see even more clearly the linkage between central-city redevelopment, as a land use strategy, and broader strategies for social good and economic vitality, a linkage surely recognized by state government leaders (Michigan Office of the Governor 2007) but in constant need of support:

- Concerning the recommendation of helping older industrial cities address issues such as schools, safety, and tax relief, the Brookings study (Vey 2007) cites education-related

275

examples from North Carolina, which offers bonuses to its teachers for working in inner-city districts, and Massachusetts, which has funded longer school days in struggling districts. The report also highlights the successful efforts in New York to reduce crime and enhance public safely, and it notes both Michigan's and Washington State's successful efforts to reduce incarceration for all but the most violent criminals and to reduce recidivism.

- Concerning basic economic strategies such as investing in downtown revitalization and competitive niches, and linking regions, the Brookings study points out that many cities are investing in downtowns, but they cite the movement by Michigan and Pennsylvania to target future state government buildings in central business districts or built-up areas as particularly noteworthy. They greatly laud any effort designed to build up economic niches, such as in Pennsylvania, where for many years the Ben Franklin Technology Partnership and more recently the Keystone Innovation Zone have striven to connect universities, leading-edge businesses, and industries with venture capital networks and foundations. To link regions, they recommend reconsideration of the concept of linking key cities through rail development.

- Regarding the use of improved urban infrastructure and catalytic projects, they reference New Jersey's efforts to create a Transit Village Initiative, linking residential development with transit stops. They also mention Pennsylvania's community action teams, designed to offer economic development advice on a short-term basis, and Michigan's Land Bank Fast Track Authority. As an example of a catalytic project, they refer to Baltimore's Inner Harbor but note that many cities have projects designed to spur investment.

- Regarding growing the middle class by building residents' skills and supporting low-income workers, possibilities include the creation of workforce intermediaries, as was done in Ohio, Pennsylvania, and California; requirements for financial literacy for high school graduates, as has been tried in Illinois and Georgia; limits on predatory mortgage lending, as is the case in New Mexico and North Carolina; and state versions of Earned Income Tax Credits, implemented now in nineteen states.

- Building "neighborhoods of choice" is in part what Michigan has been trying to do, particularly with its Cool Cities programs, as well as many housing initiatives not highlighted in this chapter. The Brookings Institution lists a number of other good suggestions, however, ranging from New York's efforts to encourage financial institutions to serve underserved communities to Rhode Island's provision of tax credits for historic preservation and New Jersey's adoption of new building codes.

Many of the ideas suggested above already cite some of Michigan's efforts, and others may already be viable components of the state's strategies, less visible to the public than initiatives discussed here (Michigan Office of the Governor 2007; Michigan's Urban Agenda 2007). Efforts to put in place support for low-income housing, workforce development, and the cost of living in cities, for example, are apparently under way, and recent changes in the Cool Cities program may have addressed many previous concerns. The challenge will be to maintain such efforts, and to enhance them, in a time of constrained governmental resources, linking all in a coherent strategy that, with perseverance, places the state in the best possible role for making creditable and lasting reforms.

In closing, it must be noted that all of Michigan's central cities are not facing the same challenges. As mentioned in the MIHELP (2007) report, for example, residents of Ann Arbor, Traverse City, and Grand Rapids face very different circumstances than residents of Muskegon, Detroit, and Flint. The first group of cities has had relative stability in population size and tax revenue, while the second group has not. The political realities of the state, furthermore, are that historically its taxpayers—part of the great suburbanizing wave outward, in many metropolitan areas—have not seen efforts targeting only the most distressed cities as popular, another reason for the broad statewide scope of the Cool Cities program and for the fairly non-specific geographic focus of the MLULC. In the final analysis, however, all residents of the state suffer when any of Michigan's cities suffer, especially since the state's most distressed cities are also its most visible, and especially since metropolitan areas are linked by bonds of transportation, economic activity, social life, and history. Building sustainable bonds of cooperation and mutual assistance, all the while balancing land use, the social good, and economic vitality, will remain an important task for the foreseeable future in this very diverse state.

Notes

1. This web-based document has not been updated since January, 2007 as we write this (October 2008), but additional legislation concerning planning and zoning has been passed since that time, most notably Act 33 of 2008, which encouraged more timely comprehensive planning and better planning coordination, as well as synchronized the state's planning enabling legislation. Legislative analyses of bills leading to Act 33 of 2008 made explicit reference to MLULC. However we refer in this chapter to the first four years after the report was issued.

2. A search of the database for the state of Michigan library system reveals no comparable report for interim governors' offices on public record. The Blanchard administration did issue a report on Lansing, and launched various programs, such as the Neighborhood Builders' Alliance.

3. In an October 2007 interview, Granholm stated: "Cool Cities is really kind of fun because these communities across the state, no matter where they are, they vie for this designation. It's really a very little amount of money, but they're all really excited about it. The people who get the designation are the ones with the best plan who show the greatest potential for community involvement as well as creating something dynamic in the city. So they all present these plans, and they have a big conference, and they're all excited about having been designated as a 'Cool City Neighborhood in Progress.' It's just a way to configure our cabinet around this goal of invigorating our cities" (Granholm 2007).

4. For a more detailed description of the Cool Cities and a few related programs, refer to chapter in this book by Hoffman and Pyne, and also see the state's Web page: http://www.mshda.info/cci. An evaluation of the Cool Cities program has been commissioned from Public Policy Associates, Inc. in Lansing, Michigan, but this may not be available to the public.

5. Federal transportation funding appears to be a major source of support for the program. Recipient schools announced in the fall of 2008 were located in four cities of Wayne

County, including Detroit, Hamtramck, and Highland Park; Benton Harbor in Berrien County; Flint in Genesee County; the cities of Saginaw, Pontiac, Muskegon Heights; and other suburban cities and villages such as Stevensville, Watervliet, Grand Blanc, Augusta, Lowell, St. Ignace, Maysville, and Grosse Ile Township (MDOT 2008).

6. Kalamazoo, Lansing, Muskegon, Pontiac, Saginaw, Traverse City, Warren, and Wyoming.

7. For instance, as a part of the MLULC deliberations, it sought white papers from several scholars and public policy consultants in 2003. Several are at http://www.michiganlanduse. org/resources/commDevelopment.htm. One report also available on a consultant's Web page and funded by two foundations is Michigan Future Inc.'s "Revitalizing Michigan's Cities: A Vision and Framework for Action."

8. Their seven categories, determined by cluster analysis of several fiscal, economic, and social variables, are seven distinct groupings of types of municipalities, arranged in ascending order of property tax base dollars per household: central city, stressed suburbs, at-risk established suburbs, at-risk low-density suburbs, bedroom-developing suburbs, low-stress suburbs, and industrial towns (Orfield and Luce 2003: 3–7).

9. They examined all U.S. cities which in either 1990 or 2000 had at least 50,000 people and were the largest city in their metropolitan area, or had at least 50 percent of the population of the largest city in that area, or had a population of at least 150,000.

10. Nelson et al. cite but critique Rusk's argument that city elasticity could help resolve the problem of sprawl, if central cities expanded their boundaries to include decentralizing residents and tax base.

REFERENCES

Belmont, S. 2002. *Cities in Full: Recognizing and Realizing the Great Potential of Urban America.* Chicago: Planners Press, American Planning Association.

Berke, P., E. J. Kaiser, D. R. Godschalk, and F. S. Chapin Jr. 2006. *Urban Land Use Planning.* 4th ed. Urbana: University of Illinois Press.

Chapple, K., A. Markusen, G. Schrock, D. Yamamoto, and P. Yu. 2004. Gauging Metropolitan "High-Tech" and "I-Tech" Activity. *Economic Development Quarterly* 18(1):10–29.

Clark, T. N. 2004a. Gays and Urban Development: How Are They Linked? In *The City as an Entertainment Machine,* edited by T. N. Clark. Oxford: Elsevier.

———. 2004b. Urban Amenities: Lakes, Opera and Juice Bars, Do They Drive Development. In *The City as an Entertainment Machine,* edited by T. N. Clark. Oxford: Elsevier.

———, ed. 2004. *The City as an Entertainment Machine.* Oxford: Elsevier.

Donegan, M., et al. 2008. Which Indicators Explain Metropolitan Economic Performance Best? *Journal of the American Planning Association* 74(2):180–195.

Filion, P., et al. 2004. The Successful Few: Healthy Downtowns of Small Metropolitan Regions. *Journal of the American Planning Association* 70(3):328–343.

Florida, R. 2002. *The Rise of the Creative Class and How It's Transforming Work, Leisure, Community and Everyday Life.* New York: Basic Books.

———. 2004. *The Rise of the Creative Class and How It's Transforming Work, Leisure, Community and Everyday Life.* Paperback edition with revisions. New York: Basic Books.

———. 2005. *The Flight of the Creative Class: The New Global Competition for Talent.* New York: Harper-Collins.

Garvin, A. 2002. *The American City: What Works, What Doesn't.* New York: McGraw-Hill.

Glaeser, E. 1998. Are Cities Dying? *Journal of Economic Perspectives* 12(2):139–160.

Granholm, J. 2007. Interview in Governing.com, September, a publication of the Congressional Quarterly Inc. Http://www.governing.com/articles/10granholm.htm.

Landry, C. 2000. *The Creative City: A Toolkit for Urban Innovators.* London: Comedia.

Markusen, A., and D. King. 2003. *The Artistic Dividend: The Arts' Hidden Contribution to Regional Development.* Report for Project on Regional and Industrial Economics. Minneapolis: Humphrey Institute of Public Affairs, University of Minnesota.

MDOT (Michigan Department of Transportation). 2008. Press Release: Lt. Governor John Cherry Announces 41 Schools." September 30. http://www.michigan.gov/printerFriendly/0,1687,7–136–3452–200984—,00.html/.

Michigan CCI (Cool Cities Initiative). 2008. Http://www.coolcities.com/.

———. Resource Tool Box. Http://www.mshda.info/cci/tools/.

Michigan Future Inc. 2003. Revitalizing Michigan's Cities: A Vision and Framework for Action. Http://www.publicpolicy.com/reports/urbanre1.pdf.

Michigan Governor's Urban Action Group. 1977. Cities in Transition: Report of the Urban Action Group to Michigan Governor William G. Milliken. Lansing, Mich.: Urban Action Group.

Michigan Office of the Governor. Ca. 1990. Working with Our Cities: Michigan's Urban Resource Directory. Lansing: State of Michigan.

———. 2007. Michigan's Cities. Http://www.michigan.gov/documents/gov/Cities_186085_7.pdf.

———. 2008. Web page at http://www.michigan.gov/som/0,1607,7–192—S,00.html

Michigan's Urban Agenda. N.d. Unattributed and undated paper posted. Http://www.michigan.gov/documents/gov/urban_173421_7.pdf.

MIHELP (Michigan Higher Education Land Policy Consortium). 2007. State of Michigan Cities: An Index of Urban Prosperity.

Mills, E. 1987. Non-urban Policies as Urban Policies. *Urban Studies* 24(6):561–569.

MLULC (Michigan Land Use Leadership Council). 2003. Michigan's Land, Michigan's Future: Final Report of the Michigan Land Use Leadership Council. Prepared for Governor Jennifer Granholm and the Michigan Legislature.

———. 2007. Michigan Land Use Leadership Council Recommendations and Related Responses. Http://www.peopleandland.org/MLULC_Recommendations/index.cfm.

Mollenkopf, J. 1983. *The Contested City.* Princeton N.J.: Princeton University Press.

Nelson, A., R. Burby, E. Feser, C. Dawkings, E. Malizia, and R. Quercia. 2004. Urban Containment and Central-City Revitalization. *Journal of the American Planning Association* 70(4):411–425.

Olson, G., and B. Kleidon. 2007. The Michigan Economy and State Budget Fiscal Year 2000–01 to Fiscal Year 2005–06: Six Years of Significant Changes. Issue Paper, Senate Fiscal Agency of the State of Michigan.

Olson, G., and T. Mangla. 2005. The Michigan Economy and State Budget FY 1994–95 to FY 2003–04: Ten Years of Significant Changes. Issue Paper, Senate Fiscal Agency of the State of Michigan.

Orfield, M. 1997. *Metropolitics: A Regional Agenda for Community and Stability.* Washington, D.C.: Brookings Institution.

———. 2002. *American Metropolitics: The New Suburban Reality.* Washington, D.C.: Brookings Institution.

Orfield, M., and T. Luce. 2003. Michigan Metropatterns: A Regional Agenda for Community and Prosperity in Michigan. Minneapolis: Ameregis Metropolitan Area Research Corporation. Http://www.metroresearch.org/maps/region_maps/michigan_1c.pdf.

Pratt, E., and M. Tyszkiewicz. 2007. *Cool Cities.* Issue Paper, Senate Fiscal Agency of the State of Michigan.

Public Policy Associates. 2008. Http://www.publicpolicy.com/cltproj.asp?ClientID=152&offset=0.

Rausch, S., and C. Negrey. 2006. Does the Creative Engine Run? A Consideration of the Effect of Creative Class on Economic Strength and Growth. *Journal of Urban Affairs* 28(5):473–489.

Rusk, D. 1995. *Cities without Suburbs.* Baltimore: Johns Hopkins University Press.

Scott, Allen. 2006. Creative Cities: Conceptual Issues and Policy Questions. *Journal of Urban Affairs* 28(1):1–17.

Thomas, J. 1997. *Redevelopment and Race: Planning a Finer City in Postwar Detroit.* Baltimore: Johns Hopkins University Press.

Thomas, J., and J. Darnton. 2006. Social Diversity and Economic Development in the Metropolis, *Journal of Planning Literature* 21(2):153–168.

Thomas, J., J. Darnton, and F. Supanich-Goldner. 2005. TIDE: Key Empirical Literature. Report prepared for the State of Michigan Cool Cities Team.

Tothero, R. 2003. The Impact of Term Limits on State Legislators' Ambition for Local Office: The Case of the Michigan House. *Publius* 33(3):111–122.

Vey, J. 2007. *Restoring Prosperity: The State Role in Revitalizing America's Older Industrial Cities.* Washington, D.C.: Brookings Institution.

280

CHAPTER 12

The Brain Drain Wars: Characteristics of Recent Movers into and out of Michigan

M. Curtis Hoffman and Jeremy Pyne

More than half the students at Michigan's three biggest universities say they'll leave the state after graduation. . . . Of those who said they plan to leave Michigan, 47% said they'd go where there are good jobs and 24% just want to try living somewhere else. . . . The 24% of students polled who said they'd leave Michigan because they want to see what it's like to live elsewhere exacerbate a so-called brain drain—the flight of young, educated workers—that Metzger [research director for the United Way for Southeastern Michigan] says is predominant in Midwest and Northeastern states. "Brains are going where the population is going" to the South and West Coast, he said. . . . No matter how well the state markets its job offerings, Robert Camaj, 21, of Farmington Hills said the key is in giving young people other reasons to stay. Camaj, who graduated Saturday from U-M, wants to live in a community with vibrant shopping, cleaner streets, better public transit and more culture. "Detroit will always be my home, but for one thing it's kind of scary—in terms of crime and things like that," said Camaj, who plans to attend law school in New York City in the fall. (Shamus 2007)

This 2007 *Detroit Free Press* story is only one example of a popular perception that Michigan is losing a "Brain Drain War."[1] The Brain Drain War has been largely framed by the work of Richard Florida, particularly his 2002 book *The Rise of the Creative Class*. Because of this widespread interest, the Brain Drain War has become a strategic priority among state and local policy makers in Michigan, and throughout the United States.

In this chapter, we look at the history and theory behind the public policy initiatives that constitute the Brain Drain War. In the first section, we review some of the Brain Drain political rhetoric and public policy initiatives from around the United States. In the second part, we look at Michigan's response to this escalating war, with special attention to its unique weapon, the Cool Cities initiative. In the third section, we examine Creative Capital theory, as developed by Richard Florida, his colleagues, and his critics. This theory is the context for Michigan's strategic response to the Brain Drain.

Finally, we use the Census Bureau's 2005 American Community Survey to assess Michigan's won-lost record in the war. By this method we hope to replace purely anecdotal interpretations of Michigan's Brain Drain with conclusions based on empirical evidence. In the last section, we examine the implications of our findings for Michigan's Brain Drain public policies.

There is much literature on international Brain Drain issues, especially the immigration of well-educated young people from the developing world to the United States and Western Europe. We are only examining migration patterns internal to the United States. We do not include in our analysis persons who move directly to or from a foreign country, although we do include foreign-born persons who move within the United States.

The Brain Drain War

The metaphorical first shot in the twenty-first century's Brain Drain War was fired by Tom Ridge, then governor of Pennsylvania, with the "Stay, Invent the Future" initiatives. In his 2001 State of the State address, Governor Ridge said:

> Ladies and Gentlemen, Pennsylvania's single greatest challenge—this year, next year, for all years—is to keep our talent at home. . . . This budget invests $10 million to turn our Brain Drain into a Brain Gain. It's a powerful investment. We'll award grants for inventive local Brain Gain ideas. We'll create new internships to bring our companies and young talent together. And we'll launch a new marketing campaign to alert young people to the extraordinary opportunities in Pennsylvania (Ridge 2001).

Brain Drain concerns have also been expressed by New Hampshire's Jeanne Shaheen (2001), Hawaii's Ben Cayetano (2001), Connecticut's John G. Rowland (2003), Michigan's Jennifer Granholm (2003), Louisiana's Kathleen Blanco (2006), and Iowa's Tom Vilsack (2007).

Some of the most recent activity has been in Indiana, Ohio, and upstate New York. Indiana governor Mitch Daniels (2007) has recommended privatizing the state lottery and using the franchise fee for "a new scholarship for top Hoosier students who remain in-state after graduation, as well as a fund that will enhance the state's key knowledge-based industries by bringing world-class researchers and scholars to Indiana's public universities" (Indiana Office of the Governor 2006: 1). To qualify for the proposed merit-based "Hoosier Hope Scholarships," students would have to agree to live and work in Indiana for three years after graduation; otherwise, their scholarships would turn into a loan that must be repaid.

In 2007, a six-university consortium in Ohio developed the Entrepreneurship Education Consortium "to avoid brain drain and stimulate economic growth." Selected students attend a summer program with the goal "to develop entrepreneurs who will remain in the region after graduation . . . form new enterprises, create new jobs for the labor force, and generate new economic activity" (Case Western Reserve University 2007). In September 2007, Silda Wall Spitzer, wife of then New York governor Eliot Spitzer, hosted the "I Live New York" summit in Cortland, New York. She said, "It has become a crippling, corrosive, chronic problem in our state for at least two decades. . . . You can call it a brain drain or you can call it a lack of a brain gain. But whatever you call it, it is time to focus on ending it" (quoted in Moriarty 2007).

A second front, the "Stem-Cell Brain Drain," opened in 2004, when California governor Arnold Schwarzenegger endorsed Proposition 71 to provide state funding to stem-cell research. Realizing that California was turning from a Brain Gain state to a Brain Drain state,[2] Governor Schwarzenegger argued that "California has always been a pioneer. . . . We daringly led the way for the high-tech industry and now voters can help ensure we lead the way for the biotech" (Schwarzenegger Backs Stem Cell Research 2004). Fearing a biotech Brain Drain to California, several states quickly initiated their own stem-cell research funding, including Wisconsin, Connecticut, Illinois, Maryland, and New Jersey (Brush 2005; Gershman 2007) After authorizing stem-cell funding through an executive order, Illinois governor Rod Blagojevich mounted a letter-writing campaign to lure away Missouri's top biotech scientists and educators (Illinois Office of the Governor 2005). Concern over the Stem-Cell Brain Drain prompted then governor Elliot Spitzer to propose a ballot initiative that would allow the state of New York to borrow money to fund stem-cell and other biomedical research (Gardiner 2006).

The Home Front

In Michigan, the Brain Drain War was anticipated by Governor John Engler in his 2000 State of the State address:

> Michigan job providers have told us that their "recurring and number one concern" is the quality and quantity of Michigan's workforce in the coming decade. To make sure Michigan has enough skilled workers to meet the needs of business, my administration has commissioned the Michigan Economic Development Corporation to launch a strategic plan. Our plan involves recruiting young skilled workers to our state, attracting bright students to study in our world-class institutions of higher learning, and luring skilled immigrants to choose Michigan as the place to pursue the American dream. We are sending the signal that Michigan has the talent to do any job. Michigan businesses will stay here, and outside businesses will move here, based on our people and their skills. The new emphasis in the 21st century must be on people retention. We cannot allow a "brain drain" to develop. (Engler 2000)

When results of the 2000 Census were released, it became more apparent that Michigan was in a vulnerable position. Between 1990 and 2000, the number of Michiganders aged twenty-five to thirty-four dropped by 212,382 (13.5 percent). Among "young, single, and college educated" movers between 1995 and 2000, Michigan's net loss was 16,018, the third highest decline after Pennsylvania and Ohio (Franklin 2003). Michigan ranked near the bottom in terms of the number of out-of-state graduates who migrate into the state (Partnership for Economic Progress 2001). Newspaper headlines began to sound the alarm: "Michigan's Population Slips More—State Stands to Lose More Political Clout by the 2010 Census" (Heath 2002); "Census: 33,371 Young People Bolt Metro Detroit—Exodus since 2000 Is Largest of U.S. Cities; Brain Drain Feared" (Heath and Wisely 2003); "Brain Drain— CENSUS: 22,000 Young Adults Leave Michigan" (Trowbridge and Lee 2006).

When Jennifer Granholm was elected governor of Michigan in 2002, the Brain Drain was no longer perceived as a potential problem, but as a crisis that demanded immediate attention with strong policy initiatives. The Brain Drain of young, educated adults had "become one of Michigan's biggest political issues" (Trowbridge and Lee 2006).

The Cool Cities Initiative

"We want to create cool cities, hip places to live and work." This single line in Governor Jennifer Granholm's (2003) first State of the State address hinted at the development of Michigan's new weapon in the Brain Drain War: Cool Cities. Throughout 2003, Governor Granholm promoted the Cool Cities idea. In August 2003, the Michigan Land Use Leadership Council endorsed policies that promoted the "benefits of walkable and rollable, compact, mixed-use, mixed-income, racially diverse, livable urban cores and neighborhoods that are characteristic of 'cool' cities." The first notable public appearance of Cool Cities was a November 2003 Web site launch. University students and recent college graduates were invited to participate in an on-line survey asking, "What will attract you and your peers from out of state to live and work in vital, lively cities throughout the state?" (www.michigancoolcities.com). In December, a Creating Cool Conference was held in Lansing, with Richard Florida as featured speaker (Range 2003). In January 2004, Governor Granholm officially declared Michigan's engagement in the Brain Drain War:

> Over the last year, we've begun an important dialogue about how we can stimulate the rise of such cool cities in Michigan—cities that attract these young workers and the businesses that rely on their talents. . . . Government can't create cool, but we can and will target existing resources to support these local efforts to create vibrant cities. . . . Young people are rediscovering Grand Rapids, Wyandotte, Ferndale, and Detroit. These coordinated efforts will accelerate that trend which is an economic imperative. For the workforce of tomorrow wants to live where it's happening and employers will not come here if that future workforce, the technology workforce, has left us for New York or Boston or Chicago. (Granholm 2004)

In 2004, a three-year pilot grant program was launched and the first Cool Cities round of funding awarded. The Cool Cities Grants and Planning Program is now administered by the Michigan Department of Labor and Economic Growth (DLEG). While Richard Florida emphasizes the "3Ts" of "technology, talent, and tolerance," the DLEG developed its own grant-making philosophy around the "TIDE" principles of economic development: Talent, Innovation, Diversity, and Environment.

> The TIDE model represents an effort to apply economic development research such as that done by Richard Florida for his book, *The Rise of the Creative Class,* and modify it for use on Michigan's small and large cities. Under the Talent category, communities should review their population and identify the education level or creative backgrounds of the residents. For the Innovation category, communities should be looking at the amount and type of entrepreneurial activity such as patent applications, new business formations, or venture capital investments. Diversity is defined as populations from various cultures and the number of highly skilled immigrants relocating to an area. Finally, Environment includes new development or redevelopment projects, and the types of amenities available in a community such as arts, cultural, and recreational destinations. Also considered is "walkability," which is the attractiveness of the area to pedestrians, including factors such as retail, commercial, and residential options within close proximity. Under additional requirements . . . the focus neighborhood must be located in a city with a community college or university, have a Local Historic District Ordinance or a National Register Historic District, and have a Local Cool Cities Advisory Group as well as an active Local Arts Agency. (Pratt and Tyszkiewicz 2007: 2)

Because of its high profile, several other grant programs initiated at the end of the Engler administration (Main Street, Blueprints for Downtowns, and Blueprints for Neighborhoods) were rebranded under the Cool Cities label. Through 2007, 105 Cool Cities grants worth $6,396,170 have gone to local governments, nonprofit organizations, and public-private partnerships. Ten of these have gone to nonprofit neighborhood and business organizations in Detroit. They have also gone to governments of small places like the villages of Grass Lake (population 1,082), Jonesville (population 2,337), Middleville (population 2,721), and Romeo (population 3,721).

The initial Cool Cities pilot grant expired in 2007, and was not re-funded. Only the absorbed programs (Mainstreet and Blueprints) and other auxiliary activities of the Michigan State Housing Development Authority remain under the Cool Cities brand. These activities include the following.

- Hosting the 2nd International Creative Cities Summit
- Creation of a T.I.D.E. economic growth assessment tool
- Working on a strategy to reinvigorate the Local Cool City Advisory Groups
- Exploring potential for a retention/attraction of young knowledge worker grant program
- Working on piloting an urban grocery store and working with the Governor's Roundtable on Urban Access to Fresh Foods
- Major updates to the www.coolcities.com website, including project pages (K. Gagnon, personal communication, 7 April 2008)

Although Cool Cities is Michigan's flagship initiative, in the "Brain Drain Wars," several other programs are, at least in part, intended to improve the attraction and retention of the residents.

- Michigan Promise Scholarships (formerly MERIT scholarships) provide up to $4,000 to Michiganians for successfully completing two years of postsecondary education at a public or private Michigan college or university. The scholarship awards are merit based, with no need requirements (Student Financial Services Bureau 2006). The funding source is Michigan's share of the 1998 Master Settlement Agreement with the tobacco industry.[3] The MERIT Scholarship program was signed into law in 1999, and the first scholarships were awarded in 2002. For 2007, the program was expanded and the name was changed to the Michigan Promise Scholarship. Public Act 42 of 2007 further amended the scholarship eligibility requirements to include Michiganians who graduate from high school outside Michigan, making the program a potential draw to in-movers (Office of Scholarships and Grants 2007).
- In 2004, the state introduced the Michigan Engineering Incentive, which provides interest-free loans to students pursuing engineering and technology degrees at state universities. The loans remain interest free as long as the recipients continue to study or work in Michigan. Eligibility extends to Michiganians attending school elsewhere and non-Michiganians attending a Michigan school. Supporters of this program tout its economic development potential. Janie Fouke, dean of the Michigan State University College of Engineering, said, "There's a strong link between science, engineering and technology jobs, and economic development or economic growth. . . . The more science and engineering jobs, the better for the state's economy" (quoted in VanHulle 2005).

- The 21st Century Jobs Fund is a plan to award $2 billion in grants between 2006 and 2015 for projects that diversify Michigan's economy, including grants for basic research, applied research, university technology transfer, and the commercialization of products in life sciences, alternative energy, advanced automotive, manufacturing and materials, and homeland security. In 2006, the fund's first year, $126.3 million was awarded through seventy-eight individual grants (Citizens Research Council of Michigan 2007). Because of the state's budget shortfall, most awards for 2007 were delayed until late in the year.

- The Angel Investment Incentive Program grants tax deductions to large investors in budding technology companies. At least $100,000 must be invested between January 2007 and December 2009, and both investor and company must be certified by a state-appointed board. According to Jody Vanderwel, president of the West Michigan–based Grand Angels, "In creating this incentive, the state has recognized a serious need in the business community and demonstrated a commitment to the growth of early stage technology companies. This type of program will lead to increased funding opportunities for young businesses most in need of financial assistance" (Michigan Economic Development Corporation 2007b: 4).

- In 2000, Michigan established ten SmartZones, collaborations between universities, industry, research organizations, government, and other community institutions intended to assist tech companies in incubating and commercializing their products. Two more Smart-Zones have since been established. According to the Michigan Economic Development Corporation (2007c), 592 companies have been assisted by SmartZones, and $774 million has been invested by public agencies and private companies.

- Michigan Regional Skills Alliances (MiRSAs) are state-supported, locally managed partnerships formed to identify labor market solutions for groups of firms operating in the same industry in a specific region. The program was started in 2004 with a start-up grant provided by the Charles Stewart Mott Foundation. As of May 2007, thirty-two MiRSAs have been created. Twelve have a health-care focus; eight have a manufacturing focus. The rest are focused on hospitality and tourism (four), construction (three), information technology (two), utilities (one), forestry and timber (one), and biotechnology (one). In support of the initiative, over $2.75 million in grant money has been awarded (Department of Labor and Economic Growth 2007).

- In 2007, Daniel G. Mulhern, husband of Governor Granholm, became chair of the new Next Great Company Project (NGCP). The NGCP is a partnership with CEOs and top management of eight Michigan businesses: Quicken Loans, Google, Plante & Moran, Bronson Healthcare, Valasis, Citizens Republic Bancorp, Cascade Engineering, and Dow Corning. Governor Granholm initiated the project because "bringing companies together to share their winning strategies in keeping and attracting a first-class workforce provides invaluable insight into making Michigan a great place to live, learn, and earn" (Michigan's First Gentleman 2007). "By fostering an attractive workplace, companies will better be able to attract and retain talent, and that will hopefully help stem Michigan's brain drain and the downslide of the economy" (Granholm, quoted in Jun 2007).

While Cool Cities and these other programs increase the capacity of local governments and other organizations to compete in the Brain Drain wars, it must be emphasized these grants are dwarfed by the money lost in cuts to state revenue sharing. Local governments receive more than $442 million less annually in 2006 than in 2001 (Plante and Morgan 2007: 2–3). According to the Task Force on Local Government Services and Fiscal Stability (2006: 16):

> Since 2001, local communities have lost over $1.5 billion in revenue sharing payments, when compared to the amount that would had been distributed had both the constitutional and statutory formula been fully funded. The constitutional portion of revenue sharing payments have only grown by 6.65% from $649.3 million to $692.5 million between 2002–2006, which is less than the rate of inflation during that time. Statutory revenue sharing reductions, on the other hand, have totaled 58% and accounted for 38% of the state's $4.2 billion GF/GP spending cuts.

Without adequate funding for basic services, local governments probably cannot effectively compete on the quality of life or economic development fronts. Their contributions to the Brain Drain War, although producing the occasional high-profile success, will likely be undermined in the long term.

Creative Capital Theory

Michigan's Cool Cities initiative and its TIDE principles are founded on Richard Florida's work, which is an extension of Human Capital theory. Human Capital theory holds that regional economic growth is now driven by concentrations of educated people rather than by proximity to natural resources or transportation corridors. Human Capital theory is associated with the University of Chicago's Robert E. Lucas (1988) and Harvard's Edward L. Glaeser (Glaeser, Scheinkman, and Shleifer 1995; Glaeser and Shapiro 2001; Berry and Glaeser 2005). Because the arguments of Richard Florida and his associates are similar to those presented in Human Capital theory, they can be referred to as "Creative Capital theory."

Creative Capital theory posits that "creativity, the ability to use human imagination and develop new or original ideas or objects, has different properties from any other input into the economy. . . . Creativity produces a limitless supply of ideas and knowledge which can be shared, used and developed by more than one person, group, organization or firm at a time" (Bell and Jayne 2006: 156).

Florida hypothesizes that tolerance (openness, diversity) enables and attracts talent; talented workers in creative occupations produce technology (innovation); and technology drives economic growth. Florida calls tolerance, talent, and technology the "3Ts" of economic growth.[4] Tolerance is the distinguishing characteristic of Florida's Creative Class Theory.

> What accounts for the ability of some places to secure a greater quantity or quality of these flows? The answer, according to the [Creative Class] theory, lies in openness, diversity, and tolerance. Our work finds a strong connection between successful technology—and talent—harnessing places and places that are open to immigrants, artisans, gays, and racial integration. These are the kinds of places that, by allowing people to be themselves and to validate their distinct identities, mobilize and attract the creative energy that bubbles up naturally from all walks of life. (Florida 2005a: 7)

The Creative Class is relatively mobile, and its migration pattern will result in stimulation or dampening of local economic growth. Thus, according to the theory, the key to a city's economic growth is improving retention and in-migration of the Creative Class.

Florida's definition of Creative Class is rather complex, somewhat like a *matryoshka* (nesting doll), with a large class containing a smaller subclass, which in turn contains an even smaller group.

Creative Professionals are almost one-third of the U.S. workforce and include those who "engage in problem solving drawing on complex bodies of knowledge to solve specific problems" (Florida 2002: 69). Creative Professionals include a wide range of knowledge-intensive occupations, from programmers to librarians; accountants to musicians; lawyers to athletes. Some critics have found this definition too broad because it includes seemingly noncreative occupations like technical support (e.g., Healy 2002: 100). Others find it too narrow, because many excluded jobs have creative possibilities (e.g., Cooke and Paccaluga 2006: 262).

A subset of the Creative Professionals is the Super Creative Core, which is about 12 percent of the U.S. workforce and includes "scientists and engineers, university professors, poets and novelists, artists, entertainers, actors, designers, and architects, as well as the thought leadership of modern society: nonfiction writers, editors, cultural figures, think-tank researchers, analysts and other opinion-makers" (Florida 2002:. 69).

Even smaller groups are bohemians (artists, writers, and performers) and gays (persons living with a same-sex partner). Despite the latter's falling outside of the occupational classification scheme, and the relatively small size of both, Florida and other Creative Capital theorists place great importance on them for several reasons.

• First, they may be a surrogate measure for a region's "tolerance," one of the 3Ts of economic growth. Florida (2004: 200) believes "diverse, inclusive communities that welcome gays, immigrants, artists, and freethinking 'bohemians' are ideal for nurturing creativity and innovations, both keys to success in today's economy." Florida (2005a: 131) finds empirical evidence that gays are associated with technology, another of the 3Ts: "Somewhat surprisingly, the leading indicator of a metropolitan area's high technology success was a large gay population. Gays, as we like to say, can be thought of as canaries of the creative economy, and serve as a strong signal of a diverse, progressive environment."
• Second, these two groups include many who Everett Rogers (1962) called "innovators" and "early adopters." That is, they are the first to embrace new establishments, new neighborhoods, and even new cities that will later be discovered and valued by the larger Creative Class. Bohemians earn a living influencing culture. Gays have a general reputation for having trendy, avant-garde tastes (Wardlow 1996).
• Third, the bohemians include, or work for, many creative entrepreneurs. Gays include many high-income couples with no children, whose above-average disposable income magnifies the impact of their tastes in the marketplace. Development within the arts and culture sector can occur when the latter supports the work of the former. In turn, a reputation for a dynamic arts and culture sector is attractive to others in the Creative Class.

Public policy in Michigan and many other states has been heavily influenced by Creative Capital theory. Because of this heavy reliance on Florida's Creative Capital theory, three questions remain open for debate: Does the Creative Class drive economic growth? Does the Creative Class care more about cool or about career? Is there a major geographic realignment of the Creative Class?

Does the Creative Class Drive Economic Growth?

Florida and other Creative Capital theorists report empirical evidence to support the relationship between creative capital and economic growth. Florida found that between 1990 and 2000, the eleven top-performing regions on his Creativity Index "generated jobs at more than twice the rate of the [eleven least-creative regions], 22 percent versus 11 percent," and between 1999 and 2002, "wages in the top-performing regions grew at almost double the rate (5.1 percent) of the laggards (2.8 percent)" (Florida 2005b: 46, 47). Creative capital is found to be more important than human capital (Market and van Woerkens 2004; Mellander and Florida 2007), low taxes (Florida 2005b), or Robert Putnam's social capital (Florida, Cushing, and Gates 2002).

These conclusions are not unchallenged. Terry Nichols Clark (2004) found that the relationship between gays and economic growth may be spurious, because gay households are highly correlated with college education. Glaeser, using data sets provided by Florida, found that human capital has a stronger association with economic growth than does creative capital:

> Skilled people are the key to urban success. Sure, creativity matters. The people who have emphasized the connection between human capital and growth always argued that this effect reflected the importance of idea transmission in urban areas. But there is no evidence to suggest that there is anything to this diversity or bohemianism, once you control for human capital. As such, mayors are better served by focusing on the basic commodities desired by those with skills, than by thinking that there is a quick fix involved in creating a funky, hip, bohemian downtown. (Glaeser 2005: 496)

Steven Malanga, of the free-market-oriented Manhattan Institute, is Richard Florida's most vitriolic critic and argues that his theory is such a poor predictor of economic performance "that his top cities haven't even outperformed his bottom ones" (Malanga 2004: 41). He believes Creative Capital theory is "completely false" (Malanga 2005a: 7) and a smokescreen for increasing government spending (Malanga 2005b). He maintains that economic growth is fostered by low taxes and small government.

Joel Kotkin (2005) argues that urban growth still depends on cities performing traditional roles: preserving sacred space, providing basic security, and hosting commercial markets. He sees the key to regional growth in healthy suburbs rather than central cities.

Cook and Paccaluga (2006) think Florida is on the right track, but believe that "in order to create knowledge-based regions we must give up the idea of knowledge being an 'essence' that can be produced and transported. Instead we should identify the different knowledge categories and their complex production and circulation mechanisms" (Cook and Paccaluga 2006: 269).

Does the Creative Class Care More about Cool or Career?

Florida argues that an important portion of the Creative Class will make their residency decisions based on a location's openness, diversity, and tolerance rather than solely on its employment opportunities. Florida's (2002: 88–92) analysis of *Information Week* survey data found that only about a third of respondents were compensation driven.

This is challenged by a number of survey-based studies. Partnership for Economic Progress (2001) tracked the migration patterns of 30,000 life science, information technology, and engineering 1997–2000 graduates from Michigan.

> Graduates that choose to accept an out-of-state job do so primarily because of better job opportunities and better salaries—not a dislike of Michigan. 53% left because of a "better job or better opportunity." 11% moved out-of-state to be closer to friends and family. 7% left to get away from the cold/bad weather and 4% cited the lack of social/cultural life. In fact, nearly half of those choosing to live elsewhere are open to relocating back to the state. (Partnership for Economic Progress 2001: 4)

Using Census data, Steven Poelhekke (2006) found that the college-educated were not attracted by diversity but rather by more conventional amenities, particularly the availability of services and home-ownership opportunities.

Is There a Major Geographic Realignment of the Creative Class?

Florida (2006: 34) finds an important geographic realignment of the Creative Class.

> Today, a demographic realignment . . . is under way: the mass reallocation of highly skilled, highly educated, and highly paid Americans to a relatively small number of metropolitan regions, and a corresponding exodus of the traditional lower and middle classes from these same places. Such geographic sorting of people by economic potential, on this scale, is unprecedented. I call it the "means migration."

However, this conclusion is not supported by studies of college graduates in the Midwest. A 2001 study of Michigan college graduates found that Michigan is relatively successful in keeping its highly skilled graduates, although it is an unpopular destination for out-of-state graduates (Partnership for Economic Progress 2001: 5). A more recent study of federal tax returns by the *Detroit News* found that the number of people leaving the Detroit area was dropping, although the number of in-migrants was dropping faster (Heath 2006). The conclusion that retention rates are high but attraction rates are low was also reached in studies on Wisconsin (Brannon and McGee 2001), Ohio (Governor's Commission 2004), and western Pennsylvania (Hansen and Huggins 2001). Thus, the demographic realignment Florida describes may be more a perception than a reality.

The April 2007 poll (Shamus 2007) cited at the beginning of the chapter suggests that graduates are currently very pessimistic about employment in Michigan. This may be due to the perception that college-educated people have been leaving the state. Could the popularity of Florida's theories and the media attention to the Brain Drain be creating a problem that previously did not exist?

Migration and the American Community Survey

A new source of information on interstate migration is the American Community Survey (ACS). The U.S. Census Bureau is phasing in the ACS as a replacement for the decennial long-form questionnaires, which went to about one in six households on census day. The ACS questionnaires go to about 250,000 addresses each month. Both ask similar demographic, social, and economic questions. The primary advantage of ACS over the decennial census is that it will provide updated information every year.[5]

After an eight-year demonstration phase, ACS data collection reached full implementation in 2005 (with the exception of Group Quarters population). For a few years, the ACS dissemination of summary data for local geographies is limited to the most populated counties and cities. Because of the sample size, summary data for less-populated local geographies will be available only after three to five years of data can be collected and aggregated.

One data set derived from the ACS is the Public Use Microsample (PUMS). PUMS files contain a sample of individual ACS records, providing the individual characteristics of housing unit and people. Although the Census Bureau has only released summary data for the most populated counties and cities, PUMS includes records from the entire country. The 2005 ACS PUMS data contain 1,259,653 housing unit records and 2,913,796 person records, which is about one percent of all housing units and persons in the United States.

To maintain confidentiality, PUMS records are stripped of names, addresses, and other identifying information. Rather than census tracts, cities, or counties, PUMS records use only special census geographies called Public Use Microdata Areas (PUMAs). Each PUMA contains a population of about 100,000. PUMAs do not cross state lines and are usually composed of combinations of counties, entire counties, or portions of counties. Michigan is divided into sixty-eight PUMAs. Larger cities may have their own PUMA. In Michigan, Ann Arbor, Grand Rapids, Lansing, Livonia, and Warren are their own PUMA. Detroit is divided into eight PUMAs.

There are a number of limitations to using ACS data. Most involve comparability issues with decennial census data (Bench 2004; Diffendal, Petroni, and Williams 2004). This study does not attempt to compare ACS 2005 to Census 2000. However, the ACS has three important limitations that complicate this analysis of the Michigan Brain Drain.

First, the ACS is best at describing the characteristics of a population, not its size. Thus, comparing the characteristics of the in-migrants and out-migrants is more reliable than determining their exact numbers. The key analysis used in this study relies on the ratio of Creative Class in-migrants to Creative Class out-migrants.

Second, the 2005 ACS did not include the population in "Group Quarters" (for example, prisons, convents, nursing homes, and college dormitories). Many young people leave or enter a state to attend a university. With dormitories excluded from the ACS sample, tracking is problematic. This study only looks at movers over twenty-five years of age. This eliminates most people moving into or out of college dormitories. While they are an important component of Brain Drain migration patterns, analysis of this group will need to wait for new ACS data collected in or after 2006, which will include the Group Quarters population.

Third, although the ACS includes those who immigrated to the United States from abroad, it cannot account for those who left the country. Thus, an ACS sample of movers will be biased toward in-migration. To mitigate this bias, the ACS sample used in this study excludes those who immigrated directly from abroad. However, this study does include foreign-born in-migrants and out-migrants as long the destination and origin of their move are both within the United States.

This chapter is based on 1,592 ACS PUMS records of Michigan in-migrants and 1,145 records of Michigan out-migrants. The PUMS records were obtained through the Integrated

Public Use Microdata Series (IPUMS) project at the Minnesota Population Center, University of Minnesota (Ruggles et al. 2007). The IPUMS project provides value-added features, which makes it a more convenient source than the Census Bureau's own PUMS files.

Migration status is determined by the response to question 14 on the ACS questionnaire, which asks, "Did this person live in this house or apartment 1 year ago?" If not, the respondent provides the city and state (or foreign country) where the respondent lived. The 2005 ACS was administered monthly, January through December 2005. Thus, the moves that are recorded by the 2005 ACS occurred during a twenty-three-month period, from January 2004 to November 2005.

Error ranges are calculated using the Design Factor method described in *PUMS Accuracy of the Data—2005* (U.S. Census Bureau 2006c). Statistical significance is determined by the method described in *Instructions for Applying Statistical Testing to ACS Data* (U.S. Census Bureau 2006b:4)

To identify the Creative Class, four nonexclusive categories are used for the population age twenty-five years and older: Degreed (persons with a four-year or advanced degree), Creative Professionals, Super Creative Core, and Bohemians and Gays. The last three closely follow the definitions used by Florida, varying only because of minor changes in the 2005 ACS occupational codes.

What does the ACS tell us about Michigan's Brain Drain? Do the facts, at least what can be discerned from ACS data, correspond to popular perceptions about the Brain Drain? Do they correspond to what would be expected from Florida's theories? Do they support Florida's critics? What do they suggest about the effectiveness of Michigan's public policies and its strategic position in the Brain Drain wars? Based on the analysis of the ACS data, we are able to make ten conclusions about the Brain Drain War in Michigan.

1. Michigan Is Not Suffering from an Unprecedented Mass Creative Class Exodus.

Florida (2005b, 2006) warns of a great "means migration." However, the evidence in the 2005 ACS suggests that Michigan suffered a rather moderate Brain Drain.

As presented in table 12.1, the out-migration for the Creative Class, age twenty-five years and older, was significantly larger (with 90 percent confidence) than the Creative Class in-migrants only for the Creative Professionals. About 1.3 Creative Professional Michiganians moved out for every Creative Professional who moved in.

2. The Creative Class Is Not Moving Out Faster Than Everyone Else.

Newspaper articles imply that the creative class is exiting fast, often featuring recent college graduates fleeing to other states for jobs. The net loss of the Creative Class (Degreed, Creative Professional, and Super Creative Core) was roughly proportional to the net loss of the general population. The ratio of out-migrating to in-migrating for the Creative Class was estimated to be about 1.3 to one, while for the general population it was about 1.4 to one.

This is good news for those who feared most college graduates could not find jobs in Michigan. But it is still disappointing news for those who hoped that Michigan's Creative Class, which benefits from initiatives like the Michigan Life Sciences Corridor, Cool Cities, SmartZones, and Angel Investment Incentive Program, would have stayed in greater numbers than the acutely suffering blue-collar workforce.

Table 12.1. 2005 Creative Class Migration—Overview

Creative Class, age 25 and other	In-Migration 2005			Out-Migration 2005			Difference p value	Ratio of out-migrants to in-migrants		
	Estimate	90% confidence interval		Estimate	90% confidence interval					
Degreed (4-year or advanced)	36,438	31,746 to	41,130	41,317	36,312 to	46,322	0.24	1.1 (+/– 0.20)	to 1
Creative Professionals	30,560	26,262 to	34,858	39,488	34,595 to	44,381	0.02	1.3 (+/– 0.24)	to 1
Super Creative Core	11,991	9,296 to	14,686	15,635	12,556 to	18,714	0.14	1.3 (+/– 0.39)	to 1
Bohemians and Gays	555	0 to	1,135	3,437	1,993 to	4,881	0.00	6.2 (+/– 6.98)	to 1
All migrants, 25 and over	79,164	72,263 to	86,065	110,521	102,336 to	118,706	0.00	1.4 (+/– 0.16)	to 1

3. A Disproportionate Number of Young Super Creative Class Workers Are Leaving Michigan.

Because of the small sample size, data on migration by age produces few significant differences between Creative Class in-migrants and out-migrants (see table 12.2). However, evidence of a Brain Drain is strong among the young Super Creative Core. An estimated 6,046 young (age twenty-five to twenty-nine) Super Creative Michiganians left the state, replaced by an estimated 3,545 in-movers.

4. A Disproportionate Number of Bohemians and Gays Leave Michigan.

In 2005, a startling 6.2 Bohemian and Gay Michiganians left the state for every one who entered (see table 12.1). Young (age twenty-five to twenty-nine) Bohemians and Gays left at an 8.3 to one ratio (see table 12.2.). Despite the small sample size, these differences are statistically significant.

The in-migration of Bohemians and Gays consists overwhelmingly of returning Michiganders or foreign-born people. Among the estimated 555 Bohemian and Gay in-migrants, only an estimated 33 were born in another state.[6]

Richard Florida places great importance on gays and bohemians as drivers of Creative Class cool and the economic development associated with it. The ACS data suggest that Michigan is very unattractive to gays and bohemians. This may be a result of perceived cultural biases or the banning of gay marriage by Michigan voters in 2004. The situation has probably not improved with the subsequent state attorney general's opinion and a 2007 court ruling holding that state universities and government agencies could not offer employee same-sex partner benefits. If Florida's theories about the Creative Class are correct, Michigan public policies on same-sex marriage and same-sex benefits are undermining those public policies aimed at creating a "cool" image for the state's towns and cities.

5. Michigan Is Not Losing Its Creative Class to the Coasts.

Again, limited sample size means that conclusions about specific states and regions must be tentative. Nonetheless, the map in figure 12.1 indicates that the West Coast and the Northeast corridor are indeed popular destinations for out-migrating degreed Michiganians. But so are the Gary-Chicago-Milwaukee corridor and the Minneapolis-St. Paul metropolitan area.

Table 12.2 shows geographic regions only when the difference between in-migrants and out-migrants is significant at the 90 percent level. As regions, neither the Northeast nor the West had statistically significant net gains against Michigan in terms of Creative Class movers. The map in figure 12.2 suggests that regional generalizations about the Brain Drain may be misleading. Michigan had net Creative Class gains from New York and Pennsylvania in the Northeast, but net losses to New Jersey and Connecticut. Michigan had net gains from Oregon and Utah in the West, but net losses to California and Colorado.

6. Michigan Is Not Losing Its Creative Class to the South.

As stated above, regional generalizations about the Brain Drain are ill-advised. Michigan had net gains from North Carolina and Alabama, but net losses to South Carolina and Georgia.

Table 12.2. 2005 Migration by Age and Selected Destinations/Origins

Creative Class, age 25 and other	In-Migration 2005 Estimate	In-Migration 2005 90% confidence interval	Out-Migration 2005 Estimate	Out-Migration 2005 90% confidence interval	Difference p value	Ratio of out-migrants to in-migrants
Degreed (4-year or advanced) and other						
25 to 29	11,863	9,182 to 14,544	12,798	10,012 to 15,584	0.69	1.1 (+/– 0.34) to 1
Michigan border states	1,925	845 to 3,005	4,118	2,538 to 5,698	0.06	2.1 (+/– 1.45) to 1
South	5,169	3,399 to 6,939	2,805	1,501 to 4,109	0.08	0.5 (+/– 0.31) to 1
30 to 64	22,553	18,859 to 26,247	25,372	21,450 to 29,294	0.39	1.1 (+/– 0.25) to 1
65 and Older	2,022	915 to 3,129	3,147	1,766 to 4,528	0.29	1.6 (+/– 1.09) to 1
South	669	0 to 1,306	2,398	1,192 to 3,604	0.04	3.6 (+/– 3.86) to 1
Creative Professionals						
25 to 29	8,233	5,999 to 10,467	11,184	8,580 to 13,788	0.16	1.4 (+/– 0.49) to 1
Michigan border states	2,014	909 to 3,119	3,977	2,424 to 5,530	0.09	2.0 (+/– 1.33) to 1
Midwest remainder	627	10 to 1,244	1,969	876 to 3,062	0.08	3.1 (+/– 3.55) to 1
30 to 64	21,007	17,442 to 24,572	27,198	23,137 to 31,259	0.06	1.3 (+/– 0.29) to 1
65 and Older	1,320	425 to 2,215	1,106	287 to 1,925	0.77	0.8 (+/– 0.84) to 1
Super Creative Core						
25 to 29	3,545	2,079 to 5,011	6,046	4,131 to 7,961	0.09	1.7 (+/– 0.89) to 1
Michigan border states	322	0 to 764	2,352	1,158 to 3,546	0.01	7.3 (+/– 9.93) to 1
Midwest remainder	199	0 to 546	1,300	412 to 2,188	0.06	6.5 (+/– 14.05) to 1
South	2,051	936 to 3,166	724	61 to 1,387	0.09	0.4 (+/– 0.38) to 1
30 to 64	7,812	5,636 to 9,988	9,426	7,035 to 11,817	0.41	1.2 (+/– 0.45) to 1
65 and Older	634	14 to 1,254	163	0 to 477	0.29	0.3 (+/– 0.69) to 1
Bohemians and Gays						
25 to 29	169	0 to 489	1,406	483 to 2,329	0.04	8.3 (+/– 20.72) to 1
30 to 64	386	0 to 870	1,805	759 to 2,851	0.04	4.7 (+/– 5.61) to 1
65 and Older	0		226	0 to 596	0.50	

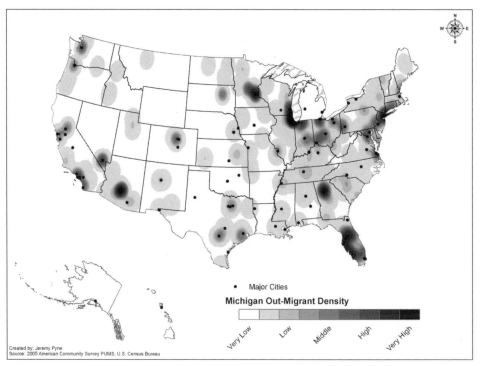

FIGURE 12.1
Destination of Creative Class Out-migrants, 2005

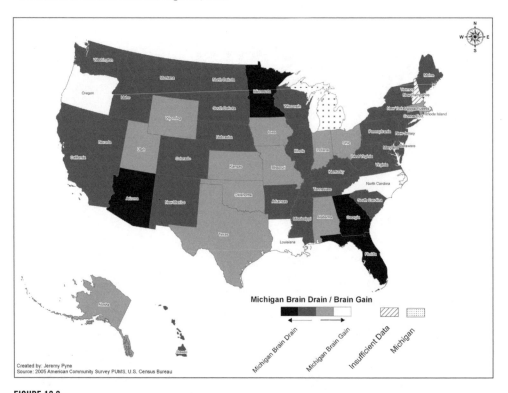

FIGURE 12.2
Net Migration (relative to Michigan) of the Creative Class, by State, 2005

Rather than a drain to the South, young degreed people moved into Michigan from the South. An estimated 2,484 young (age twenty-five to twenty-nine) degreed Michiganians left for the South, but an estimated 5,169 young degreed people made a reverse move. This is likely a temporary situation caused by Hurricane Katrina relocations, as the top two states of origin were Texas and Louisiana. Also, this effect did not show up in the Creative Professional and Super Creative Core categories, presumably because the newly arrived, degree-holding Katrina evacuees did not yet have Creative Class jobs in Michigan.

Older degreed Michiganians did move to the South. An estimated 2,398 older (age sixty-five and older) degreed Michiganians left the state, while only an estimated 564 made a reverse move. This effect did not show up in the Creative Professional and Super Creative Core categories, presumably because most of these people were retired and were not, by definition, part of the Creative Class.

7. Michigan Is Not Losing Its Creative Class to Low-Tax States.

According to Malanga (2004, 2005a, 2005b), low taxes are attractive, and low-tax states might be expected to be winners in the Brain Drain War with Michigan. However, a generalization about taxes seems as unfounded as the regional generalizations discussed above. Michigan was a net winner with many states that ranked lower on the 2005 tax burden index (Tax Foundation 2007), including Alabama, Tennessee, and Texas. Michigan was a net loser to many states that ranked higher on the tax burden index, including Minnesota, Wisconsin, and California.

8. Michigan Is Losing Its Super Creative Class to Chicago and Minneapolis.

The biggest draw for Super Creative Michiganians is not high-tech Seattle, smart-growth Portland, low-tax Las Vegas, supercool Austin, good-weather San Diego, or never-sleeping New York. The biggest draw is Chicago. It may be that only Chicago is within close proximity to Michigan, and has the size, amenities, and job market that can attract a Midwest-raised Creative Class. But all hope is not lost. Minneapolis–St. Paul—smaller, colder, and more remote than Chicago—has also become a very popular destination for Michigan's out-migrating Creative Class.

9. Michigan Holds Its Native Population, but Is Unattractive to Outsiders.

The Partnership for Economic Progress (2001) suggests that Michigan retains its native population but is unable to attract outsiders, at least among new college graduates. As table 12.3 suggests, the reality is rather more complicated. In general, the exiting Creative Class Michiganders are replaced, one for one, by entering nonnative Michiganites. However, these Michiganites do not stay. The out-migrating Creative Class population was Michiganite by half or more. Their number was much larger than the number of returning Michiganders. About 1.7 Michiganite Creative Professionals left for every Michigander who returned. This suggests that rather than marketing Michigan to outsiders, the state may need to be marketed to the Michiganites who have already moved into the state.

10. In the Long Run, Michigan Is Slowly Losing the Brain Drain War.

Analyzing the place of birth reported in the ACS data suggests that the long-term effect of migration on Michigan's Creative Class has been substantial (see table 12.4). By any definition,

Table 12.3. 2005 Migration Replacement Ratios

Creative Class, age 25 and other	In-Migration 2005			Out-Migration 2005			Difference p value	Ratio of out-migrants to in-migrants			
	Estimate	90% confidence interval		Estimate	90% confidence interval						
Degreed (4-year or advanced)											
Exiting non-natives vs. returning (native) Michiganders	11,187	8,584 to	13,790	17,498	14,241 to	20,755	0.01	1.6	(+/–	0.47	) to 1
Exiting (native) Michiganders vs. entering non-natives	18,858	15,479 to	22,237	15,615	12,538 to	18,692	0.24	0.8	(+/–	0.22	) to 1
Exiting foreign-born vs. entering foreign-born	6,393	4,425 to	8,361	8,204	5,974 to	10,434	0.32	1.3	(+/–	0.53	) to 1
Creative Professionals											
Exiting non-natives vs. returning (native) Michiganders	9,694	7,271 to	12,117	16,165	13,034 to	19,296	0.01	1.7	(+/–	0.53	) to 1
Exiting (native) Michiganders vs. entering non-natives	15,237	12,200 to	18,274	17,816	14,529 to	21,103	0.34	1.2	(+/–	0.32	) to 1
Exiting foreign-born vs. entering foreign-born	5,629	3,782 to	7,476	5,507	3,680 to	7,334	0.94	1.0	(+/–	0.46	) to 1
Super Creative Core											
Exiting non-natives vs. returning (native) Michiganders	3,455	2,008 to	4,902	6,162	4,229 to	8,095	0.06	1.8	(+/–	0.93	) to 1
Exiting (native) Michiganders vs. entering non-natives	5,786	3,913 to	7,659	6,004	4,096 to	7,912	0.89	1.0	(+/–	0.47	) to 1
Exiting foreign-born vs. entering foreign-born	2,750	1,459 to	4,041	3,469	2,019 to	4,919	0.54	1.3	(+/–	0.79	) to 1
Bohemians and Gays											
Exiting non-natives vs. returning (native) Michiganders	378	0 to	857	1,815	766 to	2,864	0.04	4.8	(+/–	5.86	) to 1
Exiting (native) Michiganders vs. entering non-natives	33	0 to	174	1,337	437 to	2,237	0.03	40.5	(+/–	499.08	) to 1
Exiting foreign-born vs. entering foreign-born	144	0 to	440	285	0 to	701	0.69	2.0	(+/–	6.25	) to 1

Table 12.4. Long-Term Effect of Creative Class Migration—Overview

Creative Class, age 25 and other	Adopted Michiganians		Expat Michiganians		Difference p value	Ratio of expat Michiganders to adopted Michiganians
	Estimate	90% confidence interval	Estimate	90% confidence interval		
Degreed (4-year or advanced)	437,675	421,749 to 453,601	899,710	876,388 to 923,032	0.00	2.1 (+/– 0.09) to 1
Creative Professionals	413,679	398,176 to 429,182	866,283	843,397 to 889,169	0.00	2.1 (+/– 0.10) to 1
Super Creative Core	147,038	137,666 to 156,410	293,232	279,904 to 306,560	0.00	2.0 (+/– 0.16) to 1
Bohemians and Gays	20,283	16,779 to 23,787	47,787	42,404 to 53,170	0.00	2.4 (+/– 0.49) to 1
All 25 and Over	1,904,928	1,874,397 to 1,935,459	2,363,261	2,325,559 to 2,400,963	0.00	1.2 (+/– 0.03) to 1

Table 12.5. Long-term Effect of Creative Class Migration by U.S. Regions

Creative Class, age 25 and other	Adopted Michiganites Estimate	90% confidence interval		Expat Michiganians Estimate	90% confidence interval		Difference p value	Ratio of expat Michiganders to adopted Michiganites
Degreed (4-year or advanced)								
Northeast	95,178	87,617 to	102,739	99,538	91,770 to	107,306	0.51	1.0 (+/− 0.12) to 1
Michigan border states	165,507	155,573 to	175,441	165,634	155,615 to	175,653	0.99	1.0 (+/− 0.09) to 1
Midwest remainder	46,798	41,483 to	52,113	45,755	40,488 to	51,022	0.82	1.0 (+/− 0.16) to 1
South	91,127	83,728 to	98,526	328,196	314,096 to	342,296	0.00	3.6 (+/− 0.33) to 1
West	34,413	29,853 to	38,973	253,506	241,112 to	265,900	0.00	7.4 (+/− 1.04) to 1
Alaska and Hawaii	4,652	2,973 to	6,331	7,080	5,008 to	9,152	0.13	1.5 (+/− 0.71) to 1
Creative Professionals								
Northeast	83,358	76,278 to	90,438	82,152	75,095 to	89,209	0.84	1.0 (+/− 0.12) to 1
Michigan border states	152,525	142,982 to	162,068	155,032	145,338 to	164,726	0.76	1.0 (+/− 0.09) to 1
Midwest remainder	41,979	36,944 to	47,014	46,726	41,403 to	52,049	0.29	1.1 (+/− 0.18) to 1
South	95,177	87,616 to	102,738	333,685	319,468 to	347,902	0.00	3.5 (+/− 0.32) to 1
West	36,669	31,962 to	41,376	242,036	229,926 to	254,146	0.00	6.6 (+/− 0.91) to 1
Alaska and Hawaii	3,971	2,419 to	5,523	6,652	4,644 to	8,660	0.08	1.7 (+/− 0.83) to 1
Super Creative Core								
Northeast	30,570	26,271 to	34,869	31,903	27,505 to	36,301	0.72	1.0 (+/− 0.21) to 1
Michigan border states	52,695	47,057 to	58,333	47,943	42,551 to	53,335	0.31	0.9 (+/− 0.14) to 1
Midwest remainder	15,054	12,035 to	18,073	17,137	13,913 to	20,361	0.44	1.1 (+/− 0.31) to 1
South	33,560	29,056 to	38,064	107,865	99,779 to	115,951	0.00	3.2 (+/− 0.49) to 1
West	14,309	11,365 to	17,253	85,935	78,717 to	93,153	0.00	6.0 (+/− 1.33) to 1
Alaska and Hawaii	850	132 to	1,568	2,449	1,230 to	3,668	0.06	2.9 (+/− 2.82) to 1
Bohemians and Gays								
Northeast	3,026	1,672 to	4,380	5,394	3,585 to	7,203	0.08	1.8 (+/− 1.00) to 1
Michigan border states	8,805	6,495 to	11,115	6,503	4,517 to	8,489	0.21	0.7 (+/− 0.30) to 1
Midwest remainder	2,519	1,283 to	3,755	2,177	1,028 to	3,326	0.74	0.9 (+/− 0.62) to 1
South	4,620	2,947 to	6,293	19,407	15,977 to	22,837	0.00	4.2 (+/− 1.69) to 1
West	1,313	421 to	2,205	13,991	11,078 to	16,904	0.00	10.7 (+/− 7.57) to 1
Alaska and Hawaii	0			315	0 to	752	0.38	

members of the Creative Class who lived in Michigan in 2005 but were born elsewhere in the United States (Michiganites) were outnumbered about two to one by members of the Creative Class who were born in Michigan, but are now expatriates living elsewhere else in the United States.[7]

The regional patterns that do not show up in the 2005 migration data do reveal themselves in the place-of-birth data. Expat Creative Professional Michiganders live in large numbers in the South and West (see table 12.5). Expat Creative Professional Michiganders living in the West outnumber western-born Michiganites by about 6.6 to 1.0. Likewise, Expat Creative Professional Michiganders in the South outnumber southern-born Michiganites by about 3.6 to 1.0. The ratios are similar for the Degreed and Super Creative categories.

The 2005 ACS data suggest Michigan has suffered a slow Brain Drain for many years, and the recent Brain Drain is not exceptional. However, the popular perception of a severe Brain Drain is growing, and may eventually prove to be a self-fulfilling prophesy. This could place Michigan's long-term recovery in jeopardy, as future economic development will depend heavily on the activities of people with both technical expertise and an entrepreneurial spirit.

The Brain Drain and Michigan Public Policy

Cool Cities is a high-profile program that has the potential to change both the characteristics and perceptions of many of Michigan's towns and cities. However, even when combined with other state Brain Drain programs noted earlier, the money gained by localities is dwarfed by losses in state revenue sharing. In the long run, deterioration of city services will likely outweigh visible improvements to city streetscapes and other investments that enhance a Creative Class environment. News reports of job losses will continue to outweigh publicity about Cool Cities grants.

Yet in her 2007 State of the State address, Governor Granholm (2007) continued to endorsed a creative capital (or at least human capital) approach to economic development: "Because the fastest job-creating states are the states that have the most educated workforces, our overriding education goal *must* be to double the number of college graduates in Michigan. That's why we created the Michigan Promise scholarship." That is also why the Granholm administration wages an annual battle—cajoling, bartering, threatening, and pleading—to get the boards of state universities to minimize tuition increases. But the chicken or egg question remains. Is fast growth attracting an educated workforce, or are educated workers producing the economic growth? Even assuming the governor is correct, the policy is compromised by the state's fiscal crisis. Just as the benefits of the Cool Cities program are undermined by reductions in state revenue sharing, the Michigan Promise Scholarship program is undermined by cuts in university funding and the perception that Michigan jobs are scarce for college graduates.

Unfortunately, no amount of cool is likely to make Grand Rapids, Ypsilanti, or Bay City competitive with Chicago. Only a revitalized Detroit–Ann Arbor metro area could conceivably compete with Chicago. As hard as that is to imagine, the Minneapolis–St. Paul area may hold the key. Understanding more about the appeal of this midwestern urban center might provide clues as to how Michigan might still win the Brain Drain War.

Notes

1. The story is reporting on a poll conducted by Selzer & Co. for the *Detroit Free Press* and WVID "Local 4" TV. Selzer surveyed 640 students by phone April 9–16 at Michigan State University, Wayne State University, and the University of Michigan. The margin of error was reported as plus or minus 3.9 percentage points.

2. The 2000 Census indicated that 2.2 million people moved out of California during the second half of the 1990s, while only 1.4 million moved in.

3. Because of the tobacco settlement, Michigan will receive $279–365 million annually until 2023 (Public Sector Consultants 2002). Other states with merit-based scholarships include Alaska, Florida, Georgia, Indiana, Kentucky, Louisiana, Mississippi, Nevada, New Mexico, South Carolina, South Dakota, Washington, and West Virginia. Michigan's is the only program that terminates at two years, regardless of merit (Duffourc 2006).

4. Florida list the 3Ts as "technology, talent, and tolerance." They are presented here in reverse order to emphasize the sequential logic of their interrelationship.

5. The information on the ACS in this and the following paragraphs was obtained from U.S. Census Bureau (2006a, 2006d) and Missouri Census Data Center (2006).

6. Because the tables combine bohemians and gays, it is worth noting that of the estimated 3,437 Bohemians and Gays who left the state in 2005, 66 percent were Bohemians, 31 percent were Gays, and 3 percent were both. Of the 555 Bohemians and Gays who entered the state, 100 percent were Bohemians and none were Gays.

7. The people of Michigan are referred to as "Michiganders" (usually by people from Michigan), "Michiganians" (usually by Michigan state officials), and "Michiganites" (usually by people unfamiliar with Michigan). We have taken advantage of having three terms for residents of Michigan and adopted the convention of referring to all persons born in Michigan as Michiganders, even if they have moved out of the state. We refer to people born outside of Michigan but who have moved into the state as Michiganites. We refer to all persons residing in Michigan, both natives and in-migrants, as Michiganians.

REFERENCES

Atkinson, R. D., and D. K. Correa. 2007. *The 2007 State New Economy Index.* Washington, D.C.: Information Technology and Innovation Foundation.

Bell, D., and M. Jayne. 2006. *Small Cities (Questioning Cities).* New York: Routledge.

Bench, K. M. 2004. *Comparing Quality Measures: The American Community Survey's Three-Year Averages and Census 2000's Long Form Sample Estimates.* Meeting 21st Century Demographic Data Needs— Implementing the American Community Survey: Report 7. Washington, D.C.: U.S. Census Bureau.

Berry, C. R., and E. L. Glaeser. 2005. The Divergence of Human Capital Levels across Cities. *Regional Science* 84:407–444.

Blanco, K. 2006. Louisiana State of the State Address. Http://www.stateline.org/live/details/speech?contentId=101167.

Brannon, J. I., and M. K. McGee. 2001. Draining Away: Who Is Leaving the State? Where Are They Going? *Wisconsin Policy Research Institute Report,* August.

Brush, S. 2005. Hoping to Avoid Brain Drain, States Push to Finance Stem-Cell Research. *Chronicle of Higher Education* 51:A22.

Case Western Reserve University. 2007. Higher Ed Consortium to Give Student Entrepreneurs Training. Weatherhead School of Management. Http://weatherhead.case.edu/entrepreneurship/.

Cayetano, B. 2001. Hawaii State of the State Address. Http://www.stateline.org/live/details/speech?contentId=16075.

Citizens Research Council of Michigan. 2007. Survey of Economic Development Programs in Michigan, Second Edition. Online: Http://crcmich.org/PUBLICAT/2000s/2007/rpt347.pdf.

Clark, T. N. 2004. Gays and Urban Development: How Are They Linked? In *The City as an Entertainment Machine*, edited by Terry Nichols Clark. *Research in Urban Policy* 9:221–234. Greenwich, Conn.: JAI Press.

Cooke, P., and A. Paccaluga. 2006. *Regional Development in the Knowledge Economy*. New York: Routledge.

Daniels, M. E., Jr. 2007. Indiana State of the State Address. Http://www.stateline.org/live/details/speech?contentId=171779.

Diffendal, G. J., Rita Jo Petroni, and Andre L. Williams. 2004. *Comparison of the American Community Survey Three-Year Averages and the Census Sample for a Sample of Counties and Tracts*. Meeting 21st Century Demographic Data Needs—Implementing the American Community Survey, Report 8. Washington, D.C.: U.S. Census Bureau.

Duffourc, D. 2006. State-Funded College Scholarships: General Definitions and Characteristics. *Review of Policy Research* 23:235–248.

Engler J. 2000. Michigan Gov Embraces State Power. Http://www.stateline.org/live/details/story?contentId=13905.

Florida, R. 2002. *The Rise of the Creative Class and How It's Transforming Work, Leisure, Community and Everyday Life*. New York: Basic Books.

———. 2003. Technology and Tolerance: The Importance of Diversity to High-Technology Growth. In *The City as an Entertainment Machine*, edited by Terry Nichols Clark. *Research in Urban Policy* 9:199–220. Greenwich, Conn.: JAI Press.

———. 2005a. *Cities and the Creative Class*. New York: Routledge.

———. 2005b. *The Flight of the Creative Class: The New Global Competition for Talent*. New York: Harper-Collins.

———. 2006. Where the Brains Are. *Atlantic Monthly* 298(3):34–36.

Florida, R., R. Cushing, and G. Gates. 2002. When Social Capital Stifles Innovation. *Harvard Business Review* 80(88):20.

Franklin, R. S. 2003. *Migration of the Young, Single, and College Educated: 1995 to 2000* [CENSR-12]. Washington, D.C.: U.S. Census Bureau.

Gardiner, B. 2006. New York Could Face Stem Cell Brain Drain. *New York Sun*, October 9. Http://www.nysun.com/article/41158.

Gershman, D. 2007. Other States More Permissive. *Ann Arbor News*, March 4. Mlive. Http://www.mlive.com/search/index.ssf?/base/news-21/1172994816257380.xml?aanews?NEA&coll=2.

Glaeser, E. L. 2005. Review of *The Rise of the Creative Class*, by Richard Florida. *Regional Science and Urban Economics* 35:593–596.

Glaeser, E. L., J. Scheinkman, and A. Shleifer. 1995. Economic Growth in a Cross-section of Cities. *Journal of Monetary Economics* 36:117–143.

Glaeser, E. L., and J. Shapiro. 2001. *Is There a New Urbanism? The Growth of U.S. Cities in the 1990s.* Cambridge, Mass.: National Bureau of Economic Research.

Governor's Commission on Higher Education and the Economy. 2004. *Building on Knowledge, Investing in People: Higher Education and the Future of Ohio's Economy.* Columbus, Ohio: Governor's Commission on Higher Education and the Economy.

Granholm, J. 2003. Michigan: Greatness Through Challenge. Http://www.michigan.gov/gov/0,1607,7–168–23442_21981–60490—,00.html.

———. 2004. Our Determination, Our Destination: A 21st Century Economy. Http://www.michigan.gov/gov/0,1607,7–168–23442_21981–84911—,00.html.

———. 2007. Our Moment, Our Choice: Investing in Michigan's People. Http://www.michigan.gov/gov/0,1607,7–168–23442_21981–161761—,00.html.

Hansen, S., and L. Huggins. 2001. *Career and Location Decisions: Recent Pittsburgh Area University Graduates.* Pittsburgh: Graduate School of International and Public Affairs at the University of Pittsburgh.

Healy, K. 2002, What's New for Culture in the New Economy? *Journal of Arts Management, Law, and Society* 32:86–102.

Heath, B. 2002. Michigan's Population Slips More—State Stands to Lose More Political Clout by the 2010 Census. *Detroit News,* December 23. Newsbank via Grand Valley State University Libraries. Http://www.gvsu.edu/library/.

———. 2006. Metro Area Lures Fewer Residents. *Detroit News,* April 20. Newsbank via Grand Valley State University Libraries. Http://www.gvsu.edu/library/.

Heath, B., and J. Wisely. 2003. Census: 33,371 Young People Bolt Metro Detroit. *Detroit News,* September 18. Newsbank via Grand Valley State University Libraries. Http://www.gvsu.edu/library/.

Illinois Office of the Governor. 2005. Gov. Blagojevich and Comptroller Hynes Encourage Missouri Scientists and Doctors to Continue Life-Saving Stem Cell Research in Illinois. Press release, August 29. Illinois Government News Network. Http://www.illinois.gov/news/.

Indiana Office of the Governor. 2006. Governor Outlines Plans to Attack "Brain Drain." Press release, December 14. Governor Daniels Press Calendar. Http://www.in.gov/apps/utils/calendar/presscal?PF=gov2&Clist=196.

Jun, C. 2007. CEOs Enlisted for Education Project. *Detroit News,* April 18. Newsbank via Grand Valley State University Libraries. Http://www.gvsu.edu/library/.

Kotkin. J. 2005. *The City: A Global History.* New York: Modern Library

Lucas, R. 1988. On the Mechanics of Economic Growth. *Journal of Monetary Economics* 22:3–42.

Malanga, S. 2004. The Curse of the Creative Class. *City Journal* 14(1):38–45.

———. 2005a. Florida Daze. *City Journal* 15(2):7–9.

———. 2005b. *The New New Left: How American Politics Works Today.* Chicago: Ivan R. Dee

Mellander, C., and R. Florida. 2007. *The Creative Class or Human Capital? Explaining regional development in Sweden Royal Institute of Technology* [Working Paper Series in Economics and Institutions of Innovation 79]. Stockholm: Centre of Excellence for Science and Innovation Studies.

Michigan Department of Labor and Economic Growth. 2007. Michigan Regional Skills Alliances Fact Sheet. Michigan.org. Http://www.michigan.gov/documents/rsa/Fact_Sheet_7_199296_7.doc.

Michigan Economic Development Corporation. 2001. Report Shows Michigan Successfully Retains Tech Graduates [Press Release, September 21]. Michigan.org. Http://www.michigan.org/medc/news/major/archive/.

———. 2006. Governor Granholm Announces 24 More 21st Century Jobs Fund Winners. Press release, October 16. Michigan.org. Http://www.michigan.org/medc/news/major/archive/.

———. 2007a. Cool Cities FAQ. Michigan.org. Http://www.coolcities.com/whatscool/faq/.

———. 2007b. Governor and MEDC Announce New Tax Incentive for 'Angel' Investors. Press release, January 18. Michigan.org. Http://www.michigan.org/angels.

———. 2007c. Michigan SmartZones. Michigan.org. Http://www.michigan.org/medc/smartzones/.

Michigan's First Gentleman. 2007. Governor, First Gentleman Launch Next Great Companies Project. Michigan.org. Http://www.michigan.gov/firstgentleman/0,1607,7–178–24380–166555—,00.html.

Missouri Census Data Center. 2006. Ten Things to Know about the American Community Survey—2005 edition. Http://mcdc2.missouri.edu/pub/data/acs2005/Ten_things_to_know.shtml.

Moriarty, R. 2007. Stopping the Brain Drain. *Post-Standard,* September 19. Http://www.syracuse.com/articles/business/index.ssf?/base/business-10/1190192765230130.xml&coll=1.

Office of Scholarships and Grants. 2007. Michigan Promise Scholarship. Http://www.michigan.gov/mistudentaid.

Park, A. 2007. The View from Florida-ville. *Fast Company* 113:43.

Partnership for Economic Progress. 2001. *Attracting and Retaining the Best Talent to Michigan: An Overview of College Migration Patterns at Michigan Public Universities.* Lansing: Michigan Economic Development Corporation.

Plante and Morgan, PLLC. 2007. Get Your Crystal Ball Out . . . What Will Michigan's Municipal Finance Model Look Like in the Years to Come? *Municipal Flash Advisor* (March):1–4.

Poelhekke, S. 2006. *Do Amenities and Diversity Encourage City Growth? A Link Through Skilled Labor.* EUI Working Paper ECO No. 2006/10. Florence, Italy: European University Institute.

Pratt, E., and M. Tyszkiewicz. 2007. *Cool Cities.* Issue Paper, Senate Fiscal Agency of the State of Michigan.

Public Sector Consultants, Inc. 2002. Tobacco Settlement. In *Michigan in Brief: 2002–03.* 7th ed. Lansing: Michigan Nonprofit Association and the Council of Michigan Foundations.

Range, S. 2003. "Hipsters," Granholm Discuss Cool Cities. *Lansing State Journal,* December 12. Newsbank via Grand Valley State University Libraries. Http://www.gvsu.edu/library/.

Ridge, T. 2001. Pennsylvania State of the State Address. Stateline.org. Http://www.stateline.org/live/details/speech?contentId=16087.

Rochester, City of. 2007. Angel Program Grants Tax Credits for Investors. *Rochester Hills Business Report.*

Rogers, E. M. 1962. *Diffusion of Innovation.* New York: Free Press.

Rowland, J. G. 2003. Connecticut State of the State Address. Stateline.org. Http://www.stateline.org/live/details/speech?contentId=16139.

Ruggles, S., M. Sobek, T. Alexander, C. A. Fitch, R. Goeken, P. K Hall, M. King, and C. Ronnander. 2007. Integrated Public Use Microdata Series: Version 3.0. Minnesota Population Center. Http://usa.ipums.org/usa/.

Schwarzenegger Backs Stem Cell Research. 2004. *New York Times,* October 19. InfoTrac via Grand Valley State University Libraries. Http://www.gvsu.edu/library/.

Shaheen, J. 2001. New Hampshire Inaugural Address. Stateline.org. Http://www.stateline.org/live/details/speech?contentId=16050.

Shamus, K. J. 2007. Most Plan to Learn, Leave: Graduates of Big State Colleges Won't Stick Around, Poll Shows. *Detroit Free Press,* April 29. Freep.com. Http://www.freep.com/apps/pbcs.dll/article?AID=/20070429/NEWS06/704290649/1008.

Student Financial Services Bureau. 2006. *Paying for College in Michigan.* Lansing: Michigan Department of Treasury.

Task Force on Local Government Services and Fiscal Stability. 2006. *Final Report to the Governor.* Lansing, Mich.: Task Force on Local Government Services and Fiscal Stability.

Tax Foundation. 2007. State and Local Tax Burdens by State, 1970–2007. Taxfoundation.org. Http://www.taxfoundation.org/taxdata/show/335.html.

Trowbridge, G., and A. Lee. 2006. Brain Drain—CENSUS: 22,000 Young Adults Leave Michigan. *Detroit News,* August 4. Newsbank via Grand Valley State University Libraries. Http://www.gvsu.edu/library.

U.S. Census Bureau. 2006a. *American Community Survey Data User Training Guide.* Census.gov. Http://www.census.gov/acs/www/Products/users_guide/acs_data_user_training.htm.

———. 2006b. *Instructions for Applying Statistical Testing to ACS Data.* Census.gov. Http://www2.census.gov/acs2005/ACS_2005_Statistical_Testing.doc.

———. 2006c. *PUMS Accuracy of the Data—2005.* Census.gov. Http://www.census.gov/acs/www/Downloads/ACS/accuracy2005.pdf.

———. 2006d. *Using Data from the 2005 American Community Survey.* Census.gov. Http://www.census.gov/acs/www/UseData/advance_copy_user_guide.pdf.

VanHulle, L. 2005. Engineering, Tech. Students Could Get Interest-Free Loans. March 25. *State News.* Http://www.statenews.com/article.phtml?pk=29258.

Vilsack, T. 2007. Iowa Condition of the State. Stateline.org. Http://www.stateline.org/live/details/speech?contentId=169994.

Wardlow, D. L. 1996. Gays, Lesbians, and Consumer Behavior: Theory, Practice, and Research Issues in Marketing. Binghamton, N.Y.: Haworth Press.

PART 4

Towards a Triple Bottom Line

CHAPTER 13

Building a Triple Bottom Line Sustainability Model in Michigan

Norman Christopher and Richard W. Jelier

Sustainable development involves simultaneously creating flourishing ecosystems, vibrant communities, stronger economies and improving the quality of life for all in the present without compromising the quality of life for future generations (U.S. Partnership for the Decade of Education for Sustainable Development 2005). Overall, when one looks at sustainable cities and communities, they reveal common characteristics, including the development of goals that are rooted in a respect for both the natural and the human environment. Sustainable development calls for the appropriate and creative use of technology that serves both of these resources, the attainment of high values and quality of life, optimization and leverage of key resources, maintenance of scale and capacity, adoption of a systems approach, support of life cycles, responsiveness and proactiveness to issues, value for diversity, and preservation of heritage (Centre of Excellence for Sustainable Development 2006).

David Brower, founder of the Earth Institute, stated, "We do not inherit the earth from our fathers, we borrow it from our children."[1] In modern times, the discussion on sustainable development was first initiated by the World Commission on Environment and Development (WCED), organized by the United Nations (UN) in 1983 and commonly known by the name of its chair, Gro Harlem Brundtland. The Brundtland Commission was created to address the deterioration of the human environment and natural resources and the consequences of that deterioration for economic and social development. The commission's final report in 1987 defined sustainability as "meeting the needs of today without compromising the ability of future generations to meet their own needs." Today, the UN Division for Sustainable Development lists forty-two different areas within the scope of sustainable development. While sustainability guiding principles have been in existence for nearly twenty-five years, only recently have many regions, cities, and communities worldwide used them comprehensively to rebuild, grow, and transform. Today, almost every major newspaper, publication, trade journal, and broadcast network has had a major story or headline focused on sustainable development or "greening." Stuart Hart (2005), in his book *Capitalism at the Crossroads,* addresses greening in simplistic terms as doing "less bad." Sustainability, on the other hand, calls us to action, which leads to doing "more good." Business, the environment, and society always exist in tension and, depending upon the issue, create varying degrees of resource scarcity, prosperity, and service conflicts.

In Europe, sustainable development principles have driven many of the European Union (EU) programs such as those that address climate change.[2] Similarly, in Australia, sustainable development principles have been elevated to something akin to a national religion. The Ecological Sustainable Development Process, Australia's first formal government initiative aimed at promoting sustainable development, was launched in 1989. By 1992, Australia produced the National Strategy for Ecologically Sustainable Development, which was endorsed by all Australian governments and the Australian Local Government Association, providing the broad agenda for sustainable development. Today, the Business of Sustainable Development Initiative (2000) also encourages environmental and economic efficiency for *all* of Australia's industry.

Similarly, New Zealand, has been a global leader in systematically advancing sustainability principles. New Zeeland is striving to become the world's "first truly sustainable nation," with an agenda that emerged from the Resource Management Act of 1991 that stresses "more sustainable practices in New Zealand households, communities, businesses, local authorities and central government" (New Zeeland Ministry of Economic Development). The agenda is anchored by six major sustainability initiatives, each of which is being spearheaded by the Ministry of Economic Development and the Ministry for the Environment. These initiatives have translated into two specific strategies to date, the New Zeeland Energy Strategy and the Emissions Trading Scheme (both were introduced in fall of 2007).

In addition to the European, Australian, and New Zealand examples, a growing number of U.S. cities have embraced sustainability guiding principles are beginning to report measurable progress that can serve as important benchmarks for further action.[3] Doug Thompson, a national sustainability expert who worked early on with leaders in Grand Rapids to advance sustainability, suggested a number of communities that could help Grand Rapids shape its sustainable development strategy. This chapter highlights a few of these cities, where sustainability efforts have already led to clear outcomes. The cities and communities that we highlight include Seattle, Chicago, Portland (Oregon), and Denver. SustainLane (April 2008) lists Portland #1, Seattle #3, Chicago #4, and Denver #11 as America's most sustainable cities. Our Green Cities (April 2008) lists Seattle #1, Denver #2, Chicago #7, and Portland #10.[4] Appendix 1 describes some of the key sustainability outcomes in these cities.

In the Midwest, Greater Grand Rapids is emerging as a model for the rest of Michigan in creating a sustainable vision of future progress. Kent Portney in updating his 2003 book, *Taking Sustainable Cities Seriously,* now places Grand Rapids twenty-second in the top twenty-five sustainable cities in the United States. Grand Rapids was also the featured city in May 2007 under "Rapid Progress" on his website (www.ourgreencities.com). In 2008, Mayor Heartwell of Grand Rapids was listed by Portney as one of the top 12 mayors in the United States that employ sustainability best practices in municipal operations.

Sustainability Grows in West Michigan

Grand Rapids, like other central cities in Michigan, has its own challenges and is burdened with a number of ongoing systemic complex problems. The public education system is in crisis. There are significantly fewer students in the Grand Rapids Public School System (GRPS), which has an enrollment below 19,300 students for 2008–2009 compared to 25,283 students for 2002–2003 (GRPS annual reports). In fall 2007, enrollment declined in the GRPS by 1,110 students. Furthermore, since 2001, the West Michigan economy, which had been relatively impervious to the loss of manufacturing jobs affecting the rest of the state, has seen the loss of more than 30,000 jobs in the region, with nearly 90 percent of those job losses occurring in manufacturing (West Michigan Strategic Alliance 2008). Increasing concentrations of poverty have reached West Michigan in many local neighborhoods and communities, with more than 15 percent of Kent County residents now living at or below poverty levels (U.S. Census Bureau 2005 American Community Survey, B17001).

In the past, attempts at solutions to these and other problems have focused on short-term, quick fixes. Leaders in the Greater Grand Rapids community have begun to recognize that a new strategic directional change needs to be undertaken. Changing demographics, globalization, recession and other financial constraints and other regional competitive factors, such as the erosion of a strong industrial manufacturing base, have dramatically altered the West Michigan workforce, neighborhoods, communities, and cities. Today, the impact of low-cost offshore outsourcing of materials that pervades the state's economy has reached Grand Rapids. West Michigan has always been built on a strong manufacturing base. Until very recently, the manufacturing sector represented over 30 percent of regional gross domestic product (GDP). Today, the manufacturing sector has slipped to just over 20 percent of regional GDP, which is still approximately twice the level of other cities and communities in the nation. Future success for the region will depend on the capability to use all forms of capital, including financial, natural, social, cultural, manufactured, community, and human capital (Elkington 1997). The future regional economic model for West Michigan will include refinements to the existing economic development strategies as well as transformation to a new business development model where value creation is based on a collaborative "stakeholder" approach. New future "green jobs" are being created in areas such as environmental engineering, renewable energy, and energy efficiency.

In the past, the traditional economic development model in West Michigan has focused primarily on economic prosperity and environmental compliance and regulations. Future economic development needs to address all components of the triple bottom line (TBL) with a balanced approach inclusively and simultaneously—with corresponding performance measurements and indicators to measure progress. Some refer to it as the 3Es (economy, environmental, equity), while others refer to it as the 3Ps (profits, planet, people). By using a TBL sustainability lens analysis, a balanced perspective can be obtained in creative

311

The Triple Bottom Line

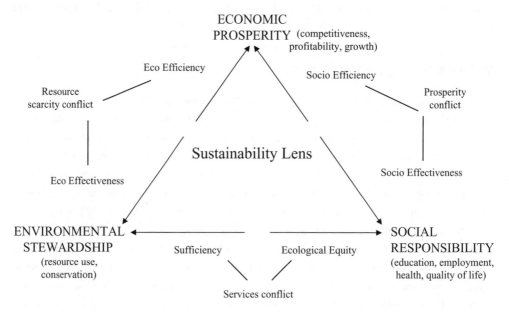

ECONOMIC
PROSPERITY (competitiveness,
profitability, growth)

Eco Efficiency

Socio Efficiency

Resource
scarcity conflict

Prosperity
conflict

Sustainability Lens

Eco Effectiveness

Socio Effectiveness

ENVIRONMENTAL
STEWARDSHIP
(resource use,
conservation)

Sufficiency

Ecological Equity

SOCIAL
RESPONSIBILITY
(education, employment,
health, quality of life)

Services conflict

Source: Adapted from Dyllick and Hockerts 2002.

problem solving. The sustainability lens allows the Greater Grand Rapids community to view systemic problems with a holistic systems-oriented analytical approach and get to "root causes."

Greater Grand Rapids has already drawn national attention through its Leadership in Energy and Environmental Design (LEED) building design and construction. The LEED building movement has mushroomed into a broader focus on sustainability in the region. The City of Grand Rapids has committed to sustainability, including being the first city in Michigan to hire a full-time sustainability manager. Grand Valley State University has also embraced triple bottom line (TBL) principles, launching a Sustainability Initiative. The business community has stepped forward by forming the West Michigan Sustainable Business Forum (www.wmsbf.org) as well as launching a Sustainable Manufacturing Initiative. Finally, the region is poised to further expand its TBL approach through the efforts of its regional sustainability organization, the Community Sustainability Partnership (CSP).

Greater Grand Rapids is rapidly emerging as a benchmark community in Michigan for advancing triple bottom line sustainability including economic prosperity, environmental stewardship and social responsibility and is gaining national exposure.

Key Accomplishments

Leading the Way with LEED

Perhaps the most significant accomplishment for Greater Grand Rapids in leading sustainability efforts statewide has been an area-wide focus on LEED construction in both new buildings and renovation projects. LEED is a building rating and certification system developed by the U.S. Green Building Council in 1993 that focuses on building materials, water and energy efficiencies, indoor air quality, landscaping and habitat, and overall resource consumption. Building owners, on a voluntary basis, can apply for four designations of LEED certification, ranging from LEED certified (lowest), to LEED silver, to LEED gold, to LEED platinum (highest), driven by design and construction guidelines developed by the USGBC (USGBC 2007b). There are a number of LEED rating systems, including new construction (LEED-NC), existing buildings (LEED-EB), commercial interiors (LEED-CI), core and shell development (LEED-CS), neighborhood development (LEED-ND), and residential homes (LEED-H).

In 2007, the USGBC's membership voted to approve a 14 percent increase in the requirements for energy performance within the LEED standards in the future, setting the bar even higher for certification. LEED-certified green buildings have superior indoor air quality, use environmentally responsible materials, save water, and are highly energy efficient, slashing utility bills and greenhouse gas emissions. Buildings are a major contributor to CO_2 emissions. Green buildings emit 40 percent less CO_2 than average. According to the USGBC, green buildings result in operational cost savings, increased productivity, reduced health care costs and an overall improved bottom line. Energy costs in green buildings are on average 30 percent lower, carbon savings are 35 percent greater, and waste cost savings average 50 to 90 percent greater than in nongreen buildings. LEED projects increased from 180 million square feet in 2004 to 642 million square feet in 2006, with a huge spike in 2007 (USGBC 2007b).

Michael Fickes, in his article "Turning Green—When Did So Much of the Mainstream Construction Industry Turn Green?" noted that this shift into mainstream construction happened sometime around 2005 (Fickes 2006). What is currently driving green and LEED construction? Forces range from rising energy costs, building material cost increases, global warming concerns, and carbon dioxide and greenhouse emissions. Green buildings now include a vast array of new features such as energy and water conservation systems; the use of Energy Star® rated products; heating, ventilization, and air-conditioning (HVAC) systems with sensors and monitors for air emissions such as carbon dioxide; roof and rain gardens; daylighting; groundwater and storm water runoff systems; use of postconsumer content (PCC) building materials; and other uses of creative and innovative green products and systems.

An incredible burst of LEED participation has occurred in Greater Grand Rapids, which dwarfs the rest of the state's activities in green building (see table 13.1). As of September 2007, the city of Grand Rapids has twenty-one and West Michigan has thirty-five of the total fifty-one LEED certified buildings (69 percent) in Michigan. The city of Grand Rapids has 58 of the 161 LEED registered buildings in the state; West Michigan as a whole has 93 (58 percent) (USGBC 2007a; see table 13.2). Grand Rapids is recognized by Rick Fedrizzi, president of the USGBC as having the most LEED-certified structures per capita and most square footage per capita of all the cities in the nation (DEQ Director Congratulates Grand Rapids 2007, Heartwell 2006; Nasser 2007).

Greater Grand Rapids has one of the most active regional chapters of the USGBC with over 300 members (www.usgbc.org). The Greater Grand Rapids is home to many "LEED first" buildings. Examples include the first LEED Young Men's Christian Association (YMCA) (Huntington), the first LEED museum (Grand Rapids Art Museum), the first LEED church (Keystone Community Church), the first LEED hospital complex (Metro Health's Eco Village),

Table 13.1. Twenty-one LEED Certified Buildings List for Grand Rapids, Michigan

Project Name	Use	Rating
Goodwillie Environmental School	Education	Certified
FHPS New Secondary Building	Education	Silver
Forest Hills Fine Arts Center	Education	Certified
Knapp Forest Elementary	Education	Silver
Bazzani Associates	Business Headquarters	Certified
Richard J. Lacks, Sr. Cancer Center	Health Care	Certified
Water/Environmental Services Facility	Municipal	Certified
Interurban Transit Partnership	Mass Transit Headquarters	Gold
Calvin College Bunker Interpretive Center	University	Certified
Martineau Project	Housing	Certified
BCBSM/Steketees Building	Health Care	Certified
Grand Rapids Metropolitan YMCA	Recreation	Gold
East Hills Center	Retail	Gold
West Michigan Environmental Action Council	Nonprofit	Certified
UFCW Local 951	Union Headquarters	Certified
East Grand Rapids Community Center	Municipal	Certified
Keystone Community Church	Faith-based	Certified
Sylvan Learning Center	Private Business	Certified
Cherry Street Health Services	Health Care	Certified
Lettinga Housing Phase 2	Housing	Certified
Kelsey Project Avenue for the Arts	Housing	Certified

SOURCE: USGBC Certified Project List 2007.

the first LEED manufacturing plant (Steelcase), the first LEED school (Goodwill Environmental School), and many others. Grand Rapids built one of the first LEED-certified municipal buildings in the state, the City Water Department's administration building, in 2004.[5] GVSU and the city of Grand Rapids have both adopted LEED building design and construction as the building guidelines for new construction. By the end of 2008, GVSU will have constructed nine buildings totaling over 650,000 square feet that are either LEED certified or undergoing the LEED certification process. GVSU has also submitted its Allendale campus for LEED certification.

Many believe that the reason that Grand Rapids is credited with being so far ahead of the rest of the state in planting seeds for green buildings is due to the ground floor interest in environmental issues by the leading furniture companies and the Business Industrial Furniture Manufacturers (BIFMA) (Gamber 2007). The furniture industry, took the lead with green and LEED construction dating back to the 1980s and 1990s. Herman Miller, Steelcase, and Haworth all have LEED-certified administration buildings and headquarters. Steelcase also constructed a LEED-certified manufacturing plant in 2001. With this construction came the establishment of many key architectural firms, all of which specialized in green and LEED building design. Early leaders by design firms such as Progressive AE, Bazzani Inc., and others led to construction firms large and small in West Michigan, such as Rockford Construction and Pioneer Construction, becoming adept at LEED-certified building. These firms have become drivers of green building in West Michigan today and now number in

Table 13.2. Fifty-eight Registered Projects List for Grand Rapids, Michigan (Including the Twenty-one LEED Certified Buildings)

Project Name	Use	Rating
101 Sheldon Building	Office/Health Care	LEED EB 2.0
Aquinas College Academic Building	University	LEED CI 2.0
Aquinas College Library	University	LEED NC 2.1
Catholic Central Gymnasium Addition	Education	LEED NC 2.2
Christian Counseling Center	Nonprofit	LEED NC 2.2
Cisco-Grand Rapids	Business Headquarters	LEED CI 2.0
DA Blodgett Children's Home	Nonprofit	LEED NC 2.2
Fairmount Square	Retail	LEED CS 2.0
Gezon M.O.B.	Health Care	LEED CS 2.0
Global Headquarters	Commercial Office	LEED EB 2.0
Grand Rapids State Office Building	Office Building	LEED NC 2.2
Grand Rapids State Office Building	Office Building	LEED NC 2.2
Grocery Building	Retail	LEED CS 2.0
GRPS Burton School	Education	LEED NC 2.2
GRPS Harrison Park Schools	Education	LEED NC 2.1
GRPS Sibley Elementary School	Education	LEED NC 2.1
GVSU	University	LEED NC 2.2
Hall Elementary School	Education	LEED NC 2.2
Helen DeVos Children's Hospital	Health Care	LEED NC 2.2
Hispanic Center of Western Michigan	Nonprofit	LEED NC 2.2
Lemmen-Holton Cancer Pavilion	Health Care	LEED NC 2.2
Metro Health ASC/MOB	Health Care	LEED NC 2.2
Metor Health Medical Office	Health Care	LEED CS 2.0
Metro Health Plaza -Cascade	Health Care	LEED CI 2.0
MSU Federal Credit Union	Business Headquarters	LEED NC 2.1
North Alano Club	Nonprofit	LEED NC 2.1
Northpointe Bank	Business Headquarters	LEED NC 2.1
Nucraft Furniture	Retail	LEED NC 2.2
Progressive AE	Architecture Firm	LEED EB 2.0
Ray & Joan Kroc Community Center	Recreation	LEED NC 2.2
South Haven Rehab and Wellness	Health Care	LEED NC 2.2
Steelcase	Global Headquarters	LEED CI 2.0
Van Andel Institute Phase 2	Health Care	LEED NC 2.2
West Catholic High School Gym	Education	LEED NC 2.2
W. MI Center for Arts and Technology	Nonprofit	LEED CI 2.0
Wolverine Gas & Oil	Business Headquarters	LEED CI 2.0

SOURCE: USGBC Certified Project List 2007.

the dozens in the region. The medical cluster (Spectrum, St. Mary's, Metro Hospitals) has joined the regional efforts to embrace and implement sustainability and LEED guiding principles in their building and construction.

Recently, Habitat for Humanity of Kent County pledged to build *only* LEED homes in all construction in Grand Rapids in a pilot program that will have national significance. Habitat for Humanity of Kent County hopes to demonstrate that a model of low-cost housing construction and green practices can become the best practice in the affordable housing market. Although it will add thousands of additional dollars to home construction, over the lifetime of each homebuyer's mortgage, future savings may exceed $50,000 for each Habitat home buyer.

Grand Rapids has also become a partner with the USGBC in promulgating the LEED for Schools program for new construction of K–12 school facilities, which addresses such areas as classroom acoustics, master planning, mold prevention, environmental site assessment, energy and water conservation, and improved air quality. In Greater Grand Rapids, there are over ten K–12 schools that are either green, LEED certified, or built to LEED standards.

Sustainability Embraced by the City of Grand Rapids

Grand Rapids mayor George Heartwell, chairman of the CSP, signaled the city's interest in embarking upon a path of transformation toward embracing sustainable development principles beginning with his State of the Cities speech on January 15, 2004. The city of Grand Rapids pledged to reduce petroleum-based sources of energy use by 20 percent and buy 20 percent of its power from renewables by 2008, a target that has been reached.[6] The city created its first Sustainability Plan in August 2006, and Grand Rapids' first ever TBL community sustainability indicator report was made available fall 2008.

The city has pledged to eliminate all use of toxic chemicals and has switched from chlorine treatment of wastewater discharge to the environmental friendly ultraviolet light treatment system. The city has pledged that all its new municipal buildings will be LEED certified. The city and Mayor Heartwell have been instrumental in helping direct environmental transformation and change in our region. Under the direction of Mayor Greg Nickels of Seattle, the U.S. Mayors' Climate Protection Agreement was drafted in early 2005. Now over 880 city mayors from all fifty states, have signed and endorsed this agreement to help reduce C02 and greenhouse gas emissions, or their carbon footprint, by 7 percent by 2012, using 1990 baseline levels (www.USmayors.org). The city of Grand Rapids was the 168th city in the United States to sign this agreement on June 28, 2005. In addition to Grand Rapids, 23 other Michigan cites have signed the agreement.[7] The most important part of the resolution are the steps that Grand Rapids will take to reduce emissions such as exclusively purchasing Energy Star® equipment for city use, increasing average municipal fleet fuel efficiency, setting reduction targets for global warming emissions, retrofitting city facilities with efficient lighting, and promoting sustainable building practices. Specific growth management strategies are being evaluated and pursued, including the goal of 100 percent renewable energy use, LEED building and construction, use of biofuels, implementation of energy conservation programs, and reducing water consumption by fifteen percent by 2015.

Another effective growth management strategy centered on environmental stewardship was the establishment of the Mayor's Environmental Advisory Council (EAC). The council is composed of about twenty volunteer community stakeholders that advise the mayor on key city environmental issues. Key recent recommendations from the EAC that have been acted upon by the city include the establishment of nontoxic purchasing guidelines, the establishment of green building guidelines and research into local emerald ash borer issues. The EAC initially focused its activities on nontoxic purchasing guidelines and procedures. A review of other nontoxic purchasing guidelines was undertaken and best practices identified. The best practices were then shared with the mayor and the city commissioners for their approval. Recent activities also include the launch of the West Michigan Sustainable Purchasing Consortium (www.wmspc.org). Green paper products are now available for West Michigan stakeholders. Additionally, Grand Rapids is creating "Green Grand Rapids," an updated master plan using sustainable principles for the Parks and Recreation Department to complement the city's most recent master plan created in 2002.

Effective January 2007, Grand Rapids was the first city in the state to hire a full-time sustainability manager, who oversees the sustainability TBL activities for all city departments. The city commissioners have approved policies stating that future new city building construction over 10,000 square feet will comply with LEED design and certification criteria. Additional environmental stewardship progress has been made by the city's wastewater treatment plant. Ultraviolet light technology has replaced chemical disinfection of wastewater, thereby eliminating 150 tons of chlorine and 125 tons of sulfur dioxide use. A geothermal system coupled with energy-efficient aeration has generated $350,000 of annual energy conservation. The city of Grand Rapids has invested over more than $210 million ($1,750 per capita) to reduce combined sewer overflows (CSOs) by 99 percent. Also to further protect the Great Lakes and St. Lawrence River, Grand Rapids, like other cities, has pledged to reduce its water consumption by 15 percent by 2015. The city of Grand Rapids is also acting in a leadership role by benchmarking other communities' best practices in developing carbon management strategies and overall energy conservation and efficiency programs.

For these efforts Grand Rapids was highlighted on MSNBC.com in June 2007 as one of the "five cities that are greener than you think," in a news article that reached an international audience. Unfortunately, Detroit was also listed as one of the five cities in the United States that "need the most help in getting green."

GVSU's Sustainability Initiative

Colleges and universities are important community stakeholders, along with the public and private sector, in advancing sustainability. GVSU has exercised regional leadership in sustainability and is one of the five founding members of the CSP. While GVSU was not the first university in the state to embrace sustainability programs, its recent involvement has been one of the keys to the sustainability movement in West Michigan.[8] The roots of the Sustainability Initiative at GVSU date back to 2004, when work began on GVSU's first TBL indicator report. GVSU completed it first baseline indicator report in 2005, "Sustainability at GVSU," including nineteen categories and sixty-four indicators and is now developing its second TBL Campus Sustainability Report (www.gvsu.edu/sustainability). After this campus sustainability assessment, GVSU had to decide which sustainability model fit best and could be adapted to add value to its future strategic plan. The decision was made to integrate sustainability on campus with a systems-oriented interdisciplinary approach adapted from Tony Cortese of Second Nature. Ultimately, the Sustainability Initiative focused on four primary pillars—affecting administration, facilities services, operations and campus dining supporting faculty curriculum and development around education for sustainability; involving students in sustainable development activities; and engaging with community stakeholders.

317

The Sustainability Initiative is focused on creating value for campus operations through savings, efficiencies, productivity, empowerments, avoided costs, reduced risks and liabilities. Some of the highlights include the implementation of Campus Sustainability Day in 2005, which became an annual Campus Sustainability Week beginning in 2006; a Student Sustainability Guidebook that is disseminated to over 5,000 first-year students each year; the development of several sustainability certificates for students; new sustainability curriculum and course development; and the establishment of more than sixty-five key community sustainability platform projects with faculty, staff students, and community stakeholder leaders. GVSU bus ridership has increased exponentially, from 98,821 rides in 2000–2001 to more than two million rides in 2008. Overall student requests for parking spaces declined during recent years as well. It is estimated that the value created by the bus ridership can be found in annual substantial savings of over $10 million on reduced vehicle fuel and maintenance costs, lower volatile organic content (VOC) emissions, and avoided costs for building new parking spaces. GVSU estimates that each parking space not built reduces costs at $25,000 per contained parking space (GVSU Pew Campus Operations 2007).

Recently, President Thomas Haas and GVSU signed the Talloires Declaration, which focuses on environmental sustainable development education. The university also signed the American College and University Presidents' Climate Agreement, which requires the development of a carbon footprint inventory as well as climate change and carbon-neutral strategies. In the recently released 2008 College Sustainability Report Card (Sustainable Endowments Institute), GVSU was one of four colleges and universities to receive national recognition for sustainability innovation. The USGBC in 2008 also recognized GVSU as one of eight colleges and universities for their comprehensive sustainability strategy. The new 2009 Kaplan College Guide highlights GVSU as one of the twenty-five most environmentally responsible and cutting edge green colleges and universities in the United States.

The Sustainable Manufacturing Initiative

We would be remiss if we focused only on the public sector's efforts in leading the way toward sustainable development patterns in Greater Grand Rapids. Indeed, the business community has modeled sustainability best practices and was the first business community in Michigan to form a Sustainable Business Forum (www.wmsbf.org). The furniture industry and BIFMA played a leadership role from the beginning in the region, from adapting green standards to the development of sustainability assessment standards for product performance.[9] Cascade Engineering, Haworth Corporation, Steelcase, and Herman Miller are just a few of the more than one hundred business members of the West Michigan Sustainable Business Forum that are leading the private sector in advancing sustainable models of development. Fred Keller, CEO of Cascade Engineering, and chair of the Department of Commerce's Manufacturing Advisory Council has, led Cascade Engineering in completing its fourth annual TBL report. The furniture manufacturers have been regional leaders in sustainability for years, and now the hospitals and food service organizations are beginning to follow. Eight companies in Grand Rapids have been designated by the MDEQ as Clean Corporate Citizens, the most of any city in the state (DEQ Director Congratulates Grand Rapids 2007). Crystal Flash Energy has embraced sustainable growth in Grand Rapids.

It is the first company to offer biodiesel fuel in West Michigan and is developing other alternative energy and fuel technologies.

The Sustainable Manufacturing Initiative directed by the Right Place, Inc., has been a significant tool in promoting regional sustainability. Birgit Klohs, president of the Right Place, Inc., has said that "sustainability is inexorably linked to innovation and without an increasing concentration of innovative sustainable companies our economy will not reach its full potential. Our support of increased sustainability and innovation capacity among West Michigan firms not only strengthens those firms but furthers our economic growth and advances our region as a premier location for similar high-performance companies" (Right Place 2007).

West Michigan has been fortunate to receive several prestigious grants, such as the federal WIRED grant and an EPA grant and a 21st Century Jobs Fund Grant. In 2005, the U.S. Department of Labor, Employment and Training Administration awarded West Michigan a $15 million WIRED grant to help assist the region in creating and implementing new economic development and business development strategies. WIRED West Michigan (www.wiredwestmi.org) is helping to provide the talents, tools, skill sets, and vision to compete in a dynamic, rapidly changing economy. These new initiatives are comprised under four innovation categories, including Market Intelligence, Innovation WORKS, Workforce Systems Transformation, and Enterprise Development.

In addition, a $398,000 Environmental Protection Agency (EPA) grant, established primary activities in several areas including participation in the green supplier's network among about twenty-five manufacturing companies in West Michigan, such as automotive and furniture suppliers. Sustainable business practices including green and LEAN manufacturing initiatives are helping to improve regional competitiveness as well as help reduce overall operating and manufacturing costs. The BIFMA organization has acknowledged in a pilot study that a green suppliers' network among key furniture manufacturers saved approximately $5 million (Christopher and Rudolph 2006). Another activity has been the linkage to Innovation Works, one of the twelve priority Workforce Innovation and Regional Economic Development (WIRED) projects, in partnership with Grand Rapids Community College, the Lakeshore Advantage and others. This program will support the development of entrepreneurial new product, market, and business activities, such as with renewable and alternative technologies, scrap and waste material reuse, use of green chemistries, and other clean technologies.

The Community Sustainability Partnership (CSP)

The development of the CSP has been the cornerstone of advancing regional sustainability efforts. Founded on August 18, 2005, the organization was established to advance TBL principles including utilizing clean technologies; improving the "quality of life" for citizens by reducing poverty, increasing education attainment levels, ensuring access to recreational amenities, attracting and retaining businesses, and conserving and preserving natural resources, leveraging community resources for economic gain and the creation of wealth. It was originally founded as an initiative of the city of Grand Rapids, Grand Rapids Public Schools, GVSU, Grand Rapids Community College, and Aquinas College. Initial seed funding was provided primarily by the Wege Foundation over a three-year period from 2005 through 2007 to establish community activities that would promote the triple bottom line. The CSP rapidly grew from the five founding members to more than 165 community stakeholder member organizations from the public, private, and academic sectors, including municipalities, businesses, public schools, colleges and universities, service organizations, nonprofits, faith based organizations and others.

The CSP is working to demonstrate sustainable progress for the region and establish transformational change based on a new multistakeholder approach. The focus is on system-oriented thinking, win-win long-term solutions, lifecycle and root-cause analysis, building of relationships and partnerships, community engagement, and lifelong learning. The CSP is viewed as a place-based model for community redevelopment efforts in the Greater Grand Rapids area and is beginning to be recognized and replicated in the rest of the state.[10]

In 2008, ongoing sustainable development activities of the CSP include recycling and waste minimization, LEED building and design, green and local purchasing, renewable energy, alternative fuels, climate change, energy and water conservation, education for sustainability, faith based programs and neighborhood sustainable development. These programs increase overall awareness and understanding about community-wide sustainable development issues, engage community stakeholders in meaningful dialogue on key sustainable development issues, grow the collaborations and partnerships, and demonstrate collective community TBL progress through key sustainability metrics.

Since 2005, the CSP and its endorsing stakeholder partners have been able to reach tens of thousands of community members with greater awareness and understanding of sustainability guiding principles and best practices. For instance, the Grand Rapids Chamber of Commerce has more than 2,500 members; Spectrum, with over forty community programs, has thousands of employees; and the MDEQ reaches statewide. Recently, the Grand Rapids Metro Ministry, comprised of thirty-one United Methodist churches in West Michigan, also joined the CSP. Even low-income central-city residents are reached through participation of nonprofit organizations such as Habitat for Humanity, the Inner City Christian Federation, and Dwelling Place.

The challenge of launching a sustainable community initiative was a daunting task that required careful planning and support. The CSP followed a process similar to the ten steps identified within the development of sustainable communities (www.smartcommunities.ncat.org). These steps are outlined as follows.

- First, conduct sustainability assessments among stakeholders and partners. These assessments allow partners to gather baseline TBL data for their respective organizations. In essence: Where is your community today? What are your demographics, crime statistics, income levels, education attainment levels, etc.? In April 2007, the West Michigan Strategic Alliance issued the first regional indicator report, known as 2006 Vital Signs (West Michigan Strategic Alliance 2007). In the fall of 2008, the city of Grand Rapids provided Greater Grand Rapids with its first TBL indicator report.
- Second, obtain stakeholder consensus on sustainable development programs and activities and share best practices. In 2007, the CSP held four community sustainability summit meetings. These summit meetings addressed topics of fostering social responsibility,

improving economic prosperity, increasing environmental stewardship, and measuring our collective progress (www.grpartners.org).

- Third, determine local "sustainability" champions. The CSP has been able to develop a cross-functional leadership effort regarding community-based sustainable development. The CSP has had both a planning team and leadership team composed of representatives from the city of Grand Rapids, GVSU, Aquinas College, Grand Rapids Community College, the Grand Rapids Public Schools and others.

- Fourth, create a vision that engages the community at large. Several entities including the city of Grand Rapids have generated future vision statements. The city of Grand Rapids used a charrette process in 2002 that helped develop elements of the current master plan for the city and Mayor Heartwell updated this vision for the city's sustainability plan in his 2006 State of the City address.

- Fifth, generate a roadmap to achieve a vision. The CSP has outlined several collaborative outcomes and expectations. The partnership has also focused on a balanced TBL strategic approach for transformational change. In the future, key community-wide efforts will concentrate on energy conservation, carbon footprints, education for sustainable development, poverty reduction, and educational attainment levels. The CSP wants to ensure that collective resources are leveraged and used efficiently to "make West Michigan the best place to live, learn, work and play."[11]

- Sixth, develop key sustainability assessments and indicators for member organizations. Some of the CSP members have spent considerable time during the last few years developing TBL sustainability indicators that can be measured and monitored. Some of the organizations that have issued indicator reports include the West Michigan Strategic Alliance 2006 Vital Signs, the city of Grand Rapids, the city of Muskegon, GVSU, Cascade Engineering, and others. Key leaders from the furniture industry, such as Steelcase, Herman Miller, and Haworth have been leaders in environmental sustainability reporting. Future sustainable development monitoring efforts will help establish more in-depth sustainability performance measurements and metrics.

- Seventh, incorporate sustainability into local policy and governance. Recently, Michigan passed a statewide energy policy that includes a renewable portfolio standard, net metering, and other regulations and standards that will help catalyze, develop, and sustain new alternative and renewable business development activities. The mayor of Grand Rapids, George Heartwell, has been instrumental in establishing grassroots visionary change for the use of renewable energy in Grand Rapids as outlined in his recent State of the City addresses.

- Eighth, identify available local resources and assets. Greater Grand Rapids is fortunate to have many philanthropic organizations, including the Wege, Frey, and Grand Rapids Community foundations, as well as others, which have been instrumental in the growth and success of sustainable development activities and programs. Additionally, there are numerous NGOs and other community organizations, such as the faith-based organizations, that can provide significant support and assistance regarding specific sustainable development programs and activities. Furthermore, another opportunity exists with colleges and universities regarding access to faculty, staff and student knowledge capital that is available to help solve systemic economic, social, and environmental community issues with community members.

- Ninth, develop a network of user and workgroups within your community. Within Greater Grand Rapids sustainable development work group areas are organized around the TBL. Economic prosperity examples include green purchasing, local food systems and sustainable business practices. Environmental stewardship groups include built environment, transportation, renewable energy, climate change and others. Social equity examples include education for sustainable development, children's environmental health initiative and health and wellness.

- Tenth, monitor progress. Many sustainable communities and cities that have achieved measurable progress on sustainable development advocate the celebration of early success. Conversations, story telling and celebrations help create awareness, increase motivation, and build confidence regarding ongoing sustainable development efforts. In the future, new media outlets will be needed to continue lifelong learning about sustainable development, including cable television, trade and business journals, and creative Web sites. Currently, the MI BIZ West, the Grand Rapids Business Journal, WGVU, and Grand Rapids–Rapid Growth (www.Rapidgrowthmedia.com) have all started coverage of the sustainability journey.

What makes a CSP model work? While it is important to have a framework and a model, it is most important to have a foundation of shared beliefs and values among stakeholder members that include trust, inclusiveness, transparency, openness and mutual accountability. If the CSP is truly going to serve as a benchmark for the rest of the state and other communities, it must continue to monitor measurable progress and communicate the progress and results through leadership, advocacy and partnerships.

Towards Transformational Change

The West Michigan region's sustainable development programs and activities are beginning to capture state and national attention in the areas of LEED building, municipal and university leadership around environmental stewardship, and sustainable manufacturing practices. Greater Grand Rapids has begun to experience some transitional progress and recognize that fundamental transformation is needed and under way. The region has been intensifying its efforts at building leadership through a "Community Sustainability Model," the CSP, to draw the region's public, private and nonprofit sector together to combat systemic quality of life issues through a balanced TBL approach.

Sustainable TBL progress in Greater Grand Rapids does not have to be an anomaly in Michigan. Grand Rapids has taken important steps to create a collective process by learning and applying sustainability best practices locally, regionally and nationally. Sustainability Manager Corky Overmyer states, "Thanks to the continued connectivity and more focused 'systems thinking,' it's not just the city of Grand Rapids that's green anymore. It's spreading through the Western Michigan Region. . . . The city and its partners are assisting many efforts in communities and municipalities around the state. . . . Can what's worked in Grand Rapids work to bring the rest of Michigan up to the same level of commitment to sustainability? I think so" (Gamber 2007).

In the beginning of 2006, Muskegon was the first region outside of Greater Grand Rapids influenced to establish its own community partnership based on sustainability guidelines, principles, and best practices. Several exploratory meetings were held at GVSU's Annis Water Research Institute. Both the Sustainability Initiative and the city of Grand Rapids shared "lessons learned," experiences, and aspirations about the CSP. In 2006, the Muskegon Sustainability Coalition was formed, based on the organizational principles of the CSP. Today, this coalition has extensive community stakeholder members in the Muskegon area, meets regularly and is developing a sustainability action plan, and just released its first TBL indicator report (The Prosperity Index). A similar sustainability partnership, known as the Holland/Zeeland 3E Sustainability Initiative, was replicated on the west coast of Michigan. The Spring Lake and Grand Haven region shortly followed with the Northwest Ottawa County Sustainability Initiative. A sustainability partnership spread to the Kalamazoo/Portage area in November 2008 and is under consideration in Battle Creek. Founders hope to generate similar interest and replication on the east side of the state with recent interest expressed by Detroit. The TBL sustainability efforts and progress have also been recognized by state government in Lansing by policy makers and statewide programs such as the climate action and energy policy groups. Out-of-state areas, such as Mobile, Alabama, have also come to West Michigan to learn more about the CSP.

An outgrowth of the CSP has been the formation of a green purchasing consortium, which has included the city of Grand Rapids, the Delta Institute of Chicago, GVSU, the Sustainable Research Group and various other CSP members and purchasing agents including Steelcase, Cascade Engineering and the Van Andel Institute. The West Michigan Sustainability Purchasing Consortium originally convened to discuss the impairments to the ecosystem in the Lower Grand River Watershed. Participants wanted to develop voluntary programs to reduce toxic loadings, minimize waste, and curtail discharges of storm water to local wastewater treatment systems. The consortium has developed a set of green purchasing guidelines and procedures that is offered to CSP members. It will leverage its collective purchasing requirements of green products, such as office products as well as other items. The consortium's goal is to identify and stimulate more widespread purchase of green products and services, and to expand local and regional market opportunities for companies that manufacture or supply sustainable products.

In May 2007, the EPA held a two-day CARE (Community Activities for a Renewable Environment) workshop for its project managers who administer national grants in Washington, D.C. The EPA had learned about the CSP model and asked if the CSP could provide an overview of its activities and programs. The EPA's objective was to understand and develop best practices to better integrate and leverage its project activities in neighborhoods and communities. Recently, the city of Grand Rapids and GVSU presented at community Greentown conferences in Illinois. The theme of these conferences was about building future sustainable communities and cities. Feedback suggests that the sustainability model in Grand Rapids is distinctive, practical, and realistic, as evidenced by the CSP activities and the use of the balanced TBL sustainability perspective.

Recently, the city of Grand Rapids and the CSP received recognition for their efforts. They achieved a designation by the United Nations University, Tokyo, Japan, as a Regional Center of Expertise (RCE) in Education for Sustainable Development (ESD). This RCE designation is the first in the United States and is one of only forty-seven such designations worldwide. An RCE is a network of existing formal, nonformal, and informal educational organizations mobilized to deliver sustainable development to local and regional communities. A network of RCEs worldwide will constitute the Global Learning Space for Sustainable Development. RCEs aspire to achieve the millennium goals of the UN Decade of Education for Sustainable Development 2005–2014 (Regional Centres of Expertise).

It may well be that Greater Grand Rapids will be looked to in the future as a harbinger of change for Michigan and in the overall advancement of sustainable TBL goals and outcomes. This is a critically important and positive first step for transformational change in Michigan, given the challenges and trends identified in this book for the state.

Notes

1. This quote, along with some of its close variants, is sometimes labeled as an American Indian proverb, or is attributed to Ralph Waldo Emerson or Chief Seattle.
2. Unlike the United States, the EU signed the Kyoto Protocol in 1997, but it has, however, fallen short of promised targets for C02 emissions.
3. In the United States, Rachel Carson's 1962 book, *Silent Spring*, ushered in the modern environmental movement.
4. Similar to the large number of organizations and publications that track comparative business climates, there are a number of entities that are beginning to track sustainability. These include, but are not limited to, Sustainlane (http://www.sustainlane.com/us-city-rankings/) and Our Green Cities (http://ourgreencities.com/).
5. In 2005, the state of Washington became the first state to require that public buildings and schools be built to at least LEED silver standards (Seattle Metropolitan 2006).
6. Michigan is one of the states that recently passed a 10 percent renewable portfolio standard. Governor Granholm also appointed a 2008 Michigan Climate Action Council to focus on transportation, land use, energy, the built environment, and cross-cutting issues related to reductions in Greenhouse Gas emissions.
7. Most of this activity is recent. At the beginning of 2007, only five cities, Ann Arbor, Ferndale, Marquette, Berkley and Southfield, had signed the protocol (Kelly 2006).
8. The University of Michigan took the early lead in establishing the Erb Institute for Global Sustainable Enterprise in 1996. The institute fosters interdisciplinary research and education initiatives. The university also created a task force in 2003, recommending eight areas the University of Michigan could improve upon sustainability through key environmental and performance areas. At Michigan State University (MSU) the Office of Campus Sustainability was spawned in 1998 when a group of faculty, staff, and students presented a proposal to implement a campus environmental assessment. They developed their first campus report card highlighting TBL indicators in 2001–2002. Their second Campus Report Card, in 2007, is a comprehensive TBL report with specific sustainability indicators and measurements. They publish a monthly "Footprint" newsletter, offer a sustainability speaker series, and generally promote sustainable development within the MSU community.

9. BIFMA with hundreds of members around the United States, is headquartered in Grand Rapids. It is the second industry to develop sustainability assessment standards regarding product manufacture, setting a leadership example for other trade and industry groups.

10. The place-based protocol was adapted from the Base of the Pyramid Learning Laboratory in the Johnson Center for Sustainable Global Enterprise at Cornell University. (Johnson Center 2007).

11. This is the vision statement for the region as developed through the West Michigan Strategic Alliance.

APPENDIX 1
Sustainability Outcomes of Leading U.S. Cities

Seattle

According to the Seattle Climate Action Plan (2007–2008), key sustainability outcomes in Seattle include the following.

- Energy use by homes, businesses, and industries has actually decreased since 1990, while the city witnessed an unprecedented economic boom. Climate-friendly policies at City Light, the nation's first zero net emissions utility, further shrunk the city's carbon footprint.
- Seattle's efforts to address global warming are paying off. A recently compiled inventory of Seattle's greenhouse gas emissions shows that Seattle is meeting their Kyoto Treaty targets, for reducing climate pollution to seven percent below 1990 levels by 2012. The city is producing eight percent less carbon dioxide and other gases than they did 15 years ago.
- The "Complete Streets" ordinance was initiated by establishing new requirements for street and sidewalk lighting, requiring pedestrian and bicycle safety improvements, and increasing the number of trees along streets. It puts walking, bicycling, and transit on the same level as cars when the city improves streets and arterials. A New Bicycle Master Plan will add miles of new lanes and safety improvements.
- Mayor Greg Nickels initiated the "Center City Strategy," a vision for encouraging economic growth, transportation, and new housing in Seattle's downtown core and the nine adjoining neighborhoods. In the next fifteen years, these neighborhoods are expected to boast 69,000 new jobs and 56,000 new residents. Northgate, a city designated "Urban Center," is an example of plans becoming reality.
- Seattle has piloted the use of a higher blend of biodiesel (B40) with an eye toward using this blend throughout its fleet. Citywide fuel use is down 12 percent from 1999. Of the city's approximately 1,000 diesel-powered vehicles, all but 3 percent run on biodiesel. And nearly 80 percent of new light-duty vehicle purchases are now either hybrid or biodiesel vehicles.
- Seattle is leading the nation in city-owned Leadership in Energy in Energy and Environmental Design (LEED)-certified buildings, with ten and more than 100 green buildings are already in development around Seattle. In January 2007, Seattle led the nation with 26 LEED certified buildings within city limits, representing 8.1 million square feet and over two billion dollars of capital investments (www.nyclimatesummit.com).
- Founded in 1991, Sustainable Seattle is a nonprofit organization whose mission is to advance an integrated vision of urban sustainability by measuring progress, building diverse coalitions, and undertaking key initiatives. Its vision is an interconnected group of healthy, compact, livable urban centers across the Center Puget Sound region, where people work together to restore and improve the vitality of their communities, the economy, and the environment.

Chicago

Sustainlane.com gave Chicago high scores nearly across the board in its index of Most Sustainable Cities: "knowledge base (#1), city innovation (#5), energy and climate change policy (#5), commute

(continued)

to work (#6), and regional public transportation ridership (#2). The city has been moving toward a new type of urban environment since Mayor Richard M. Daley's administration began almost maniacally planting trees, about a half-million since Daley took office in 1989 while planting more than 80 miles of landscaped medians. Mayor Daley's plan to make Chicago 'the greenest city in America' soon blossomed into urban roof gardens, starting with City Hall in 1999" (Sustainable Circles Inc. 2007). The Environmental Action Agenda (2006) lists 188 accomplishments achieved by more than forty city departments and sister agencies in advancing sustainability in Chicago. According to the most recent Chicago Climate Action Plan (2008) the following has recently been accomplished.

- The city registered twenty-two of its buildings for LEED certification, including schools, libraries, and police and fire stations. Over two hundred and fifty buildings are currently working towards LEED Certification in Chicago.
- Chicago's 2.5 million square feet of green roofs was recognized as being more than all other U.S. cities combined. As of 2008, there are 400 additional green roof projects in various stages of development totaling nearly four million square feet. Chicago plans to increase the number of green roof projects to 6,000 by 2020. Energy savings for buildings with roof gardens is estimated at twenty percent.
- In 2007, more than 20 percent of the electricity used in City buildings was purchased from green power sources. Chicago has retrofitted fifteen million square feet of public buildings to lower energy usage by a minimum of thirty percent. The City and its partners distributed more than one million compact fluorescent bulbs through the Smart Bulb Program to residents for free.
- The Department of Housing funded 237 affordable housing units in environmentally friendly residential developments.
- Chicago's 100 hybrid vehicles will use an estimated 10,000 fewer gallons of fuel per year. Additionally, Chicago has transitioned 1,200 of its municipal fleet to alternative fuels.
- In the last decade, the Department of Water Management has reduced water consumption in its service area by 160 million gallons per day. For every 5 percent reduction in the amount of water used, Chicago taxpayers save approximately $1.2 million in costs to treat and pump water. Such conservation also helps the city save on future infrastructure costs, as a result of the reduced wear and tear on the water distribution system.

Portland

Portland maintained its top ranking on the 2008 list of the fifty most sustainable cities in the Sustain-Lane rankings, SustainLane City Rankings 2008). The Office of Sustainable Development in Portland advocates "a better future, a better now!" Its mission is to provide leadership and contribute practical solutions to ensure a prosperous community where people and nature thrive. Sustainable development programs and activities focus on garbage and recycling, green building, energy and biofuels, global warming, and sustainable food. According to the Office of Sustainable Development (www.portlandonline.com/osd), key Portland sustainability outcomes include the following.

- Portland through its Local Action Plan on Global Warming is doing its part to reduce greenhouse gases. Per capita carbon dioxide emissions are down 13 percent since 1990—more than in any other U.S. city. Total emissions are down 1 percent, while the national average is increasing rapidly.
- Portland city government energy bills have been reduced by a total of $14 million since 1994— with $2 million in savings in 2004. This taxpayer savings is a model for other communities.
- Portland with more than 270 miles of bikeways was named "most bike-friendly major city in the U.S. by the League of American Bicyclists with an estimated sixteen percent of Portlanders who commute on bikes.
- Portland's residents and businesses recycled more than 55 percent of their waste this year, leading the nation.

APPENDIX 1
Sustainability Outcomes of Leading U.S. Cities (*continued*)

- Portland is now home to the most LEED-registered projects of any U.S. city. Record numbers came to the U.S. Green Building Council (USGBC) annual conference, Greenbuild. Nearly 8,000 people from twenty-seven countries flocked to Portland for Greenbuild 2004.
- One hundred percent renewable energy goal—city government bought or generated 12 percent of its electricity from wind power and an innovative project that uses waste sewer gas from the wastewater plant to generate power in microturbines and a fuel cell. The city council has committed to own or lease a wind farm to generate 100 percent of government power needs in the near future.

Denver

Greenprint Denver is a long-term citywide strategic plan and initiative that advocates the importance of sustainable development and ecology-friendly practices throughout the community. Specific plan activities focus on the reduction of greenhouse gas emissions; increase of city forest coverage; reduction of waste; utilization of renewable energies; increase of green-built and affordable housing; implementation of city green building policy; expansion of city green motor fleet; promotion of mass transit; conservation and protection of water; and green industry economic development. According to Greenprint Denver 2008 (www.greenprintdenver.org), key sustainability outcomes to date include the following.

- Denver created the first "Green Fleet" program in the nation by purchasing alternative fuel vehicles. More than forty-three percent of the fleet is powered by alternatives, including 138 hybrid electric vehicles.
- Denver has one of the largest light-emitting diode (LED) traffic light inventories in the country saving the city nearly $800,000 per year.
- Denver Water's new recycling plant once complete will deliver 450 million gallons of recycled water each year via fifty miles of purple pipe for non potable uses such as irrigation, golf course and wildlife preserves. Denver's Parks and Recreation use twenty eight percent less water today than in 2001, since replacing outdated irrigation systems.
- The city's single-stream recycling program has seen an 18 percent increase in tonnage in the first year.
- A cornerstone of Greenprint Denver's energy management and energy efficiency goals includes the development and implementation of an updated Greenhouse Gas Reduction Plan (GGRP). The GGRP will monitor the emissions impacts of the city's work over time, including adoption of high-performance building practices, reducing materials use and waste production, support for growth patterns that de-emphasize reliance on cars, and development of more renewable energy sources for the city.
- Denver continues to be a world leader in solar research and the hub of natural gas exploration and development throughout the Rockies. The city has recently added wind energy incentives.
- The metro area FasTracks project, approved by voters in seven Colorado counties in 2004 and managed by Denver's Regional Transportation District, is a unifying element in regional community-planning efforts. The $4.7 billion, twelve-year plan will link Denver's suburbs together with comprehensive mass transit service through 119 miles of new light rail and commuter rail, 18 miles of bus rapid transit service, 21,000 new parking spaces at rail and bus stations, and expanded bus service. The expansion is the largest build-out in U.S. history, and will make metro Denver one of the top five regions in the country in terms of miles of fixed rail.

REFERENCES

Anderson, S. 2005. Annual Report Cover Letter. City of Portland, Oregon, Office of Sustainable Development. Http://www.portlandonline.com/shared/cfm/image.cfm?id=130429.

Brower, D., and S. Chapple. 1995. *Let the Mountains Talk, Let the Rivers Run.* Dunmore, Pa.: Harper Collins.

Business and Institutional Furniture Manufactures Association (BIFMA). 2006. ANSI/BIFMA Safety and Performance Standards. Http://www.bifma.com/standards/index.html.

Centre of Excellence for Sustainable Development. 2006. Sustainable Cities Characteristics. www.rec.org/REC/Programs/Sustainablecities/Characteristics.

Christopher, F. N., and B. L. Rudolph. 2006. The Business and Institutional Furniture Manufacturers Association International (BIFMA) Sustainability Guidelines, An Industry Case Study. Twelfth Annual International Sustainable Development Research Conference, April 6–8, in Hong Kong City's Economic Development Office, 2006, Brownfield Redevelopment. Https://www.ci.grand-rapids.mi.us/index.pl?page_id=558

City of Chicago Department of Environment. 2006. Environmental Action Agenda Executive Summary: Building the Sustainable City 2006. Http://egov.cityofchicago.org/webportal/COCWebPortal/COC_ATTACH/Action_Agenda_Exec_Summary_06.pdf.

City of Denver. 2006. *Greenprint Denver.* Http://www.greenprintdenver.org/.

City of Seattle, Office of Sustainability and Environment. 2007. *2007–2008 Seattle Climate Action Plan: Progress Report.* Seattle, WA.

DEQ Director Congratulates Grand Rapids for Sustainability Efforts. 2007. State of Michigan. March 29. Http://www.michigan.gov/printerFriendly/0,1687,7–135–3308–165477—,00.html.

Dyllick, T., and K. Hockerts. 2002. Corporate Sustainability: Beyond the Business Case. *Business Strategy and the Environment* Published online in Wiley InterScience www.interscience.wiley.com 11(2):130–141.

Elkington, J. 1997. *Cannibals with Forks: The Triple Bottom Line of 21st Century Business.* Somerset, NJ: John Wiley & Sons.

Environmentally Preferable Products (EPP) Procurement Program. 2007. Massachusetts EPP Glossary of Terms, Sustainability. Http://www.mass.gov.

Fickes, M. 2006. Turning Green—When Did So Much of the Mainstream Construction Industry Turn Green? *Michigan Constructor* (Summer/Fall 2006):12–18.

Gamber, J. 2007. Going Green in Michigan. *Planning and Zoning News.* August.

Grand Rapids Business Journal. 2007. Spectrum, VAI Form Molecular Center. Grand Rapids, Mich., March 19.

GrandWalk. 2006. Http://www.grandwalk.com/.

Guy, Andy. 2006. Go for the Grow. Http://www.mlui.org/transportation.

GVSU (Grand Valley State University) Pew Campus Operations. 2007. Http://www.gvsu.edu/operations.

Hart, S. 2005. *Capitalism at the Crossroads: The Unlimited Business Opportunities in Solving the World's Most Difficult Problems.* Philadelphia: Wharton School.

Healthy Homes Coalition. 2006. Get the Lead Out! Http://www.healthyhomescoalition.org.

Heartwell, G. 2006. State of the Cities Address. Grand Rapids, Mich.

Johnson Center for Sustainable Global Enterprise. 2007. Base of the Pyramid Initiatives, Base of the Pyramid Learning Lab. Http://www.johnson.cornell.edu/sge/boplab.html.

Kelly, C. 2006. Traverse City Eyes Cooling Agreement: Will Town Become Michigan's Seventh to Tackle Global Warming? Michigan Land Institute. Traverse City, Mich. November 12.

Libby, L., and A. Nalukenge. 2001. *Metro Growth: A Mandate for Reinventing Regions in the 21st Century.* AEDE. Columbus, OH.

Local First. 2006. Http://www.localfirst.com.

LOHAS. 2007. LOHAS Background. Http://www.lohas.com/about.htm.

Nasser, H. 2007. Mayors Unite on the "Green" Front. *USA Today,* February 1.

Natural Step. 2006. Http://www.ortns.org/framework.htm.

New Zeeland Ministry of Economic Development. N.d. Sustainability. Http://www.med.govt.nz/ templates/ContentTopicSummary____27750.aspx.

Our Green Cities. 2008. Http://www.ourgreencities.com.

Portney, K. 2003. *Taking Sustainable Cities Seriously: Economic Development, the Environment, and Quality of Life in American Cities.* Cambridge, Mass.: MIT Press

Regional Centres of Expertise (RCE). 2008. Http://www.ias.unu.edu/sub_page.aspx?catID=108&dd] [D= 183.

Report of the Brundtland Commission: Our Common Future. 1987. New York: Oxford University Press.

Right Place. 2007. About the Right Place. Http://www.rightplace.org/about/.

Seattle Metropolitan. 2006. Green Builders. October. Http://www.vulcanrealestate.com/content/Docs/ SeattleMet_greenbuilding_1006.pdf.

Smart Communities Network. 2006. Http://www.sustainable.doe.gov/.

Smart Growth by Collaboration. 2006. Partnerships for Smart Growth. Http://www.epa.gov/ smartgrowth/univ_collaboration.htm.

SOURCE. 2007. The SOURCE, Leveraging Resources, Creating Opportunities, Keeping Promises. Http:// www.grsource.org/about.php.

Sustainable Circles Inc. 2007. Chicago: The Wind at Its Back. Http://www.sustainlane.com/us-city-rankings/chicago.jsp.

SustainLane City Rankings. 2008. The SustainLane 2008 City Rankings. Http://www.sustainlane.us.

Urban Land Institute. 2008. UrbanPlan, Glossary, Economic Development. Http://www.urbanplan.org.

U.S. Census Bureau. 2005. American Community Survey, B17001. Http://www.cridata.org/ communityprofiles.aspx?cp=ct Community Research Institute. Grand Rapids, MI: Grand Valley State University.

U.S. Conference of Mayors Climate Protection Center. 2008. Http://usmayors.org/climateprotection/ listofcities.htm.

USGBC (U.S. Green Building Council). 2007a. Certified Project List. Http://www.usgbc.org/LEED/ Project/CertifiedProjectList.aspx?CMSPageID=244.

———. 2007b. USGBC Web Home Page. Http://www.usgbc.org.

U.S. Partnership for the Decade of Education for Sustainable Development. About the Decade. 2008. Http://www.uspartnership.org.

WMSTA (West Michigan Strategic Alliance). 2008. WMSTA Web Home Page. Http://www.wm-alliance.org.

Contributors

Soji Adelaja is the John A. Hannah Distinguished Professor in Land Policy and the director of the Land Policy Institute at Michigan State University. He also directs the Michigan Higher Education Land Policy Consortium and is co-director of the People and Land Initiative funded by the W.K. Kellogg Foundation. He holds joint faculty appointments as professor in the departments of Agricultural Economics; Geography; and Community, Agriculture, Recreation, and Resource Studies. Dr. Adelaja previously served as Executive Dean of Agriculture and Natural Resources, Dean of Cook College, Dean of Research and Executive Director of the New Jersey Agricultural Experiment Station at Rutgers University. His more recent research has focused on strategic growth policy, renewable energy policy, growth modeling and organization of public-private partnerships. Adelaja received his Ph.D. in Economics from West Virginia University.

Charles L. Ballard, professor of economics at Michigan State University, has been on the faculty since he received his Ph.D. from Stanford University in 1983. In 2007 he became director of the State of the State Survey, in MSU's Institute for Public Policy and Social Research. Also in 2007, he won the Outstanding Teacher Award in MSU's College of Social Science. He has served as a consultant for the U.S. departments of Agriculture, Health & Human Services, and Treasury, and for research institutes in Australia, Denmark, and Finland. His books include *Michigan at the Millennium* (2003) and *Michigan's Economic Future* (2006).

Annalie Campos is a Ph.D. candidate in the Department of Geography at Michigan State University. She completed a master's degree in Resource Development–Urban Studies at MSU, with a specialization in Environmental and Natural Resources Policy. She has conducted research in urban metropolitan environments including household waste management, community development, ethnic diversity and spatial inequality, and urban decentralization. Her dissertation focuses on public spending on transportation and sprawl in the Southeast Michigan region.

Jered B. Carr is associate professor and director of the Graduate Program in Public Administration in the Department of Political Science at Wayne State University. His current research focuses on political consolidation, municipal service cooperation, and metropolitan governance. He is co-editor of *Reshaping the Local Government Landscape: Perspectives on City-County Consolidation and its Alternatives* (2004). He earned his Ph.D. in 2000 from the Reubin O'D. Askew School of Public Administration and Policy at Florida State University.

Norman Christopher is currently executive director of sustainability at Grand Valley State University, after serving as an executive manager for several chemical companies and most recently as president of Haviland Enterprises in Grand Rapids. At GVSU he is responsible for coordinating and developing the university's Sustainability Initiative, including activities within campus operations, dining, and administration; faculty and curriculum development; student involvement; and community engagement. He also teaches an MBA course in sustainable business practices. Mr. Christopher received an undergraduate degree from the University of North Carolina and an MBA from the University of Connecticut. He also was a graduate in the Program for Management Development at Harvard University. Mr. Christopher also is active within the Grand Rapids community serving on a number of boards, councils, and commissions.

Betty Gajewski received a B.S. in Environmental Sciences and a M.S. in Communications, both from Grand Valley State University. Additionally, she pursued post-graduate work at Michigan State University in Resource Development, emphasizing environmental planning and park and recreation planning. At the Annis Water Resources Institute, Ms. Gajewski is working on many watershed projects. She also has worked as an environmental engineer with a large manufacturer with domestic and international operations, as well as performed environmental consulting for both business and governmental clients on a wide variety of projects. Ms. Gajewski served for many years as the chairperson of the Ottawa County Planning Commission and as a member of the Ottawa County Parks and Recreation Commission.

Elisabeth R. Gerber is professor of public policy at the University of Michigan's Gerald R. Ford School of Public Policy and research associate at the Center for Political Studies, Institute for Social Research. Her current research focuses on intergovernmental cooperation, transportation policy, state and local economic policy, land use and economic development, local fiscal capacity, and local political accountability. She is the author of *The Populist Paradox: Interest Group Influence and the Promise of Direct Legislation* (1999), co-author of *Stealing the Initiative: How State Government Responds to Direct Democracy* (2000), and co-editor of *Voting at the Political Fault Line: California's Experiment with the Blanket Primary* (2001) and *Michigan at the Millennium* (2003). She received her Ph.D. in Political Science from the University of Michigan.

Yohannes G. Hailu is visiting assistant professor and associate director of the Land Policy Research Program at the Land Policy Institute of Michigan State University. He provides programmatic leadership of research initiatives and conducts research in areas of New Economy strategic policy, the economics of talent and population movement, renewable energy policy, land policy, and strategic economic growth policy. He holds a Bachelor of Arts in Economics and Finance from University of Asmara, Eritrea, a Master of Science in Agricultural and Resource Economics and a Ph.D. in Natural Resource Economics, both from West Virginia University.

Elsie Harper-Anderson is currently serving as the Ariel Investments Visiting Research Fellow at the Chicago Urban League. Her research focuses on the impact of macroeconomic transformation on regional labor markets. Harper-Anderson's recent work focuses on the connection between economic development and workforce development examining the role of sector-based strategies in uniting the two. Other research investigates the effects of economic boom and bust cycles on racial inequality patterns. Harper-Anderson has previously served as a faculty member at the University of Michigan and taught at the University of California, Berkeley. She has also worked in local government, administering economic development and housing programs. She earned her Ph.D. from the University of California, Berkeley, and a master's degree from the H. John Heinz III School of Public Policy and Management at Carnegie Mellon University.

M. Curtis Hoffman is associate professor and director of the School of Public and Nonprofit Administration, Grand Valley State University. He received his Ph.D. from the Maxine Goodman Levin College of Urban Affairs, Cleveland State University. He has published in *Public Voices and Public Administration Review*. He received the 2002 William and Fredrick Mosher Award for best article by an academician appearing in *PAR*. Prior to moving to Grand Rapids, he was a research associate with the Northern Ohio Data and Information Service and the Housing Policy Research Program at Cleveland State University.

Richard Hula is professor and chair of the Department of Political Science at Michigan State University. Before becoming department chair in 2001, he served as the director of MSU's program in Public Policy and Administration (1991–1996) and associate director of the Institute for Public Policy and Social Research (1991–1998). He received his Ph.D. from Northwestern University. He has served as president of the Policy Studies Association (1997–98) and was selected as a Distinguished Scholar Teacher by the University Maryland. Hula's research and teaching interests focus broadly on environmental policy and urban politics. His books include *Market-Based Public Policy* (1988), *The Color of School Reform* with Jeffrey Henig, Marion Orr, and Desiree Pediscleaux (1999), and (with Cynthia Jackson-Elmoore) *Nonprofits in Urban America* (2000).

Richard W. Jelier is professor in the School of Public and Nonprofit Administration at Grand Valley State University. He received a dual Ph.D. from Michigan State University in Political Science–Urban Studies. He teaches and directs a summer Urbanization program at Kingston University, London, and created and directed the Public Affairs and Planning in Sydney, Australia, program, summer 2000 to 2007. Dr. Jelier served as a research fellow at Kingston University, London. He is a founding member and investigator of the Michigan Higher Education Land Policy Consortium, a partnership with Michigan State and Wayne State

333

Universities. He has published other book chapters, and his publications have also appeared in *Urban Education, Urban Review, Journal of Public Affairs Education,* and *International Journal of Economic Development.*

Angela Lazarean is a recent graduate of the Master of Urban Planning Program at Wayne State University. She completed a one-year Americorp stint with the Resource Assistance for Rural Environments, working as an assistant planner for a small rural town in the Willamette Valley, Oregon. She is currently an urban planner with the State of Oregon Department of Land Conservation and Development, responsible for doing plan reviews on proposals that come in to amend the comprehensive plan on economic development, housing and urban growth boundary adjustments. She is also the project manager for updating the statewide UGB coverage layer in the state Geographic Information System.

Eric W. Lupher has been with the Citizens Research Council of Michigan since 1987, where he has worked as a research associate and is currently director of local affairs. During his time with the CRC, he has conducted studies on a number of different state and local government policy issues. In addition to his research responsibilities, Lupher manages the CRC website, and he has served as treasurer of the Governmental Research Association. He is a member of the Governmental Accounting Standards Advisory Council, where he represents the user community on behalf of the GRA. He received a Bachelor of Arts from James Madison College at Michigan State University and a Masters of Public Administration from Wayne State University.

Jeremy Pyne is the geographic information systems specialist for the Community Research Institute at the Dorothy A. Johnson Center for Philanthropy and Nonprofit Leadership, Grand Valley State University. He holds a MPA degree with an emphasis in urban and regional policy and planning and a Bachelor of Science degree with a major in geography and planning, both from GVSU. He has coauthored two volumes of the *Ethnic Atlas of West Michigan.* He has presented his work at Arizona State University's fourteenth annual Nonprofit Conference and the 2005, 2006, and 2007 IMAGIN conferences. He is also the project leader for MAPAS, CRI's online interactive mapping and data application tool.

Laura A. Reese is a professor of political science and director of the Global Urban Studies Program at Michigan State University. She has authored four books and more than forty-five academic articles on local economic development. Reese has conducted national evaluations for the Department of Commerce, Economic Development Administration, providing assessments of such development tools as business incubators, industrial parks, community planning processes, military base conversion, and various types of small business lending. In Michigan she has conducted policy assessments of Tax Increment Financing and PA 198 Tax Abatements.

Gary Sands, an associate professor of Planning at Wayne State University, has more than thirty years of experience as an academic researcher and consultant to government agencies in the fields of housing and economic development. He has undertaken funded research on a variety of local economic development programs, including Renaissance Zones,

Neighborhood Enterprise Zones, Industrial Property Tax abatements, and Tax Increment Finance Authorities. His research has examined the relationship between local government regulations and incentive programs and the characteristics of private development activity.

June Manning Thomas is Centennial Professor of Urban and Regional Planning at the University of Michigan, Ann Arbor; she is also professor emeritus at Michigan State University. In 2003 she was inducted as a Fellow in the American Institute of Certified Planners. Her books include *Redevelopment and Race: Planning a Finer City in Postwar Detroit* (1997), *Planning Progress: Lessons from Shoghi Effendi* (1999), the co-edited (with Marsha Ritzdorf) *Urban Planning and the African American Community: In the Shadows* (1997), and the co-authored *Detroit: Race and Uneven Development* (1987). Dr. Thomas writes about diversification of the planning profession, planning history, and social equity in neighborhoods and urban revitalization.

Dale E. Thomson is an assistant professor of political science at the University of Michigan–Dearborn. He teaches courses on public administration and public policy. He also is director of the Institute for Local Government, which trains local, elected officials on matters of policy, practice, and professionalism. He has served as director of the Community Development Research Unit at Wayne State University's Center for Urban Studies; as a social science analyst for the U.S. Department of Housing and Urban Development; and as HUD's policy representative on the President's Council on Sustainable Development and the White House Task Force on Livable Communities. Thomson's current research foci include community development policy, the knowledge needs of local elected officials, and administration in local government and nonprofit organizations.

Katharine Trudeau is a graduate of Wayne State University's Master of Urban Planning Program with a concentration in Housing and Community Development. As a research assistant in the Department of Geography and Urban Planning at Wayne State, her research topics included evaluating the use of industrial tax abatements in Michigan through geographic information systems and tax increment financing as a tool for neighborhood revitalization. She currently works as a program manager at Citizens' Housing and Planning Association, a nonprofit housing organization, in Boston. She has a Bachelor of Arts in Political Science and Sociology from the University of Michigan.

Eric S. Zeemering is an assistant professor in the Department of Public Administration at San Francisco State University. He teaches classes on intergovernmental relations and urban administration. His research on interlocal cooperation has appeared in *Public Administration Review* and *State and Local Government Review*. He served as a city council member in Rockford, Michigan, from 1999 to 2001.